dandelions for DINNER

*Greece at War
and a Family's Dreams of America*

Sam P. Stamatis and
Peter S. Stamatis

iUniverse, Inc.
Bloomington

dandelions for Dinner
Greece at War and a Family's Dreams of America

Copyright © 2011 Sam P. Stamatis and Peter S. Stamatis

All rights reserved. No part of this book may be used or reproduced by any means, graphic, electronic, or mechanical, including photocopying, recording, taping or by any information storage retrieval system without the written permission of the publisher except in the case of brief quotations embodied in critical articles and reviews.

iUniverse books may be ordered through booksellers or by contacting:

iUniverse
1663 Liberty Drive
Bloomington, IN 47403
www.iuniverse.com
1-800-Authors (1-800-288-4677)

Because of the dynamic nature of the Internet, any Web addresses or links contained in this book may have changed since publication and may no longer be valid. The views expressed in this work are solely those of the author and do not necessarily reflect the views of the publisher, and the publisher hereby disclaims any responsibility for them.

Any people depicted in stock imagery provided by Thinkstock are models, and such images are being used for illustrative purposes only.

Certain stock imagery © Thinkstock.

ISBN: 978-1-4620-5674-3 (sc)
ISBN: 978-1-4620-5675-0 (hc)
ISBN: 978-1-4620-5676-7 (e)

Library of Congress Control Number: 2011919550

Printed in the United States of America

iUniverse rev. date: 12/4/2012

It's a good thing to be well descended
but the glory belongs to the ancestors.
—Plutarch

Contents

Preface ix
Acknowledgments xi
Introduction xiii

Part 1
GARGALIANI

Chapter 1. Death Is in the Air 3
Chapter 2. Escape to Gargaliani 6
Chapter 3. Will Someone Please Marry My Daughters? . 21
Chapter 4. The Rise of Nitsa 35
Chapter 5. Chicago 50
Chapter 6. Good Times 58
Chapter 7. Hard Times 79
Chapter 8. Patras 94

Part 2
WAR!

Chapter 9. School 111
Chapter 10. New Neighborhood 136
Chapter 11. Italians! .153
Chapter 12. In Business 167
Chapter 13. Mouzaki .180

Chapter 14. The Mati. 195

Chapter 15. Life Goes On 221

Chapter 16. The Oracle. 236

Chapter 17. Kanella 248

Part 3
GOOD RIDDANCE

Chapter 18. Arrivederci, Roma 259

Chapter 19. The Day After 272

Chapter 20. Stoupas 288

Chapter 21. Surviving a War 300

Chapter 22. Divesting Assets 312

Chapter 23. Return to Mani 322

Chapter 24. The Battle of Gargaliani 333

Chapter 25. Nothing But Hope 350

Chapter 26. Lying Low 360

Chapter 27. Getting Ready 373

Chapter 28. Good-Bye 388

Chapter 29. Athens 395

Chapter 30. America 408

Bibliography 417

Glossary 419

Preface

When Sam Stamatis, my logical and easygoing father, retired after a long career as an electrical engineer, I (Peter Stamatis) worried about what this always active gentleman might do to keep himself occupied. So I suggested that dad stay busy by writing down the events of his childhood—things he never talked about—and told him that I would put it all together, perhaps for future generations of our family. Sam seemed to like my suggestion and before long, he began mailing me pages he had hand-written in his engineer's sure penmanship on yellow legal pads. For the next several years, I was swept away by his secret boyhood life and together, we wrote this book.

Before then, I had heard little about Sam's (or Sarantis, as he was called as a boy) childhood; he *never* talked about it. Of course, I knew he was born in a small city in southwestern Greece called Gargaliani. I also knew that he was the grandson of the town's priest and the child of a taciturn carpenter and a charming mother. And I was well aware that he left Greece for the United States on a boat around 1946 when he was 13.

But what I didn't know is how close he, and so many other Greeks like him, had come to dying on so many occasions. In the pages that follow, we recount what really happened to Sam, the story of his youth, but perhaps more importantly, the story, in so many ways, of the survivors of World War II. And we tell it in Sam's own voice, as he remembers living it.

From here on out, Sam is the "I" of this story. Note that with the exception of the background information on the World War II years, this memoir is essentially his memory of his youth. Some of the events depicted in this book, especially those in the early chapters, took place a century ago or more, and the events of the Great Depression and World War II happened well over half a century ago. Sam did his best to remember and recount what he had been told of things in Greece before he was born and the things that happened to him. He also drew heavily upon his mother's oral and written description of the events of her life.

In some cases, we reconstructed dialogue from Sam's personal recollection, or at times, as the conversations had been written or described to Sam by his mother or others. Also, some of the names have been changed, where we thought appropriate.

Peter Stamatis

Acknowledgments

A special thanks to all of those who helped us, including

Dr. George Alexopoulos
David Brinton
The late Michael W. Coffield
The late Dr. Plato Deliyiannis
Anastasios Ghikas
Danny Halazonitis
Christ Halazonitis
Greg Hides
Gust Kapernekas
Eleni Lemberis
George Mathew
Niki McIlvain
Jane Powers
John Powers
L. Edward Purcell
The Staff of the National Hellenic Museum, Chicago
Rev. Fr. John Rallis
Ioanna Salta
Katherine Stamatis
Steven ("Stathi") P. Stamatis

Introduction

During the middle ages, communities built on the sea were prime targets for pirates. To avoid being looted, those in danger often abandoned their seashore dwellings and sought refuge at higher ground. In the southwest Peloponnese, a town now known as Gargaliani served as such a sanctuary.

Gargaliani sits roughly six kilometers east of the Ionian Sea and atop a steep plateau that rises some three hundred meters above it. Sixty kilometers to the east of Gargaliani, well beyond the majestic mountain the locals call Ayia, is the city of Kalamata, the Peloponnese's second largest. To the north of Gargaliani are the two smaller towns of Filiatra and Kyparissia. Kyparissia is home to the region's train station. To the south is the strategically significant port town of Pylos, the site of many naval battles centuries before.

Gargaliani's western view overlooks an idyllic valley of olive groves peppered with patches of vineyards and ornamented with whitewashed farmhouses that run all the way to the azure Ionian. Few places on earth enjoy a view so beautiful. But from Marathos, the tiny coastal town situated directly to the west and right on the sea, Gargaliani is barely visible.

I spent the first thirteen years of my life growing up in this place, which according to the 1940 census, had roughly 9000 inhabitants. This made it, by Greece's standards, more populous than most. And while the town has no doubt changed over the last seventy years, everything about Gargaliani for me is suspended in time. In my memory, it has been spared the decay of evolution. Its wartime aura is always in my thoughts and is permanently ingrained in my soul. Though for sixty years I have rarely talked about my youth, I have never been able to forget it.

The Gargaliani that I visit while in my late seventies—and some seventy years after the events described herein—is foreign to me and lacks the corrosiveness of the bygone era we write about. It looks like every other sleepy Greek agrarian town, spicy yet common. Its residents argue in cafés, lazy stray dogs sleep in its *plateia,* and the sunny Ionian Sea's waves endlessly curl onto nearby shores. Though the things I remember seem to have been forgotten by the current residents, buried beneath life's trinkets and frivolities, the memories of this arid place are front and center squatters on the mantles in all the rooms of my mind.

My youthful peers, people who never left Gargaliani, have been somehow able to forget the calamities of the 1930s and '40s—calamities caused by famine, Italians, Germans, and then perhaps worst of all, by the Greeks themselves. These people have always been a curiosity to me. But those times left an indelible mark on me, shaped my view of the world, and imposed on me a frame of reference I have spent the rest of my life arguing with. Perhaps I am the curiosity.

Sam Stamatis

To my children and their children.
Sam Stamatis

To my parents and their parents.
Peter Stamatis

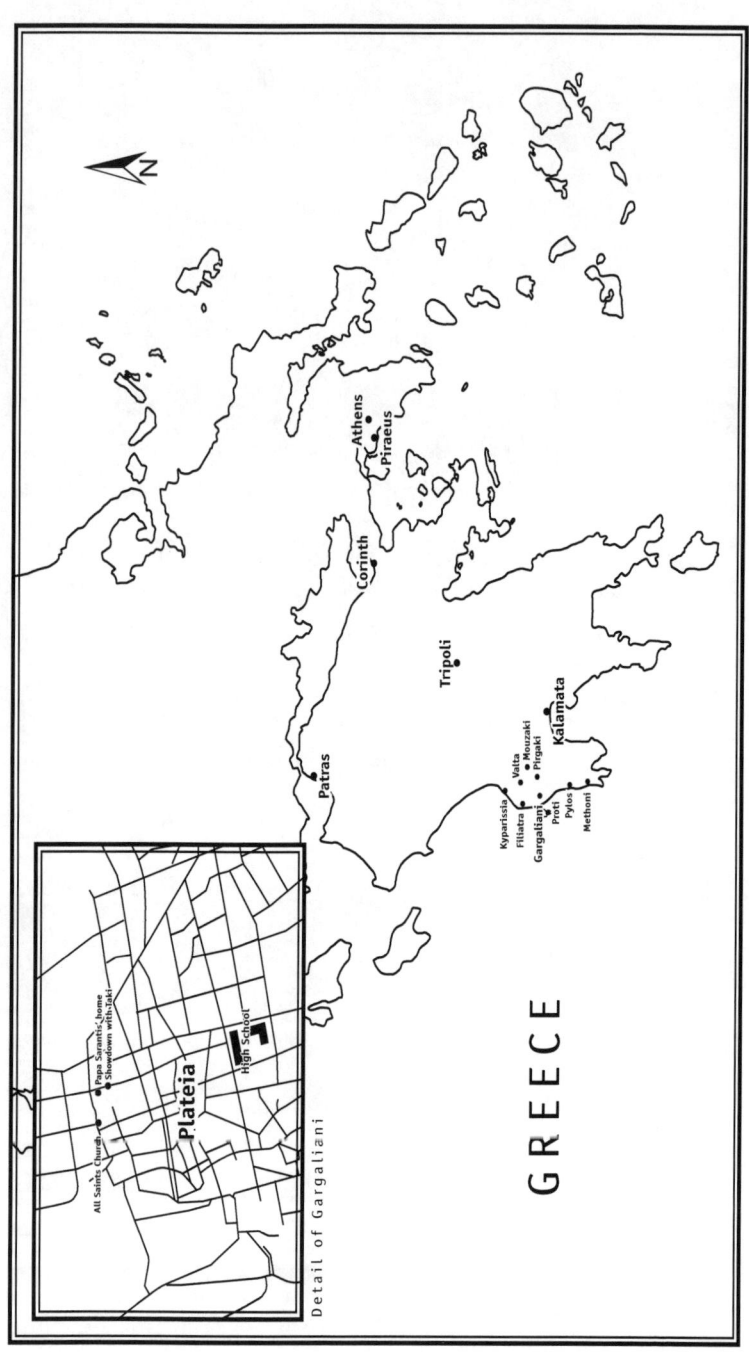

PART 1
Gargaliani

Chapter 1
DEATH IS IN THE AIR

The battle had begun quicker than I expected, and the chaos was a surprise. We knew our lives might be at an end as soon as haphazard cannon shots fired by members of the *Andartes*—Greek Communist guerilla fighters—began to rain down near our home in the early morning's darkness on September 22, 1944.

Though I was only eleven years old, I was well aware that others, certainly many more worthy, wealthy, and able than us, had not made it. I also knew that whether we would survive this dark day was no sure thing. In fact, the odds were heavily against us.

When a shell, luckily a dud, crashed through our neighbors' home and slammed into its kitchen, Mother grabbed my younger brother Stathi.

"We are leaving," Father said and directed the four of us through a maze of narrow streets to my uncle's home several blocks away.

There, along with a number of other traumatized, war-weary people, we huddled in a storage room, temporarily safe from the random and sloppily aimed explosions.

From that bunker, we trusted that our side—the Royalists and their "Protective Forces"—was winning, that the invaders would not take our town, and that we would be able to continue our lives in the same rhythms that we had always lived them. But these notions were promptly dashed when we saw a soldier, one of ours and dressed in his street clothes, walking away from the fight. Father asked him how we were doing and if Gargaliani had been able to defend itself against the Communist attack. The man scoffed at us and declared that the battle had ended and the invaders had prevailed.

Before long, we began to see more and more of our fighters abandon Gargaliani's defense—an even more troubling, foreboding sight. In minutes, bearded Communists filled our street. The conquerors ordered us, along with everyone else, to move through the town, and they herded us past its *plateia*, the main square and center of community life; Father and I moved together while Mother kept a grip on Stathi, who was only five years old.

We were funneled into Gargaliani's high school, where the victors undertook to sift their supporters from the crowds. The Communists spoke of reconciliation, but it quickly became clear they were in no forgiving mood at all. We watched for hours as they separated their sheep from the goats, and they mercilessly eliminated problem people who failed their makeshift loyalty tests. It was only through a gift of fate that we were passed when, as supporters of the Royalists, we should have been failed. They set us free onto the streets.

Unsure what to do, we stood before the house of the leader of the Protective Forces. If to the victor belong the spoils; to the vanquished belongs woe—the heroic warrior was on the run, his residence in flames. Communist guerilla fighters moved quickly through the streets and crisscrossed the plateia. Whatever rules had previously governed our civilized town had disintegrated. We were on our own, and there was no one to turn to—anarchy had triumphed. For us to survive, Father knew we had to get off the streets and to the safety of our home. But that wouldn't be easy. Before us, we could see that Andartes intoxicated by bloodlust filled the plateia. They moved everywhere throughout the square as each of their unmerciful deeds fueled other, more incomprehensible and unconscionable ones.

Father led us quickly and quietly through the streets of our town as the bone-jolting cracks of all-too-close firearms serenaded us. The streets were littered with the discarded dead, our neighbors frozen in random poses of horror. When we were only twenty or so meters from our home, we recoiled at the sudden appearance, directly in front of us, of a teenager we knew named Takis. Two barely pubescent Andartes, armed with pistols and holding rifles, stood beside him.

Mother never cared much for Takis or his family. Over the years, our relationship with him had been perfunctory and inconsequential; he wasn't part of our world, and we weren't part of his. Prior to that moment, Takis's existence had never mattered to us one way or another.

But when Takis saw Father, the young man's eyes darted back and forth and, as if he had finally located his prey, he pointed at Father.

"There's one. There's one right there. He is one of them."

Father froze.

"Shoot him; shoot him now," Takis ordered.

The obedient Andartes raised their rifles and took aim at Father.

Who could have imagined we would have arrived at this brink, to such an unceremonious end to year after year of struggle and suffering? How was it that we, Greeks who had spent the previous decade surviving famine, war, and foreign occupation, suddenly stood face to face with our executioners, other Greeks no less, people who like us had struggled through those same years of suffering?

To understand how my family, not to mention Greece itself, had descended to this mindless place, we must start at the beginning.

Chapter 2
ESCAPE TO GARGALIANI

Around 1860, my maternal great-grandfather, Spyro Petropouleas, then in his mid-twenties, arrived in Gargaliani after fleeing from the only home he had ever known, an area called Boliana in the Mani region of Peloponnesus. Mani, about a hundred kilometers to the east of Gargaliani, is a rugged mountainous area replete with free-spirited Greeks, famous for never being subjugated during the four-hundred-year Ottoman occupation. Even well after the rest of Greece had been taken over, the Maniates, as Mani's citizens are known, successfully repelled the advancing Turks so many times that the invaders decided that conquering them wasn't worth the effort and moved on. The rugged Mani terrain, combined with the fact that the Maniates were loud, obnoxious, and stubborn, made the Turks realize that even if they conquered Mani, maintaining control over it would have required too much manpower. So, other than the occasional incursion, the Turks left Mani alone.

Great-grandfather Spyro left Mani because it was his only alternative to death. Vendettas amongst Maniates were common in the late nineteenth and early twentieth centuries. To a Maniate, a family's pride and reputation were paramount, and feuds amongst them could last for generations. One action would lead to a reaction, which would demand a retaliation, and so on, which caused the participants to live in a state of perpetual conflict. Violence begot violence, and while vengeance often came hard and fast, retribution could also be delayed for years. It wasn't unusual for someone to be shot as payback for something his father had done a decade before.

But despite their apparent inability to forgive and forget, the Maniates were unsurpassed in *filotimo*, the Hellenic notion of hospitality that is deep seated in Greece's psyche and predates Homer, who wrote about it at length in *The Iliad* and *The Odyssey*. Those who welcomed and helped Odysseus on his journey back to Ithaca after years of war in Troy exhibited *filotimo*. *Filotimo* is the foundation of a Greek's character and leads him to treat a stranger like a long-lost brother, often embracing him at the first meeting. Most Greeks have *filotimo* to a degree, and the Maniates seemed to have been given several extra doses.

For reasons that have been forgotten over the years, young Spyro was set to become the latest victim of a Maniate family vendetta when he thought better of it and chose to leave Mani instead. As the story was told, Spyro and his new bride Maria took a few personal belongings and set out onto the Aegean in a boat on a nocturnal escape, moving their way westward along the Peloponnesian coastline. They passed a number of coastal towns and sailed past Pylos, the famous port town and the site of many great naval battles of antiquity. Fatigued, Spyro and Maria were eventually seduced into exiting their craft by the plush vegetation and vineyards of the coastal village of Marathos. They came ashore and continued moving a few kilometers due east toward Gargaliani.

Despite Spyro's and Maria's sincere attempts to remain incognito, word of their arrival spread quickly through the area. It was an unusual event when a stranger came to town, and because he was from Mani, all assumed Spyro was a fierce warrior. The town fathers assembled and determined it was best to avoid a fight and offered Spyro a job instead. He accepted and became a deputy police officer. They charged Spyro with capturing guerilla fighters who roamed the nearby mountains and countryside terrorizing the area's villages. They were the descendants of the fighters of the Greek War of Independence who never returned to docile civilian life. Spyro lived up to the Maniate reputation and used his wits, practicality, valor, and *filotimo* to bring many wanted men to justice. His success helped him make a name for himself, giving him fame and respectability.

As years passed, young Spyro and his bride accumulated a considerable amount of wealth that included vineyards, olive groves, and wheat fields, not to mention a spacious house with a plush garden not far from the Gargaliani market. They were blessed with six children – three daughters (Poulia, Tasia, and Eleni) and three sons (Antonis, Dimitri, and Sarantis). Sarantis, born around 1865, was my grandfather. Three of these children died during childhood and another married and left Gargaliani, leaving behind only Spyro and his two remaining sons Sarantis and Dimitri to care for the family's agricultural holdings. This was a formidable task considering the family's properties were substantial and scattered throughout the area.

Spyro's sons grew into upright and thoughtful men and helped their father greatly in the handling of the family's affairs. Indeed, locals began to call on Sarantis and Dimitri when they needed their help to perform various law-enforcement tasks. One such request came in around 1885 when the local police needed assistance capturing a criminal in the town of Pirgaki, six kilometers due east of Gargaliani. When the wanted man was captured, all in Pirgaki rejoiced. One whose rejoicing was especially ebullient was Pirgaki's retired schoolmaster, a man named Michael Stavropoulos. This vocal law-and-order advocate was so elated with the capture that he invited the posse and various Pirgaki dignitaries to his house for a celebration.

It was at the Stavropoulos celebration, on an airy star-filled night with the whistling sounds of the Peloponnesian breezes whirling through the vineyards and the scents of roasting skewered lamb, jasmine, and the sweetness of the summer breeze in the air, that Sarantis saw, for the first time, the retired schoolmaster's daughter. Naturally, her name was Eleni. Throughout history, Greeks have idolized women named Eleni, which is rendered in English as "Helen," and young Sarantis was no exception. It was an Eleni whose face "launched a thousand ships" and who was to blame for the decade-long bloodbath known as the Trojan War.

This Eleni had a similar effect on Sarantis. She was young, still in her teens, but had already developed into a stunning specimen of feminine perfection—Venus on her shell. She was like one of those statues an ancient sculptor would carve out of white marble. All Eleni was missing was the urn, but that didn't matter. Sarantis loved her and wanted to marry her. He spent the rest of the evening contemplating things he would someday say to this Helen of Pirgaki, if ever given the opportunity. Sophoclean phrases entered his mind, and they all rhymed and their meter was perfect, until, of course, Eleni came near him and he was immediately dumbfounded.

Sarantis did not speak to Eleni that night or for the next two years. But he continued to answer the call of his elders and participated, more than he cared to, in various reconnaissance missions into the countryside. And the more he did it, the less he liked it. What bothered Sarantis was that the so-called law-enforcement missions served as the cover for his colleagues to satisfy some perverted personal desire to inflict pain on others. He wondered what it was in a person that caused him to derive corrupt pleasures from making others suffer. Of course, most people will justify their own barbaric behavior by focusing on some higher cause, say, law and order, the common good, or the supposed deterrent effect of their actions on others. But these justifications were never sufficient, and Sarantis knew that the worst actions of man bubbled forth from some fundamental condition of the human soul. Sarantis became a detached participant in the expeditions to capture criminals, and from his perch, the difference between the captors and their adversaries began to blur.

Sarantis never saw his religious conversion coming. To him, the mission was like every other—he and a team would head to the hills and capture some bandit. But, in the days leading up to a proposed mission, Sarantis decided he had enough. What bothered him was philosophical in nature—theological, actually—and arose from the thought that even though most men recognized that they were creations of the benevolent God, they failed to recognize that others were as well—whether posse member, bandit, farmer, or sheep herder. And out of this ubiquitous blind spot was born cruelty, the justification for a person's lack of compassion and mankind's never-ending capacity to inflict harm on others. Most disturbing to Sarantis was that the blind spot caused one's vanity to swell as he partook in the demise of another.

As the dozen-person posse moved, all these thoughts raced through Sarantis's mind, and he began to lag behind. His decreased pace was imperceptible at first until he realized he began to lose sight of the team. It was then that he noticed what the group must have ignored: that he was about to pass a chapel. And he saw that in front there was a monk tending to flowers.

There was certainly nothing special about passing a chapel, or a monk for that matter, as Sarantis passed them all the time. Churches were everywhere in Greece and being, like everyone else, a Greek Orthodox Christian, seeing one for Sarantis was a non-event. But for some reason, Sarantis started wondering about the monk and the

dandelions for Dinner

world he lived in, a place that seemed so different from his own. He thought about how the monk must have once been like himself, in a worldly life, with a family, obligations, desires, ambitions, loves, and lusts. What was it that caused that monk and others like him to trade the world for the church? Thoughts spun wildly through his mind, and he contemplated the posse and what it was likely to do if its latest mission was a success. He wondered what he would do if his comrades again became brutal for the sake of brutality, whether he would remain silent as he had in the past. Suddenly, Sarantis could no longer justify being the detached observer and knew he had to act. So with dawn settling, the gang on the march now well ahead, and the monk absorbed in his gardening, Sarantis stopped and introduced himself. And just like that, he walked out of the only world he had ever known and into a new one.

Sarantis spent the next few days at the chapel talking with the monk and helping with various chores. When finally he returned home, was a changed person and casually announced to his parents that he had decided to become a priest.

There is a quirk in Greek culture that almost always surfaces when a young man tells his parents he has decided to enter the clergy. Usually, the parents, despite the fact that they have spent their lives giving priests honor, respect, and kisses on their hands, greet such proclamations with horror. Typical responses include, "Are you joking?" "Who told you to do that?" "The kid's lost it," and so on. The assumption is usually that someone has "gotten hold" of the young man or, in Sarantis's case, some charismatic monastic had brainwashed him.

Sarantis heard all this and more from his parents that day. For Spyro, there was distinct separation between the life people lived in the world and the life priests and monks lived in their churches and monasteries. A different set of rules applied to each. Life in the world was a constant struggle in which people employed whatever means necessary to survive. Lying back in some prayer-induced trance was for him the surest route to poverty. God and religion were, in a way, on the back burner for Spyro. They were something to draw upon when he ran out of ideas as to how to handle a certain situation—a moral fire extinguisher, used only in cases of dire emergency. Curiously, this was precisely that type of emergency and circumstance in which

Spyro would suggest that Sarantis talk to a priest or perhaps be exorcized. But of course, that wasn't an option here.

"Why would you, my son, possibly want to become a priest? You are from a family of means. The priesthood is not for you. The priesthood is for people with nothing else."

"It's a decision I've made," Sarantis replied, "I have been called. What can I do?"

Responses like these exacerbated Spyro's anger, and his questions became a tirade as the implications of Sarantis's choice began to coalesce in the father's head. If Sarantis became a priest, he would no longer be involved in the day-to-day maintenance of the family's agricultural holdings, which would be a huge blow. Spyro had counted on Sarantis and Dimitri not only to take over these operations, but also to build on them. He had planned for his children to live a better life than he had and saw no nobility in being poor. He had pictured his son Sarantis much as *The Iliad's* just warrior Hector saw *his* son, as growing to be "a better man" than he was. And now Sarantis, his own flesh and blood, was going to stoop so low as to become a priest? Spyro took the decision personally.

"What is everyone going to say about Petropouleas's son becoming a priest? Eh? Tell me that. What have I done to you to make you do this to me?"

At one point, Spyro determined that Sarantis's decision was an act direct from the Almighty, one designed solely to settle some outstanding score He had with Spyro.

"Why me? What have I done to you?" he exclaimed as he looked skyward.

Eventually however, Spyro saw that Sarantis, having emerged from the monastery calm, focused and enlightened, was intractable. He had made his decision and it was final.

There is something else that Maniates like Spyro had in common in addition to the vendettas and the *filotimo*. It's that their word was their bond. Once they made a decision or a commitment, the matter was finished; it was closed, and there was no need to revisit it. So after Sarantis's announcement settled, Spyro and Maria understood they could not change their son's mind. Practical thinking quickly set in as neither Spyro nor Maria were the type to brood over anything, and they immediately understood they were presented with a new challenge—to ensure that Sarantis was properly married prior to his ordination as a priest. To allow him to be ordained while unmarried would bar Sarantis from *ever* marrying and relegate him to life as a celibate. If Spyro and Maria frowned upon Sarantis becoming a priest, his becoming a celibate priest was anathema. It was time for action.

Although he hadn't seen beautiful Eleni of Pirgaki in almost two years, Sarantis thought of her often. In fact, despite his parents' fears, Sarantis came to another decision during his time away: that the moment to marry Eleni had arrived. But this posed a challenge. With the division between the sexes clear, both young men and young women understood their roles in this strict society and only spoke to one another cautiously when adults were present and rarely if ever when alone. Even in Gargaliani, young men had seen Maniate-style vendettas play out, which deterred them from disgracing a girl and her family.

For a wedding to take place between people forbidden to freely converse, the parties required help. Enter the marriage broker, the indispensable ingredient in every union. Matchmakers came in many shapes and sizes, and although such persons were typically women and related to at least one of the interested parties, any male or female could quickly assume the role when circumstances required. Indeed, most people relished the impromptu opportunity to play matchmaker and to receive the accolades associated with success. Marriage brokers served at least two purposes. First, they introduced the parties. Second, they negotiated the nuptials, particularly the nature and extent of the *prika* or bridal dowry, often the most important aspect of a potential wedding. Most parents would begin accumulating a daughter's *prika* from her birth and would encourage her to do the same as soon as she could understand its importance. By the time a girl was of marrying age, her *prika*, having been added to for years, would often include her wardrobe, blankets, sheets, pillows, kitchen utensils, embroidered tablecloths, and so forth. If her family had means, it could sweeten the pot with some proportion of its total wealth, usually swatches of land, animals, farms, and sums of money.

Sarantis never discussed Eleni with his parents. With Spyro and

Maria thrown into a panic that Sarantis would be ordained a priest prior to marriage and with Sarantis mum on his intentions with the girl he saw two years before but had never spoken to, the parents began pushing girl after girl on their son. Their suggestions were subtle at first, as Spyro would point out at the cafés how this or that man's daughter had grown into quite a woman. But Sarantis knew his father, and he could immediately smell out such maneuvers. Lest he give the wrong impression, he met Spyro's observations with bland indifference.

The more Sarantis ignored his parents' recommendations, the harder they pushed; and the harder they pushed, the more Sarantis ignored them. Sarantis grew tired of the machinations and in the end, the household exploded into conflict as the family members put their cards on the table.

"But my son," said Spyro, "we only want what is good for you. We are trying to find a solution to your problem."

"What problem are you talking about?" retorted Sarantis.

Maria said, "You claim you are ready to be ordained a priest, and if it is God's will, then so be it. But your father and I both think that this desire you have to be ordained a celibate is a mistake—that life as a celibate priest is not for you."

"Who said anything about being ordained a celibate? Where did you get that idea? I don't believe that is God's will for me. To tell you the truth, I have decided to marry and have even chosen the girl."

Sarantis told his parents about the Pirgaki posse, about Michael Stavropoulos, the party at his house, and about his daughter, Eleni.

Spyro and Maria listened closely and as soon as Sarantis finished his story, Spyro turned to Maria and said, "Aren't the people in Pirgaki a bunch of barefoot villagers? And who's this Stavropoulos character? And who's his daughter? What kind of people are these?"

The following day, Spyro went looking for an acquaintance in the plateia by the name of Kyriakos, who was a well-known merchant from Pirgaki who came to Gargaliani several times a week and was someone with whom Spyro was friendly. When Spyro asked him about Stavropoulos, he learned that he was a born to a well-known and well-to-do family that had lived for generations in Smyrna. His parents educated Michael at the best schools and even sent him to the university in Paris. And after completing his studies there and with his head filled with new thoughts and ideas, Michael first went to Smyrna, but he then decided to return to Greece to help in the struggle to maintain its independence from the Turks and to rid Greece from its many Turkish influences. He had seen the world outside of Ottoman influence and wanted to do his part to westernize Greece. He promised his parents he would return to Smyrna the following year but never did.

Once he arrived in Greece, the Greek minister of education recognized him as a person of letters and immediately hired him. Eventually, the government sent Michael to Pirgaki to teach and ordered him to set up an education system. Michael started a school that emphasized Greece's classical history, designed to show the Greeks that certain parts of their culture were not Greek at all, but Turkish.

Spyro also learned that Michael had retired and that he had worked hard all those years for little money but somehow, he was able to raise his four children and even sent his first three to study at the University of Athens, including a daughter, which was quite unusual for that time. But, Eleni, as the youngest, would watch her three older siblings leave Pirgaki to pursue their education while she would remain in Pirgaki to look after Michael and Eugenia in their old age. Nevertheless, Kyriakos thought that young Eleni was the smartest of the lot.

Spyro listened closely to everything Kyriakos said that afternoon. And the more he heard, the more he liked. Satisfied that Stavropoulos was a respectable person and not just some "villager," Spyro and Maria determined that Spyro would request Kyriakos to approach the Stavropoulos family with a formal marriage proposal. That conversation took place within a few days when Kyriakos, thrilled to be entrusted with this important responsibility, went to the Stavropoulos's home. Like Spyro, Michael interrogated Kyriakos. And as Kyriakos satisfactorily answered each, a gloom settled over Michael as his great fear began to materialize.

"What is going to happen to us without Eleni? Who is going to care for us as we get older? We have learned to depend on her so much!"

Later, Michael gave what he considered sad news to Eugenia, which prompted a shriek of pure joy to shoot from her mouth.

Eugenia castigated her husband for his selfishness, told him that despite whatever plans for Eleni he might have concocted in his mind, that the girl indeed would get married, and if she approved of Sarantis after meeting him, that she would marry *him*. And that was it.

"Eleni is not a slave," she said, "but a young woman who is entitled to live her own life and to have her own family."

Eugenia discussed the Petropouleas' proposal with Eleni and told her everything she knew about Sarantis and his family. Eleni, surprised, agreed to meet the suitor, and within days, the families got together. She immediately liked Sarantis, who she perceived as a gentle soul who projected compassion and kindness, qualities she was smart enough to know were the ones she wanted in the man who would become her husband. That Sarantis was to become a priest was for Eleni the icing on the cake. The perfect situation for Eleni was one that would allow her to pursue the philanthropic impulses that constantly picked at her. As for Sarantis, he thought that Eleni was even more beautiful than he remembered. Less than two days later, the two became betrothed to one another with the wedding set to take place within the month.

Concerning *prika*, Sarantis fell in the category of those whose negotiating position suffered as the result of his strong affections. There would be no parcels of land, no homes, and no money for him. On his wedding day, Sarantis would just get Eleni, who came with no more than some clothes and a few other belongings. But for a young man who was preparing for a life as a priest and accordingly a life of limited luxuries, Sarantis had found the ultimate woman, a diamond in her own right, humble, beautiful, and satisfied with the little that was hers. And as he pondered it all, Sarantis was confident that God was raining his blessings upon him.

Eleni had wondered if she would ever get married. As the youngest of four children—five years younger than her next older sibling and a full fifteen years younger than the oldest—Eleni had watched as the three of them, one by one, left Pirgaki for Athens to be educated at the university, never to return. Of course, while for her the adventure and thrill of such escapes carried the most seductive allure, Eleni knew that being the youngest in her family caused her to bear the responsibility of caring for her parents in their senescence. Eleni undertook this duty with a peaceful grace that only highlighted her internal elegance.

When thoughts of her future entered her mind and when she contemplated the type of man she might marry, Eleni was conflicted. On the one hand, she had her share of romantic thoughts of a strong and protective man sweeping her off her feet, one who shared her father's erudition and certitude and augmented it with physical strength and ability. On the other hand, Eleni dreaded marriage to one of those domineering males who seemed to be everywhere and who would no doubt endeavor to hold her by the back of her neck, directing her every action. While such conflicts have paralyzed many into inaction and perpetuated a day-to-day acceptance of the status quo, Eleni knew that her world was in a state of flux, and she was ready to go with the flow of whatever came her way. And so she remained open and even anticipated the potential for emancipation that only marriage could bring her, much in the same way that the world of academia had freed her older siblings.

Prior to meeting Sarantis, Eleni prayed constantly to Panagia, the Virgin Mary, and put in her order for a faithful groom, a person who she could marry and then walk, hand in hand, her life's path toward Christ. And while she waited for his delivery to her, Eleni stayed with her parents and patiently took care of them, fully expecting her spouse's arrival at precisely the preordained time. So when out of nowhere, young Sarantis appeared and was focused, pious, and ready not only to marry Eleni but also to enter the priesthood, Eleni knew that her prayers had been answered. From the moment she first saw Sarantis, she loved him and loved him deeply. She loved his piety, his faith, and his charity. But Eleni's love for Sarantis was neither the flighty nor the calculating types found in Sophoclean plays, but originated in the recognition that Sarantis was her spiritual brother, a person who viewed the world through the same lens as she. Eleni understood Sarantis, his points of view and his frames of reference and therefore had no fear of leaving her parents, no fear of leaving Pirgaki, and no fear of marrying a man she had just met.

Sarantis and Eleni were married in Pirgaki. No one now knows the exact year of the couple's marriage, but it was around 1890. After the wedding and its ensuing festivities, the newlyweds made the six-kilometer journey from Pirgaki to Gargaliani on the back of a mule and entered their new home and their new life together. Of course, for Sarantis, the new home wasn't new at all but was the same home he was born and raised in, the rectangular two-story, three-bedroom house cut into the side of an incline, just one and a half blocks from the Gargaliani market and three blocks northwest of the plateia. As for Eleni, it was all new, and she was not only living with a new husband but with his mother, father, and brother. But Eleni, who had been taught obedience and respect for her elders, didn't mind. Indeed, it was the very system of deference to elders that allowed the household to function as smoothly as it did, with Spyro serving as the ultimate authority on all matters concerning the family's affairs, even those that involved Sarantis and his new bride.

Over time, the family renovated the house and added an additional wing to accommodate the two families separately and comfortably. Eleni and Sarantis moved to the new wing, built with three bedrooms, a large dining room, a kitchen, and, most importantly, an indoor toilet, the era's ultimate luxury item. When Dimitri married years later, Spyro and Maria left the house altogether and moved to a small apartment a few blocks from their two sons. By 1910, Spyro and Maria had passed away.

Eleni's early years as Sarantis's wife were full of blessings. Shortly after their marriage, the Bishop of Kyparissia ordained Sarantis a priest and assigned him to the church of All Saints in Gargaliani. From that point on, people would no longer call Eleni's husband Saranti, Aki, Taki, or any of the many nicknames for the name Sarantis, but would call him "Papa Sarantis," that is, the "Priest Sarantis." In subsequent years, Eleni watched her husband evolve into a fine priest with a loyal following. She saw him become the deliverer of exemplary sermons, usually totally extemporaneous, and she was in awe of his ability to convey in the simplest terms God's messages of humility, charity, chastity, and above all, love for Christ. Eleni marveled at his piety and the fruit it bore, how it drew people to him.

Eleni gave birth to three daughters. Theano, the oldest, was born in 1892. Tasia was born four years later in 1896. Then, sometime around 1900, Nitsa, my mother, was born. The exact year of Nitsa's birth has never been certain. Indeed, later in life she always lied about her age when asked. I remember when I once inquired as to why she never gave a straight answer.

She said with a look of great satisfaction, "Anyone foolish enough to ask me my age deserves the lies I tell him."

Eleni watched Papa Sarantis became a leader, always in charge and always the center of attention. He became the person in Gargaliani to see and to be seen with. Visiting dignitaries always paid him their respects when passing through and praised him for his humility, extraordinary grace, and finesse. Papa Sarantis was not only an impressive moral presence but a physical one as well. At five foot eleven, he was taller than most, built with a broad-shouldered stance, and had a clear-eyed stare. Indeed, with his charisma, most agreed that Papa Sarantis's singular abilities at diplomacy rendered him overqualified to serve merely as a rural priest from a small and obscure town. His advice was quick and sure, his authority unquestionable.

A mere example was the occasion when the family of a local girl had learned that a young man in town had slept with her. When the news made its way to Papa Sarantis, he was unequivocal.

"Marry her immediately," he ordered the adolescent.

But the boy waffled, and a week later, the girl's brother shot him dead in the plateia. Papa Sarantis performed the funeral service at All Saints, and at the end of the service, in a display that warned others about engaging in similar conduct, he stood before the casket on the altar of the church of All Saints.

"Yianni, I told you what to do!" he said sternly and in full voice, "but you wouldn't listen to me!" The priest took several steps, then momentarily turned back. "Now sleep!" he commanded the corpse.

All the while, Eleni's position as *presbytera*, the priest's wife, put her in the ideal position to become the area's leading philanthropist. She distributed food and other items to less fortunate locals. Because he was the town priest and because word of Eleni's willingness to help others had spread, guests and sometimes total strangers often made their way to their home for a meal and a place to sleep, which made their house, over time, a refuge for transients, some noble and some not. Once, some locals recognized and arrested a felon disguised as a monk who had taken up residence in the priest's home.

As the decades passed, Eleni noticed subtle changes in her

husband and watched Papa Sarantis devolve, through his forties and fifties, into a self-centered and domineering person. At first, these traits came out faintly and piecemeal as aberrations—a little impatience here or a lost temper there. But, over time, what had begun as aberrations grew more frequent and intense. Eventually, these negative traits began to characterize most of his actions. Of course, Papa Sarantis, consumed in the events and the obligations his life seemed to have assigned to him, didn't realize what was happening or what he was becoming. People rarely do. To himself, he was just focused on his church, his congregation, his family, whatever land he inherited, and raising his children.

When those burdens were set before the backdrop of Papa Sarantis's celebrity status, his unmatched oratorical abilities, and the respect everyone paid him, the combination collectively fertilized the deadliest sin for any person, let alone a priest—hubris. Intense pride has a way of isolating a person, of driving others away, slowly and one by one, until the prideful person, in competition with all, conquers all. When it appears there are no longer people with whom to compete, having in his own mind conquered all, the prideful person turns his attentions to a contest with the Almighty Himself. Of course, this is usually done unconsciously and it is only after some great calamity that a person obtains the perspective to see just how far down the wrong road he has traveled. So, as Papa Sarantis's pride grew, he became more and more an island, and the more isolated he became, the more his pride grew.

Eleni watched as locals continued to offer the priest's family their alms, dropping off produce, cheeses, clothing, and other items on her front door. But she longed for the lost joy that had once accompanied the donors' actions—the smiles, the banter, and the overflow of brotherly love. Eleni watched with increasing awareness that people's smiles no longer carried the spontaneous delight they once had. She also knew that their gifts, which had dwindled over the years, were no longer motivated by love, but by a desire to placate the demands of a martinet—to do just enough to remain below her husband's purview and to avoid his condemnation. And no matter how hard she tried, Eleni's efforts couldn't replace the void Papa Sarantis's pride left behind. As for the donors, most just longed for the smile Papa Sarantis used to give, the memory of which, year after year, decade after decade, faded and faded. Gone was that focused, bright-eyed smile that looked directly into a person's soul and said, without words, "I know and see your true self; who you really are under the masks you wear; and I understand you and love you unconditionally."

Chapter 3
WILL SOMEONE PLEASE MARRY MY DAUGHTERS?

Over the years, the changes in Papa Sarantis affected Eleni as well as his girls. The three daughters of Papa Sarantis and Eleni grew up as celebrities in Gargaliani, the most conservative of social environments. As the children of a famous priest, Theano, Tasia, and Nitsa's social position, in modern terms, was akin to being the offspring of a governor or a mayor. Everyone knew the girls and envied their social standing. Locals watched them and discussed what they had heard about what this one said about this or what the other one said about that. While this scrutiny provided the locals with conversational fodder, it created a constraining atmosphere for the girls, one where these judges evaluated, discussed, and eventually criticized their every word and action, no matter how frivolous.

And Eleni solemnly watched, year after year, how Papa Sarantis's bloating vanity bore fruit—bruised fruit to be sure—personified in the personalities of his three daughters. As this happened, there was less and less Eleni could do as she slowly lost her role in raising her children. By 1910, when Theano, Tasia, and Nitsa were eighteen, fourteen, and ten years old, respectively, the priest had reduced Eleni's role to little more than chef and chambermaid as Papa Sarantis obstructed her efforts to counteract his influence.

Knowing full well that he and his children lived under the microscope of the Gargaliani demos, Papa Sarantis urged his daughters to be examples for others and to be worthy of emulation for their superb behavior and good manners. What people would say or think about him and his family was always of prime importance. In their early years, Papa Sarantis's daughters complied fully with his commands and were impressively obedient young girls. He taught them fastidious behavior and manners and made certain that his training would prepare them to be able housekeepers. Despite the innumerable restrictions the three lived under, they idolized their father and instinctively responded to questions about him with adoration. They were always quick to note there was no other man like him, and they snapped at anyone who dared imply anything to the contrary.

The priest raised his daughters with an eye always on the ultimate goal: their marriages. But raising daughters was precarious. People in the Gargaliani social caldron gossiped constantly, and just like in Mani, every Father knew that loose talk could quickly compromise the reputation of a girl and thus her chances for marriage. While there was never any question about their chastity, by the time Theano, Tasia, and Nitsa reached their twenties, the priest was faced with a devastating situation—his inability to find them husbands. That Theano was twenty-eight and unmarried was an enormous challenge because a father had to marry off his oldest daughter first. Allowing a younger daughter to marry before her older sibling would, in effect, write off the older sister. So, Papa Sarantis took a firm position and on several occasions turned away suitors who had asked for both Tasia and Nitsa's hand. The family would sink or swim together.

Though Theano grew into the most intractable of young women and there wasn't a single suitor inquiring about her, Papa Sarantis blamed himself and the priesthood for her ill fortune, assuming the problem was his lack of sufficient dowry to offer a potential groom. Still, he was surprised that despite his charisma and star power, not to mention his allocation of the large vineyard for Theano, she kept coming up empty. And so Papa Sarantis prayed that God would send Theano a good Christian not so preoccupied with material things.

As Theano approached thirty, Papa Sarantis began noticing she wasn't helping the situation as she had become difficult to handle and reason with. And so, he panicked. He knew that if Theano hit thirty without being married, all hope would be lost for her, and so he began to connive to resolve his dilemma. He found a new appreciation for Laban, the Old Testament character who, when in a similar predicament, agreed to give his younger daughter Rachel in marriage to his nephew Jacob, but before the wedding, Laban swapped Rachel for her unmarried older sister Leah. Rachel, covered from head to toe during the wedding ceremony, made it all the way through consummating the nuptials and to the following morning before Jacob discovered to his horror what had happened.

Such fleeting fantasies were the only comfort Papa Sarantis had during his fruitless hunt for a groom, and though he was aware of the nefariousness of his own machinations, he longed to pull a similar maneuver. He would have readily traded Theano for Tasia or Nitsa at the altar, if he could only figure out the logistics.

Around 1919, with Papa Sarantis convinced that none of the local bachelors would marry Theano, he resolved that his only hope was to look outside the country, to a person who neither knew of Theano and her challenging personality, nor would this person need a significant dowry from Papa Sarantis. So, in the fall of that year, he wrote a friend named Matsukas who had left Gargaliani several years earlier for Chicago. He told Matsukas about Theano and, in confidence, inquired about potential Chicago suitors. It only took a few letters for the matchmaker Matsukas to zero in on a wealthy American with roots in Gargaliani, a man by the name of Nikolaki Papachristofilou. Papa Sarantis had hit the jackpot.

Nikolaki was an elegant, forty-five-year-old businessman who dressed conspicuously in the latest American fashions, fully equipped with gold pocket watch, fob, and three-piece suits. He moved with the air that he was a man of means and intelligence. Papa Sarantis was elated, and Matsukas arranged for Nikolaki to come to Gargaliani to find a wife the priest hoped would be Theano.

In the spring of 1920, Nikolaki returned to his hometown. He had been told repeatedly of Theano, how lovely, loving, and eventempered she was, and he liked the idea of marrying the daughter of the famous Papa Sarantis. Like the clothes and accessories he coveted, a bride who was the child of a celebrity was an adornment he could not resist. Theano, on the other hand, had been told of Nikolaki and his intentions and inwardly resolved to avoid such a set up at all costs. She spied the would-be suitor walking with friends in the plateia shortly after his arrival, and reacting without thinking, she told her father, in blunt, no uncertain terms that showed her total lack of appreciation for his efforts, that she was *not* marrying Nikolaki, or any other man, let alone leaving Gargaliani for Chicago.

Even Theano could never have predicted what would follow in that fateful discussion, and Papa Sarantis, seemingly unaware that he was playing the parent in the same skit in which he had once played the child, pulled out all the stops.

"You're not going to marry him?" he shouted at her one afternoon.

"Oh yes, you will! You are about to turn thirty. If you don't marry this man, let me tell you what your fate will be—you will become an old maid. You will never get married, you will never have children, and you will spend the remainder of your years living here and taking care of your mother and me. But if you don't want to do that, you can still go to a monastery and become a nun. Do you want to become a nun? Eleni, the girl wants to be a nun!"

Of course, Theano didn't want to become a nun, and after a heated exchange, she finally confessed to her family her true reason for not wanting to marry the American—she had been secretly in love with someone else for at least a decade and "wanted to wait to see the outcome of that relationship."

"Wait to see the outcome of that relationship?" Papa Sarantis asked incredulously. "What relationship? What are you talking about?"

Papa Sarantis wondered whether someone had compromised his daughter's virtue.

"Are you insane? This man has come all the way from America. He risked his life on a ship, and you talk about some other relationship? What relationship? Who is he? What are you talking about? What has this person done to you?"

"He's not from here," Theano quietly and solemnly replied.

"Who's not from where? What are you talking about?"

"He's from Mani."

"Mani? Who's from Mani? You found someone from Mani? You have never even been to Mani! My father left Mani and those lunatics decades ago, and you found someone from there? Who are you talking about?" he begged.

"It's Elias."

The priest's mind silently raced. Then he crossed himself.

"Your cousin? My aunt's son? Is that who you are talking about?"

Theano's statement was a bombshell. She told her family how she had fallen in love with Elias, her cousin from Mani who she met a few years earlier when he came to Gargaliani on business. She reminded everyone how Papa Sarantis brought this cousin to their house for dinner. She had instantly fallen in love with him. She also described how she was convinced that he experienced the same instant affection and, as evidence, mentioned how Elias had suggested that it wasn't right for the families to live so far apart and that they should move closer to one another. Theano took this statement as a veiled yet obvious declaration of Elias's love for her.

If only for a moment, Papa Sarantis could relate to Theano's amorous feelings and couldn't help but recall the fireworks prior to his own nuptials. But Theano having a relationship with her cousin was not an option, and he determined he had to shake the insanity from her. He ranted about how, in the last ten years, not a single soul had called for Theano and scoffed at how she could so quickly dismiss an exceptional man like Nikolaki for no more than an insane, unreciprocated episode of imagined love. He pushed so intensely that in the end, Theano had no choice but to acquiesce to his wishes.

Later that year, Nikolaki and Theano were married at the church of All Saints in Gargaliani with Papa Sarantis officiating. Only a week after that, the newlyweds left Gargaliani to begin their new life in Chicago. Once she was gone, Papa Sarantis rejoiced and savored the fact that a major problem, one that had consumed him for a decade, was finally solved.

But the priest's troubles with Theano didn't end with her marriage and her removal from the European continent. Nikolaki and Theano moved into his mansion in Chicago's Hyde Park neighborhood, a swanky and affluent part of its south side and home to the University of Chicago. Theano had difficulty adjusting to her new life, one that couldn't have been more different from her old one. When their train arrived at the LaSalle Street Station, for example, Nikolaki's three brothers met the couple as they disembarked. One of them handed Theano a fur coat as part of the family's welcome. But apparently not wanting to give the impression that Nikolaki could buy her so easily, Theano threw it to the ground. It was downhill from there. Despite the chauffeur-driven car, the full-time maid, and the instant gratification of all her requests, Theano's irrational demands came one after the next, and in the end, she proved insatiable. She became a dissatisfied loner in a mansion which, for the next four years, she stuffed with everything imaginable: statues, rugs, paintings, and so forth. The first fruit from Papa Sarantis's tree appeared to be a bruised one indeed.

What was worse, Theano treated Nikolaki terribly. And the man just heroically absorbed it all. Though he complained about her bitterly in letters to Papa Sarantis in which he implored his father-in-law to intercede, there was little the priest could do. Rumors spread around Gargaliani that Theano had lost her mind in Chicago. And there was a degree of truth to them. For Theano, the Chicago skies were always gray, its smoke stacks always blew pollutants, and the tall buildings in the distance were mere mocking reminders of the cemetery evergreens in Gargaliani. She nagged Nikolaki endlessly to leave Hyde Park and to return to Gargaliani. No amount of material wealth could placate her. And after only four years, Nikolaki sold his share in the family businesses to his brothers, and the couple, along with their two-year-old son John and six-month-old daughter Eleni, returned to Gargaliani.

When they arrived, Papa Sarantis was happy to see his grandchildren, but embarrassed and disappointed at what Theano had become—a loveless and irrational creature and the topic sentence of every paragraph uttered by the Gargaliani gossip circuit. Even so, Theano's marriage made her someone else's problem, and Papa Sarantis kept his attentions focused on marrying off his next daughter, Tasia, a task that became a four-year effort.

As the middle child, Tasia felt starved for her father's affection which Theano, the black hole of attention, had sucked away. Tasia complained that no one ever told her they loved her or expressed compassion for her. She seldom experienced hugs or kisses, the affectionate expressions of love that every person craves. Indeed, Tasia lived in a house where her older sister dominated her father's attention and her younger sister monopolized whatever little love was left over. Although she wanted to be recognized, accolades came in dribbles and caused her to take a position of defiance and independence—traits that gave the impression she was unapproachable and cold. But deep in her heart, Tasia wanted to extricate herself from her father's grip and find freedom in the arms of a husband who would take her away from Gargaliani, a petty place she despised. Regardless of how she actually felt, she fervently wanted to appear to the world to be someone who had everything. It was this fictitious feeling that she was somehow different from all those around her that ultimately mattered most to Tasia, and she cherished the gulf of separation she created between herself and everyone else.

Ultimately, Tasia found peace when Papa Sarantis learned of a possible suitor from Tripoli, a city northeast of Gargaliani near the center of the Peloponnesus. The parties met at a pastry shop in Kyparissia and, as fate would have it, found an instant affinity for one another. Indeed, they liked each other so much that the matchmaker, a friend of Papa Sarantis, reported that the suitor, Spyros Mothonios, vehemently refused to take any *prika* whatsoever because Papa Sarantis's vocation understandably made it impossible for him to be in a position to offer a *prika* worthy of Tasia. Papa Sarantis married the couple at All Saints and they then moved twenty-five kilometers north to the town of Kyparissia.

Marrying off two of his three daughters, and indeed the more problematic ones, provided a respite for Papa Sarantis as he found himself in his late fifties. Despite the fact that he was a priest, a person who one would only assume spent a portion of each day in the struggles of self-examination, it wasn't until the marriage of Tasia that he had the time or even the inclination for a little self assessment, a process that proved more painful than he ever expected.

One morning in the fall of 1927, within a few weeks of Tasia's wedding, Papa Sarantis found himself seated alone in one of the Gargaliani cafés that lined the plateia. Things the priest had been unable to see came finally into focus. As the hustle of the plateia's coffee houses ramped up, Papa Sarantis's right hand grasped his prayer rope, and his right thumb counted off, one by one, the endless circle of knots. Drifting deeper and deeper into a daze, he ignored the greeting of those who passed and mechanically sipped one of his several daily cups of coffee. In an earlier time, Papa Sarantis would have been involved in a heated debate with the other men, exchanging remarks on politics and current events. He always took great delight in unleashing his ever-ready lethal bursts of rhetoric, effective at disarming any adventurous scout who dared challenge his oratorical superiority. In the past, Papa Sarantis saved his most lethal salvos for the moments just before his customary abrupt departure, cleverly eliminating the opportunity for any counterstrike.

But such verbal militancy was not on that day's agenda. Humility, or in Papa Sarantis's case, humility's negative relative, humiliation, has a way of revealing the emptiness of such staged triumphs. For sure, the difficulties he experienced in marrying his daughters heaped upon him hefty doses of the latter. He had always suspected that when he wasn't around, the locals mocked his obvious difficulties. He knew all too well how people tend to derive pleasure at the misfortune of others and how other's tribulations can often make one feel better about his own lot. But until that moment, Papa Sarantis never realized how good *his* troubles really made others feel. And as he thought through his life, he began to see things clearly and was taken aback at how his many sins had returned to haunt him tenfold. It occurred to him that during his darkest moments, his café "friends" offered him neither a helping hand nor an encouraging word, but only sneered, gossiped, and silently cheered each of his crosses as they emerged.

Where were they when I was struggling to marry off those girls? Why did they abandon me? he wondered. *I never abandoned them.*

As these thoughts swirled through his head, he began to do the only thing he knew how to do—pray. And as he prayed, more thoughts entered his mind with a clarity that had eluded him for decades. When he spontaneously recognized that his suffering was his own creation, a tension clamped onto to his lower stomach. It tightened as he contemplated the obvious effect his newly discovered sins had on his children. His prayer intensified.

Oh, God, have mercy on me, a sinner.

He thought of Tasia and especially Theano, recalcitrant albatrosses who though now thrown from his neck, offered him no freedom. Guilt had become his new captor—guilt for his own actions and for theirs. His mind raced to Nitsa, his youngest. Despite his inattention, he marveled at how she had never been a problem for him.

I have ignored the girl all these years and she's the best of the lot, he thought. *Could it be that the less I interfere, the better things turn out? Oh, God, have mercy on me! The girl wanted to study in Athens like her cousins, and I said no, good girls stay with their families. And she has attracted a number of suitors already, and all of them laughed at my attempts to turn their attentions to Theano and then to Tasia. But I don't blame those boys at all for scattering. I wouldn't have wanted either of them. Or their father, for that matter. Oh, God, have mercy on me, a sinner!*

His thoughts returned to his café friends, and only now did he see what everyone else in Gargaliani had known for a decade, that all the men with sons of marrying age had stayed away from him. Despite the unending flow of pleasantries, Papa Sarantis and his family had become pariahs.

If I had only shut my mouth and permitted others to speak. If I had only listened with compassion to others. Why did I have to win every argument? Why did I want everyone to marvel at me and my wit? Why did I always have to be the center of attention? Get behind me Satan! Oh, Jesus Christ, have mercy on me, a sinner.

The priest saw himself as the Gospel's boastful Pharisee who he had preached about so many times, the one who was damned the very moment he thanked God that he was better than those less virtuous than he.

His prayers continued as he sat at the café, staring into space. Random memories knifed in and out of his thoughts, uncontrollable and violent. He thought of Eleni.

My sweet wife, my presbytera has never complained about a thing. I brought that flower here from Pirgaki and treated her as if I was doing her a favor, when in fact she was doing me the favor. Oh, God, have mercy on me. I've lived with a saintly person my entire life, all along thinking it was she who lived with the saint! What a fool I am!

Papa Sarantis's thoughts drifted to Theano's poor husband Nikolaki, whose lamentable life had created an endless flow of gossip, the most recent bit involving Theano's eviction of Nikolaki's mother and mute sister from their home and then the claiming of the house as her own. He realized he had raised a misfit, one he cleverly disguised as the dignified daughter of a respected priest. When he considered that his silence about Theano's madness amounted not to passivity but to active enabling, a flow of new questions charged into his mind.

How did my problems become so big? When did I become so common?

When it occurred to him that bad fruit must fall from a bad tree, he looked at himself again.

Did I become corrupt? When did I become corrupt? How did I become corrupt? What did I do to my wife? How did she endure the cross of living with me? And what did I do to my children?*

Papa Sarantis slowly began to see that *he* was the cause of his own troubles, that he terminally suffered from what he knew was the worst sin of all, the grievous sin of pride. This sin had caused him, little by little, to distance himself from God and to replace God with himself. He realized that it happened because he mingled too closely with the laity. He saw how people's endless accolades had led him to believe that his abilities were his own, not gifts from God. Somewhere, Papa Sarantis had allowed his focus to turn to himself. The more others had praised and complemented him, the more he had allowed the serpentine pride to slither into his psyche. Indeed, he realized how pride, with its manipulative arms of conceit and deceptions, had captured and ruled his heart with a tenacious grip that choked off any humility. He thought back to his conversion and to his early days of piety.

When did I forget those lessons? When did I become my own God? When did my nourishment stop coming from the Holy Spirit and instead from the daily praises I received? Oh God, have mercy on me the sinner. I am an idolater, worshiping the false God of me! Oh, thank God my poor parents didn't live to see this—I have become a true disgrace.

Papa Sarantis concluded that as bad as Theano and Tasia were, he was worse. To undo what he had done, he knew, would require agonizing work. But he would start immediately. Of course, he would confess everything to his father confessor, the bishop, but that wouldn't be enough. He would need, as he had told others so many times, ceaseless prayer to disassemble his armaments, piece by piece, as each represented an impediment to Divine Grace. He had to destroy them. The effort seemed Herculean, since each impediment had deep roots that would require great suffering to unearth. But he had to do it to restore his inner spiritual life. Papa Sarantis trembled with fear at what he faced because he knew that his pride was the root of his identity.

What will happen to me if I destroy the image of myself that I have created? Who will I become?

In a way, Papa Sarantis had been comfortable in his misery— misery that carried the familiarity of an old friend. He was confused and yet able to settle on the thought that only by being humble, as life circumstances had forced him during his early years, would he be redeemed. After all, it is the meek who shall inherit the earth. The contradictions were almost too much for him to swallow over a single cup of coffee, and so he decided it was time to go.

Papa Sarantis left a few coins on the table, rose from his seat, and drifted toward his home. On his way, he kept to himself. He did not talk or bless anyone, and he did not make his regular stops. Others must have thought it odd that he didn't say hello as he passed and that he neither worked the crowds nor acknowledged those who came to kiss his hand.

Perhaps I'll return to the church where I found my salvation, he thought.

When he arrived home, Papa Sarantis told Eleni everything he discovered that day—his thoughts, his actions, and about his desire for redemption. He apologized for pushing her aside and dominating her. He asked her forgiveness. Eleni, though evicted into the background for so many years, knew that she and Papa Sarantis would have this conversation one day and had long waited for him to see things for himself. So she rejoiced at the return of her prodigal husband, immediately forgave him, and the two spent the next few hours talking like old friends who hadn't seen each other for years.

But while Eleni had hoped for and even predicted this rapprochement, neither she nor anyone else could have predicted that Papa Sarantis would die that night in his sleep. But he did. He was sixty-two years old.

It is ironic that Papa Sarantis left when he did, having realized his sins but unable to make amends with the rest of his family, his friends, and his flock. Perhaps even worse was that my grandfather was never able to really personally impart the lesson he learned to his daughters, to imprint in them the obvious secrets he had so painfully discovered. But there are those who say that everything happens for a reason and that God takes people when they are at their best. Perhaps, in that moment of clarity, Papa Sarantis was as good as he was ever going to be.

The night following his death, Papa Sarantis was placed in state in the church of All Saints. As word of his passing spread, priests from the entire region quickly made their way to Gargaliani to perform the ceremony Papa Sarantis had performed hundreds of times for others, the funeral service. The service reached its apex when, in the church packed with mourners that spilled out its doors, the twenty-odd clergy that included the local bishop, priests, deacons, and monastics, surrounded the silenced Papa Sarantis lying in his casket and asked God to help their colleague complete his final journey:

> O God of spirits and of all flesh, You have trampled death and have abolished the power of the devil, giving life to the world. Give rest to the soul of Your departed servant, Sarantis, The Priest, Our Brother and Co-Celebrant, put him in a place of light, in a place of repose, in place of refreshment, where there is no pain, sorrow, and suffering. As a good and loving God, forgive every sin he has committed in thought, word or deed, for there is no one who lives and does not sin. You alone are without sin. Your righteousness is an everlasting righteousness and Your word is truth.

The priests, one by one, paid their respects to Eleni and her three daughters. All others who came, and there were hundreds, hugged and kissed them. The women cried and hugged each other. All somehow seemed to forget that, in the last decade, their affection for the deceased priest had faded. A person's death tends to finally make others love him unconditionally, perhaps the direct result of the elimination of the opportunities for the dead to hurt and disappoint.

Papa Sarantis's passing was a severe blow to Eleni and Nitsa, both emotionally and financially. The priest had made no contingency plans whatsoever for this, no provisions set aside for his wife nor for his remaining unmarried daughter. On the contrary, Papa Sarantis died with so many balls in the air that when he left, most of them, except for a few that Eleni and Nitsa were able to catch, crashed to the ground. Income from the vineyard and the olive grove was small and insufficient to sustain the lifestyle the two had grown accustomed to. Eleni and Nitsa lacked the money to buy food and clothing and were forced to turn to their immediate family for help. Despite his problems, Theano's husband Nikolaki, who always displayed great *filotimo*, did whatever he could.

Tasia, on the other hand, was nowhere to be found. While she attended her father's funeral, she showed little emotion and returned to Kyparissia as soon as it was over. For Tasia, her old life in Gargaliani was behind her, a role in which she had been terribly miscast, its characters an embarrassment, and the life there a community-theater production for which she refused to volunteer. Tasia's coolness devastated Eleni, but with too many of her own problems, she put that worry on the back burner and refocused her efforts on her and Nitsa's survival. Nitsa couldn't put aside Tasia's rejection as easily and that, combined with her father's passing, caused her to fall into a deep depression. When Nitsa finally emerged from it, she let her pride became her sword and shield. While the pride of some can leave them unsatisfied with everything, Nitsa's would prevent her from complaining or taking any action she perceived beneath her. Griping was not an option. After all, no matter what happened and no matter how bad things would get, she would always be the daughter of the great Papa Sarantis.

In the months that followed the funeral, the village began to move on after Papa Sarantis's passing, and Eleni and Nitsa found themselves more and more isolated. Little by little, guests stopped visiting and gifts, money, and tidings stopped coming in. With their house in a perpetual state of mourning, Eleni and Nitsa closed their home to the world and became like hermits. Papa Sarantis had handled all major household decisions, made all judgments regarding the family's properties, dealt with the town of Gargaliani, brought money into the family, and so forth. In their state of dark isolation, neither Eleni nor Nitsa could manage the family's affairs.

Then, the situation of the two mourners went from bad to worse. Within a year of Papa Sarantis's death, Eleni developed an intense cough, one that made her sound like a barking seal. When the cough did not resolve after several weeks but worsened into one that produced blood, doctors quickly diagnosed her condition as tuberculosis. Nitsa did what she could to halt the disease's progression by caring for her mother, but her attempts were fruitless. Before long, Eleni could not rise from her bed, the result of a gradual loss of appetite and a fever that kept her shivering, week after week.

dandelions for Dinner

Locals knew tuberculosis well, that this relentless bacterial infection had attacked Eleni's lungs and that to go near her would be to risk infection because Eleni could easily transmit the disease to another just by coughing or sneezing in their presence. When visitors did come, they would wash themselves with alcohol before and after entering the room, and even then, could only enter like bandits, with handkerchiefs covering their faces. Month after month, the beautiful Helen of Pirgaki coughed, spat, sighed, and eventually faded from this world. When she finally passed and joined her husband, she was no more than a wizened flesh, draped over a horizontal collection of aged and tired bones.

Chapter 4
THE RISE OF NITSA

After burying her father and mother in just eighteen months, my mother, Nitsa, walked alone onto the stage of her adulthood and into a role for which her privileged childhood had not prepared her. Despite being the youngest—and accordingly the recipient of the attention Theano and Tasia couldn't wrestle away—Nitsa always claimed that her parents had starved her for attention. Whether or not she actually was, is a matter for debate. Nitsa was an obedient child who spent most of her time under everyone's radar even though her good behavior was taken for granted and went unrewarded.

She told a story later in life that served as the metaphor for her childhood. On New Year's Day just after her eighth birthday, Papa Sarantis entered the house in a happy mood and while wishing everyone a happy new year, gave Theano and Tasia each a gold coin for good luck. When young Nitsa asked about her coin, the befuddled priest removed an old five-drachma piece from his pocket and handed it over. Nitsa acted happy to receive the coin, while hiding her anguish at the oversight that burned her insides.

As for her vocation, Nitsa's mother and grandmother had trained her in the domestic skills. Because she was the youngest daughter, her parents had expected her, much more than her two older sisters, to cook, clean, sew, and care for Papa Sarantis and Eleni in their old age. The lessons were all courses in the skills required for her to become a wife and the matriarch of her own family. They taught her how to conduct herself in public, to be always cognizant of her surroundings, alert at all times, and like the women before her, *never* be with the opposite sex unless other adult females were present. Maintaining her chastity was crucial. Nitsa took these lessons seriously. She used to tell me how if, for example, a man passed by her window, she would quickly close the shutters until he was gone. If she was outside the house and a man came walking her way, she would swiftly retreat and close the door behind her until he passed.

Her mother's death was an acute psychological blow for Nitsa. It hit her with an uppercut that was delivered while she was already falling from the knockout blow of Papa Sarantis's death. She was twenty-eight years old and alone. With little help from her sisters, who were consumed with the responsibilities of their own families, the duties that she had been sheltered from became Nitsa's alone. Of course, it was now up to Nitsa to continue to take care of mundane tasks like buying food, cooking, and cleaning. These, she could handle. But she also had to function in the world of men, the very men society trained her to shun. This was exceedingly difficult. Shrewd tenant farmers tended to Gargaliani's grape and wheat fields, and Nitsa knew they would be quick to cheat her wherever and whenever they could, despite any tenant agreements. Her mind was a blank slate about how to manage such matters. The responsibilities of the household and the demands of others seemed to howl as they spun around her. The accumulated burden of all these new responsibilities was overwhelming. No longer could she say, "talk to my father about this" or "talk to my mother about that."

In order to survive, Nitsa became the perpetual mourner, always dressed in black and quick to accept the condolences of others for the rapid and sudden passing of her parents. Most found it difficult to come down too hard on her, having just suffered back-to-back losses and Nitsa used this opportunity to learn how the world of men worked and how she would navigate through it, something she would do alone, unless God sent her a husband.

Nitsa vowed she would not marry just any man and wanted one who was decisive and sure, cut from the same swatch as her father. But she would keep such matters in God's hands. If he sent her the right groom, she would marry him. If not, then she would complete the remaining years of her life alone.

Others possessed a much higher level of urgency about Nitsa's matrimonial plans, and sometime after Eleni's death, several family friends sprang into action. The most determined of these matchmakers was a former mentee of Papa Sarantis, Papa Ntres. Following Papa Sarantis's death, Papa Ntres began bringing Nitsa a number of potential husbands, all of whom she one by one dismissed as uneducated farmers. His queue of bachelors seemed endless as Nitsa's rejections were at first not greeted with exasperation; he just produced the next suitor in line. Papa Ntres was determined to carry out what he knew were his former mentor's wishes—one way or another, he would see to it that Nitsa settled into the safety and sanctity of family life.

After a dozen or so rejections, Papa Ntres's list of grooms began to thin, and he realized his task was much greater than he originally thought. After a year of trying, he began to feel the weight of the cross that was Nitsa, often expressing his frustrations to Theano, asking questions.

"What's the matter with her? Doesn't she realize her situation? Doesn't she know she's almost thirty, unmarried, and living alone in that house? Doesn't she see that she's running out of options?"

His string of questions ebbed and flowed from week to week and led him to raise both his arms, look toward the heavens, and pray, with the conviction he typically reserved for announcing the resurrection of Christ at the Anastasi service, "Dear Mother of God, open her eyes to the situation!"

Disturbed by his own exasperation, Papa Ntres prayed for the strength to keep on.

As the months passed, Nitsa began to avoid Papa Ntres, tired of feeling guilty about rejecting him over and over again. Indeed, her almost reflexive rejections led her to believe she would never get married, that she was just one of those people who were surprised to learn that marriage wasn't for them. She figured that her expectations for a groom were either too high or too narrow to be fulfilled by an actual living human being. She often contemplated what she would do with her life if she didn't marry. And as she progressed down this train of thought, she avoided Papa Ntres more and more, since he was a man she thought could only suggest one bucolic bumbler after another.

But on one afternoon, Papa Ntres caught up with Nitsa and told her he had found the perfect mate for her, a young man named Panagiotis Stamatis, who had just returned from living in America. When Nitsa heard his family lived near St. Spyridon, located on the east side of Gargaliani, she recoiled at the proposition of settling for a farmer. As the daughter of Papa Sarantis, she would have to marry someone with at least *some* status, stature, and wealth. If the prospective groom was without a minimum of these qualities, she would prefer not to marry.

Though she initially balked, Papa Ntres was undaunted and convinced her that marrying was likely a now-or-never proposition.

"Nitsa, what's the matter with you? You don't like this one, and you didn't like that one. Remember something. Your years are passing and with them, so are your options. You are already twenty-nine years old. And every day that passes makes you a day older. You don't want to end up a spinster, do you? Your parents have been gone for two years now. Stop mourning and get on with your life. And stop wearing all that black. You're not a nun, and you have mourned too long. It's not too late to marry. Get on with your life."

She eventually acquiesced to the priest's requests and agreed to meet Panagiotis in the plateia.

Panagiotis Stamatis was born in Gargaliani in 1893. The son of Antonis, a raisin farmer, Panagiotis spent his youth running and playing in the streets of Gargaliani. By the time he reached the age of thirteen, he not only stopped growing at a mere five foot two inches tall and he had also finished all the formal education he would ever receive, the equivalent of a junior high-school diploma. During his teen years, Panagiotis helped his father and other siblings tend to the family's properties, first by planting and trimming grape vines and then by harvesting, processing, and selling raisins. Year after year, Panagiotis watched his siblings leave Gargaliani for greener pastures elsewhere. Each knew that neither Gargaliani nor Antonis's meager raisin farm would ever provide enough of a livelihood for them or the families they would inevitably create.

Panagiotis grew into a pious person and though often taken advantage of, avoided harboring ill feelings toward anyone. Not surprisingly, this trait often made him an easy target of those willing to lie, cheat, and steal for their own advantage. When asked why he tolerated such behavior, he would say something like "things must be bad for them if they have to resort to such tricks." Panagiotis was the salt of the earth, and no matter how bad things were, he neither formed devious plots against others nor needed to have the last word in any argument.

Despite his fundamentally good character, Pantagiotis was fated to become a pawn in the conflicts that rent Greece during his lifetime. Around 1913, during a period when Greece was involved in the complex maneuvers of nations that lead to full-blown war in Europe, the Greek army drafted Panagiotis. He was twenty years old.

At that point, Greeks were polarized into two factions: one devoted to King Constantine (the descendant of the Austrian-born Greek King Otto) who favored the Central Powers of Germany, Austria, and Turkey, and an opposing faction made up of supporters of the Greek Prime Minister Eleftherios Venizelos, a man who was generally sympathetic to Great Britain and France. The division between the factions—known as the National Schism—cut through Greek national life and essentially resulted in the creation of almost two separate nations. This fundamental conflict continued in one way or another for decades and directly affected the lives of my family and almost all Greeks.

Although Panagiotis was young and loyal to no one other than his own family, he found himself in an army regiment that favored the king, who, in 1914, ordered Panagiotis's unit to leave Greece for Munich, Germany. Even though Greece was officially at war with Germany, the king had found a way to keep army units loyal to him out of World War I and far from the fighting between the Germans and other Greek army units. Prime Minister Venizelos had actively inserted Greece into the war on the side of the Allies. Panagiotis's superiors dragged him and his unit to Germany, and he spent the next four years cutting down trees in the Black Forest and using the lumber to build houses for the Germans. War taught Panagiotis carpentry.

After the signing of the Treaty of Versailles in June 1919, Greek soldiers in Germany were released and ordered to return home. Unfortunately for them, they were given neither money nor train tickets. An odyssey ensued, as Panagiotis and some of his fellow soldiers walked the entire way from Munich to the Italian port town of Brindisi, stopping along the way to ask friendly farmers for some food or helping themselves to whatever they found growing. Once they made it to Brindisi, Greek ships ferried them eastward to

Patras in the northwest Peloponnese, 130 kilometers due north of Gargaliani.

When Panagiotis and his mates caught the first sight of Greece, they cheered. When they first stepped on Greek soil, they kissed the ground. And when they raised their heads after so doing, the police arrested them. The current government was belligerent to Greeks who it felt deserted the homeland during the war, not to mention those who built houses for the enemy, and shipped them to the island of Crete to be jailed and tried by military tribunal. Panagiotis thought that he and the others would be quickly convicted and sentenced to death by firing squad. But for reasons none of them could explain, the days in prison stretched into weeks and the weeks into months. After half a year peeled off the calendar, government officials sent Panagiotis and the six hundred other prisoners to Athens for immediate trial. Panagiotis spent his boat ride to Athens asking God to help him avoid the impending doom. Just before the trial was to start, and as if on cue, an unexpected and unexplained power shift occurred in the government. The new officials freed Panagiotis and the other military prisoners. Not wanting to press his luck, Panagiotis returned to Gargaliani, gathered some belongings, said good-bye to his parents, and immediately left Greece for the United States. He would remain there for nearly a decade.

Panagiotis entered the United States on March 10, 1920, through Ellis Island and moved in with his sister Tasia in the Logan Square neighborhood of Chicago's northwest side. Happy to be in a place not at war and ready to get to work, he quickly found employment in the restaurants and candy shops of Chicago's more established Greeks. Though he was an experienced carpenter, the Irish dominated the building trades and weren't hiring Greeks, regardless of their skill and training. And so Panagiotis worked where he could and saved everything he earned in the jobs he could find. His ability to survive on the bits of the Gargaliani raisin fields helped him accumulate a tidy sum of money before he knew it.

Panagiotis was an industrious dreamer. He worked with his head down and was unaffected by world events. When for example, Adolph Hitler became leader of Germany's Nazi party in 1921, he didn't pay much attention. When Benito Mussolini became prime minister of Italy the following year, he didn't care too much about that either. Indeed, over the following decade, Panagiotis became an American citizen and was able to save four thousand dollars, money he kept deposited in savings accounts he held with two different financial institutions, a bank in Logan Square, and the United States Post Office, which at the time offered postal savings accounts. Panagiotis's new-found financial independence allowed him to rent an apartment and save enough money to start his own business, something he had always intended to do and for which he suffered no shortage of grand ideas—ideas that he often shared with his peers only to hear them recite a litany of reasons why this one or that one was impractical. Such negativity would inevitably let the air out of Panagiotis's enthusiasm, at least until the next idea hit.

After a decade of toiling, Panagiotis realized that he needed a partner whose enthusiasm had more stamina than his own. And because he knew he could trust no one outside of his own family, he decided that it was finally time to find a wife, someone to not only care for him and to give him children but also to help him tend to the business he would soon open. Panagiotis longed for someone who would offer him understanding and strength, someone who would inspire him to heights beyond his own abilities and someone who would watch his back with an eye perhaps slightly more cynical than his own. He understood that his own meekness required that he be pushed and prodded to commercial success. Without periodic shoves in the right direction, he would never make it.

In the fall of 1928, Panagiotis told his employers that he was leaving for Greece and that he would return only after he found a wife. His employers, Greeks who had at one time or another done the same thing, wished him luck and gave him gifts, money, and messages to take to their loved ones back home. A month later, Panagiotis walked into Gargaliani for the first time in a decade. When he and his parents saw each other, they all kissed, hugged, and wept in the most joyful of homecomings. Late into the night, Panagiotis regaled them with stories of his sister and her children, people about whom they would continue to hear stories, but would never again see. Panagiotis told them about America and its unending opportunities and riches. He also told them about Chicago, a place where trains traveled above the ground and buildings were so high that you entered special cabins that whisked you to their top. Like children listening to a fairy tale, Panagiotis's family soaked up his stories well into the night.

The following day, Panagiotis ventured to the plateia of the town he missed for so long, a place whose smells and sounds he savored. Papa Ntres was waiting for him, told him that he had settled everything, that he had selected a bride for Panagiotis and that the bride was the daughter of the great Papa Sarantis. He told Panagiotis about what had befallen Nitsa, about the sudden death of her father and about the illness and passing of her mother. Panagiotis listened quietly, growing more and more excited over the prospect of matrimony with the offspring of a man he remembered as sure and strong. In fact, he couldn't believe that someone of Papa Ntres's stature would even consider *him*, the son of a raisin farmer, as a potential groom for one of the great celebrities of the town. Surely, he thought, only the cream of the crop would be available for Nitsa. For the first time, Panagiotis was in the game—the prospect of marrying Papa Sarantis's daughter was a prize far beyond anything he had ever imagined.

Panagiotis marveled at the priest's depiction of Nitsa and her family's piety. He quickly ran home to tell his parents the good news, about Papa Ntres, about Nitsa, and about the godliness others said she possessed.

"Of course, we don't know the girl, Panagioti," his father Antonis opined, "but chances are she's not for you. As the daughter of a priest, she comes from a family that hasn't ever gotten their hands dirty. Papa Saranti, God rest his soul, was a good man. But the children of clergy are always difficult. Their life is lived on the stage and with high expectations. Ours is not. And we don't understand it. We are farmers, Panagioti. If you marry that girl, you will likely not be happy. She is accustomed to a certain way of life that you are unfamiliar with. You will not be able to give it to her. Take a woman from a family like ours, and if you give her more than she's used to, she will appreciate and love you for it. A humble woman will be happy just to have the riches that are you."

Panagiotis listened carefully to his father's words but refused to permit anyone to let the air out of his excitement for he felt an exuberance he had never before known. He realized that his parents assumed he was the same person as he was when he left Gargaliani years earlier, but his years abroad had changed him and had opened his eyes to a larger world of risks, potential, and bigger rewards. Panagiotis wasn't alone in this view. In the eyes of possible mates like Nitsa, his experiences over the previous decade and a half had made him a contender, and he knew it. There and then, he resolved, for the first time in his life, that he would be aggressive, regardless of the reaction of others. He would reach for the big prize, a crazy scheme for sure, but also an act of defiance against not only his family, but against his own inclinations, against his habit of predictability and never leaving the safe harbors of his mind.

    Better still, Panagiotis knew that reaching up and marrying into Gargaliani's elite class would give him a sense of accomplishment, one that he had never before experienced. He ruminated over what his future would bring with Papa Sarantis's daughter at his side. He thought of Nitsa and himself in a business partnership and imagined that he would perform the work, whether it was making pastries or performing carpentry while the daughter of the charismatic priest would serve as the face of the enterprise, focusing on sales and customer relations, business skills he knew he lacked. Suddenly, wealth and fame were within Panagiotis's grasp, and closed once and for all would be the mouths that had spent the previous three and a half decades reminding him of his limitations and predicting his demise. Suddenly, the possibilities seemed endless.

    Though the parties lived within a few blocks of the plateia and of each other, it took Papa Ntres several days of planning and shuttling between Panagiotis's and Nitsa's houses to orchestrate the location and timing of the meeting. Not wanting to seem too interested, or even too available for that matter, Nitsa declined the first few proposed dates claiming she had to travel to nearby Theano's beach house or to neighboring Kyparissia to see her sister. When she offered alternate dates, Papa Ntres proposed them to Panagiotis who immediately accepted them all. Papa Ntres, not wanting Panagiotis to seem available, played coy on his behalf, declining one but accepting another, which Nitsa then declined, and so on, until finally a date and time was set.

    The formal introduction of Nitsa and Panagiotis took place in the plateia at Kokonis's café. That evening, well after siesta time, the café was filled with its usual clientele of older mustached men, all of whom sat at tables. Though such meetings were always designed to give the appearance of casualness, especially when the eyes of the town watched them, they were serious affairs. The participants understood that the outcome would not affect only them, but generations to come.

Nitsa and Panagiotis showed up that evening, each with a support group. Nitsa arrived with Theano and Nikolaki, while Panagiotis's mother and father flanked him. The group sat outside at one of the few large rectangular tables with Papa Ntres at the head and Nitsa's family to his right and Panagiotis's to his left. Sitting furthest from Papa Ntres were Nitsa and Panagiotis, positioned directly across from each other.

Papa Ntres understood very well that fate had dealt him an uneven hand as matchmaker, with Panagiotis too anxious to marry the famous priest's daughter and Nitsa too negative toward the entire proposition. The priest knew he needed extraordinary finesse to simultaneously play up Panagiotis, play down Nitsa, and negotiate a *prika* that would be acceptable to both sides. But he relished the challenge and prayed that God would help him see the transaction to its conclusion.

Over the next hour, the families discussed everything from the news of the day to gossip and then to the plight of Greek refugees from Asia Minor. All along, Panagiotis and Nitsa sat awkwardly across from one another, silently feigning participation and enjoyment of the conversations. Panagiotis said nothing. That made Nitsa wonder whether he was so urbane that all the country talk bored him or that perhaps his international travels might have bred arrogance in him. But as the evening continued, she saw that Panagiotis's countenance gave away the real reason for his lack of participation. In fact, it didn't take too long for Panagiotis's terror and discomfort to be palpable. This led Nitsa to wonder whether Panagiotis's international travels were the result of an adventurous spirit or more likely something forced on a passive personality by winds beyond his control. This suspicion didn't sit well with Nitsa, who sought someone like her father—talkative, sure, and determined—one whose personality made him the leader and prime mover of every circumstance.

If he is just a victim, she thought, *then he's surely not for me.*

Gargaliani

And yet, as the evening wore on, Nitsa's calculated casual glances caught something she liked about Panagiotis, a quality he possessed that intrigued her. She eventually realized that he reminded her of the Papa Sarantis of her childhood. She saw his gentle posture carried an almost saintly appearance, a quiet and content innocence that spoke to her much more loudly about his character than cocky self-promotion ever could. His eyes conveyed a hidden wisdom.

In the several days after the meeting, Nitsa barricaded herself in her home and thought much about things: about Panagiotis, his lack of status and stature, his piety and his poor yet noble parents.

Several days later, Papa Ntres unexpectedly stopped by Nitsa's home.

"Nitsa, Nitsa, where are you, my child?" the priest called as he knocked on her front door.

"Where do things stand with *Kyrio* Panagioti?" (*Kyrio* is the Greek term for "Mr."; *Kyria* means "Mrs.").

"Where do things stand? Things don't stand anywhere. I am not in a position to marry that man, and that's all."

Despite his readiness, the sureness of Nitsa's response surprised the priest.

"I can't say anything bad about *Kyrio* Panagioti," she said. "Really. But he lacks everything I am looking for in a husband. He has none of the things necessary for a wedding to take place here. Most importantly, the man that I will marry must have deep roots here in Gargaliani. I was born here, and I was raised here. I am in no position to go to America to see if I have some sort of future there. Forget it. I will not repeat Theano's mistakes."

"My Nitsa, what are these things you're saying?" the priest responded. "We are talking about your future. You're not thinking straight. Panagioti is a steady man, calm and sure. He has made a great name for himself in America with his work ethic and his character. And he came here to find a wife. And I think his wife should be you. Your father would want you to get your family life started. And that will start with you getting married. Panagioti is the man you should marry and with whom you will build a strong foundation for your new life. Now is the time for you to do this, Nitsa, before you turn thirty. Every day that passes makes you a day older. You don't have the options you did when you were nineteen.

When you wake up to this fact, the decision will be an easy one for you. If you wait too long, you won't have *any* options."

"Please don't insist; he doesn't have the wherewithal for us to live here as I am accustomed to, growing up a priest's daughter. Can't you see who I am? Why would you push this farmer on me? If I marry him and stay here, I will become the town joke. I will fall very low. I'm better off alone."

"Forget about all that nonsense Nitsa! Panagioti has a golden heart; he is sincerely pious and faithful. He is not afraid to get his hands dirty and has big plans in America. Whether you realize it or not, my Nitsa, Panagioti is precisely the person you are looking for. Remember what I have told you today. Panagioti's gifts are hidden for now but will be obvious to you later."

As he left that afternoon, the priest told her how excited he was for her. The priest walked out the door, down the five stairs and onto the street.

"This is a wonderful new beginning. A wonderful new beginning for you, Nitsa! Your father himself has sent you Panagioti, and just because you can't see our beloved priest anymore doesn't mean you don't have to listen to him."

This threw Nitsa's decision into a tailspin. She found herself in a position and a situation she was unable to control, even though it involved her future so acutely.

Who is that crazy priest to tell me who and when I should marry? she thought. *What does he know about what my father would think about all this? My father was a real man, a sophisticated man, a cosmopolitan saint! And just because this goat-priest chased him around for a few years makes him wise enough to tell me who to marry and what to do?*

Later that same afternoon, Theano visited. She was for once calm and reserved and could see the wild look in her sister's eyes. Nitsa remained silent for several moments. For sure, the last thing she wanted to do was to justify herself again, not to Theano or to anyone else.

"Did you hear what that lunatic told me?" Nitsa asked.

Theano shook her head.

"He told me I should marry that raisin farmer's American son. Can you believe that? And he acts like I have agreed to do so. I haven't agreed to anything. Oh, Mother of God, help me!"

Nitsa looked at her sister and waited if not for an answer, then for some clue that the two were on the same page. Theano gently gazed back at Nitsa with a look of infinite compassion and understanding. Then she rose.

"Nitsa!" she loudly exclaimed, startling her sister. "The priest is right!"

"Look at yourself! You've gotten fat—you've gotten ugly—your beauty has long since left you. Go look at yourself in the mirror. Go! You're wearing black—your hair's going gray—you are twenty-nine years old, and you look like you're fifty—and you have been wearing black for the past two years, well beyond the appropriate time. Everyone is laughing at you. Wake up, Nitsa! You have a life to live and you can't keep putting it off. You can no longer find refuge in the black you have been wearing. Get rid of it and fix up your face. Put on some powder and color your lips so that you will be at least somewhat attractive to the opposite sex. Don't think you are going to get married looking like that!"

Nitsa stared at her sister, frozen, as Theano continued.

"Do you think Panagioti is just waiting for you? Everyone knows he's looking elsewhere for a bride. Wake up!"

Theano's words tore at Nitsa's core.

"Nitsa, you must get married and get married quickly. Now is the time. God has sent you this Christian man from America. Get moving. Our parents are dead and gone from this place. We're going to bury you with them soon if you don't wake up."

Nitsa began to cry.

"It's all my fault, Theano," she said. "How did I get here, abandoned and not provided for, left to make these decisions on my own? This is a decision father was to have made for me. Why did he leave me? How did things get so dark, with me abandoned here in the endless night of this desert?"

"Nitsa, everything is going to be fine."

Theano began to cry also.

"Look at me. Yes, I had Father's help, but look who I ended up with—Nikolaki! You should be thankful you get to make this decision on your own."

"How am I making this decision on my own if you and that priest are making it for me?"

"Oh, stop complaining, Nitsa. Wake up to the world that you have been dead to since our mother died!"

Theano arose from her chair and walked out of the house without saying another word.

In the days that followed, Nitsa lugubriously locked everyone out of her life and spent her days lamenting the black hand she had been dealt.

How did things get so bad? she wondered. *Who are all these people who claim to know what is best for me? Even my own sister thinks I should marry that nobody.*

But, as each day passed, Nitsa realized that her life needed to change and a pragmatism arose in her. To continue in the same routine, she knew, was intolerable. She feared that her sister and the priest might be right, that her advanced age might make Panagiotis her last chance to marry. She ran through scenarios of what might happen if she did not marry him and then what might happen if she did. It became clear that if she married him, the couple could never live in Gargaliani. Nitsa was unwilling to abandon her place of prominence in her hometown in exchange for little, if anything. Marrying Panagiotis would no doubt drop her to the lowest caste, the status of peasant farmer.

But she *could* marry Panagiotis if after the ceremony, the couple immediately moved to America, to that unknown and remote place that she had only heard tales about, the place that people disappeared to forever. Nitsa developed an appreciation for the folk song that many locals sang at festivals, the sorrowful song of a country that mourned each of its daughters who left to marry its sons who had left before them:

Don't send me, Mother, to America
Because I'll wither away and die there;
Dollars, I don't want. How else can I say it?
All I need is bread and onions,
And the one I love…

But Nitsa saw that living as a married woman in America could not be any worse than being single in Gargaliani. In her quiet, contemplative moments, she realized that there was no alternative to Panagiotis—it would be either him or nobody. And there was nothing worse than living her life alone and conceding to Gargaliani that she was a woman no man wanted.

When Nitsa finally emerged from her home, she told Theano and Papa Ntres that she had decided to marry Panagiotis and that they would immediately leave Greece for America. When the two heard it, each let out an enormous sigh, relieved that Nitsa's life would at last get out of neutral. When Panagiotis heard it two days later, he was thrilled that his mission had succeeded, and even more so that he was finally joining the group of winners: the married.

The town quickly caught word of the pending nuptials. When she spoke to people in the town, Nitsa portrayed her future in America with Panagiotis as bright and full of adventure. Inside, of course, she feared what lay ahead, what the result of abandoning the comfortable status quo would bring. And yet, her reckless act carried for her an air of newness and adventure. Nitsa was perhaps most relieved to be leaving Gargaliani and the burning spotlight under which she had lived for nearly three decades. This in particular caused her to experience a reborn feeling of sunny days to come and pleasure at the prospect of being liberated from the town's piercing and judgmental eyes. And perhaps even more important was that no matter how bad things might go in America, Nitsa knew she would be able to maintain majestic appearances to those she left behind by spinning her circumstances any way she wanted.

Panagiotis was simultaneously elated and terrified, unable to believe he was about to marry Papa Sarantis's daughter, while at the same time totally unsure about whether he could rise to the occasion.

What do I do next? he wondered. *Will I be able to give Nitsa a life she will be satisfied with? Will I be able to make it on my own in that land of giants? Will Nitsa be happy living there with me?*

Papa Ntres performed their marriage ceremony in June 1929 at All Saints church, and afterward, the newlyweds agreed that Panagiotis would leave Gargaliani for Chicago to prepare a home and to set on course the business plan he had devised. They decided that Nitsa would stay behind to wrap up her affairs in Gargaliani and handle the endless paperwork required for her to leave Greece and to enter the United States. When the time was right, Panagiotis would send for her.

Chapter 5
CHICAGO

Panagiotis returned to Chicago's Logan Square in August 1929, and he moved back into his sister Tasia's home. He spent the next few days speaking to a number of people about the business idea he had devised, selling boxed candy on consignment in display cases he would build inside already established businesses. He figured that business owners, who would share in his profits in exchange for giving him room for his cases, would welcome him in their stores. He was right. Most especially liked that Panagiotis would make daily rounds to replenish inventory and promptly divide up any proceeds. In only a week, Panagiotis received commitments from five storeowners, all enthusiastic about the new venture and complimentary about his innovative idea. With the enthusiastic responses, Panagiotis was energized and settled on a nougat recipe and a design for his cases. He also interviewed people who could help him service his customers.

Panagiotis spent the month of October 1929 arranging for the installation of his first counter, measuring the space, and acquiring the necessary building materials. On November 1, 1929, he arrived at a north-side diner ready to begin the counter's construction and to schedule some last-minute details. When he walked into the empty restaurant that morning, he noticed that this once calm and confident owner looked as if he hadn't slept in several days; his formerly clear eyes were now unfocused and bagged.

"What's going on?" Panagiotis asked.

"What's going on? What do you mean what's going on?" the owner replied.

"I'm ready to install the candy case we discussed. I'm going to purchase the materials today and want to measure the space so I can get things going."

As these words came out of his mouth, Panagiotis could see

something had gone very wrong in the world of that Greek's restaurant.

"Install your silly counters?" the man said. "After what's happened?"

Panagiotis froze.

"You don't know what's happened, do you? You must be the only person in America who doesn't know what's happened."

The man grabbed Panagiotis's shirt with both his hands.

"The stock market has crashed, you silly fool! We're ruined! This country is ruined! Look around you! There's nobody here! We're finished! Can't you see I am finished? I am selling everything and returning to Greece as quickly as I can. There are dark days ahead. Dark days! You'd be smart to get out of here too."

Panagiotis, silenced and dumbfounded, stumbled out of the restaurant and boarded a streetcar to Greek Town where he stopped at one of its cafés to catch up on the horrible turn of events. Once there, those he hadn't seen since his return from Greece told him about the stock market crash, about how economic conditions in America were going from bad to worse, about how people were losing fortunes, and about how many of the formerly rich had jumped out of windows. They also told him about Greeks who had already closed their businesses up in anticipation of hard times ahead.

For the next week, Panagiotis contemplated the state of the world, his business plan, and most importantly, Nitsa, who was waiting for him to send for her. After speaking with some other prospects, most of whom reneged on their prior commitment, Panagiotis decided to shelve the candy counter idea until the economy improved. He reconnected with one of his old bosses who hired him back as a candy maker. For the next eighteen months, Panagiotis worked hard, at least ten hours a day, six days a week, saving whatever he earned with the exception of the money he sent Nitsa in Gargaliani. He lived frugally and in a year and a half, despite the depression that had settled in the country, Panagiotis was able to accumulate another twenty-five hundred dollars, most of which he deposited in one of his accounts. All in all, Panagiotis showed forty-five hundred dollars in his Logan Square account and another twenty-five hundred with the Post Office. This respectable sum was the nest egg upon which his life with Nitsa would be built, an amount that despite the world's tumult, made him confident and sure about his future.

In the spring of 1931, after almost two years of separation, Panagiotis began making arrangements for Nitsa to come to Chicago. He rode streetcars and trains to downtown Chicago, completed document after document, day after day, and was ready to book her passage. But, that summer, everything fell apart. Panagiotis heard that people had gathered in line at the Logan Square bank to withdraw whatever money they had deposited there. After racing there and waiting endlessly in line, Panagiotis learned that the bank had run out of money. Almost all of Panagiotis's savings were wiped out with a single indifferent announcement that the bank was closed.

Depressed devastation did not begin to describe Panagiotis's new view of the world. For the first time, doubt chipped away at his assumption that despite what happened elsewhere and to others, the benevolent God always protected and guided him. Though his twenty-five hundred dollars at the Post Office were still safe, Panagiotis was at a loss as to how to break news of this enormous defeat to Nitsa. To make matters worse, Panagiotis's brother-in-law lost his job, and so whatever money Panagiotis earned went to support his sister's family.

Circumstances deteriorated even more when Panagiotis lost his job after his boss announced he decided to give up on America and return to Greece. Despite all his efforts, Panagiotis could not find employment, and in order to survive, he began drawing down his savings. A letter every few days provided Nitsa with a blow-by-blow accounting of the unprecedented pessimism that had become life in America, the lack of opportunity, the joblessness, and worst of all, the loss of hope. Left with no choices, Panagiotis determined that life in the states was worse than life in Greece. He wrote Nitsa that *he* had lost hope in America, and that he was returning to Gargaliani. The couple would live there as long as necessary to survive. He packed his belongings, bought his wife some gifts, including a Singer sewing machine, withdrew all his money from the Post Office in a single cashier's check, and boarded a ship for Greece.

Hopeless melancholia cocooned Nitsa when she read Panagiotis's declaration that he was returning to Gargaliani. Her greatest fear had arrived, and she knew that a life in Gargaliani without the wherewithal to maintain her appearances was a humiliating one of despair, not to mention one that would no doubt be laborious and meager. Nitsa imagined her future as one of ridicule and condescension.

"I'm like Prometheus," she told Theano, "destined for nothing but suffering. *This* daughter of Papa Sarantis will have to live here and be a farmer's wife for all to see. I don't know why God has sentenced me to be chained to this rock, helpless as the buzzards of this town land on me and pick at my liver daily. He must have placed strength in me of which I am unaware."

As had become her pattern, Nitsa's lamentations gave way to calculations and dramatic action. When she recovered from her shock, she prepared for her husband's arrival. And she prepared in a way so as to show the world, as if it cared, that the obvious change in plans was a thoughtful step up, not a desperate maneuver.

Yes, I will live humbly, she declared to herself, *but that can be something to be proud of, something impressive.*

So, Nitsa cleaned and whitewashed her house to give the impression of the joyful anticipation of her husband's arrival. When he appeared weeks later with all his belongings in several wooden boxes, Nitsa prepared a loud feast. And she showed off to all the things Panagiotis had brought, first and foremost the sewing machine, something no one had ever seen or even heard of before.

The return to Gargaliani was in a way even more difficult for Panagiotis than it was for Nitsa. His first order of business was to claim his portion of the family's small properties from his brother George, who alone had been barely surviving off them with his wife and three children. Panagiotis took half of his family's house, a vineyard of roughly five acres as well as another acre of raw land, moves that stung his brother. When added to Nitsa's inheritance—four acres of vineyards that produced high-quality eating grapes, a field of thirty olive trees, and her family's house—the couple's assets were small but at least somewhat respectable. While they would not be rich, both held out hope they would at least be able to support themselves.

Right away, in the summer of 1931, it became obvious that Panagiotis would have a hard time making ends meet as a farmer. It is not easy to learn farming on the fly and from the very beginning, Panagiotis struggled to keep up. It had been twenty years since his last harvest, and his inexperience led to costly rookie mistakes. He wasted time among the wheat fields, the vineyards, and the olive grove, trying to tend to them all, but in the end, he was unable effectively to tend to any. He struggled to cut deals with tenant farmers, all of whom were much more land-savvy than he, which resulted in his overpaying for underperformance. These burdens were at times too much for Panagiotis to carry alone and unlike his brother George, Panagiotis lacked the assistance of his wife in the day to day tending to the fields. In fact, while George's wife Eurydice planted, trimmed and harvested, Nitsa never dirtied her hands in the fields. She thought her pedigree precluded it.

Panagiotis was inundated and overwhelmed in those first two years and was never able to catch up. What little income he was able to extract from the harvested wheat, raisins, and olives was enough to sustain him and Nitsa for only a few months. By February 1933, the couple had spent the money Panagiotis brought back from the States. Panagiotis and Nitsa found themselves in a true struggle for survival in the face of diminishing returns in a world beset by depression. With nothing to fall back on, Panagiotis borrowed whatever he could from the agricultural cooperative in Gargaliani, posting his next summer crop as collateral. While such loans were designed to provide poor farmers like Panagiotis with money to buy seeds to plant and harvest, Panagiotis spent it on groceries and other necessities that he and Nitsa needed to live.

In the midst of all this, on March 2, 1933, my mother, Nitsa, gave birth to me in my grandfather Papa Sarantis's home, the same place where she was born over three decades earlier. One of Mother's neighbors served as the *mamee*, the midwife who helped her deliver me. Though she didn't see it coming, my birth marked Mother's rebirth. It returned to her what the death of her parents and then her marriage to Panagiotis had taken. I gave my mother something truly her own, something larger than herself, and something that instantly replaced the despair that poked at her for years. My appearance marked a new day in her life, and Mother quickly resolved she would not only take the lead in raising me but would do everything she could to mold me herself. While I happened to be born into a farming family, Mother considered that circumstance only temporary and vowed to make sure the farmer's mentality would never take root in me, and that her son's time as a farmer's child would be only the first scene in the first act of an epic with many costume changes. She determined that I would be raised to be a man of logic and letters, like Papa Sarantis and her erudite grandfather Michael, that my psyche would not become infected with the apathy and cynicism of her husband's kin, poor people she had written off as obtuse and crass. She would protect me by proceeding through life as if they did not exist.

Following my birth, Mother's first order of business was to make sure I was properly named. Giving me my name would officially take place at my baptism, a year or so later. Prior to that, I would be known only as "baby," as was customary. The tradition in Gargaliani, not to mention the rest of Greece, has always been to name the first male child after his father's father. This tradition is so hardened into the culture that it remains to this day, and it is not uncommon for names to alternate back through time for centuries—George is the son of Nicholas, who was the son of George, who was the son of Nicholas, and so on. So there is little doubt that I should have been named Antonis, after my paternal grandfather. But with Mother at the controls, that was never going to happen. And though she knew she could not unilaterally impose her will when it came to something as profound as my naming, she prepared to do what was necessary.

Shortly after my birth, Father and his family began to make preparations for my baptism in Gargaliani. Out of respect for Papa Sarantis, they all assumed Papa Ntres would perform the sacrament at All Saints, and my father's family gleefully marveled at the thought of having another Antonis in the family. Though all called me "baby," Panagiotis's parents would from time to time purposefully slip and call me "Antonaki," little Antonis, in anticipation of my naming. But though Mother politely smiled at these games, she secretly plotted. After I turned six months old, Mother made her move.

"Panagioti!" she said one September morning as the two sat at their kitchen table, "Saint Dionysius visited me in my sleep last night."

Saint Dionysius was perfect for this situation. He was born to the ruling class on the Ionian island of Zakinthos in the sixteenth century, a time when the island was under Venetian rule. As a child, he was educated with the aristocracy, a process that made obvious to all his enormous intellect. By his early adulthood, people had recognized Saint Dionysius as a man of letters, a deep thinker of great wisdom who had mastered several languages. Tonsured a monk while in his early thirties, the church hierarchy named him archbishop of the Aegean island of Aegina a decade later. Talk of his enormous piety and wisdom quickly spread through the region. While alive, Saint Dionysius took on such celebrity status that he was, in the end, granted permission to return to the quietude of Zakinthos where he died at the age of seventy-five. For four centuries, his body has been there. And it has never decomposed.

"Really?" Father replied.

"Yes. And he told me that I must take the baby to Zakinthos to be baptized at his church."

"He told you that?" Father asked sardonically. "And did he say anything else?"

"Oh, yes. He told me that he has already selected his godparents and that we will find them by placing the baby at the front of the altar. The godparent that approaches is the one he selected. Also, we are to name the baby Dionysius!"

"Dionysius? We can't name him Dionysius. We have to name him Antonis. What will my relatives say? C'mon now Nitsa, please. Don't do this."

"I'm not doing anything. It's all the work of the saint. If they have a problem with any of this, then they should take it up with him."

Several weeks later, my parents, accompanied by Mother's sister Tasia and her husband, began the trek to Zakinthos. After their arrival, Mother reported seeing another dream.

"Panagioti, the saint came to me in my sleep again last night."

"Which saint?" asked Father.

"Saint Dionysius. He told me that he wanted me to name the baby after the Holy Forty Martyrs of Sebastia. He said it has been written and that it must be so."

"He wants us to name the baby 'Saranti?'" asked Father. "After *your* father? So you're telling me that Saint Dionysius wants us to name the baby not after my father, not after himself, but after your father?"

"What can I say?" asked Mother. "That's what he said. If you don't like it, you should take it up with him."

And that was how it went. On the day of my baptism, Mother placed me on the altar at the Church of Saint Dionysius on the island of Zakinthos, and as my parents waited to see who would pick me up, Mother's sister Tasia ran to the altar and grabbed me, to Mother's delight and feigned surprise. Father, to his credit, only smiled and shook his head when he realized he had been set up and that his wife was craftier than he could ever have imagined.

The following year, 1934, Father once again sought loans from the agricultural cooperative. But because he hadn't paid back the previous year's loan, the cooperative allowed him only half the amount it had before, which he once again used to buy food, not seeds. Unable to borrow any more money, Father worked as a hired hand for other farmers, which enabled him to put at least some food on our table. But, this afforded him less time to tend to his own fields, and they floundered.

By the winter of late 1934, Father knew he had to take drastic action in order to ensure his family's survival. Our neglected lands produced nothing except the olives his heroic trees gave forth and whatever grapes he could gather from his wild vines. When Father couldn't find work, even as a laborer, he felt compelled to either ask his brothers in America to send him money or to sell family assets. After he tried the former and failed, Father sold to Papa Yianni, the priest from the nearby town of Floka, two acres of vineyards Father had written-off as worthless. The income from the sale gave my parents room to breathe and the means to try to bring another harvest to market the following year. That summer, 1935, Father convinced his reluctant wife to move us from Papa Sarantis's home into Father's half of *his* family's home. Despite the embarrassment, Mother knew she had no choice and reluctantly agreed to rent out Papa Sarantis's home. Though leaving that home was a terrible blow to Mother for all the obvious reasons, caring for me trumped everything, and *that* couldn't be done without the rental income. But the hardest part of it all for Mother was that her ability to maintain appearances had ended—it was next to impossible, even for her, to put a positive spin on the move, one that meant living in a small, single-family dwelling with Panagiotis's twenty-nine-year-old brother George, his wife, and three children.

Chapter 6
GOOD TIMES

It was in this context, as the firstborn son of a mismatched couple whose union occurred only after all other options were exhausted, that I snuck into this life and into a world whose offerings, though I scarcely realized it at the time, were just barely enough to keep me alive. From my earliest years, a life of perpetual shortage was the only life I knew, a life where I considered one drachma a boon and a single fig a feast. The site of my early world was the second floor of one of the family's properties, a two-story, corner building located two blocks northwest of the plateia and four blocks southwest of Papa Sarantis's home.

Living in that building was difficult. Because its first floor was a cellar the family had used for storage, the structure's only living space was on the second floor, a recently renovated, three-bedroom, single-family apartment that we shared with my *Theo* George's family. (*Theo* is the Greek term for "uncle"; *thea* means "aunt.") Fitting two families onto that floor was not easy under the best of circumstances. In our case, however, the situation was especially awkward as the relationship between Father and his brother soured once Father announced we were moving in. And as time passed, their rapport decayed further. To accommodate one another, the two decided that the large hallway that ran east to west through the unit would serve a boundary and separate the floor into two homes, each with its own entrance. We were to live on the south side of the apartment and they on the north. Though that sounds easy enough, complicating that clear division was the fact that too many people lived in the flat, not to mention that one of our allotted rooms was on Theo George's side of the hallway and the only commode and kitchen on ours.

We ended up with one bedroom, a parlor, a room with a table for eating, and one of the building's balconies. Our bedroom and the parlor were the most inviting of rooms, both airy, well furnished, and lined with illuminating windows that when opened, provided walls of natural light. Our eating room however, was a dark and foreboding windowless cavern. Without the square meter skylight in its ceiling, an opening that provided at least some usable light but only when the sun was directly overhead, the room would have been perpetually pitch black. This was a room I avoided at all costs, a place whose darkness and location (it was the closest room to Theo George's side of the house) made it hostile territory and a place my mother had warned me never to venture near. Theo George's family lived in two bedrooms, one for him and his wife, another for his children, and a third room that doubled as both parlor and dining room. The brothers divided the kitchen in halves.

That left the final shared room of the home, the bathroom, located in the southwest corner of the building adjacent to the kitchen. Two families, eight people in all, shared that one bathroom. The only room in the house not renovated, it was a foul and unkempt place whose filth was surpassed only by its stench. To me, that room was the worst place on earth. At its center sat a waterless toilet from which emanated an awful aroma that lunged to the other rooms of the house, making it unapproachable for anyone but those too old or too desperate to care. Ventilating the bathroom was a sole small square opening several meters off the ground at the rear of the room, just under the ceiling, one that provided no relief for those in the house. As for me, I don't believe I ever used that facility as I was never able to overcome my reflex to wretch and gag whenever near.

So when the need arose, I opted to use the family chamber pot, a dented metallic container that resembled the bottom half of a flowerpot. Mother kept it under the family bed, covered with a piece of cardboard. Every night, she would place it next to her bed for everyone to use when the urge hit in the middle of the night. There it would remain until morning when Mother, as part of her daily routine, would carry it down the hall to the bathroom, empty it in the toilet and then rinse it in the kitchen sink.

I remember one morning, when I was not yet four years old, Mother removed the cardboard cover and directed me to pick up the commode, carry it down the hallway and empty it in the toilet. Though horrified, I complied, picking it up by its lip with both hands. But as I walked down the hallway, the heavy pot became difficult for me to control and its weighty contents began to swish around inside. The further I walked, the more momentum the excrement picked up which soon splashed my fingers and legs. More and more spilled on the floor as I approached the bathroom and when I made it to the door, I was gagging, on the verge of vomiting.

I peered into the bathroom and my eyes fell upon a horrifying site. Seated on the toilet in black garb was a hooded figure, dark and unrecognizable. I froze so fast that the waste in the commode began to move more violently. When the figure silently motioned to me with her finger to approach, I could neither move nor speak but immediately recognized the phantasm to be none other than Baba Yanka, the evil witch from a Russian fairy tale. Mother had read me that story many times, and I heard how this witch used to travel from town to town in a garlic press from where she terrorized the locals.

After several frozen moments, I blurted out, "It is Baba Yanka!" and dropped the commode to the floor.

With a loud, splashing "dong," the container sent its contents flying everywhere—on me, the wall, the floor, and into the bathroom.

I ran back down the hallway toward our bedroom screaming, "Mana, Mana, Baba Yanka's sitting on our toilet! Baba Yanka's sitting on our toilet!"

Mother hurried into the hallway, saw my soiled condition, and ordered me to stand and wait for her in our bedroom. She sped to the bathroom only to see my Theo George's Mother-in-law sitting on the toilet. Mother spent the next ten minutes cleaning up the mess, all the while apologizing to our outraged housemates and promising them I would be more careful in the future. When she returned to our bedroom, she was upset.

"You're old enough to know better. Don't' you ever go near that toilet again, understand?"

"Yes, Mana."

Eventually, my parents' relationship with Theo George and his family became so awkward and edgy that Mother simply avoided any contact with them, which didn't help the situation. For Mother, living with people she considered bucolic and uneducated made even the most casual encounter a chore. Saying "good morning" became too much and so she avoided the hallway, kitchen, and bathroom

Gargaliani

whenever she thought one of them might be around. Her distaste got to the point that she loathed drawing water from the open barrel on the first floor because she thought she might run into them and instead walked outside and a full block just to fill a pitcher with water. But her aversion for the farming class was not aimed solely at Theo George and his family. Eventually, she avoided going to the neighborhood faucet all together; she no longer wished even to socialize with others like them.

Eventually, tensions mounted on all sides, and the locals began to dislike Mother and her obvious superciliousness. Their odium reached its acme when Mother once sent me alone to fill a pitcher of water at the fountain. As I struggled to fill and then handle the weight of the bulky decanter, the other women at the fountain began to criticize Mother, gossiping at how terrible she was for sending a little boy like me to do a grown woman's work. As I struggled home, one of the women shook her head, snatched the pitcher from me and carried it to our front door where she placed it down. Mother covertly watched the entire scene through a window.

It was from that same balcony, certainly my favorite part of our home, that the Gargaliani of the 1930s, with all its flowers and all its weeds, unfolded before my eyes. The first memories of my life go back to when I was three years old or so. I remember sitting on the balcony for hours either alone or with a friend occupied by things like cutting figures from heavy paper or making necklaces from beads Mother had collected from some tree near the plateia. I loved that balcony, its warped gray planks and its black corroded iron rails, and liked nothing more than being out on it and the sunny freedom it gave me. It was the perch from where I was able to watch the world below. From there, I learned how our town operated and how its inhabitants coexisted.

The safety of the rickety balcony was questionable, and so Mother laid a soft cotton blanket on its floor to not only cover the entrance and a few of its planks, but to set out the boundaries that I was not permitted to venture beyond. When noises from the street created a temptation too large for me to resist and Mother would find me beyond the blanket poking my nose through the rails, she would mildly reprimand me, reminding me of the risks of venturing too close to the edge. But her warnings couldn't quell the allure of the commotions and noises below, and if there was one constant in my life over the next several years, it was that I had to see what was going on in the street. The constant parade set forth below me was as entertaining to me as any circus. Every day, I watched conversing people coming and going to and from the plateia; women, with their arms loaded full of groceries, heading home from the market; older boys on the street playing games that I spent hours trying to figure out; and men navigating their loaded horses and donkeys through the town's streets. I thought this spectacle was designed personally for me and was a daily carnival I never wanted to miss.

The cavalcade began every day when, out of the morning's silence, I heard the familiar scraping and clapping sound of a wood and steel-wheeled platform that made its way down my street, always passing under our balcony. Atop that impromptu vehicle sat a double amputee who used his hands to scoot himself through town, from street to street.

"Mana, it is Bousoulas again. He's going to the plateia!" I would shout when I saw him.

"Yes, my boy," was her typical reply as she performed her daily chores.

Bousoulas, who had been given a nickname that literally means "crawler," was dirty and sorrowful looking soul who had lost both his legs just below the groin when, while serving in the Greek army during one of the country's skirmishes with Bulgaria, he stepped on a land mine. He was now destitute, and he survived only by shining shoes near the plateia. Though from our balcony he seemed docile and pitiful, a closer look revealed that Bousoulas lived with the constant terrifying snarl of a rabid wolverine. Even worse, his life was an unending rant about the tragedy he had become. Though surprisingly unsympathetic, Bousoulas was, from my safe distance, a most curious character, and his appearance signified the beginning of my day.

Soon after Bousoulas, another invalid would traipse through town, this one unable to hear or speak and accordingly was called "Mougos," a word that literally means deaf-mute. Mougos typically traveled around town with a basket of fruits and vegetables lodged under his arm and was always on his way to, or just returning from, the agora. When I asked Mother why he couldn't talk, she explained that a person born deaf cannot learn to speak, though his mouth and vocal cords are able to generate sounds. When I pressed my palms against my ears to try to understand what she was saying, I was still able to hear myself speak though I couldn't hear my Mother's words as well. Whenever I saw Mougo, I struggled to understand his disability. The fact that he never learned how to speak because he could not hear was a great revelation that I spent hours on that balcony pondering.

After Bousoulas and Mougos, a distinguished-looking man dressed in a suit would make his first of several daily passes in front of a bakery that was one door to the south of our building. This urbane man, with his greased and slicked back hair, smoothly and with great agility moved through our street. And he did so with such intense purpose, as if he was always on his way to give throngs of waiting vassals an important speech.

"That's Kyrio Katritsis," Mother once told me. "Every day he goes to one of the cafés in the plateia to have his coffee and to play cards."

"Every day at noon, just as the bell-tower clock at the Church of Panagia rings, he arises from his usual chair and passes in front of the bakery, on his way home to have lunch. If our clock ever broke," Mother laughingly said more than once, "we could set it by the appearance of that man."

Though I always laughed with her at this comment, I never understood what she was trying to say. We never owned a clock.

Another one of our street's regulars was a deranged man in his early twenties everyone called Bililis. Each morning, Bililis would station himself for peddling across the street and a block to the south of our balcony, near the bakery and in front of a store that sold fabrics and other textiles. Always an interesting person to watch, it was obvious to me, even back then, that there was something very wrong with Bililis.

Bililis's very existence caused a commotion. Older boys in town with nothing else to do chronically picked at and teased him, pestering him to perform one indecent act or another.

"Bililis, pull your pants down!"

Sometimes, poor Bililis would comply with the vulgar urgings and sometimes he wouldn't.

On occasion, the boys would chant to him in unison, "Throw your money in the air! Throw your money in the air! Throw your money in the air!"

Even though he had spent hours collecting his few drachmas, Bililis couldn't resist the juveniles' chants and would inevitably enthusiastically spray his drachmas high into the air, only to watch the vultures gather up his loot and run off. On our way to the plateia, Mother used to hasten as we passed Bililis. Nevertheless, I would stare at him, never able to take my eyes off such a curious yet handsome creature. And as I eyed him, with Mother dragging me alongside her, Bililis would, with a childlike wave and an innocent smile, say hello and good-bye to me all at once.

Once, when I was playing alone in front of our home, I began unknowingly drifting toward Bililis's station. I suddenly found myself standing directly in front of him, speechless and at a loss as to what to say, afraid and surprised that I had gotten so close and unsure about how I should act or how I could be nice to him.

And so without thinking, I took a deep breath and yelled at the man-child the same thing I had seen the older boys yelled at him so many times, "Toss your money in the air! Toss your money in the air! Toss your money in the air!"

I must have been quite a sight to Bililis because when he saw me standing before him and then heard what I was yelling at him, his face lit up with an angelic smile as he gently shrugged his shoulders and showed me his two empty hands.

Looking back, it is obvious that the people saw this young man as someone less than human and treated him worse than the town's multitude of itinerant dogs. Bililis's docility seemed to bring out the evil side of almost everyone, save the kind souls who gave him alms. What surprises me most today is that I never saw anyone come to Bililis's aid. People like Bililis, those who lived on society's fringe and only survived through the alms of others, were marginalized and would face a great challenge in the rough years ahead.

Woven in the swatch of characters were a number of my peers, children who would one day become the town's merchants and farmers, its future Kyrios Katritsises, Bousoulases, Mougos, and Bililises. First among them was the loud, persistent, and omnipresent Aliki, a little girl roughly my age that lived across the street.

Gargaliani

Almost every day, Aliki would call up to our balcony over and over, "Come down, Sarantis, so we can play. Sarantis, come on." As soon as Mother heard her, she would sigh and decline my request to play in the street in between our houses.

When Aliki's demands became too much for Mother, she would sternly snap back, "Aliki, go home, your Mother's calling you."

And Aliki would ramble back into her house, as Mother would close the balcony door. When I once asked Mother why she always turned Aliki away, she told me she didn't want me to be too close to her family because there was something wrong with her teenaged sister, Vasso. I never understood what Mother was talking about because to me, Vasso was always nice—quick to stroke my hair, to offer me treats, and to tell me what a nice boy I was. On an occasion when Mother relented and let me play, my friend and I were startled to see Vasso standing up at the ledge of her family's second floor window, with her long straight hair tousled and a far-away, wild look on her young face. And then, I watched Vasso throw herself from the window and heard her body crack as it collided with the unyielding sidewalk. Vasso died later that day at Gargaliani's doctor's office. I never learned what caused that young girl to kill herself, and no one ever spoke of what happened that day again.

Usually, I played with Spyro, a charismatic young boy who always seemed to be involved in the mischief of children five years his elder. But there were plenty of other children, all of whom spanned the town's socio-economic scale. For example, the day I returned covered in lice from a neighbor's home, Mother forbade me from ever visiting him or his dilapidated house again. But as all things are relative, there was also Dimitra, the product of the union of Gargaliani's dentist and one of its strictest, most demanding schoolteachers, Kyria Dina. They forced this poor girl always to wear neatly pressed clothes, to keep her hair perfectly coifed, and to parade around in perfectly shined shoes highlighted by perfectly folded stockings. They forbade Dimitra to play with me or any of the other local children, street rats her Mother considered too dirty.

And though all the adults in our town seemed to suffer from hyper-class-consciousness and while almost all Gargaliani's families were on the poorer end of the world's economic scales, we were part of a colorful cast playing roles in a Hellenic farce that, though part comedy and part tragedy, allowed us to live in a bucolic simplicity that is rare today, if not extinct.

When Mother was able to get me off that balcony during those early years, she often took me for long walks through town. During one of our strolls, we ended up at the home of a woman who, years before, was my grandmother Eleni's housekeeper. Stassa, as she was known, lived on the other side of town, a few blocks east of Thea Theano. When we arrived at her house, Stassa greeted us and made her usual fuss over me. Suddenly, a dog appeared out of nowhere and darted at me, began jumping around, and then jump upon me, scratching at my face. I panicked and ran. The dog came after me and nipped at my backside, which only made me run faster until I tripped, fell, and hit my head on a rock covered in horse manure. Blood gushed from the dirty wound. Mother ran to me, kicked the dog out of the way, and took me to Stassa's home where several women held me down as one poured hydrogen peroxide directly on the open wound and wrapped my head in a bandage.

By the time we arrived home that day, Theano and several of our neighbors were waiting for us. They placed me in our bed and several minutes later, Father appeared with Dr. Zorbakos, one of Gargaliani's physicians. The doctor removed the bandage, examined the wound, and told everyone he had to give me a shot. I looked at Mother and begged her to intercede on my behalf but knew, from the look on her face, that I was on my own. Dr. Zorbakos lit a kerosene burner next to me, and I watched him boil a needle and syringe that looked huge, like the ones I had seen used on horses. When everyone's attention was momentarily diverted, I snuck away from the bed and walked out of the bedroom, down the stairs, and onto the street. I ran west, toward the bluff upon which Gargaliani sat, and planned to hide from everyone including that horse doctor with the syringe. Though I ran as fast as I could, I heard Father's voice behind me.

"Sarantis, stop!"

I kept running.

"Come on Sarantis, let's go to the plateia. I'll buy you some candy there."

I knew he was lying and kept running, with all my might, as fast as I could.

"Sarantis, stop, right now!" Father's loud voice revealed he was right behind me and had become agitated. His run became a sprint, and I felt his hand clamp onto my arm. I screamed and squirmed, an action that prompted him to beat me with a tree branch he picked up. He dragged me back to the house and brought me back into the bedroom where, without a word, Mother stripped my pants down and a half a dozen hands held me motionless. From the corner of my eye, I saw Dr. Zorbakos slowly moving toward me like a mad scientist, waving his enormous syringe with its endless needle toward my buttocks. I screamed and cried for what seemed like eternal moments, endless torturous eternities. After he administered the shot, I couldn't believe that no one showed any compassion for me. Where was my Mother's endless and unconditional love? Two of the hands that held me down were hers. And then to add insult to my injury, after they released me, I heard everyone whispering about how I had a lot to learn, about how I had overreacted, about how I shouldn't be afraid of little puppies and shots. That experience made me ultra-sensitive to the presence of all dogs, as if that particular beast had informed the entire canine population that I was an enemy. And so from that time forward, I was ready to battle with every dog I met, no matter how docile.

During those days, Mother often took me with her on her visits to Theano's home, just on the other side of the plateia from us. Once there, the two would talk and knit by the bay windows in Theano's dining room, an area that overlooked her backyard. While their conversations covered just about everything, they mostly gossiped about various people in town, so intently that I was left free to wander and explore Theano's abode. My favorite room was the parlor, a warm and lace-filled room that contained a phonograph with a winding arm, which was an artifact Theano and Nikolaki had brought with them from Chicago and an item that, to my surprise, Theano let me play with.

The machine fascinated me, and I quickly mastered how to wind it up and how to start and to stop it and how to make it generate sound. Theano's son, my cousin Sarantis, was several years my senior and the only other person I knew with the name Sarantis. A boy whose obnoxiousness was surpassed only by his hilarity, Sarantis would furnish me with records to play and showed me the subtleties of the contraption. But what impressed me most was not that it created sound, but its mechanics—how the turning of the crank led to the turning of the table which led to the creation of sound. My love affair with that machine continued until one day, I arrived, and perhaps a bit too enthusiastically pulled a chair in front of it, climbed it and began winding. When I attempted to place a record on the turntable, the disc slipped from my hands, fell on the floor and shattered. Just then, Theo Nikolaki entered the room.

"Don't you ever go near that record player again!" he said with a stern and angry voice.

And that was that.

So on further visits, I had no choice but to stay near Mother and listen to their gossip. And I learned all about the people in town. When we returned home and we ate dinner, I heard Mother repeat simplified but spiced up versions of the gossip to Father. Once, Theano caught wind of the how deeply consumed I had become with what she was saying and abruptly expelled me from the room, ordering me to go in the backyard.

"Go see what your cousin Saranti is doing."

On that particular day, I meandered out of the house and onto the back porch, which overlooked the backyard. There, I saw a large brown donkey at the foot of the stairs, literally eating the banister. Smart enough to know that the donkey would kick and bite me if I got too close to it, I stayed at the top of the stairs from where I could see the rest of the activity in the yard. I saw Sarantis and several of his friends cleaning the barn, the donkey's usual abode, and discarding various useless items and whitewashing both its interior and exterior. I was puzzled as to why these boys would make such a fuss about cleaning out a barn and why they were working so hard to improve the living conditions of a stupid donkey.

As I pondered this, the donkey kept eating the stairs and with a loud crack, dislodged one of the banister posts. I rushed into the house and made a full report. Theano ran to the porch.

"Hey, big head! You obviously took after that lunatic Father of yours! The entire house is ready to fall and you are cleaning out the donkey's barn? What's wrong with you? Don't you have a brain in the enormous head of yours?"

Sarantis was unfazed by his Mother's words.

Gargaliani

"No, no, Mana!" he replied laughingly. "I took after you! You're a priest's daughter and everyone knows that you women are insane. I am your product! So don't blame poor Father!"

"Now listen to me you bed wetter, I am going to tell everyone what you are. Everyone will know about you! Get that damned donkey back in the barn."

"Don't even think about that, Mana. I'll tell them about you and what a twisted beast you are!"

Though Sarantis was only eleven years old, he possessed a remarkably advanced vocabulary. As the two traded vulgarities, he kicked the donkey in the belly and pushed it back into the barn. That caused Theano to deride her son some more.

"You kick that donkey bread head? I should kick you!"

Sarantis said something back and the two began to argue. Mother grabbed my arm.

"C'mon, Saranti. We're going home. Good-bye, Theano. We'll see you tomorrow," Mother said as we made our quick escape.

Several blocks from the scene, I turned to Mother.

"Why were Sarantis and his friend's cleaning the donkey's barn?"

"I hear they are turning it into a theater."

"What's a theater?"

"A theater is like the cinema, Saranti. Like what we've seen at the movies. And also a little like Karagiosi."

Karagiosi was a traditional Greek children's puppet show.

I thought about this for a moment, and my mind raced to the cinema I had seen, movies from another world depicting horses, carriages, and trees. Most recently, I had seen many images of men speaking to throngs of people from balconies. I could never figure out why they always seemed to be yelling. Mother could see that I was confused.

"It is not all that complicated, Saranti. Next week, when your cousin's theater is finished, we'll go see his play."

When that day came, we arrived at Theano's house and I ran to the barn to find it filled with people. When I tried to enter, a young girl I had never seen before stopped me.

"Where's your ticket?" she demanded.

When I took a close look at her, I realized that the "girl" was really my cousin Sarantis in drag. When he looked up and realized he was talking to me, a look of displeasure came over him.

"Get away from here! Go to your Mother, Saranti, and stay with her."

I ran into the house and dragged Mother to the barn.

"Mana! Saranti is dressed like a girl," I reported. "Why? Why is he dressed like that?"

When we arrived at the barn, Sarantis was gone, the barn door open and the play about to begin. Mother and I entered and took our spots against the back wall and the curtains opened. Quickly and with great vigor, actors began entering and exiting the stage, some talked and others gestured. In the middle of it all was Sarantis, dressed as a maid and carrying a broom. He spoke and gestured louder and more intensely than everyone else. He was a natural. Though the entire spectacle confused me, others found Sarantis hilarious and laughed whenever he spoke.

One of the actors gestured to the ceiling and said, "What a beautiful moon."

All the other actors looked and said, in unison, "Yes, what a beautiful moon."

Then the audience looked up and nodded, as if they all agreed that the moon was beautiful. When I looked up, all I saw was a dingy rafter full of cobwebs. I didn't understand why I didn't see what everyone else did.

Suddenly, a commotion began on the stage, and its curtains began to close, pause, hesitate and then open again. Loud voices emerged from behind the curtain. Without warning, the curtain rod and all of the curtains fell to the stage from the rafters with a raucous thud. There, in full view of the entire audience, was Sarantis, clad in his girl outfit, wrestling with another boy. Both cussed profusely at one another over who was allowed to open and close the curtains. When the fighting and the invectives escalated, Mother grabbed me by the arm and dragged me out of the barn.

Days like these were typical in the Gargaliani of my youth, but no matter what happened, our walks would end when, just a few blocks toward the west by the last incline of the main road on its way in and out of our town, Mother would take me to watch the sun set over Gargaliani's valley. That magnificent sunset, with its orange and purple-fingered hues, was a marvelous site. And from there we could see the foot of the mountain below us and our town's farmers and their animals climbing its steep slopes returning home before dark.

The older I became, the more I realized that the name Sarantis, even in Greece, is an unusual one. It translates to the number forty and commemorates the Holy Forty Martyrs of Sebastia, Roman soldiers of the fourth century who refused to renounce their Christian faith and were stripped, tied, and martyred by being thrown into a freezing lake. Few people have my name. Of course, there was my cousin. Though both of us were named after the same person, he wasn't around all that much. So when people made fun of my name, calling me things like "forty pancakes," there was usually no one to stick up for me.

Many times, when Mother took me on our afternoon walks, friends and relatives would inevitably make a big fuss over me, tell me what a cute little boy I was and tousle my curly black hair. When they mentioned my name, I would always feel uncomfortable and self-conscience. My name embarrassed me, and for sure, I didn't know what to say about it. And so I would blush and find refuge hiding in Mother's dress. Oftentimes, young girls would give me a lot of attention, hug me, and eventually ask me my name.

I always sheepishly replied, "My name is Saranti," an answer that would only prompt them to giggle, pinch me in the cheek, and ask me to say it again.

If they teased me too much, I would inevitably cry.

"Don't worry about them, Saranti," Mother would say. "They're just having fun."

When my cousin Sarantis, who lived with the name for much longer than I had, saw how embarrassed I became, he was disgusted.

"Listen, Saranti. When these girls giggle about your name, don't become embarrassed. Never be embarrassed. Instead, you're going to tell those broads exactly where they can go. Here's what you're going to do. Spread out all your fingers in your right hand."

I did as instructed.

"Bravo. Now spread them all the way out, so your hand is all the way open, like this. The next time one of those girls gives you a hard time about your name, hold out your hand just like this, right toward their face, and say, '*Na poutana*.'"

"*Na poutana?*"

"Yes, *na poutana*. Now let me see you do it."

"*Na poutana*."

"Very good. That's good. But I want you to say it like you mean it. Be strong about it. '*Na! Poutana!*' Like that. Now do it again."

"*Na! Poutana!*"

"Not bad. Actually, that's pretty good. Now you do that and no one will bother you again."

Within a couple of days, some of the neighborhood girls began to pick on me.

"What's your name? Tell us your name."

This time, I did as Sarantis taught me.

"*Na poutana!*"

Of course, I had no idea I had just called the girls whores, an action that made everyone, including the girls, roar with laughter. My response only made them ask me my name some more and caused a crowd to gather. Apparently, no one had ever seen a boy my age put ten-year-old girls in their place. Then, things spun out of control. People were everywhere asking me to say my name, causing me to curse even more, causing them to only ask me again. Thankfully, Mother appeared.

"Get out of here all of you," she scolded. "You should all be ashamed of yourselves. This a just a little boy. Get out of here!"

"Where did you learn that, my boy? Who told you to say that to those girls?"

"Saranti told me," I replied. "He told me that's what he does."

"That figures," said Mother as she shook her head and walked away.

The Gargaliani of the mid-1930s was a lively place. I remember how I could smell the aroma of fermented grapes, a smell that remains carved into my memory. Winemaking season hit Gargaliani every October, and when it came, our neighborhood bustled with activity. Harvested red grapes were in abundance, and I would watch for hours as donkeys and horses loaded with huge baskets of them passed

Gargaliani

under our balcony on their way to make our town's red wine, most of which would be consumed locally and mostly in Gargaliani's tavernas.

I remember one occasion when there was a great commotion around the house as Aliki and I saw of one of our neighbors, a man named Kosta but who we respectfully referred to as Barba Kosta (Barba roughly translates to "uncle"), had received loads of grapes in large baskets and stacked them up in an open courtyard. As soon as I caught sight of them, the balcony couldn't contain me, and without asking Mother for permission, I ran out our front door and down the stairs where I found myself standing next to Aliki. For several minutes, we stared at the wall of stacked baskets of grapes. When someone asked Barba Kosta for a few to eat, he was too busy tinkering with a platform and some kind of squashing vat to pay any attention. So, a few kids began eating his grapes. Some others followed suit, and before I knew it, everyone but Aliki and me were enjoying a feast.

When Barba Kosta realized what was happening, he snapped, "Get out of here you little bastards before I cut all your throats!"

The children scattered, leaving Aliki and me curiously watching to see what Barba Kosta was going to do with the grapes and the contraption he was building. After a few moments, he looked up from his work.

"What are your names?" he asked.

"My name is Aliki and this is Saranti," Aliki replied.

I was too shy to utter a sound.

Barba Kosta nodded, and after a few seconds, a big smile lit up his oily, dark, and gruff face. He reached into one of the baskets and used his knife to cut two bunches of grapes. He handed us each one.

"Move in a little closer and I'll show you what I'm doing," he said.

We watched as Barba Kosta emptied several of the baskets into his vat, and then as he climbed inside bare footed and stomped on them. Aliki and I marveled at the unlikely hilarity of what we saw.

That evening, Father explained the importance of grapes to Gargaliani and to everyone's survival.

"From grapes, we make three things, Saranti—wine, *petimezi*, and ouzo."

Though I knew that *petimezi* referred to the sweet grape syrup we used to sweeten our foods and deserts, I didn't understand the connection between the grapes, wine, and ouzo. They all seemed so different to me.

"Well, if you can make all three of those from grapes, then why don't we use our grapes to make wine or ouzo?"

"Because we don't have the equipment, Saranti. But even more important is that winemaking requires skill. Many try, only to find when they break the seals of their barrels that instead of making wine, they made vinegar!"

But grapes weren't the only product of Gargaliani—there were also olives, a regional staple from the time before *The Iliad* and the commodity that dominated the economy of our city. Next to the side door of our home was a *litourvio*, an olive-processing center, one of several in town that converted the city's olives into oil. During olive-harvest season, late in the fall, our neighborhood hummed with activity. Horses and carts loaded with heavy sacks of olives came and went. Gruff and husky men carried bags around and eventually into the *litourvio*. From the first time I saw those cussing men lug their dirty burlap sacks to the center on their backs, I was extremely curious see what happened to them inside. Spyro and I would watch as much of it as we could.

From time to time, Barba Nionios, the *litourvio's* supervisor, would catch sight of Spyro and me and invite us to warm ourselves by the processing center's giant fire. Sometimes, he even offered us his famous treat, a piece of toasted bread dipped in fresh sweet olive oil. We would watch with awe as Barba Nionios would remove several large pieces of bread from a nearby bag and then toast them near the huge fire that burned under the boiler. Then he would walk the toasted bread over to a wooden oil container, remove its lid and dip each piece carefully into a pool of fresh olive oil. After that, he would return with the bread, add some fresh oregano he kept in a bag near the boiler and top it off with a pinch of salt. I remain amazed at Barba Nionios, at the time and care he took in making us our treat and how good it tasted when he was finished. Maybe it's just a kid's memory, but none of us has ever been able to reproduce the taste of that man's creation despite repeated attempts. Exasperated, Mother once concluded that the remarkable taste came from the

Gargaliani

flavor released by the fuel source for the boiler's fire, the residue of the olives after their final pressing.

One day, I asked Father to explain how people produce clean oil from olives on trees. Pleased to hear such a question, he explained how Gargaliani processed its olive oil in a manner that hadn't changed since antiquity and relied on certain basic physical laws.

"Oil and water never combine. If you take a cup of water and mix it with a cup of oil, no matter how much you shake the bottle, the two liquids will never mix. When you stop shaking, they will come to rest separate from one another with the water at the bottom of the bottle and the oil at the top. Do you know why the oil is on the top?"

"Because it's magic?" I replied as I shrugged my shoulders.

Father laughed as he patted me on the head.

"For sure, Saranti, the olive oil has magical powers: it keeps us alive; we cook our food in it; we eat it; and we use it as fuel for our lamps. But that's not why it rises to the top of the bottle. It rises because it is lighter than the water, which drops to the bottom. It is that simple. Now what does that have to do with getting the oil out of the olives? Tomorrow, we will be running our olives through the *litourvio* and you'll see what it takes to make oil."

When we arrived at the *litourvio* the following day, Father took me to the rear, near a huge circular container mounted on a cement platform. Father and Barba Nionios walked me through the plant pointing out the two giant stone wheels that crushed the olives, the multi-toothed gears that turned the stones, the lever that turned the gears, and the mules that pushed the lever. They showed me how they took the pulp, placed it into porous sacks that resembled envelopes, and set them in an enormous press that crushed them. The press caused the olives' oil to ooze out through the pores into a collection reservoir.

"The oil from this first pressing is always the best oil, Saranti," said Father. "It's the greenest and best tasting. Watch now how we clean it."

They poured the oil into water, just as in antiquity, and the two liquids separated. Then the oil's impurities began to descend through the oil, continuing down through the water. Then, Father showed me how they used boiling water from a huge tank, in conjunction with the press, to extract the remaining oil from the crushed olive pulp in second and sometimes third pressings. From there, Barba Nionios, with the help of a special skimming vessel, removed the oil from the tank and stored it in his customers' individual containers. What remained in the tank was a mixture of water with traces of oil that they finally discharged into Gargaliani's open sewers, which led to creeks and out of the city. Father took me outside and showed me how some of Gargaliani's poor had diverted a small stream of that water and set up a primitive contraption to capture bits of oil from the dirty water.

"Why are they doing that?" I asked.

"These women use the oil bits to make soap."

When I stepped toward the women, Father grabbed my arm.

"Don't say anything and stay away from them, Saranti."

"Why?"

"Because they are extremely superstitious—all of them. They're like a bunch of witches. Be careful because if you cross them, they'll give you the *mati*."

He was referring to the evil eye.

The manufacture of soap from the *litourvio's* residue was one of the more bizarre sights to behold. Women of the town made it in crackling pots, and for reasons that remain a mystery to me, its manufacture was among the most superstitious of processes. Women who made it muttered various prayers as they stirred their caldrons and gave the impression that, without the prayers, some force would corrupt the manufacturing process. Once, I wandered into the home of one of my aunts when she and some friends were making soap in a large bubbling pot. When they heard me comment that the soap looked like pasta soup, I sent them into a panic, causing them to scurry to recite a litany of prayers designed to undo whatever harm my innocuous statement had caused.

The soap witches marked the end of my lessons in olive oil but only the beginning of my education in superstitious ways. In fact, such superstitions were part of the fabric of our town and were indoctrinated in us from our earliest years. People discussed them after dinner and late into the evenings, when children would gather after dark under the corner street light across the street from our home. And it was under that light, in the stillness of the night, that the older children would tell the younger ones stories, the same stories that they had been told several years before by the children older than them—stories about Greece, legends about the town, and rumors and innuendo about various people, some alive, some dead. I always loved listening to the storytellers and would become totally absorbed in the tales they relayed. Oftentimes, Mother would take over the storytelling, and because of her combination of charisma, theatrics, celebrity, and deviousness, she was always a favorite amongst the children.

One night, one of the local elderly women stumbled across such a gathering and started telling us about the ghosts, or *fantasmata*, that occupied our town. The harridan immediately noticed that her audience was all ears.

"Children, you must know that our *fantasmata* are extremely dangerous," she began, "and you must all do everything you can to avoid them. *Fantasmata*, children, are the lost spirits of the dead who were unkind to others and have been exiled from heaven, left to wander the earth in an endless search of something they are doomed to never find."

As she spoke, the petrified children stared at the shrew and followed her eyes as they widened and squinted as accents to her tale.

"*Yiayia* here is correct," interrupted Spyro's authoritative nine-year-old older brother. "I've seen *fantasmata* myself, here in the plateia, wandering and looking. On the grave of my grandmother I swear to you that I've seen them."

The children all nodded their heads in agreement, affirming that ghosts were everywhere, and that they had seen them too.

"More than any other place," the woman continued, "the *fantasmata* of Gargaliani gather by the creek under the bridge at the entrance to the town, near the slaughterhouse and the old schoolhouse at the plateia. So be careful, because—" and the woman stood up straight and her eyes widened, "if you see one, you are destined to die."

All of our eyes widened, and we must have looked horrified because she then added, almost as a footnote, "Unless, of course, you are carrying a crucifix."

Hearing this, Mother was finished with the old woman, scolded her for scaring the children and ordered everyone to disperse.

Despite my Mother's casualness and her assurance that the old woman was out of her mind, I was certain that ghosts were as plentiful in Gargaliani as were men in coffee houses. In fact, I was sure that *fantasmata* were all around *me* and had determined that the number you might find in a certain place depended on the environment.

"For sure, they are all over our vineyard," I told Spyro that night. "And I think the most are there around midnight, because there's no one around."

Spyro agreed without hesitation.

"I also think that they are in our dining room, near the entrance to our building, and near the area under our stairs."

"There's no doubt about that, Saranti. I agree that they like areas where there are no people."

Chapter 7
HARD TIMES

By the summer of 1935, Father was struggling to keep us fed. He was a dreadful farmer who had not taken to his new vocation very well and was never able to make his fields productive enough to satisfy our needs. And so, we perpetually lacked the basic things we needed in order to live. I often overheard conversations between Mother and Father and from my very earliest years, I understood that there was something chronically missing from our house. When times were especially trying or our budgets unusually tight, Mother would become more protective of me than she already was, keeping me even closer to her and telling me stories about people in poverty and the heroic efforts of children who were able to cope with the trauma of not having enough food to eat. Her stories always ended happily, usually with some superhero-like benefactor entering the scene and saving the family.

Like her stories, Mother and Father's conversations around our dinner table typically involved the hope of some letter arriving from America, usually whether such a letter would come, whether it was on its way, or where it might be at that very moment. Though I didn't understand everything that was happening, I could oftentimes see that these conversations were stressful and saddened Mother, who, whenever she noticed I was picking up on her distress, would end the discussion and quickly snap back to her happy demeanor.

As for our finances, we were barely able to keep ourselves nourished under pre-World War II conditions, an era that by all accounts would be considered affluent in light of what was to come. So by the mid to late 1930s, a pattern took root in our family that continued until the day we left Gargaliani for good. Only months after the 1935 grape and olive harvests, we had eaten whatever food we had farmed and our very survival depended on handouts from Father's oldest brother, Stathi, the only one of his siblings who was unmarried. Because Stathi lived without the financial burdens and obligations of family life, he became Father's go-to-guy. Over three decades earlier, around the turn of the century, Stathi had decided he would rather not share his family's few acres with his siblings, and so at the age of twenty, he permanently left Greece for America. His first employment was as a laborer on the transcontinental railroad, and after that, he settled near Detroit where he worked as a candy maker. When the Depression hit, Stathi stayed in Detroit, choosing to slug it out in the States rather than return to Gargaliani.

Stathi remained a lifelong bachelor and by most standards wasn't much of a financial success in America. He never owned any property and never made much more than he needed to live on. But from our perspective, Stathi was a tremendous success. We saw him as an urbane man of means, a Rockefeller. And we placed upon this poor laborer our burdens, making him not only our backup, but also our savior. When times got bad, my parents' hope always lay in the fact that they knew they could always ask poor Stathi for help.

By 1936, Mother and Father began to rely more and more on Stathi. And, as their need for extra cash continued to increase, Stathi began to bristle at the idea of sending more money, losing patience with what he perceived as Father's inability to support his family. Things got worse when Stathi learned in a letter from my Theo George's family that Father had sold a prime strip of the Stamatis vineyard the year before. Stathi wrote Father an invective letter, castigating him for selling family assets when what he should have been doing was buying more of them. Obvious that he didn't understand the extent of our plight. Father wrote his brother that he sold the land only because he was desperate and did it only to feed his family. Father's letter fell on deaf ears, and Stathi cut us off almost completely. In the months after that, whatever funds we received from Stathi were sporadic and at best, meager. This prompted Father to enter into a new letter writing campaign, whereby he would send Stathi letters requesting aid, which would prompt Stathi to send only some token handout, an action that would in turn cause Father to write Stathi again, turning up the heat by augmenting the description of our poverty with tales that someone had taken ill or that the local agricultural cooperative was about to take over some piece of our property.

Gargaliani

Though in theory, we had enough land to produce the food that we needed to survive, Father attributed his ineptitude to his inability effectively to combat the pests that preyed on the wheat and corn he had planted. I remember how, time and time again, when he discovered insects were quietly eating our crops, Father's face would turn red and his eyes would cynically sharpen.

"*Gamimene* beasts; you dirty insects; you are eating my corn?"

Often, the sight of insects would cause him to take his plea directly to the crops.

"Grow! grow! hurry up and grow! I beg you to grow before these accursed insects eat you. Hurry!"

Other times, with Mother and I silently staring at him, Father would begin to stomp at the insects while he helplessly swore at them and his rants turned into a staccato one word per stomp: "Take – that – you – dirty – scum – of – the – earth."

When he eventually wore himself out with his unheeded screams and stomps on the arid ground, Father would plead with the insects themselves, "Okay, fine. Eat if you like, but I beg you, please leave some for us."

What would have certainly worked better for Father would have been the pesticides that others used to spray their crops. But he was always playing a financial game of catch-up, robbing Peter to pay Paul, so such preventative measures were beyond his comprehension and means. During the harvest of 1935, for example, Father had gathered a modest quantity of raisins, most of which he sold in the Gargaliani market. He used those proceeds to pay his prior year's debts and saved a little for us. As for the olive oil we produced, more than enough to satisfy our needs, Father sold that off bit-by-bit as we ran out of food to eat.

By March 1936, we used up our money and reserves from the previous year, and left with no other choice, Father wrote Stathi again and like before, went looking for work, a move that continued to be a double-edged sword. When Father didn't work our land, no one did. So, he did his best to alternate working for others and tending to our fields, a strategy that would keep us alive but would never be profitable enough to extract us from what had become our intractable downward spiral. And what made the spiral worse was the effect it had on our dignity, stripping it off layer by layer as one would peel an onion. This hit Mother especially hard and she lamented how she and her family were becoming even lower than the migrant workers who came to Gargaliani during planting and harvest seasons.

My parents' psyches were delivered another blow when their ability to feed us wavered. Once that happened, Mother began sending me to Thea Theano's house for lunch, a way to ensure I would have at least one decent meal a day. Though the thought of eating lunch every day at my aunt's house was horrific, I went anyway and tried not to complain, even though I knew I was at the mercy of Theano. Indeed, going to that tense place without Mother left me totally exposed to Theano and her family's mercurial natures. So, every day at noon, I left our house, passed the church of Panagia with its bell tower that chimed the noon hour, moved through the plateia, past Kokonis's café, Galata's dairy, and then Skountzos's emporium. When I arrived at Thea Theano's home, I would run up its few stone steps, walk into the house through the front door, and announce my presence. Even though I tried to act natural, like I was a member of their family, I sensed that an irrational and unpredictable hostility always hung in the air and could never get very comfortable.

I could always count on Sarantis and his older brother John to greet my presence with superior smirks. As for their father, Theo Nikolaki, he was just completely indifferent to me. So, whenever there, I gravitated toward my cousin Eleni, the middle child and nine years older than me. Eleni always welcomed me with a maternal smile whenever she saw me. On Sundays, Thea Theano served meat and made sure I didn't waste any of it. She also served us *kefalotiri*, a hard cheese made from cow's milk that I had never seen before.

When I once asked Father why we never ate *kefalotiri* at home, he replied that it was "Too expensive and feta is more nutritious and plentiful anyway, so do your cross and pray that we have enough money to buy a little feta every once in a while."

For a full month, all went well at Theano's home until I arrived one Sunday. I checked in the house and saw that Theano hadn't finished cooking.

"Wait outside Saranti," she said. "I'll tell you when the food is ready."

I did as I was told. I wandered down the back steps and began floating several pieces of wood in a barrel of water that sat in my aunt's backyard. Out of nowhere, Theo Nikolaki appeared and when he saw what I was doing, scolded me to "get out of there" which, because of his anger, I interpreted to mean "get out of *here*." I promptly went home. When I told Mother what happened, she listened quietly. That was the last time I ever went to Thea Theano's house for lunch.

Though I'm sure Nikolaki didn't mean to chase me away for good, after a couple of months, I had apparently worn out my welcome—we weren't the only family in Gargaliani living through hard times. Because they were the only relatives we had, Mother never made a big deal about my expulsion but handled her sister and her family adroitly. Indeed, poverty had brought to light Mother's singular abilities at theater, manipulation, persuasion, and crisis management, skills she would not only use to handle her sister, but to keep us alive in the years to come.

The pressures to get food eased up on us during the summer of 1936 when Mother sold off a piece of her dowry, a vineyard located at the foot of the plateau just below the chapel named after the Prophet Elia. Father used the money to stock up on provisions, buying foods like beans, lentils, flour, fruits, and pastas. The day he brought the first bags of food home, Mother snatched them, raced into the kitchen and cooked us up an enormous bowl of *hilopites*, square pasta in red sauce. Though the rations cost us dearly, they would keep us going at least until the end of the harvest that fall.

That summer, Father worked our fields around the clock. Because they were over a kilometer from our home and there weren't enough hours in the day for him travel back and forth several times a day, he brought Mother and me to stay with him at the farm. And so we lived there day and night for three months that July, August, and September. To partially spare us from baking under the red-hot Grecian sun and freezing in the often-cool Grecian nights, Father built us a hut from ferns that grew wild near the farm's enormous fig tree. Though a valiant effort, the hut provided neither shelter nor protection from the elements, and we remained exposed to the sky, its blistering summer sun and from time to time, its short drenching bursts of intense rain.

We spent those days and nights on a bed Father made from straw that Mother had covered with sheets and blankets. I hated sleeping in that damned hut, a place where wildlife of all kind would venture in and out at all hours of the day and night. Mosquitoes were everywhere and screamed in the ears of anyone who sat even for a minute. Geckos moved about with impunity and ran back and forth over the faces of the sleeping. Though Mother thoroughly inspected our surroundings, I was frantic at the thought of so much as a beetle crawling on me while I slept.

And as each of those days ended and the sun dipped into the Ionian with all its splendor, a chorus of sounds dominated the fields, an arena that served as an orchestra hall for thousands of creatures: cicadas screamed their endless sirens, crickets strummed for mates at triple forte, dogs barked, cats shrieked, and unknown creatures burrowed under the earth. When I complained about the noises to Father, he told me that all these animals slept during the day and waited until the cool of the night to socialize. The noisy wildlife, he said, was probably upset that we had encroached on their world. As dusk settled into the night's blackness, the racket would resolve into a hum, an etude that served as my personal lullaby.

Mother could no longer afford to be too good to work and she and I were responsible for tending the garden, our family's future food source. Together, we planted peas, beans, okra, and tomatoes. In that searing sun, keeping the ground moist was an enormous challenge as the plot's only water source was located near the edge of our farm in a makeshift hole that Father had dug to collect rainwater. The hole was several meters wide and at least two meters deep, though it looked deeper than it was because Father had dumped the dirt he dug out of it around its perimeter. All sorts or weeds grew around the hole, making it attractive to a plethora of wildlife. From that pit, Father lugged bucket after bucket of water the fifty or so meters to the garden, where he would dump them until all our plants were irrigated.

Father spent his days working our field from sunrise to sunset, trying to grow wheat and raisins, crops he hoped would earn us a profit that fall. He worried endlessly about the weather and about how our wheat was most vulnerable to destruction the two weeks before harvest, a time when its seeds harden and are most delicate. He especially worried that a heavy wind from the south known as a *livas* would blow its red-hot air over our crops and destroy our wheat seeds before they could mature. Those twenty-five kilometer-per-hour

North African winds that heated up in the Libyan desert and raced northward across the Mediterranean were the fear of every farmer.

In the second week of July, Father began to prepare for the wheat harvest. I watched him clear a ten by ten meter square of brush near the hut, level it, and spread atop the ground a mixture of water and cow manure. He laid down layer after layer of the spread until it dried into a hard and smooth cement-like surface. This area became our threshing floor, our *aloni*, the place where Father would separate the grain from the wheat stalks and where he would later dry our grapes into raisins. After the *aloni* was prepared and the wheat seeds had hardened and with no Libyan winds in sight, Father commenced the harvest. He enlisted the help of Barba Stavros, a neighboring farmer, and his two sons. The four of them spent the next week hand cutting the wheat stalks and tying them in large bundles. Using a technique that Socrates himself must have invented, Barba Stavros tied his horse to a post in the center of the *aloni* and began walking it in a circular path around it. As the horse walked, Father and Barba Stavros's sons placed the bundles at its feet. When the horse stepped on the cluster spikes, the wheat seeds sprang free. Round and round the horse walked until all the stalks were smashed and reduced to small pieces. Meanwhile, the men utilized homemade pitchforks to shovel the crushed stalks up into the air where the wind blew away the chaff, leaving the heavier grain on the *aloni*. Using this archaic method, Father and his helpers harvested the grain and swept it into piles and then into four large sacks.

I loved the action, and from my vantage point under the fig tree, I watched every move the horse and the men made. I asked Mother if the four sacks of wheat by the side of the *aloni* were ours and couldn't believe it when Mother told me that we could keep only two of them as the other two belonged to Barba Stavros and his sons, payment they had earned for the work they performed. When it was over, we piled our two sacks on the horse and Father and Barba Stavros led it to our home for storage.

After he stored the wheat sacks and then repaired the trampled *aloni*, Father began preparations for the raisin harvest. For this, he would need Mother's help, and on a moonless warm night in the beginning of August, the three of us sat alone outside our hut and as novas and super-novas illuminated the star-speckled black sky, I listened as he gave her his final harvest instructions.

"You are in charge of the *aloni*," he began, "my helper and I will bring you the baskets of grapes and place them there. You will empty the basket and lay out each cluster side by side. And make sure you allow some breathing room between the clusters."

When I quietly asked Mother if I could help her perform this obviously crucial task, she gave me a silent, affirmative nod. I became flushed with the pure joy of anticipating my involvement in a holy effort. My time had finally come.

When Father finished instructing Mother, he finished his coffee and smoked a cigarette.

"It's time to go to sleep," he said as he rose.

"Please, Mana, please, can I stay up a little longer?" I pleaded.

She silently acquiesced, and Father reached over, took my hand, and led me a few meters away from the *aloni* near some rocks. We watched the stars.

The brightness of the moonless August sky was breathtaking. Father lit another cigarette and after we sat silently for several minutes, I turned toward him.

"Where is the moon when it is not here?"

Father smiled. "The moon is on the other side of the world. In a few hours, it will rise from the east."

I thought about his answer for a moment but couldn't comprehend what he meant when he said the world was a ball with sides. His answers sparked many questions, most of which I could not verbalize.

"Where is the other side of the world?"

"The world is an enormous ball," he began, "and people live all over it. So though you may be on one side of it, there are people on the other side as well."

He drew on his cigarette.

"At the bottom of the world, do the people fall off?"

"No." Father replied. "The ball we live on spins, and because of gravity, everything is held onto it. Nothing falls off."

I had no idea what he was talking about, and apparently noticing this, Father smiled.

"You will learn these things when you grow up."

In silence, we looked at the sky, and its brilliance quickly hypnotized me. A blanket of shimmering stars projected its flickering, bright beauty. As we looked up, lying on our backs near the *aloni*, Father pointed out various patterns and shapes, stars he suspected others had grouped together and named.

I was unable to understand and couldn't differentiate one group from another. In fact, I couldn't pick out even one of his stars. But I was mesmerized by the magical phenomenon that in a number of ways, I had just noticed for the first time. The brilliance of the illuminated sky suspended over the black fields gave me a feeling of detachment, and I became an obscure observer who, though engulfed by darkness, remained dazzled by a phenomenon that transcended human explanation. Even the flickering oil lamps from far away farms were no longer discernable as they gave the illusion of being a continuation of the sky's canopy.

On August 4, 1936, with the support of a friendly military, General Ioannis Metaxas removed King George from the throne and established a military dictatorship in Greece. The dictatorship, which as a practical matter included the king, was a totalitarian, anti-Communist state with its claimed foundations of support in agriculture and labor. We couldn't pay too much attention, because by mid-August, it was time to harvest the vineyards, which were no more than a couple of acres filled with tangled and haphazardly planted grape vines. Because certain grapes were ready to harvest sooner than others, Father and a helper systematically walked through the vineyard and detached, bunch by bunch, those that were obviously ripe. They set the grapes into large baskets, and they carried them to the *aloni* for drying. When they dropped off each load, Mother and I took over and carefully lay each bunch on the *aloni*, one next to the other, so that the hot sun would dry each bunch into raisins.

Because I would spend much of the day in the sun, Mother dressed me in sandals, short pants, and suspenders and tied a large straw hat to my head, one designed to protect me from the penetrating rays. But even well after the work began, while Mother was on her hands and bare knees lining up the grapes, something she swore she would never do, I was consumed with the hat, frustrated that I couldn't get it to sit properly on my head. When I moved to place down a grape bunch, the hat shifted and I had to stop what I was doing to straighten it. Mother hurried to keep up with Father, and urged me to take a break and rest under the fig tree. And so I stayed out of the way by sitting under a tree and drinking water from our canteen.

I watched as Mother moved quickly and with ease—her days of being too good for such work were over. As Father and the helper continued to dump baskets onto the *aloni*, Mother spent the entire day organizing them into straight columns. After laboring the entire day, Mother was exhausted, and her knees were raw and her back throbbed with pain. I still cannot fathom from where she found the strength to prepare for us that night's dinner, a large tomato salad with cucumbers, onions, and olive oil. But as we ate it, Father explained that we had harvested whatever grapes were ripe and that further harvesting would be deferred a couple of days.

"Thank God." Mother replied.

The grape harvest continued in this manner for the next couple of weeks—intense work for a day or two, followed by a few days off. Soon, all of the grapes were harvested and a thick blanket of them covered the *aloni*. Though pleased with the number of grapes the vines had produced, Father's worries shifted once again to the weather.

"Any rain at all will destroy everything. Say a prayer that conditions will remain dry."

At night, neighbors would meander over and along with Father, read the sky to formulate disastrous meteorological predictions.

"You see that red sky? It means we will have a terrible rain tomorrow," one would say.

"Forget the rain, that blurry moon means terrible winds tomorrow," another would reply.

Father spent those days walking around the *aloni*, looking at the sky, and spouting his endless rant of predictions, all dire.

"Oh, my God, it's going to rain. God protect this crop from the rain. How could you let it rain? It cannot rain. I don't think it's going to rain. The damn winds are coming. Look, it's going to rain."

Despite Father's dread, the weather remained perfect for drying the grapes. In fact, after only a few days in the sun, the grapes began to shrivel and take on the appearance of raisins. Once that happened, Mother flipped them with a rake to help the drying. Then, she agitated them to separate the fruit from the stems. Once the sun completely dried the raisins and the agitation set them free, Father swept the fruit into a large conical pile.

By the first of September 1936, my parents had finished the raisin harvest and had lined up our raisins in four one-hundred kilo sacks on the side of the *aloni*. Father was ecstatic over what he considered our surprisingly high yield, a result he attributed to our unusually good weather and to something he had added to the soil the year before. On the evening before we were to transport the sacks to town, Barba Stavros and some other neighbors who had walked over after a day of work to chat, were surprised to see what our vines had produced. Father took great satisfaction in our output, and as he described to them the highlights of the harvest, he was obviously pleased that he was able to get the family's land, the source of his and every other Greek landowner's pride and identity, to produce such a crop.

I loved talk of our family's success. When the conversation switched to the latest exploits of the local gypsies and robbers, fear overcame me. That there were gypsies near, people who Mother had repeatedly threatened would kidnap and torture me if I didn't listen to her, disturbed my very existence. When I looked at Father for reassurance, I couldn't figure out the man's apathy. Either he was unaware that gypsies might take me, or he didn't care. Either way, I went to bed that evening with my head filled with images of tall slender robbers overwhelming us, stealing our raisins and tools, and kidnapping me.

Soon after I fell asleep, a ruckus in the field awakened me. When I looked through a hole in the hut's wall, I saw several men struggling to hoist our heavy raisin sacks. I saw another man picking up Father's tools and another filling other bags with raisins. I turned to yell, to wake up Mother and Father but could not generate any sounds from my mouth. Mother and Father continued to sleep.

Finally, and with all my strength, I yelled, "The gypsies are stealing our raisins!" and I swung my hand and hit Father in the face who, despite the blow, didn't budge. I became frantic as the robbers had secured our belongings and feared that they were coming for me next. Unable to rouse my parents, I was desperate and alone—abandoned and at the mercy of the gypsies who Mother had warned me about so many times before.

I screamed with all my strength, only to realize that Mother was talking to me. And as she spoke, she pressed something cool onto my forehead.

"Everything will be all right, my boy. You are hallucinating. You have a fever," she said as she pressed cold compresses on my head.

"Mana, they are stealing our raisins—the robbers are stealing our raisins," my subconscious sluggishly murmured.

"No one is stealing anything. Everything is all right."

I slowly opened my eyes and saw daylight.

"You have been dreaming. You've been sick and had been delirious all night with a high fever. You have malaria," she said.

Apparently, our ubiquitous water holes had become breeding grounds for the anopheles mosquito, the common transmitter of that disease.

The disease caused me to hallucinate and put me in a dimension of total delirium. Though what I saw seemed so real and immediate, when I awoke, I was unable to describe what I had just seen. In the midst of my confusion, Mother assured me that in just a few days, my illness would pass. That day, Father borrowed a neighbor's donkey, loaded me atop, secured me with a rope, and moved me back to town. Once home, Dr. Zorbakos visited me and administered quinine tablets. With Mother at my side, I remained in bed for a week on a strict regimen of quinine, food, and sleep.

By December, we had harvested everything and completed our outdoor work for the year. Whatever our fields had produced—four sacks of raisins, two sacks of wheat, and two large urns of olive oil—lie in our ground floor storage room. But before he could sell any of it, Father had to first pay back at least part of what he owed the agricultural cooperative. In order to keep that amount to a minimum, he underreported what we harvested.

Father hoped our unexpectedly high raisin output would be a small boon for the family. But his dreams were dashed when he learned that everyone else experienced similar production, causing a raisin glut to drive down prices to only a little more than the government-set minimums. Metaxas tried to stimulate a rally in the raisin market by issuing an edict: first, all bakeries were to bake large quantities of raisin bread; and second, each Greek had to buy a loaf of raisin bread with each loaf of regular bread he purchased. Though the bakers complied and the country was now enjoying regular quantities of raisin bread, the move did little to affect the price of raisins nationwide and nothing to help my family's lot.

In the first weeks of 1937, Father had sold off most of our raisins. Whatever wheat we had, he rationed. Though we still had enough olive oil to last us a few months, we were penniless and unable to purchase anything at the agora, with the exception of whatever money Father earned as a day laborer for others, income which was at best, sporadic. Father found himself up to his ears in an endless cycle of desperation. Of course, other farmers were in a similar predicament, but somehow, they seemed able to handle their affairs better. We rationalized that they had what we lacked, the proper equipment: a plow, a horse, a donkey, a real shelter, and canvases to protect the harvest from the elements.

The truth was that we were out-of-place town folk, reluctant farmers who confused our ineptness with fate. Just watering our plants on a daily basis was a formidable task for Father and backbreaking work he struggled with every day. The glee we felt when the beans, peas, tomatoes, and other vegetables we planted sprang optimistically from the ground turned sour; we were often forced to watch the leaves of the young plants curl and turn yellow. Though Father employed a number of frantic efforts to reverse the slow death—he cultivated the soil around each plant and he changed the time of day the plants were watered—the plants still died. Father's need to bring in Barba Stavros and the rest to help us with the harvest took huge bites out of our take. Our rudimentary farming methods gave us much lower outputs than we might otherwise have had, and unlike other families, we had no reservoir of relatives or friends to assist us. With the exception of Mother and me, Father was alone.

Painful irony was always only a few meters away. Papa Yianni, the priest who owned the farm adjacent to ours, was an excellent farmer, an agricultural alchemist who seemed to turn every piece of land he touched into gold. We watched how he and his two sons seemed to spend their days idyllically tending to their fields. They were always ahead of the game, effortlessly working the soil to air the roots of their plants, always grafting, pruning, dusting, spraying, and, in the end, harvesting more than they could handle. When Papa Yianni watered his garden, he did so by emptying buckets directly into tiny canals that led the water down a prescribed path to the roots of each of his plants. His richest crops seemed to come from the piece of land that Father sold him. And to make matters worse, Papa Yianni discovered water and then dug a well on that very same strip.

On the home front, our relationship with our housemates continued to deteriorate. Mother was never comfortable around them and continued to avoid the entire family. Her discomfort made its way down to me, and I avoided them as well. Even though I lived in the same house with cousins my age (Antonis was only two years older than me, his sister Voula only one year older, and Takis was my age) and they seemed willing to play, I avoided them.

Then one evening in late December of 1936, Theo George returned from the vineyards with a high fever. His family called the doctor and though he announced my uncle would soon recover, Theo George died two days later. The doctor said it was from pneumonia. Theo George was only thirty-four years old. Grief filled every crevice of the house as we mourned the loss. We adorned the doors of our building in black, and people blocks away could hear the lamentation cries of our housemates.

They shrieked things like, "Why did you have to go?" and "Who's going to bring me my coffee?" and "You were so young!" and "Why did you have to take him now?"

When relatives from both sides of the family gathered around Theo George's corpse, they lamented endlessly, sang the memorial for the dead, and spoke of his virtues. But not even Theo George's death could bring our families together. Even though Mother took no part in the lamenting, she was nevertheless stricken with grief and prayed for her brother-in-law's family. She couldn't figure out how his widow, Eurydice, and her three fatherless children would survive. As for me, I found the lamentation screams curious and watched the spectacle from the top step of the stairs, just across the hall from the bedroom where my dead uncle lay. When Aliki heard the cries, she wandered in and watched along with me. We watched people from all over the area come into the impromptu wake and join in the lamentations. Eventually, Aliki and I began repeating what we heard. Our wails grew louder and bolder until one of Thea Eurydice's relatives heard us.

"Are you making a mockery of your uncle's death, Saranti? I thought you knew better than this. And to think you are the grandson of Papa Saranti! You little bastards, you should both be ashamed of yourselves."

My actions didn't help mend any fences. When Father heard the lamentations morph into the adults venting their grief onto Aliki and me, he ran to our defense and became ensnared in an argument with his deceased brother's family, right in front of the corpse.

The death of my Theo George had little effect on us. As for the effect it had on his wife and children, I have no idea. All I remember is that Theo George's death saddled Eurydice with the burden of maintaining that family's farm in addition to raising her children alone while the daily rhythms of my family continued as they had before.

Chapter 8
PATRAS

The early months of 1937 were rainy, which meant a time of little work for the area's farmers. As most had plowed their fields and waited for the spring planting, those months were a time for a little light work, hibernation, and coffee. Most of the men spent at least part of their days talking and playing cards in the plateia's cafés. Though Father would still head to our fields somewhat regularly to pick up some firewood, gather dandelions for dinner, or make preparations for the coming season, he always ended up at one of two cafés, either the one that belonged to Kyrios Kokonis or the one next door that belonged to Kyrios Tsironis. And while there, Father passed his time like everyone else, smoking cigarettes, drinking coffee, playing cards, and talking politics. Mother, of course, remained home performing domestic chores and often sent me out to find Father and to relay to him some message. When she did, I knew I could find him in one of those smoke filled arenas.

As the spring approached, Father decided we would harvest only grapes that season. Not having any money to plant anything, Father said we would leave that portion of our land idle for a year.

"Perhaps it will make the soil stronger," he rationalized.

As for our vineyards, Father had to prepare them to bear fruit. The winter had dried and blown away the leaves, leaving behind a chaos of medusa-like branches that reached everywhere. When the tangle of vines began to bud in the spring, Father got back to work and began the arduous process of trimming each branch back, one by one, with his curved knife. He cut back every single vine in that field, careful to leave three buds on each finger that shot off from its base. And after he meticulously piled the cut branches near the *aloni*, he grafted each vine by making a cut with his knife, which was a surgery he said helped it grow property. Father had to perform all this work quickly, before the beginning buds matured into branches, something that happens fast with grape vines—so fast, you can almost watch them grow. What made the work harder for Father was that *his* father never planted any of the vines into rows, but scattered them randomly around the field, requiring him to hoe each vine individually and by hand. Had my grandfather planted the vines in rows, Father could have quickly run a plow through the field. So it was only after he finished agitating the dirt around each vine by hand that he proclaimed the field ready.

Pessimism, that most terrible corrosive, filled our dinner-table discussions. Despite Father's claim that strengthening the soil in our wheat fields was in our long-term best interest, Mother couldn't stop harping over the folly of leaving that land bare. Father listened and maintained it wasn't necessary but quietly wondered how the family would survive that year with no more than a raisin harvest, especially when the previous year's raisin *and* wheat harvests were not enough. Finally, and as if a prayer were answered, a ray of hope beamed into our home that March when Father received a letter from his youngest brother, Dimitri. Dimitri worked as a cobbler in Patras, an Ionian port town and the largest city in Peloponnesus, approximately a hundred thirty or so kilometers to the north of Gargaliani. In Patras, Dimitri explained, the government was financing the construction of an enormous school complex known as the Arsakion, an institution built to educate girls to become Greece's future teachers. Dimitri told Father that he could certainly obtain a construction job there if he wanted one.

With little thought and even less hesitation, not to mention Mother's enthusiastic consent, Father shut down the house, abandoned our newly pruned grape farm, packed up his carpenter's tools, and stuffed our personal belongings into our single large black leather suitcase, a luxury item he had brought back with him from America in 1932.

"We are going to Patras," he said.

Within a day, we boarded a bus for the twenty-five or so kilometer drive to Kyparissia, where we would then board a train that would take us the remainder of the way. What a trip! When we arrived in Kyparissia, I asked Mother if we would visit her sister and my Godmother, Tasia. Mother, who was not on speaking terms with Tasia because of some squabble over money, made up an excuse as to why we couldn't see her. We spent that night with some of Mother's friends and woke up early the next morning to catch the train to Patras.

The train station was a carnival to me, a collection of people, metal, smoke, and anticipation. Everyone there seemed to have a purpose and people busied themselves with nervous looks at their watches, stares at the tracks, and peeks at the giant clock on the wall. I buzzed with excitement and my head spun with adventure. I felt I couldn't possibly wait a second longer to finally see up close what I had only seen in pictures— an actual train. As departure time approached, people began to stand up, and an invisible energy streaked through the air as everyone began to move toward the tracks. With so many people in front of me and with everyone so much taller than me, I struggled to see what was happening. Mother gripped my hand. A sea of legs surrounded me. When Father realized I was drowning, he swooped me onto his shoulders.

Then I saw it, a black steam engine in the distance roaring toward us. As it chugged toward the station, its smokestack filled the crisp and clear atmosphere with dense mushrooms of black smoke. For a moment, it disappeared behind a curve, only to reappear right in front of us, a sight so sudden that the only thing more horrifying than its harsh size was the screeching soprano blasts of its massive whistle. With a sense of urgency, the passengers boarded the train, and it pulled out of Kyparissia. On the way, the locomotive stopped frequently and every time it did, peddlers ran on-board to hawk various things: kabobs, cigarettes, candies, cookies, and so forth. Only when the train began to pull out did they jump off.

After several hours and a dozen or so stops, we finally arrived in Patras. When we stepped off the train, Father's brother Dimitri graciously greeted and led us to his home. I met his wife, my thea Vasso, and their three children, my cousins, Costas, Yianni, and Eleni for the first time. With my cousins, it was love at first sight. Costas was the oldest of the three and only a year older than me. Like me, Yiannis was four years old, and Eleni, a year younger. When I asked Mother why metal cages surrounded Yianni's legs, she told me that he had a disease called polio that kept him from walking properly. We ran and played until we collapsed with exhaustion.

Gargaliani

The following day Father went to the construction site. When he returned several hours later, we rushed to meet him.

"Did you get the job?" we asked, almost in unison.

He didn't answer but turned his head from us. When we ran around to look at his face, we could see that his lips that were tightened and that he was holding back a smile, the sure sign he was trying to keep a secret or play a joke on us.

"You're smiling, you're smiling," we said, and Father told us that he had accepted a well-paying job as one of the project's master carpenters.

Things were looking up. Within days, we rented our own one bedroom apartment, which was spacious and equipped with a kitchen. It was a ground-floor unit and had one entrance that led directly onto the street and another that led into the building's circular rear courtyard, the place where the tenants gathered to wash their laundry and in the evenings, assemble, talk, smoke cigarettes, and drink coffee.

Mother had difficulty adjusting to life in Patras. In Gargaliani, putting aside our financial struggles, Mother was still somewhat of a celebrity, still Papa Sarantis's daughter. In Patras, she was isolated and anonymous. Though she thought of herself as above all of her neighbors and spent little time associating with them, she performed her various chores with at least one eye and one ear on everyone. And when Father came home from work at night, she would relay the day's soap opera—what this woman said, who came to see that neighbor, or who she heard yelling. Her tales were replete with embellishments and mockery. Partly because her disposition was one of perpetual sarcasm and partly to keep others from knowing to whom she was referring, Mother gave everyone in the area a nickname. When she noticed how one lady couldn't stop ordering people around, she branded her "Bouboulina," after the female folk hero who during the Greek Revolutionary War of 1821, built and captained ships, directed her own army, negotiated with Turkish sultans and Russian admirals, and performed great feats on the high seas. When Mother observed how another lady read people's future in her guests' coffee grounds in such a way that she ended up extracting more information from her patron than she conveyed, Mother labeled her *"magissa,"* the sorceress. And as for the one pitiful elderly neighbor, a woman who seemed to be afraid of her own shadow and always agreed with everyone, Mother reserved the moniker, *"theema,"* the victim.

An endless parade of rats filled the apartment in Patras. No matter how many of them Father killed with traps, with a hammer, or just with his feet, the damned rats were everywhere. They terrified Mother, and I remembered more than once waking up at night to see her standing on a chair pointing and screaming while Father moved around the unit crouched over and holding a hammer over his head.

"*Ai gamisou*, you bastard!" and "Get lost, you dirty beast!" Father scolded as he chased the panicked and shrieking vermin. And when his hammer finally crushed the head, the spine, or some other part of a rodent, Father would pick it up by the tail, open our front door and throw it into the street. Because there were infinitely more rats than Father could kill, this scene played out almost every night. By the time we left that apartment for a better one down the street, there were at least a dozen rodent corpses in front of our door in varying degrees of decomposition. Some were even squashed, by passing wagons, horses, and pedestrians.

When Father was at work, I spent my time watching Mother perform her chores. When she finished, she took me for walks around different parts of the town. We often visited the grounds of the Church of St. Dionysius, a massive and attractive place where many mothers brought their children to play. Other times, we headed down to the port, a busy and bustling place filled with people scurrying in every direction, trucks moving about and ships being loaded and unloaded. There were so many people at the port that whenever there, I was overwhelmed, confused and scared, and I held my Mother's hand very tightly out of fear that if I got lost there, she would never find me.

Mother often took me to Patras' beaches, where I played on the sand and waded into the shallow water while trying to catch minnows that darted here and there. Once, while we sat on the beach, we watched a majestic sailboat moving toward us on the shore, its sails up and tight. Just before it ran aground, the captain slowed his vessel and brought it to a sliding stop on the sand. He began unloading boxes of flopping and gasping fish onto the beach. With a big smile, the gruff and charismatic angler offered Mother a paper cone filled with small fish, which she graciously accepted and hurried home to cook.

Our afternoon walks often brought us to one of Patras' parks, another place where people gathered to socialize. Children played in that pine-filled yard while women chatted, the elderly sat on benches reading newspapers, and the men argued about politics. Whenever there, Mother gathered pinecones into a bag and using a knife, extracted and fed me pine nuts one by one.

On the days we ventured near one of the city's main parks during the noon hour, we were sure to hear a cacophonous marching band plow through, a corps fully loaded with trumpets, low brass and drums. That cadre destroyed the tranquility of the park, caused pigeons to take flight, and instantly energized the area. The buglers were Italians, students at a Roman Catholic middle school leading their classmates from the classroom building to the cafeteria building for lunch. Greeks took positions around the park and admired the spectacle, pleased by the flashy uniforms, the music, and the students' innocent enthusiasm.

When I first saw the overwhelming band, I exploded with excitement. Unable to contain myself, I begged Mother to one day let me play a trumpet.

"Maybe, but not at that school. That's a private school, and it belongs to the Roman Catholic Church."

"What?"

"It belongs to the Papa in Rome, Saranti." Mother proceeded to tell me about Constantinople, the Patriarch, east and west, the Great Schism, excommunications, one church, two churches, and other topics that meant nothing to me. I had heard about Italians before, in Gargaliani's cafés, and there it was always negative. But these Italians didn't look so bad to me. They were playing their instruments for us and looked like they were having fun.

Our afternoons often ended near the Arsakion job site where Mother and I struggled for a glimpse of Father at work. Sometimes we would see him, and when he saw us, he always smiled and waved. Working hard, being successful, and earning a generous wage gave Father a confidence that he had not experienced in years; it gave him dignity. He was happy in Patras, a different person. On the job site, he had authority and I was proud when I saw him confidently telling others what to do. At work, he developed friends and with his self-esteem restored, became a proactive person, someone who seemed to anticipate and control the events that unfolded before him. He was in charge and spoke with a forceful voice, a tenor that made Mother and me feel secure and made me want to be with him. At times, when he saw us and could get away from his work for a few minutes, he would explain what was happening that day. But to me, it seemed to be the same thing every day. When I asked him why the job appeared to be progressing so slowly, he smiled.

"Everything happens in sequences, Saranti. First, we build the foundation. Then, only after the frame is ready do we build the walls. If you build it out of order, it will not stand."

Evenings in Patras were idyllic festivals of happiness. With nothing to occupy us in our apartment and no light after dark except our kerosene lamp, nightfall brought all of Patras outdoors, onto its sidewalks and into its cafés and squares. Usually, we ended up strolling in its plateia and then relaxing at one of its cafés or pastry shops. Father passed those nights socializing with friends from the job site, and I remember that everyone made a big fuss over me, hugging me, messing up my hair, and giving me coins to buy candy. Mother rarely let me spend the coins but bought me a piggy bank to store them.

"When this is full," she promised, "we will break it open and use the money to buy you a tricycle!"

That thought gave rise to a number of tricycle-related fantasies and made me religiously place whatever coin I received into that piggy bank. I spent hours staring at it and was amazed, just as Father predicted, at how when shaken, the sound it emitted deadened as we added more coins. I carried the piggy bank everywhere and wondered about how many coins it held. Eventually, it became so heavy that I couldn't carry it anymore, and its permanent resting place became Mother's dresser. After it filled and when the day arrived for us to open it and buy the tricycle, the piggy bank disappeared. We searched everywhere for it, in the courtyard, around the plateia, in the apartment, but to no avail. In the end, we couldn't find it and Mother declared it stolen. But even then, I could tell by Mother's attitude, her feigned concern, and most importantly that ironic smile, that no one had stolen the piggy bank but that she had taken it.

Gargaliani

Apparently, she found a better use for the money than buying me a tricycle.

By the end of that summer, Father's work at the Arsakion project had finished, and he was once again unemployed. Though he tried to find other work in Patras, his efforts proved futile. His reprieve from scraping and dejection was over and suddenly, my parents were talking about returning to Gargaliani. Soon, it was obvious that there was even less for us in Patras than there was in Gargaliani, and we prepared to return. But though Mother and Father were sad to be leaving our reprieve from struggle, there was at least one good omen that we would take back to Gargaliani. Mother was pregnant. My days as an only child were numbered.

It was November of 1937 when we returned from Patras, and the raisin harvest was complete. Our wheat fields were useless—they were a mess after a summer of inattention and wild growth, especially after Father had failed to plow them the previous year. Once again, Father focused his efforts on preparing the vineyard for the following season. And like before, to put a few drachmas in his pocket, Father worked as a day laborer for other farmers and as a carpenter whenever he could. But this time around, and with another child on the way, Father knew that an inordinate effort would be required to keep us from becoming completely destitute, an effort that would include the commencement of letters to his brother Stathi in Detroit and his continued sale of family assets, whether land or otherwise.

Mother was worried, but couldn't pay too much attention to any of it. She remained preoccupied with her pregnancy and seemed to make sure everyone knew what she was going through.

"My sacrifice is so great," she would say. "No one but a mother can possibly understand it."

When she was stricken with a morning sickness that wouldn't subside, and the aroma of almost any food made her nauseous, she would look at Father or me and ask, "Do you see what a mother goes through? Do you see my suffering." As her body expanded, she wondered aloud, "When will the day come when I can deliver this child? When will God free me from this burden?"

Her suffering reached its acme one afternoon when Mother and

I were walking to the home of one of her distant cousins, my thea Agni, who lived on the other side of the plateia. As we were about to turn on a street adjacent to the plateia and continue toward her home, we approached the pastry shop of Kyrios Hilas. I saw several young ruffians sitting on the straw chairs in front of that store. They were the type of men Mother certainly considered low-lifes. As we neared the shop, the men began to catcall Mother, who at the time was eight months pregnant and wearing some sort of makeshift maternity dress. What they were saying to my Mother, I didn't understand, and she didn't alter our gait or even look in the direction of the cacophony, but became very angry and squeezed my hand hard as she pulled me past them. When my hand began to hurt, I pulled away from her, and she suddenly lost her footing and fell forward to the ground, directly onto her belly.

Kyrios Hilas ran out from his shop and a crowd of people circled us. The men who were talking to Mother became curiosity seekers and meandered over. Kyrios Hilas took charge of the situation.

"Everyone move back. Make room for the lady. Let the lady get some air." Mother, obviously shaken, ordered everyone away.

"I don't need any help. Please leave me alone."

She rose to her feet. Then, as if nothing had happened, she placed her purse back onto her left forearm, took me by the hand and we continued our walk down the street. When we reached the end of the block and were finally out of sight of Kyrios Hilas and his customers, Mother made a circular detour and we quickly headed back home. When we arrived, she sat on her bed and sobbed uncontrollably, terrified that her fall might have injured the baby. That was one of the few times I ever saw my Mother cry. And as she lay in her bed, I watched her pour rubbing alcohol onto her stomach and rub it into her skin as she mumbled some prayers to herself.

Mother laid low for the remainder of her pregnancy, and I recall how on one winter night just a month shy of my fifth birthday, a date I now know to be February 2, 1938, I was suddenly awakened to hear her screaming in pain. When I got my bearings, I realized that I was in our bedroom and in my bed, which sat a meter or so from my parents' bed, against a wall and underneath a cluster of icons. The *mamee*, our town's midwife, Thea Theano, and Dr. Zorbakos filled the room. The *mamee* was a tall, skinny woman, around forty years old who had somewhere picked up the know-how to deliver babies. A sense of urgency filled the room, and everyone talked quickly to Mother as she screamed in pain with each contraction. When her wails subsided, I fell asleep again only to be awakened again by more of Mother's screams and more loud voices only moments later. For what seemed to me hour after hour, this pattern continued: every few minutes, Mother's screams stirred me, I would fall asleep, only to be awakened again.

Despite the presence of Dr. Zorbakos, brought in by Father as a precaution, the *mamee* was in charge. She barked out orders to everyone like an army sergeant, commanding one person to fetch hot water, another to get more towels, and another to get her something else. Mother complained at every turn,

"God free me from this struggle. Panagia, you are a Mother, why must I suffer so? I am dying and nobody cares."

The *mamee* was even more stern toward Mother, ordering her to breathe a certain way, to turn her body this way and then that way, to get up and walk, and then to lie back down. So sure of her actions was the *mamee* that even Dr. Zorbakos stayed back, preferring not to interfere and not wanting to upset the woman as she performed her thaumaturgy. As for me, I think I suffered more than Mother. I knew Mother was delivering a baby and so what bothered me the most was that her screams kept me from sleeping. And what made it all worse for me was that Father had borrowed a number of additional kerosene lamps so the *mamee* could see what was happening. All the light and the noise and commotion made my brain hurt. And for reasons I will never know, no one had the sense to remove me from the room, to take me somewhere else to sleep. So I spent that winter night in the room with my Mother and a number of others while she gave birth, jarred into consciousness every few minutes or so until finally, the room fell silent.

When I woke up the next morning, I saw Mother lying in bed with a baby on her left arm. Though the custom at the time was to wrap newborns tightly in gauze like a mummy to ensure their proper posture later in life, Mother pooh-poohed that as an old wives tale and had the baby swaddled in a small white blanket.

"Saranti, come and meet your brother," she whispered.

When I took a look at him, I noticed his white skin, his slanted eyes, and marveled at his full head of bushy black hair. As I stared at the kid, Mother reached under the blanket and pulled out a red toy car.

"Sarantis, look at what your brother brought for you from heaven."

I took the car, looked at Mother, then at the baby who I mostly considered an interloper, and then at the car.

"How did he get out of your stomach?" I asked.

Mother paused and thought for a second. Then, with her ironic smile, she slowly raised her right hand and pointed to her open mouth.

Everyone rejoiced at my brother's arrival. Relatives paraded through the house to see and to admire the newborn. When they saw his slanted eyes, they called him the *kinesaki*, the little Chinese boy. Most agreed he looked like Father but when I looked at Father and then at my brother, I didn't see any similarity at all.

Within a few months of his birth, Mother began to arrange for my brother's baptism. Of course, finding suitable godparents was the first order of business, and Mother settled on some neighbors of Theano, the Prevezanos family. It was decided that the Prevezanos' two children would serve as godparents. The Prevezanoses were a highly respected family in Gargaliani, and Mother considered it a great honor to bring them into our circle. In addition, the family, unlike us, had means, and Mother hoped that in a time of great need, they would be there to help their godchild. So with the issue of the godparents settled, the only thing left to decide was the baby's name. Of course, since mother named me after her father, the natural thing to do would have been what she should have been done with me: to name him after my paternal grandfather, Antonis. But once again, Antonis would lose out.

My brother's baptism took place at All Saints. Present were Papa Ntres, dressed in his celebratory white baptismal robes, and my mother's and father's families.

At the beginning of the ceremony, Papa Ntres walked from the altar to the narthex of the church began the ceremony, "In the name of the Father, and of the Son, and of the Holy Spirit." He laid his hands upon my brother's head:

"Let us pray to the Lord. In Your Name, O Lord God of Truth, and in the Name of Your Only-Begotten Son, and of Your Holy Spirit, I lay my hand upon this Your servant…"

Papa Ntres looked at the godparents to provide him with the baptismal name of the baby. Though everyone in the room expected to hear "Antonis," the Prevezanos siblings replied, in unison, "Efstathios." Papa Ntres continued the ceremony,

"Efstathios! who has been accounted worthy to flee unto Your Holy Name and to be sheltered under the shadow of Your wings. Remove far from him that ancient error, and fill him with faith and hope and love that is in You, that he may know that You alone are the True God, and Your Only-Begotten Son, our Lord Jesus Christ, and Your Holy Spirit."

With her in-laws dead, Mother had decided some time before the baptism that naming my brother after her father-in-law would serve little purpose above and beyond conforming to the customs of the day. She thought that naming the baby after Father's brother Stathi (short for Efstathios), our donor in times of need, was a much better choice. Her reasons were obvious. First, the name was more than an appropriate thank you to Stathi for the financial help he had given us over the years. Second, Mother calculated that it was a quick way for our family to mend fences with Stathi and return to his good graces, something that we desperately needed since he was still upset over Father's sale of the family's land years before. Third, odds were that we would need the man's help again.

In the subsequent months, Mother lamented aloud more than once how disappointed she was at the Prevezanos family. It was quickly apparent that the Prevezanoses never took their vows seriously and the close relationship that Mother's move was intended to establish never materialized. On the contrary, it seemed obvious that the Prevezanoses sought to avoid us after Stathi's baptism, never inviting us over, forgetting Stathi's birthdays and annual celebrations of his saint's day, and generally exhibiting indifference toward their vows. In the end, Mother said the Prevezanoses were like Greece's politicians, vote-getters who made their appearance in towns before elections, baptizing babies, making unctuous promises, and forming illusory relationships, only to vanish after the votes were cast.

Stathi grew quickly, much faster than I had expected. For example, Mother had placed his crib in our bedroom, across from my cot and under an enormous mirror that had been with Mother's family for years. I saw that as Stathi grew, he began to stand in his crib and the taller he became, the closer he grew to the mirror. One day, when we thought he was napping, we heard a thunderous crash from the bedroom and when we rushed in, saw that Stathi had pulled at the mirror causing it to fall square atop the crib where Stathi sat, shattering into a thousand tiny little pieces. And there was little Stathi standing nonplussed inside his crib, one hand holding onto the rails, his hair full of broken pieces of glass, and his thumb in his mouth. Mother whisked him away, cleaned him up and lit the oil lamp that hung in front of the wall of icons in our room, thanking God that her son hadn't even been scratched.

As anyone with a younger sibling knows, Stathi's birth ended my role as the family's epicenter of attention. I was grateful for this, and with Mother distracted, I discovered a freedom to maneuver that I had never before known. I developed a private life for the first time. Suddenly, Spyro and I moved with impunity and with Aliki usually trailing behind, lived a life most succinctly summarized as one escapade after another. Though the secrecy of our adventures was usually short lived as Aliki, despite her sincere assurances that she wouldn't ever tell anyone what we were up to, could never resist the urge to run home and report to everyone what she had seen. Often, Aliki's news reports would earn me a spanking, but I learned to take my punishment from Mother and Father without complaining very much, and though I would agree not to play with Spyro again, or any other boy she considered as unsuitable, my promises were ephemeral. Before long, Mother referred to all of my friends as *alites*, hoodlums, the scum of society and to Mother, the sludge at the bottom of Gargaliani's barrel.

Mother may have been right when she told me that the kids I ran around with would become nothing but soil tillers, or even worse, pumpkinseed peddlers. But my friendship with them comprised my life's early relationships and our adventures the scenes of some of my life's most profound discoveries. Once, around my sixth birthday, we sat under one of the town's bridges and watched an oily stream trickle its way downhill to the Ionian Sea. We joked, we threw rocks in the stream, and floated leaves that we watched swiftly move downstream. Then, for no apparent reason, I experienced a sudden and unique revelation. I realized that I was an independent entity, a completely self-contained human being separate and apart from both my friends and from everyone else. I looked at my hand and moved my fingers. I thought about Spyro and how he was who he was a distinct entity in his own right, with his never-ending running nose and his dirty face. Aliki was one as well, with her perpetual look of wonderment and her eyes that were always filled with *tsibles*, sandy dried mucous. Why I suddenly realized this in the midst of playing that day I do not know, but I was dumbfounded by the fact that I was a unique, solitary, and alive person. I was neither of them nor anyone else. I was me. I began to notice Spyro and Aliki, and had a new respect for them, each were individuals, unique, solitary, each with unique wishes, needs, and originality. Overwhelmed by this realization, I interrupted their play.

"I am me," I said.

They looked up from their play.

"And you are you."

Aliki and Spyro stared at me, and I tried again.

"I said, 'I am me, and you are you.' "

They looked at each other and then back at me and then, with no reaction whatsoever, continued whatever they were doing without saying a word. For sure, we didn't have a meeting of the minds on this esoteric metaphysical concept. And though I knew I had discovered something profound that day, I decided to keep it a secret from that point on, realizing that I might never be able to explain it to anyone.

Part 2

WAR!

Chapter 9
SCHOOL

"Look Nitsa, look! Metaxas is coming to Gargaliani! Metaxas is coming!" father said in April 1939, as he ran into the house holding a newspaper. The man was excited.

General Metaxas had proved himself a heavy-handed rightist dictator, one who was not shy about using brute force to instill law and order. Despite the fact that he had many supporters, including Father, Metaxas's truculence had also earned him many enemies on the left.

Father told us that Metaxas would be passing through the Peloponnese, stopping in towns where he had enjoyed the most support. Gargaliani, a place that generally leaned right, would be amongst them. In the days before his arrival, pictures of the general were everywhere. In each, he was happy, usually smiling as he stood with open arms, ready to hug everyone, or handing a flower to a child. The country's schoolbooks pictured him, giving children the impression that he was someone who loved and cared about them; like an uncle they had never before met.

Father particularly liked Metaxas's no-nonsense, law-and-order style.

Though he preferred a democracy in Greece, Father would privately tell Mother that "We Greeks need a strong leader to keep order. At least now, there is respect for people's property."

But Father also thought Metaxas had crossed the line when he began jailing political opponents.

"He'll be making a big mistake if he hits his adversaries too hard. People have long memories. He'll only be feeding a future fire."

The news of Metaxas's visit brought great excitement to Gargaliani. The president of the Gargaliani Council issued a proclamation, which announced the General's arrival along with an edict of things to do that required immediate attention, including the whitewashing of homes on the route and the mandatory display of the Greek flag. Those who refused to fly the flag were taken in for questioning before a magistrate, and their refusal taken as a sign of disloyalty to Greece. We didn't have a flag. When Father was interrogated, it took him a while before he could convince the magistrate we were too poor to buy one.

"Give me one of your flags and I will gladly display it," he told them as he pointed to the numerous flags displayed around the room. They complied.

Father put his carpentry skills to use when Gargaliani commissioned him and some others to build an enormous arch under which Metaxas's motorcade would pass. After officials learned that Metaxas would enter Gargaliani after a stop in Kyparissia, they directed the carpenters to build the structure on the west side of town.

Metaxas's entrance would be a triumphant one, not unlike the entrances of the generals of antiquity in their victorious returns from battle. As we lived nearby, I visited Father daily and watched the arch take form. When it was completed, it was a magnificent, huge structure that spanned the width of a street and towered as high as an adjacent building. Father was very happy and proud of the work.

Not long after that and only two weeks before the general's arrival, Gargaliani officials received a telegram that the general planned to enter from the eastern end of the city, en route from Kalamata. Pandemonium broke loose when officials read the letter, and they directed Father and the other carpenters to dismantle the arch on the west and move it to the east. Time was of the essence. So with teams of horses and wagons, they transported and reconstructed the arch near the eastern entrance, not far from the church of St. Spyridon. Again, they decorated the arch with banners and political slogans and made every effort to clean up and whitewash everything on the new route. All was well.

When his arrival was only days away, town officials received a new telegram, one that said the original route was back on, that the general would once again be entering Gargaliani from the west. And Father, the crew, wagons and animals were dispatched to move the arch from the east back to the west and its original location.

When the big day finally arrived, General Metaxas entered

War!

Gargaliani from the west, traveled under the arch and headed toward the plateia as the bells of the churches rang, sirens blew, and myriad people waived and ran after him. When he arrived in the plateia, he was ushered up to a balcony from where he gave a rousing speech. Mother and I were too far to hear what he said, and I was too little to see anything. But with each of his applause lines, I could hear the excitement of the crowd and could feel each clap, whistle, and cheer.

For many, Metaxas's visit was no more than a politician's stop in our town. But for Father, it was much bigger. Metaxas's appearance was a harbinger of things to come, of a return of our country to a military mindset. Father was worried, and warned us that Metaxas was getting the country ready for war. And he was right.

Despite the Munich Agreement between Germany and England that had been reached the previous year, Hitler ordered the invasion of Poland on September 1, 1939. Two days after that, Britain and France declared war on Germany and World War II was underway. By June of 1940, German soldiers had marched into Paris and only a few weeks later, began bombing Great Britain.

Though Father carefully followed these events in newspapers he studied while drinking coffee in the plateia, I was oblivious to it all. Greece was not yet at war, and my family seemed consumed with more mundane things, like our survival. Father never seemed to make enough money and never realized whatever pie-in-the-sky plans he would make. Our vines did not produce enough grapes, our wheat field not enough grain, and our olives never enough oil. The prices at which we sold our goods were too low, and the prices at which we purchased our food were too high. Though making ends meet was always a struggle, Mother and Father, alone but with occasional checks from my Theo Stathi, were somehow able to pull it off. The world had made us survivors, accustomed to hard living. Though our continued existence was filled with struggle and uncertainty, we continued to live on. Whether I ate lentils or meat for dinner, I still played with my friends in the streets, Mother still took care of the home, and Father still farmed, smoked, played cards, and argued politics in the plateia.

Though Gargaliani lived with the agony of what tomorrow might bring, the life of the town continued, its farmers always planting, pruning, or harvesting and its plateia always bustling. And the fuel that kept us moving forward was hope, hope that circumstances would change, hope that Greece could avoid the war, hope that our fields would produce more, hope that just over the next hill was an oasis, hope that God had bigger plans in store for us. Perhaps even more importantly, hope kept us from despair, life's unforgivable sin. Looking back, though our life was hard and uncertain, the love in our family unit was unconditional, paramount, and to the death. And though we didn't realize it at the time, that alone made it a good life; a blessed one.

The fall of 1940 was time for me to begin school. I knew all about school, having listened to endless updates from Spyro after his forced attendance. One day the previous year, he appeared in front of our house in an unusually dour mood.

"My mother told me that I have to go to school," he murmured.

"Why?" I asked.

"Well, I have just turned seven. You don't have to go until next year, Saranti. You are very lucky."

"Why don't you want to go to school?" I asked. "Don't all the kids your age have to go?"

"Don't you know what happens there, Saranti? The teachers there have a mission, and it is to beat all the children. If you don't learn to read, they beat you. If you don't learn to write, they beat you. If you talk in class, they beat you. My parents are sending me to that place to get beaten."

I felt great empathy for Spyro and fortunate that I was able to defer my beatings for another year, having missed the cut off by six months. Every day, Spyro would fill us in on the latest school happenings. The typical story involved some corporal punishment administered to one of the older students and went something like this:

"Michael (or whomever) kept talking in class and when Kyria Galata told him to cut it out, he didn't listen. Then she grabbed him by the arm, dragged him out of class, and summoned a male teacher who pulled his ear out from the root, and beat the crap out of him."

Sometimes Spyro would tell us about a brave soul who fought back, or better yet, escaped, say out of the window. We revered such children as superheroes. One story involved a nine-year-old boy named Antonopoulos, who, after his teacher slapped him, turned to her with a sneer and said:

"You hit me? Not even my Father hits me. *Ai gamisou poutana!*"

The room gasped in unison.

"And your mother and your father too!"

Antonopoulos ran out of his class and down the school's stone steps still swearing: "And the ass that gave birth to you! *Ai gamisou!*"

Antonopoulos never returned to school.

Hearing such stories on a daily basis left me in a desperate state of total intimidation. Sometimes, I would tell Mother of my concern, and she would do her best to encourage me, by either explaining that the stories were exaggerations or by eulogizing the merits of school and pointing out the great achievements of local personalities, even though some had difficulties in the first grade.

"You see Kyrios Papageorgiou, the pharmacist? If you study hard now, you can be a great success like him. He had a hard time in first grade, but he stuck with it and look at him today. Everyone respects him. Saranti, school will make you a better person. Always remember what Alexander the Great said, 'I owe my life to my mother and my better life to my teacher, Aristotle.'"

Mother reminded me of these words often, pointing out that school was of paramount importance and that if I wanted a better life, I would have to focus on my studies. But even then, she was quick to point out that as important as school was, even Alexander agreed that a mother came first.

"Remember always, it is school that will give you a better life. A much better life than farming. Do you see how hard your father works for so little. That will not be your fate, Saranti. You will go to school, be an excellent student, and you will become a pharmacist. Just like Kyrios Papageorgiou. He finished grammar school, high school, and the university. You will do the same."

It seemed Mother and I had some version of this conversation daily. She repeated how hard I would study, how much work I would do, how successful I would become, and that I would grow to be a well-respected person with my own pharmacy in the plateia.

"You'll be famous," she would say, "and you will do it without having to till the soil. You will become an educated person. You will grow to have a better life, the life of a selected few, a life that will insure you stability and respectability. People will look at you with admiration, Saranti, and they will come to you to for advice."

In a way, I suppose, I became Mother's obsession, her hope to fulfill her own incomplete life and the hope of our family, the one who ultimately would extricate us from our present condition, the one who would move us out of the poverty that we lived in.

"Some day, I will stand next to you as others adorn you with accolades and bravos," she would tell me.

When the time arrived for me to go to school, Mother took me to a store in the plateia and purchased my school supplies: a satchel, a first-grade reader, a little slate board, and a composition book. The reader's cover pictured a cartoon of a young, sweat-soaked student carrying an oversized bag stuffed with the letters of the alphabet. When I looked at that boy, his enervated condition, and the obvious weight of his bag, I was intimidated and assumed that I would never be able to do whatever it would take to learn to read. As for the composition book, it was adorned with its own propaganda, a photograph of General Metaxas, his arms out-stretched and ready to embrace all of Greece's bright young students.

Father showed me how to use the slate board, and he began to draw figures and fancy curves. I tried to copy him, but my attempts were to no avail. My hands were too inept to hold the writing stick, a large, dark, chalklike instrument that placed erasable lines on the writing board. Sensing my struggle, Father picked up a pencil and with our kitchen knife, sharpened it to a fine point. I took it in my hand and began to scribble randomly in the composition book. The point broke. Then I took the knife and I tried to sharpen it as did Father. I quickly became frustrated because with every cut of the wood, I broke the pencil's tip until, cut after cut, most of the pencil was gone, in slices on the floor. Once again, Father sharpened another pencil to a nice point and after a few moments of trying to teach me to write with it, returned the pencil and the paper to satchel.

"You'll learn to write in school," he said and walked away.

Mother walked me to my first day of school. The building, one that was home to six grades in separate classrooms, had no electricity. Mother led me through its hallway, up its staircase, and to my classroom, which had already been divided into halves. Similar to the seating arrangement in church, the boys sat on the left side and girls on the right. An aisle separated them and served as the runway that the first grade teacher, Kyria Tasia Prosiliakos, walked up and down. When Mother handed me off to her, Kyria Tasia motioned to me to take a seat in the rear, near the left-hand corner of the room. By the time class began, roughly fifty students filled the class, with two children seated at each of the room's large desks.

Kyria Tasia sat me next to a boy I had never seen before, one from a different neighborhood. When I looked around, I realized that I didn't know a single person in my class. Who were these people? Where did they all come from? What a vulnerable and lonely feeling. Everyone seemed hostile and unfriendly, and so I sat there silently. I quickly realized that I was completely unprepared for school. The others seemed so much more comfortable in the environment, as if they had long been students and already knew the material we would cover in class. On the contrary, I was truly beginning as a blank slate and didn't know the first thing about reading or writing. I had no clue even where to begin. Though I could add and subtract numbers in my head, reading words and numbers appeared magical to me.

I will never be able to decipher such puzzles, I thought.

Kyria Tasia's first act that day was to place a few letters on the blackboard.

"Class, this is *Alpha*, the first letter of the alphabet. Everyone repeat after me, *Alpha*."

"*Alpha*," repeated the class.

"*Alpha* makes the 'aaahhh' sound. Everyone say Aaahhh."

"Aaahhh," the children repeated.

She said it again, and we repeated it again, until we convinced her that we knew the letter. Then she proceeded to the next one.

"Children, this is the letter *Veta*. *Veta* is the second letter of the alphabet. Everyone repeat after me, *Veta*."

"*Veta*," said the class.

"Now write the letters in your composition books."

Takis, the boy next to me, and I took out our books and did our best to copy the letters from the blackboard. Takis began to write sluggishly oversized letters and for whatever reason, I assumed he knew what he was doing so I began to copy him.

I quickly realized I possessed no writing skills. Though I wrote what I thought were correctly drafted and nicely rounded letters, I realized I was only writing mirror images of what Takis had written, with my left hand moving from right to left while Takis moved his right hand from left to right. The more letters Kyria Tasia introduced to us, the more I realized I could not discern in which direction the letters were supposed to open. Half of them faced one way and the other half the other. I was at a loss to figure out why the inventor of the alphabet didn't just design all the letters to point the same way. Overwhelmed and in a class that was so large, my ineptitude went unnoticed for several days, until Kyria Tasia finally made her way over to me to examine my work. When she flipped a few pages in my composition book, she let out a big yell and with a loud smack, slapped the back of my hand with her long stick.

"What kind of a mess is that?"

I sat dumbfounded, unaware of which of my inadequacies irked her the most. She snatched the pencil from my left hand and forced it into my right.

"From now on you will write with your right hand. Is that clear? I don't ever want to catch you writing with your left hand again. Do you understand?" I nodded as the whole class looked at me and felt a warm flush of blood fill my face.

Kyria Tasia turned to the class.

"There is no place in this world for left-handed people. Remember that, children."

As the year went on, Mother and I developed a routine whereby I would come home from school and tell her about my day. Then she worked with me, teaching me to hold my pencil and giving me various writing exercises like drawing circles, squares, and triangles. At first, I found the tasks nearly impossible, and because I was left-handed, my right hand had little coordination. It could barely hold a pencil. But over time, it gained dexterity and strength, and I improved tremendously and caught up with my classmates. Though I continued to reverse my letters and even more so my numbers, Mother taught me to slow down and to think before I wrote.

"All numbers, except the four and the six, open to the left, Saranti. Keep practicing. Practice makes perfect."

Eventually, I was able to write all the numbers and the letters correctly. Though at times, usually when I wrote fast, I reversed a number or two, I got to the point where I quickly recognized the error and corrected it. As the months passed, my confidence increased, and school was not nearly as awful as I had expected, even though I had my share of encounters with Kyria Tasia. Once, when she was at the blackboard writing letters, she wrote a "μ" and then placed directly next to it an "α."

Then, she turned to the class, and pointing to the "μ," asked "What sound does this letter make?"

"Mmmm," repeated the class without hesitation.

"Very good." Then pointing to the "α," she asked, "What sound does this letter make?"

"Aaahhh."

"Very good. Now, who can tell me what sound these two letters make when they are placed together?"

Everyone raised their hands and struggled to get Kyria Tasia's attention to answer what was obviously an elementary question. Caught up in the enthusiasm of the moment, I raised my hand as well. And then, to my horror, with fifty hands waiving in the air, Kyria Tasia did what I never wanted her to do. She pointed directly at me.

"Saranti! What sound does the "μ" and the "α" make when they are placed together?"

I froze. Kyria Tasia waited impatiently for my answer.

"Saranti, what sound does the 'μ' and the 'α' make when they are placed together?"

More silence. My classmates turned to look at me, and suddenly, all I could think about was that everyone was staring at me. I forgot the question I was supposed to answer.

"C'mon Saranti, what sound do you get when you combine the 'mmmm' sound with the 'aaahhh' sound?"

By this time, the sound of my teacher's voice was a blur. Terror and embarrassment paralyzed me. Now frustrated, Kyria Tasia ordered me to the front of the room. I rose from my chair and walked to the blackboard. She once again pointed to each letter with her long wooden stick.

"Saranti, what sound do the 'μ' and the 'α' make when they are placed together?"

The children began to pity me, and as Kyria Tasia spoke with her back to the class and pointing to the cursed 'μ' and 'α,' my classmates began to silently mouth to me the answer, "mmmaaa, mmmaaa, mmmaaa." Though I heard them, I thought it would be wrong for me to give Kyria Tasia an answer that I had gotten from others so I continued to stand silently in front of the class, dumbfounded. Finally, Kyria Tasia ran out of patience and began to hit my legs with her stick. And as she continued to hit me, she peppered me with the question.

"What sound do the 'μ' and the 'α' make when they are placed together? What sound do the 'μ' and the 'α' make when they are placed together?"

The school's bell rang, literally saving me as the whole class rose and in unison, got behind me, and pushed me toward the door.

When I found Mother waiting for me nearby outside the Church of Panagia, I told her what happened. She listened quietly.

"Saranti, every once in a while, a person needs a good beating to wake him up a little bit. Don't worry about it too much. Kyria Tasia did you a favor. Men of great character have endured many beatings, and most of the time, they are divinely inspired. It's likely that God sent your beating directly from paradise. You need to be more attentive in school. Listen to your teacher and follow her instructions. That way, you will learn your lessons and you won't get beaten."

I listened to my Mother, and that day marked the last time Kyria Tasia beat me. I was sure to stay out of her way and never to raise my hand unless I actually knew the answer.

Eventually, I became so acclimated to school, its lessons and its routines, that I actually began to like it. My classmates, initially strangers, became my friends, those with whom I joked and played. Our school day ended at noon, at which time we were sent home for lunch. Some of my classmates, however, didn't leave the school until after they were fed lunch, usually a bowl of soup and a slice of bread. I learned that those children were the *apori*, or "those without means"—the poor. When Mother learned about the free lunch, she handed me a plate wrapped in a dinner towel and told me to eat lunch with the *apori*. When I arrived at the school's kitchen the next day, a lady stopped me, asked me my name, and then checked it against her list. When she didn't find it, she checked another list and then informed me that I was not one of the *apori*, that I couldn't have a bowl of soup, and that I should go home to eat. When I arrived, I showed Mother my clean dish.

"Why didn't you eat lunch at school like I told you to, Saranti?"

"I tried, but the lady there wouldn't let me. She says we are not *apori* and the food there is only for them."

Mother began laughing hysterically.

"We are not without means? Is that why we lack almost everything?"

The following day, Mother came to school with me and approached the lady who had denied me lunch. When she tried to tell Mother that as landowners, we were by definition not *apori* and did not qualify for the free meal, an argument ensued. The next day, Mother gave me another plate and once again told me to eat lunch at school before I came home. When I hit the lunch line that day, the lady just waived me through. Despite my discomfort, not to mention Mother's, the grandson of Papa Sarantis was now officially considered to be among Gargaliani's *apori*.

For rich and poor alike, Gargaliani's evenings were convivial festivals set in the plateia. Anyone who walked the town's streets eventually made his way to that energized, tree-lined square block, with its perimeter surrounded by a generous sidewalk and the round, metallic tables and straw chairs of the town's cafés. The plateia was the magnet that attracted everyone. It was where Gargaliani spent its evenings, where its people, dressed in their best clothes strolled with friends and sat at cafés, where its children played. The plateia emitted a constant energy, one that forced whoever stepped upon it to begin to walk back and forth over it. In fact, for reasons unknown, few could step onto the plateia without commencing these *voltes*, as the strolls were known. The *voltes* had no order, and some people walked in one direction while others in another. They were interrupted only when one stopped temporarily to greet friends. But such conversations were usually cut short, and the walking quickly resumed, as if the person was on his way to somewhere important.

We were no different and usually after we regained our bearings from our afternoon nap, Mother would put Stathi into his stroller, one Theano had brought from Chicago, and walk us to the plateia. Once there, she would meet her sister and some other women and pass her time pushing Stathi around and gossiping. As for me, I would immediately make a break for my friends and spend such evenings running around the square, kicking a ball, and playing games like tag or hide-and-seek. If Gargaliani's plateia was its center, the cafés were the plateia's foci. These were raucous and bustling places, their chairs always filled and their customers stopping in regularly. The cafés were where the town did most of its public living, where they constantly stopped in, ordered coffees, sweets, or some jellied fruit preserve, sat and talked.

Whenever Mother sent me to find Father, I knew exactly where to find him. And looking for him was always an exciting adventure because whenever I found him playing cards, he would pull up a chair for me and let me watch. It didn't matter that I didn't understand what the players were doing or what made them pick up or throw down cards. There were few things I liked more. I loved being part of the action. I especially loved how Father would reward me with something sweet after each game. So as not to become a nuisance, I would sit quietly and listen to the men talk with one another. At a young age, I noticed a large contrast between what the men at the cafés talked about and what the women discussed when they got together. Every Greek man considered himself a PhD in politics, and those in Gargaliani rarely gossiped about mundane household matters or the town's petty interpersonal relationships. Their discussions focused on major world affairs, on the Greek government, its leaders, places called England, America, Germany, and so forth. And that the men were generally uneducated farmers in the middle of nowhere in southern Greece didn't prevent any one of them from speaking with authority on any of these subjects. In all my years at the town's cafés, I never heard anyone respond to a point by saying "I don't know" or "you may be right about that" or "I want to think about that." On the contrary, the men seemed to operate from a perspective that they had long ago researched and thought through the most demanding and difficult issues of the day and come to conclusions that were not only correct, but etched in stone—conclusions they would defend to the death. So no man was at a loss to describe, say, life in America, even if he had never left the Peloponnese. And that he was describing it to a person who had spent ten years living there didn't matter, so long as some uncle or cousin of his had given a thirty-second oration on the matter he adopted as his own.

As a boy, I learned a lot about current events in the town's cafés. I listened to the men talk about an Italian named Benito Mussolini and how he invaded a place called Ethiopia the year before. I heard them talk about how the leader of Germany, a man called Hitler, was a friend of Mussolini's and was building a large army, about an apocalyptic war that was coming, and that Hitler's army would fight the armies of France and England. Though I couldn't understand most of what I heard and the names those men bantered around were only empty words, the few names I retained provided me with enough ammunition to speak with equal authority on these subjects to my friends. Indeed, the know-it-all attitude made its way down to me.

One day while I was playing with Aliki underneath our balcony, I began telling her about Italy, Ethiopia, Germany, Hitler, Mussolini and some of the other characters I heard about. Though the girl had no idea what I was saying, she listened as I stressed to her the importance of these people and what they were doing. The more I spoke, the more animated I became, my eyes wide and my arms waiving for emphasis until I saw Mother was watching my oratory from the balcony above. Suddenly, I became flush, embarrassed that I was speaking so authoritatively and embellishing on an adult subject I wasn't expected to know anything about. On Mother's face was that ironic smile, the part-disapproving, part-mocking expression, the look that had the effect of alienating me, of making me feel abandoned by her, as though she had seen a part of me that she chose to mock, rather than to love unconditionally. I instinctively pretended that nothing unusual had happened and changed the subject by asking Mother for something to eat. She disappeared into our flat and when she returned, lowered a round cookie with a string. I shared it with Aliki and we returned to playing. But from that point forward, I avoided talking about adult matters with other children, especially when Mother or another grown-up was around.

I also learned some of life's most important lessons at the plateia's cafés. Once when I was playing with a friend around Kokonis's café, Father sat nearby, drinking his Greek coffee and socializing as he always did. Every ten minutes or so, I would interrupt him and ask him for a one-half drachma piece so I could buy a piece of candy. Every time I asked, Father gestured "no" by lifting his shoulders and opening his palms. I must have been an incorrigible pest because finally, Father's friend, Kyrio Themis, motioned me to come over to him. He dug his hand deep into his pocket and removed a twenty-drachma coin, gave it to me and told me to go to the newspaper stand to get some change. When I turned the single coin over to the stand's owner and in return received two handfuls of coins, I was amazed. I stared at all of them and thought that since there were so many, there wouldn't be any harm in keeping one. When I returned to Kyrios Themis, I emptied the contents of my hands onto the table and then watched as Kyrios Themis, one by one, separated each of the coins and stacked them into neat and uniform piles. Then he counted each pile, and then each coin in each pile, and then each pile again. After he performed this ritual a number of times, he turned to Father.

"One-half a drachma is missing," he reported.

Father turned toward me, grabbed my arm, and fished through my pockets. A terrified shame flushed over me and my stomach tightened as the gravity of my sin confronted me. When Father pulled the missing half-drachma from my pocket, he yanked me by the ear toward him.

"Saranti, go home!" he yelled.

Then he smacked me across my face. The impact of his calloused hand onto my tender face gave off a firecracker smack that echoed through the plateia.

I sobbed as I ran, and when I arrived home, I told Mother everything. She listened quietly, talked to me about the importance of obeying the Ten Commandments and gave me a slice of bread with fig marmalade to quiet me down. When Father arrived sometime later, I lay awake in bed and could hear Mother castigating the man for mistreating me.

"Have you gone mad hitting the boy over that? Don't you ever do that again."

But Mother's defense gave me no peace because I knew in my heart that what I had done was wrong.

All this living occurred in the midst of the plateia's jovial commercial atmosphere, with waiters operatically shouting orders, rushing with trays over their heads, and serving their patrons coffee and ouzo. The cafés' waiters were men in their thirties and forties who hustled when the cafés were busy. They never bothered to write down their orders, but instead shouted them directly to whomever was making the coffee inside.

"One coffee medium sweet" or "Two coffees heavy and no sugar" was the music of the plateia.

Oftentimes, the waiters bellowed in code to the coffee maker who knew that the waiter's inflection or that his inclusion or exclusion of a certain vowel would mean the coffee should include or exclude some ingredient. Peddlers like Nikitas, a fixture in the plateia, added to the cacophony by advertising aloud whatever they might be selling that night.

"Peanuts, almonds, pumpkin seeds! Peanuts, almonds, pumpkin seeds!" he would cry.

Men seated at cafés drinking ouzo would call him over and buy or gamble for some of whatever he sold, snacks just salty enough to perfectly accent the taste of whatever aperitif they happened to sip.

In the midst of all this was our town's crier, Bakas, who for whatever drachmas he could negotiate from the town's merchants, would walk the perimeter of the square and air his commercials.

"Ladies and gentlemen. Be advised that the store of Kyrios Ladas just opened a new barrel of sardines."

Then he would move down twenty paces or so and repeat, "Ladies and gentlemen. Be advised that the store of Kyrios Ladas just opened a fresh barrel of sardines."

Then another twenty paces down and a repeat of the same pitch.

Off in the distance, one could hear Kyrios Ladas's clerk, who stood in front of a curtain of salt-cured cod that hung from the door at the front of the store, counting off fish as he dug them from a barrel of sardines embedded in salt, "Sardine number one. Sardine number two. Sardine number three."

And with every number he shouted, he slapped a sardine into a piece of wax paper he held in his other hand, only to hear the customer remind him to shake off the salt before he weighed the purchase. Even when Kyrios Ladas had no customer, the clerk would still loudly count fish off the same way, just to give people the impression he was selling something others wanted.

By eleven o'clock, the plateia usually emptied as people headed to their homes for dinner and sleep, its gaiety suspended until the following evening. The plateia was the location of our entertainment, where the town did most of its living, and, a community center where people socialized.

On October 28, 1940, events that took place hundreds of kilometers away shifted the rhythms of our plateia and changed Gargaliani, and even more so my family, forever.

Hanging from one of the trees that encircled the square was a static-riddled speaker wired to one of the town's only radios. The device, short wave and AM, broadcast news and music from Athens's only radio station. Based apparently on cloud patterns, the radio's reception drifted in and out and all too often morphed into a jarring static squeal, one that would prompt a waiter to hit it with his fist or retune it until it recaptured reception. That day, news trickled into the plateia over the radio confirming what had hit Gargaliani's telegraph office earlier that morning. Greece was once again at war, this time with Italy. The information was spotty and as the day wore on, we learned that Mussolini had demanded Greece's surrender or else suffer immediate invasion. The news took the town by surprise, despite heightened world tensions and an endless stream of talk from Mussolini's mouth. But bellicose posturing and garrulousness were one thing; an invasion something else entirely.

Following Italy's adventure in Ethiopia and in line with the Fascist Il Duce's dreams of resuscitating the corpse of the Roman Empire, Mussolini ordered the invasion and occupation of Albania in April of 1939. The following year, on August 15, 1940, the day of the

War!

celebration of the Assumption of the Virgin Mary, an unidentified submarine torpedoed and sunk the Greek cruiser *Elli* as it sat anchored near the harbor of the Cycladic island, Tinos. Though everyone knew the submarine was Italian, the Greek government never officially confirmed it, choosing to try to calm sentiments instead. Now, in a move that not even the Fuehrer knew about, Mussolini, tired of playing second fiddle to Hitler and wanting to flex a little Italian muscle, called Italy's invasion of Greece into action. But even though the *Elli's* sinking was so recent, the invasion took almost all the Greeks, even the political aficionados in our plateia, by surprise.

Throughout the day, we heard bits and pieces, how Mussolini had told Metaxas to immediately surrender Greece or face the Italian army, and claims that Metaxas made a heroic one word refusal, "*Oxi!*" or no!

In his short but stirring speech to the Greek people, broadcast over the speaker in the plateia, Metaxas mobilized Greece for the struggle ahead.

"The moment has come to fight for the independence of Ellas, her identity and her soul. Although we kept the most strict neutrality and equality to all, Italy, ignoring our right to live as free Hellenes, asked me today at three o'clock in the morning to surrender parts of our national grounds, as dictated by her and that, but for the occupation of these grounds, the Italian army would attack by six o'clock in the morning. I answered to the Italian ambassador that I consider this request and the manner it was made as declaration of war by Italy against Greece.

Now we must prove we are worthy of our ancestors and the freedom they gave us! The whole nation must stand up as one body! Struggle for our country! Our women! Our children! And our holy traditions! Now, above all, struggle!"

Though inspiring, Metaxas's bravado-filled words were not necessary to motivate Greeks to fight. Word of the invasion caused the country to spring into action. With Greece's independence little more than a century old, still in the psyche of every Greek was the understanding that freedom carries a price and that Greece's freedom wouldn't be squandered. "Liberty or Death" was a line people repeated over and over, and when the call came in, army veterans across the country gathered their uniforms and made their way back to their units.

I learned of the invasion when I arrived in school that morning. When my class settled, Kyria Tasia stood in front of the class with a sober announcement.

"The Italians have declared war on us," she said.

When she realized that none of us knew what she was talking about, she continued, "Let me start that again. The Italian army has invaded Greece from Albania and our country is now at war. They want to take our country. They want us all to be Italian, not Greek. Many men from Gargaliani will leave this town and go fight them. There will be something for all of us to do. That includes you. Greece will never die. *Zito i Ellas.*"

For the remainder of the morning, other teachers entered our classroom and addressed us, each one a little more belligerently than the one before.

"That jackass Mussolini thinks he can conquer us?" one asked. "Those Italians now will see how we Greeks fight."

"We will fight the Italians in the same way we fought the Turks and the Bulgarians and everyone else!" exclaimed another.

"We are going to destroy those dirty Italians, we'll eat those plates of spaghetti alive," said yet another.

It seemed everyone concluded every sentence uttered that day by repeating, *Zito i Ellas,* long live Greece. I think I must have heard it several thousand times. When all the speeches had ended, Kyria Tasia returned to the front of the class.

"School is closed until further notice. You must go home now."

When I walked outside, I saw people all over the plateia who were trying to get a handle on what was happening. Near Kokonis's café, Father sat talking with his lugubrious friends about the invasion, the Italians, that Greece was once again at war, the Germans, and about what lay ahead. Everyone spoke only about the state of the world—there would be no card playing. By late afternoon, people remained in the plateia under a veil of somberness. Gone were the earlier displays of saber rattling and gaiety. A dark sobriety caused everyone to realize that they were hesitant to make the same swap as Achilles, to trade a mundane family life for glory. People speculated as to who would be included in the mandatory draft and at what age the cutoff would be placed. Some said the line would be at fifty years of age while others said forty. Father, who was forty-seven, was not concerned.

"Who would want an old guy like me?" he asked.

One thing everyone knew was that while the people would do their duty, wars had no winners, and that in this conflict, there would be many victims—that our town would be a victim.

"When everything is said and done," one man pointed out, "Metaxas and his family will be fine, but people like us will pay the ultimate price. Just look around here, the widows and orphans from other wars are too many to count."

That evening, several young men entered Kokonis's café. They were from the army. One of them got everyone's attention.

"All Greek Army veterans, ages twenty-two to forty, are hereby immediately called into military service. You will receive word of when and where to report. Because there is no time now to train anyone, those of you who have not previously served will not be called into action at this time. You should await further instructions."

When we heard the ages of mobilization, Mother was overwhelmed with happiness. She knew we would need Father at home to survive the war.

The next morning, Gargaliani had sprung into action with busses, trucks, and taxis zooming in and out. Newspapers from Kalamata over sixty kilometers to the east, brought war news. Many of our town's young men were leaving, heading toward staging areas in places all over the Peloponnese. Women cried and clung to their husbands and sons as they boarded busses.

Those who were leaving held back their tears and said things like "I'll be back soon," or "make sure you do x, y, or z when I'm gone," or "if this or that happens at the farm, be sure you call this person," and so on.

At the cafés, the men discussed how since antiquity, the Italians had always been out to cheat the Greeks and were in fact responsible for the demise of Greek civilization and the fall of Constantinople. Quips and songs from unknown poets had already landed and would continue to appear almost as regularly as the newspapers. One of the more popular ones involved a Greek official personally sticking it to Mussolini:

Mussolini is a jackass
The Italians are a saddle
And our Koritsis will mount him
And ride him all the way back to Rome!

For the next several days, war mobilization accelerated, and traffic in town increased. Good-byes were everywhere—our streets flowed with tears. After a week, the shock of the sudden change of everyone's fate seemed to wear off, and the town began to lock into its new war paradigm. This caused a degree of normalcy to return. The schools reopened, and people resumed their previous routines. Most had a greater ability to adapt than they knew.

Within a couple weeks, the town returned to some degree of normalcy. We were back in school and news of the war became the most coveted commodity. People purchased early morning newspapers from Kalamata as soon as they arrived, as they did the afternoon papers from Athens. War updates spread through the town. We quickly learned that at the front, the defense of Greece went much better than everyone had expected. When the Italian army moved south into Greece from Albania, it was never able to achieve any sort of breakthrough. By mid-November, the Greek Army mounted a counter-offensive that pushed the Italians back into Albania. After it crossed the Albanian border, it continued on, conquering town after town. Gargaliani rejoiced with news of each victory, and with each Albanian city that fell, our church bells rang and my school held assemblies commemorating our soldiers' valor. Kyria Tasia pointed out how our capturing of new land was merely taking back territories that had always belonged to Greece.

"Our soldiers are welcomed as liberators in every village they enter," she said.

Letters from the front trickled in, replete with stories of bravery and heroism. They typically involved tales of small bands of outnumbered Greek soldiers capturing a cadre of Italians. We heard that we had captured scores of Italian prisoners, so many that our army didn't know what to do with them. Surprising enough, these tales were for the most part true. One such story described how one of our town's soldiers, on patrol with eight other men, came across an Italian hiding behind some boulders, waiving a white flag. Though the Greeks feared a trap, the Italian soldier, who kept repeating

War!

"*bono Greco, bono Greco,*" kept waiving his flag and led the Greeks around a bend to a cave, where, to the Greek's amazement, a pile of rifles and pistols lie at its entrance. And behind the weapons stood some three-hundred Italians soldiers with their hands raised. The eight Greeks secured the weapons and marched the three-hundred Italians back behind Greek lines. At their camp, a Greek officer, still enraged from fighting at the front, began to swear and shoot at the unarmed Italians.

"Stop! Stop!" the Greeks shouted at the irate officer.

Then, a Greek jumped in front of the officer.

"If you want to shoot someone, shoot me. But not these unarmed men," he ordered.

They restrained the officer and avoided a massacre. Prisoners like these were removed from the front and distributed all over Greece. They sent a dozen of them to Gargaliani and put them to work planting evergreens near the chapel of the Prophet Elia. Feats such as these made us feel proud and invincible.

Greece gushed with ebullience over its victories in Albania. While we expected the Italians to be a more formidable enemy, it didn't take much to figure out that despite the bluster of Il Duce, the average Italian's heart wasn't in conquering Greece. Few wanted to leave their bones in Albania for the imperialistic rants of a buffoon. Indeed, while Mussolini's grandiose plans for the revival of the Roman Empire may have had an intellectual appeal amongst certain Roman elite, they lacked much popular support. Many laughed at how Mussolini once impressed Hitler with a military parade that featured endless columns of soldiers and artillery, when in fact the army was only the same thousand or so troops doing lap after lap around the block. But though he could fool Hitler, Mussolini couldn't fool his own people, and few were convinced of the nobility of their mission in Albania or their invasion of Greece. Indeed, the Italians were surprised by the strength of the unbending Greek lines, and their enthusiasm faded even more when they discovered they faced Greek soldiers who never questioned the nobility of defending their country from invaders and who drew upon an endless reservoir of Hellenic heroes when the time to act arrived. In this war, the immortal Spartan phrase, *e tan e epi tas*, which roughly translates to "return from battle as a victor or as a corpse on your shield," was never too far from any Greek's lips.

When the winter fighting arrived, Albania sunk into a deep freeze. Conditions became intolerable, and the poorly equipped and dressed Greek soldiers paid a great price. Frostbite and amputations were common. Though our soldiers could defend against the Italians, no amount of bravery could protect them from the cold, and the government instituted a massive effort to knit garments for the soldiers. Every available female in Gargaliani volunteered to knit stockings, sweaters and gloves that were transported to the front. Mother did her part. When more letters arrived with complaints that our commanders were fighting only a war of containment and that they could easily push the Italians all the way into the Adriatic Sea if permitted, the town cheered.

But as all good things must come to an end, so did this twentieth-century installment of the story of Greek heroism and valor. By early spring 1941, the Italian army's invasion of Greece had officially become a complete fiasco, and in April, Hitler came to the aid of his diminutive Italian counterpart. Through the friendly and unprotected Yugoslavian border, Germany drove roughly one-hundred fifty-thousand troops into Greece, surprising the Greek commanders who assumed that any German invasion would come through Bulgaria. The tanks of these German Panzer Divisions were generally unopposed, and after only a few skirmishes, Greece quickly submitted, and one of our generals signed Greece's surrender to Germany. But as appearances are everything, at Hitler's direction, the generals repeated the signing ceremony; the second time, Greece surrendered to Italy.

With Greece's capitulation, our army was immediately disbanded and each soldier ordered to return to his village. Chaos ensued as the men began to walk home. Over the next several weeks, soldiers straggled into Gargaliani. Though many were unscathed from the war, some had wounds and still others had left certain parts of their bodies at the front. Many never made it back. A few of the more enterprising soldiers returned with booty, such as a horse, a mule, or some other animal the army had seized to assist in the fight against Italy. But with the collapse of the army and the resulting chaos, most of these animals never returned to their original owners but fell into the hands of black-market speculators. A few soldiers with

War!

vision realized that surviving during the coming occupation would be difficult had the gumption to walk an animal back to their homes.

After Greece's surrender, Gargaliani began to brace for the Italian and German occupations. Town officials feared the worst and announced that our schools would close several weeks early. As classes wound down, Kyria Tasia announced that our intrepid school would neither cancel our year-end assembly nor its presentation of diplomas. So a week before the end of classes, Kyria Tasia walked around our class.

"I am handing out poems to several students in the class. Those of you who receive them are to memorize and prepare to present them at the assembly next week. You should practice them with your parents until you can perform them without any help. Any questions?"

Kyria Tasia handed me the last sheet she carried. When I arrived home, I removed the paper from my satchel and threw it at Mother's feet.

"Kyria Tasia gave me that today and says I have to recite it to everyone at the assembly. My answer is no! Under no circumstances will I get up on any stage. And for sure, I will not read that ridiculous poem before the school."

My breathing was labored and my heart pounded. Mother picked up the paper, and I saw in horror the curling up of her lips into that damned ironic smile.

"Sarantis, this is what happens to good students," she began. "Good students are given poems to read. Kyria Tasia gave you a poem to read. That means that you are a good student!"

"I don't care. I don't want to be a good student."

Mother ignored such drivel and immediately began to teach me the poem. When I resisted, she tried bribes. When those didn't work, she downshifted to threats, which turned out to be a much more effective strategy. Despite my resistance, I began to learn the lines, and Mother said that it wouldn't be enough for me just to recite them, I had to act them out, to modulate my voice and make gestures that corresponded with what I said. When I offered my halfhearted attempts at drama, my difficulty coordinating the words with Mother's gestures became obvious. On several occasions, I became so frustrated that I ran out of the house and vowed that I was finished with the poem and that I would never recite it to anyone. But Mother stayed the course, and little by little, things began to stick.

When I was eight years old, future events seemed extremely remote to me, even those that were only a day away, that I was able to put them out of my mind and act as if the day of reckoning was so far off that it would never come. So remote were my tomorrows that when they finally arrived, I was always surprised that some miracle had not intervened to save me, that things actually went as planned.

When the morning of the assembly arrived, Mother kept a close watch on me, fearing that I might make a run for it at the last moment. She escorted me to the school and, never leaving my side, escorted me to the stage. Terror pulsed through and froze my body. Mother and Kyria Tasia dressed me in my costume by tying a towel around my head that began under my chin and terminated with a big knot atop my head. When they shoved a piece of cloth in my mouth, they told me I was ready.

"Now, Sarantis Stamatis will tell us about his terrible toothache," the teacher announced.

I couldn't move an inch and was totally unable to walk onto the stage. It remained empty and I could hear the children begin to giggle at my failure to appear.

"Come on out, Saranti. It's okay. You have nothing to be afraid of," the announcer said.

The audience giggled some more, and Mother sprang into action. She grabbed my arm and pulled me on to the stage. When the audience saw Mother manhandling me, they roared with laughter and applause. Realizing that I had no choice and that resisting would only worsen my fate, I stopped, acquiesced, and moved toward the middle of the stage. And as I stood there, with the towel on my head and the cloth in my mouth, Kyria Tasia signaled me to begin. When the laughter finally subsided, I took a deep breath and began:

Oh, oh, oh, that tooth has started to hurt me again,
And it has caused me dizziness,
Stinging and pain.
I had a paper sack, filled with candies and sweets,
And before I could eat them all,
My tooth broke with a loud crack!

With every line, I held my jaw in a gesture of pain and then pointed to my head and then back to my mouth. The audience loved it. I didn't expect that reaction, and it frightened me, causing my voice to trail off to a squeak. The more I spoke, the more the cloth in my mouth interfered with my speech and I covertly tried to push it back in its place with my tongue. I began the second stanza with vigor only to have it peter out like the one before. The audience could not stop laughing. The audience sprayed bursts of laughter at me in between each sentence, which sparked even more laughter. When I completed the last sentence and realized that I had forgotten several lines, I felt obliged to go back and to recite those too. By now, even Kyria Tasia and the rest of the teachers were laughing and clapping. When I finished, Mother came on stage and rescued me, frozen as I was in shock in a pool of perspiration.

From all indications, my performance went extremely well. Mother was pleased and smiled the entire walk home. Though for sure my delivery did not go as *I* had planned, the comedy of the spectacle trumped any disappointment in the lines I blew here and there. Without trying, I gave that poem about my toothache a new twist that went beyond the simple lamentation of a little pain.

Much later in life, I looked back and realized that all I was trying to do was to complete an abhorrent task that others had forced upon me, and my struggle apparently offered those in the audience a reprieve from the challenges that were moving toward our town. But I was not so philosophical at the time, and I remained traumatized and for years suffered through dream after dream of being on stage delivering that damned poem.

Chapter 10
NEW NEIGHBORHOOD

Despite the war, by the early summer of 1941, my family's relationship with our housemates had deteriorated to the point that we had become prisoners in our own home. Mother refused to go into the kitchen or the bathroom unless she was sure that no one from my late uncle's family was nearby. I'm sure they must have felt the same way. But whether Theo George's family was still upset over my Father's claiming of his half of their home or whether it was Mother's aloofness toward the struggles they faced after Theo George's death, I cannot be sure. But no one could deny that our living arrangements had become unpopular with everyone. When some tenants in Papa Sarantis's old house moved out, Mother insisted it was time to gather our belongings and return to that more spacious dwelling. Adding to the urgency of the move was the fact that the enemy occupation forces were only a few weeks away and that the birth of my brother had placed four of us in the same bedroom. That arrangement was unbearable because when Stathi cried, everyone woke up. When one person was sick, everybody suffered.

Talk of the move filled our house and caused me great distress. Though I knew they were altering my entire world and comfort zone, I quickly realized there was nothing I could do to stop them. And though we were moving only four blocks to the southeast, just a quarter turn around the plateia to its east side, to me the new house was a million kilometers away. I had long before identified myself with my neighborhood and had become a fixture there, as much a part of it as the *litourvio* or Bousoulas. I knew of nowhere else and was incapable of visualizing any life outside that cocoon.

"How can I abandon my friends?" I nagged Mother. "How can we leave our home, my school, and our neighborhood? Why don't we move next year?"

I repeated questions like these endlessly while Mother tried to neutralize my concerns as best as she could.

"Trust me when I tell you that where we are going is much better," she'd say. "We are moving to a much bigger house, one with three large bedrooms. You and your brother will have your own room together. We are moving to the house that I grew up in, the house that the great Papa Sarantis and his father built. He would have wanted you to grow up there. After we move, you will go to an even better school, and you will make new friends. It will only take you a few days to forget everything about this old neighborhood."

And so without much further conversation, I understood that I would soon start life over again and began to prepare myself mentally for the change to come. Mother handled the physical logistics of organizing the move. When the big day finally arrived, Father borrowed a horse-drawn cart and hired a man to help him move our larger items: the bed, a dresser, and our kitchen table. After only a couple of trips back and forth, our side of the apartment was empty. Mother swept out our home for the last time, closed the shutters, and without saying good-bye to Theo George's family, unceremoniously locked the door. We left, never to return. I followed her as she carried Stathi down the stairs. When we emerged on the empty street, we silently began to walk. No one approached us, and no one said goodbye. And with each step, I severed my ties to the only neighborhood I knew a little more. I knew that I would rarely see Spyro and Aliki again, and even when I did, my absence from the old set would alter our friendship forever. Yes, we would recognize each other as friends, but our days as comrades were over.

But being the child that I was, I couldn't hold on to such dramatic thoughts for long, and as we walked, my mind drifted to other things. I watched a group of birds fly and settle on some wires next to a utility pole. I wished I had a slingshot to shoot one; I felt like they were just begging me to fire at them. Mother tugged sharply at my arm.

"Stop daydreaming," she ordered.

We passed the community fountain and then the office of the other doctor in town, Dr. Papathomopoulos. As I had finished the first grade, I tried to sound out whatever signs I found in front of me, "*i-a-tros Nee, Nee,*" I said.

"*Nilos,*" Mother corrected.

A little further, just on the edge of the agora, I noticed an old dilapidated house, one I had seen many times before

"*Mo, Mor, Mour – ya, Mor, O geros tou Morias!*" I said as I read the worn out inscription engraved across the face of the building. With Mother's help, I sounded out the words.

"Do you know who was the *geros tou Moria*?"

"No, Mana."

"*O geros tou Morias,*" Mother began, "was the old man of Moria, the name given to the Greek revolutionary hero Kolokotronis. 'Morias' means mulberry tree and many years ago, the Byzantines grew mulberry trees here. In those trees, they raised silk worms that they brought from China. In the end, there were so many Mulberry trees that the Byzantines called all of Peloponnesus 'Moria.'"

Mother led us through the agora and then onto a narrow side street. From there, we walked across a rectangular field that was home to several horses. That clearing was filled with the piercing pounding "clang...clang...clang" of Gargaliani's blacksmith. When Mother grabbed my hand tightly to keep me from wandering near the horses, I remembered that I had been in this neighborhood before. The previous year, Father had sent me to deliver a note to Kyrios Stelios, our tenant at Papa Sarantis's old house. Father walked me most of the way that afternoon and then stopped on a corner a block away. Then he motioned for me to go ahead alone.

"Walk straight ahead and go to the house on the corner. Make a quick left and then knock on the door and hand this note to Kyrios Stelios," he ordered.

I knew Kyrios Stelios well as he had been our neighborhood's mailman for years. When I arrived at the home, I knocked as Father had told me and before I knew it, the towering Kyrios Stelios stood in the doorway. I handed him the note. He read it and with a huff, motioned me to follow him. In the house, he disdainfully reached into his pocket and removed a handful of coins. Then he selected three five-drachma pieces and threw them onto his dining room table. Silently, he motioned for me to take the money. I gathered the coins and without looking back, ran out of the house. I found Father later in the agora and handed him mailman's advance on his next month's rent.

"Bravo," he said and took the money and bought us a bag full of food.

As we exited the clearing, I turned to Mother. "I know where the house is."

"Lead me to the place you remember," she replied and let go of my hand.

I ran ahead, through a narrow alley and immediately fell upon the backside of our new home. Before I could get too close however, I saw a group of women hovering in front of the adjacent house. Though I had never seen them before, they opened their arms and ran in our direction when they saw me. If their greeting surprised me, it surprised Mother even more.

"Welcome, welcome. Nitsa and the children are here! Nitsa and the children are here!"

They hugged and kissed Stathi and me and then Mother. The encounter shook Mother and froze her dead in her tracks. She was speechless.

The women were Mother's first cousins, Maria, Katina, and Eleni, the three daughters of Dimitri, Papa Sarantis's younger brother. All these years, they had lived in the old wing of my great grandfather Spyro's house, and though they were my aunts, I had never met them. Now, they would be our neighbors, along with their brother Christos and their parents, who were still alive. Prior to that day, I didn't know that my grandfather, Papa Sarantis even had a brother, let alone that he was still alive. I learned later that we had never visited my uncle because Mother had become upset with him and his family following the death of her parents. For whatever reason, she felt that Theo Dimitri and his family had either turned their back on her or not helped her to the extent she deemed appropriate and wrote them off. But not even Mother's decade of coldness could withstand such a show of affection, and though she tried to remain reserved and to pull us close to her, the love melted her heart and I remember thinking she looked like she might cry. It seemed that time can in fact heal all wounds.

After the hugs, my cousins led us to my aunts' courtyard, a garden full of roses. There, seated above us on a large, second-floor balcony that overlooked the area was Papa Sarantis's younger brother, my Theo Dimitri.

"Who-is-there?" he asked in his overly loud, staccato voice.

"It is Nitsa and the kids," one of his daughters yelled back as we walked toward him.

Theo Dimitri felt for his cane, pushed it into the floor and rose from his chair.

"Wel-come, wel-come. Come-up-here-to-the-bal-co-ny-so-I-can-talk-to-you."

His speech was like a loud machine gun.

His daughters led us through their home's main door, up a flight of stairs, through a dining room, then a bedroom and out to Theo Dimitri's balcony. When we stepped outside, he stood there facing us, looking at us but seemingly past us. Mother moved toward Theo Dimitri, took his hand and out of respect, kissed it. Then she pushed me and Stathi in front of her to do the same. When I kissed his hand, Theo Dimitri turned it around and started lightly to feel my face with his fingers. I looked up and saw that his eyes were colorless, his pupils clouded over, making his eyeballs appear almost totally white. Years of untreated cataracts had blinded him.

"Damn-these-cur-sed-eyes. What–I-would-n't-give-to-be-able-to-see-my-bro-ther's-grand-chil-dren."

Theo Dimitri's voice filled and bounced around the courtyard.

And with his hand holding my chin, he turned to me and shouted, "What-is-your-name?"

The louder he spoke, the softer I wanted to speak.

"My name is Saranti," I mumbled.

His eyes widened and an enormous smile erupted on his face.

"Sa-ran-ti!" he exclaimed.

Tears rolled down his cheeks.

He patted me on the head and said "Sa-ran-ti, you-will-come-visit-with-me. Okay, Sa-ran-ti?"

"Yes," I replied.

Theo Dimitri had four children, none of whom were married.

War!

Maria was the oldest, in her mid-twenties and had been named after Theo Dimitri's mother, my great grandmother. Katina was twenty-two. Christos, partially paralyzed from polio, was eighteen, while the argumentative and ill-tempered Eleni was fifteen years old. As for Dimitri's wife Fotini, she was a dour and unapproachable woman. Endlessly mourning the death of her mother, she always dressed in black and spent her days cursing everyone including her daughters for being unmarried and her son for being an invalid. She never combed her hair but preferred to keep her head covered under a black scarf. When she actually removed the scarf, her head resembled an abandoned bird's nest.

After we reconnected with my uncle, we entered our new home, a rectangular dwelling that was much larger than what we were used to. It sat directly to the east of Theo Dimitri's square dwelling and ran lengthwise along the west side one of the town's main roads ending at a small gravel alleyway that headed to the west. As soon as we entered the home, we marveled at its brightness, at the number of windows that lined the street side of the house and at the light they let in. The house was equipped with three large bedrooms, spacious dining and living rooms, and on the north end, a bathroom and a kitchen fully equipped with a wood burning stove. We quickly learned that the largest bedroom shared a wall with Theo Dimitri's home through which we could hear the din of our new neighbors' voices.

The kitchen comprised a table, some chairs, and a wood burning stove. Though connected to the home, it was obviously constructed afterward and stood upon four pillars. The north end of the kitchen butted up to a stone wall over which we had a direct view through large bay windows into our neighbor's backyard. At the northeast end of the kitchen was a small staircase that led down to a side door and exited into the main street. Two more steps to the left led to an open space under the kitchen and another step to the left into the basement under the home.

Our new home was definitely a step up. After we settled in, our first order of business was to have the house blessed. Mother and I headed to All Saints and acquainted ourselves with the priest just brought in to replace Papa Ntres, who had died a year or so before. Ordained while unmarried and accordingly an "archimandrite," Papa Christodoulos was in his early thirties and had been named the priest in charge of my grandfather's former parish. After kissing his hand, Mother made her first meeting with the priest her time to flash her priestly pedigree and to display her knowledge of ecclesiastical matters. Papa Christodoulos was delighted to meet Mother and told her he would take her up on her offer to mend his vestments as the need arose.

"You must also, Kyria Nitsa, allow this fine son of yours to become one of my helpers at the altar."

"Of course, Father! Saranti is looking forward to following in the footsteps of his famous grandfather."

Though it was not apparent to me, Mother immediately pegged the new priest as insincere, definitely not cut from the same cloth as her father or even Papa Ntres, and accordingly nicknamed the red bearded priest "Javer," after the relentless and irrational investigator who endlessly tracked Jean Valjean in Victor Hugo's *Les Misérables*. On our way home, Mother sized up his darting eyes as calculating and his over-alertness to be the sentry he stationed to guard his secrets. But Mother also knew that she had to stay close to Papa Christodoulos, that this relationship could help us in a time of need.

As the days passed, I realized that Mother was right when she told me I would forget the old neighborhood. It surprised me how quickly I adapted to change. Fleeting nostalgic thoughts about my old friends quickly evaporated from the heat of the constant activity in our new neighborhood, and perhaps even more so from the anticipated arrival of the occupation forces. Though children filled the new neighborhood, I became closest with two named Niko and Kostas. Niko lived across the street from us, a few houses to the south. We were the same age, and he was the youngest of seven children with five older sisters and a brother two years our senior. Niko's family owned several vineyards, all of which were located near the sea and just a block or so southeast of Thea Theano's beach house. Because he was from a family a few notches above us on the socio-economic scale, Mother loved him and encouraged me to play with him.

Shortly after we moved into the new neighborhood, Niko's father was killed at one of the tavernas in the plateia. Neighbors told us that suddenly and without any provocation, a drunk plunged a knife into his stomach. The next day, I watched the funeral from our bedroom window and saw my new friend as he walked in the procession with his family, a black band tied around his sleeve and his eyes swollen from crying. When Niko came around to play a few days later, he told me in confidence that his father died protecting the honor of his family. I felt sorry for Niko. I could not comprehend what he was going through and knew not to bring up the subject. We never discussed his father again.

As for Kosta, he was also my age and lived a block down the street. In contrast to Niko's parents, Kosta's family members were migrant workers who had settled in Gargaliani several years earlier. In further contrast to Niko, Kosta lived near the bottom of the socioeconomic scale. Of course, Mother kept telling me to stay away from the boy. She particularly didn't like the fact that every morning, Kosta would linger outside our house, as if he had nothing else to do, waiting for me to come out and play. And Mother's objections reached a fever pitch when our fathers became friends and she saw the four of us happily returning home in the evenings from the coffee houses.

"You are setting a bad example for Saranti by associating with those people!" she yelled. "What's the matter with you? Is this how far we have fallen? Now we are truly associating with the bottom remnants of our society."

Father paid no attention to Mother's criticism.

"You know, Saranti, listening to your Mother about everything is no way to live."

Though we were only eight years old, the impending occupation caused politics to dominate even my discussions with my friends. Niko, Kostas, and I spent hours under an enormous oak tree that stood adjacent to our home discussing what we had heard about Greece, the invaders, and how our lives would change. Convinced that Greece was the very hub of the world and that everything revolved around it, we determined that every other country had betrayed us. We talked about the occupiers' arrival, and all conversations eventually led to speculations of what they would be like, how they would look and act and how they would treat us. After discussions and wild suppositions, we agreed that the Italians couldn't be all bad if they ate tomatoes and pasta. Even the name "Italia," when said properly, was melodic and pleasing to the ear. We decided we would not be able to hate a people who, like us, enjoyed good food, especially when they had such a happy sounding name.

But the Germans were another matter altogether. The word *Germania* contained no melody at all and carried with it a harshness that induced fear in our hearts. Father told us often about the Germans and about how he had lived in Germany during the last war.

"They are an arrogant people, lack compassion, and are difficult to approach. Stay away from them," he said.

When we learned that the Germans preferred to eat potatoes and sausages, we couldn't figure out how anyone could like a German. But whether Italian or German, we plotted how we would spy on our invaders and settled on where we would create lookouts in trees and areas from where we could survey the area and report on their movements.

As busy as my friends and I were preparing ourselves for the occupation, the real action on our block was at our neighbor's house, the home of Kyria Garifalia Halazonitis. From our kitchen window we could see straight into her backyard, and from the day we landed in our new home, Mother and this woman, roughly ten years her senior, became fast friends. They conversed endlessly about everything from the Gargaliani of their childhoods to Papa Sarantis to the gossip of the day. They would always finish their conversation with praises and a prayer for the deceased priest, always commemorating his good deeds and holiness. But from the day of our arrival, Kyria Garifalia bore one of the greatest weights any mother could carry—concern for her son, Nikos, a young man in his early twenties who several months earlier had left Gargaliani to fight the Italians.

Every day, Kyria Garifalia visited the plateia hoping to receive some word on what had happened to him. All she knew was that Nikos was a pilot somewhere in northern Greece, and as soldiers trickled back home, she interrogated each for some piece of news.

"Where were you stationed? Did you see my Nikos? Did you hear anything about him?"

The reverberation of her voice through the crowds became common, as she moved from one cluster of soldiers to the next: "Has anybody seen my Nikos?"

War!

Day after day, the woman returned home depressed and with no more information than she had when she left her house with that morning. Like the many women looking for sons that no one had seen, Kyria Garifalia needed someone to cry with, someone to give her hope that her son would be home soon, and someone to carry at least some small piece of her cross. Mother became Kyria Garifalia's companion, her confidant and counselor, and from our kitchen window, would speak to the anxious mother as she hung laundry in her backyard.

"For sure, he's on his way back," she'd say, "I'll bet he's on the next bus. Any day now, he'll burst through your door."

Barely two weeks after our move and in a way that lent a great deal of legitimacy to Mother's insights, Nikos Halazonitis burst through the door of his mother's home and into her backyard. Bushy haired, slender, and still dressed in his Royal Hellenic Air Force uniform, Nikos's demeanor was not the dourness of defeat that soaked the psyches of many others who straggled back into town. Nikos arrived in an explosion of charisma, all smiles, laughing and talking faster than the words could leave his mouth. He reported on the war, the Albanians, Italians, airplanes, prisoners, and the dead. He told us how even though the Italian soldiers were completely equipped and how their forces were overwhelming, they still could not beat the Greeks.

"They didn't have any *psihi,* their hearts were not in this fight; they lacked the soul and determination to win it," he said. "We were fighting up there to protect our land, our women, and our families. They fought because that little lunatic forced them. They never had a chance against us. They were a beaten force from the beginning."

After he tired of telling us his tales from the front, he said he'd had enough, retreated into his house, and emerged in his yard with a guitar. He sat in a straw chair and began to strum and sing, his voice loud enough for the surrounding houses to hear. Some of the songs he sang were famous while others he just made up as he went along.

Duce, Duce, don't pretend you're a tough guy,
Because Nikos was there—
Flying his airplane, for all of Greece
We ate them,
We ate them alive,

dandelions for Dinner

We ate those plates of spaghetti alive.

Nikos had so much energy that he seemed to have trouble containing it all. He was the life of any party, a person with an inexhaustible number of ideas, and he offered them often and with conviction.

Nikos Halazonitis became my hero. I looked at him, his uniform, his charisma, and his ostensible ability to control events around him with a sense of awe. When Nikos once saw me staring at him as he told one of his tales from the front, he reached into his pocket tossed me a piece of candy.

"My boy, we ate them alive."

His attention made me feel like part of the action. "When I grow up, I want to be just like him," I told Mother later.

Mother had other plans for me, and for sure, they weren't that I be like Nikos.

"Be very careful who you select to be your hero, Saranti. Nikos is a lot of fun, but there are so many others much greater than him. Socrates spent his life in search of God and truth. Your grandfather, the great Papa Saranti, spent his life selflessly serving others. Solon gave Athens its laws and helped her find democracy. Nikos is a nice young man, but you will grow up to be much greater than he. There are much greater people you should try to be like."

Mother liked Nikos and he certainly entertained her, but she considered him a garrulous self-promoter. She was certainly pleasant to him and conversed with him often, but there were parts of his personality that she preferred I not adopt. Most importantly, he could be so talkative and so impetuous that she feared for his safety and the safety of those around him.

"Saranti, Nikos is a lot like Pausanias," she told me. "Many, many years ago, Pausanias was the generalissimo of Athens. When the Greeks once asked the Oracle of Delphi about him, the Oracle declared that Pausanias was capable of doing both great good or great harm to Athens. In the end, it was great harm. Saranti, we all love Nikos, but he is reckless. He has to be careful. If he survives the war, it will be a miracle."

When Father overheard Mother's commentary, he laughed.

"Oh, Nikos is like Pausanias? Oh, sure, now, your Mother

has made this neighbor of ours immortal, just like the gods of Olympus."

Soon after the dust settled from Nikos's arrival in Gargaliani, Mother encouraged me to visit my Theo Dimitri. Perhaps out of shyness and for sure frightened by his overenthusiastic daughters, I resisted. Over the next few days, Mother told me about him, about how he had not always been blind and about the type of active person he had been only a few years earlier.

"He used to take care of the rose garden and his vineyards and had the respect of everyone including his family and his neighbors. Now that he is blind, Theo Dimitri needs his family more than ever. He needs a lot of attention. Your theo is a good man and his family cannot ignore him. If we don't pay attention to him and if he were cut off from the family's business activities, it would be his end. It is very important that his children consult him on all family matters."

The more I heard about my uncle, the more I liked him.

"His children are all decent and hard-working people, Saranti."

Then she paused and seemed to measure her words.

"But watch out for Eleni. She treats her Father very poorly and God will punish her for that. Don't be like her. If you visit Theo Dimitri every day, God will bless you with many gifts."

One day, with nothing else to do and perhaps out of curiosity, I wandered into Theo Dimitri's rose garden. When his daughters saw me, they made a big fuss over me and eventually led me up to his balcony. Theo Dimitri sat in a chair next to a small table and when he heard my voice, he smiled.

"Wel-come-my-Sa-ran-ti. I-have-been-wait-ing-for-you! Come-sit-ov-er-here."

I climbed into the chair across from him.

"Sa-ran-ti, I-am-so-hap-py-you-came-to-vi-sit- me. What-a-bles-sing-it-is-to-have-my-bro-ther's-grand-son-here-with-me. Do-you-know-that-you-are-the-grandson-of-my-bro-ther, Pa-pa Sa-ran-tis?"

"Yes," I replied.

"If-he-were-al-ive-today, he-would-be-very-proud-of-you. Your-grand-fa-ther-was-a-great-man. A-saint-ly-man. Did-you-know-that?"

"Yes." I said.

After a moment of silence, he continued. "And-did-you-also-know-that-your-grand-fa-ther-didn't-have-any-brains?"

"No!" I said, surprised.

"It's-true." My uncle took a deep breath. "Ev-ery-thing-the-people-gave-him, he-gave-away. He-didn't-have-the-sense-to-take-care-of-him-self-and-his-fa-mi-ly." He looked off and sighed, "Oh-my-bro-ther."

We sat in silence.

Several minutes later, he turned to me wide-eyed. "Who-is-Mu-ssu-li-ni?"

"The spaghetti eater? He's the president of Italy," I replied.

My answer must have delighted Theo Dimitri because he let out a laugh loud enough for all of Gargaliani to hear.

"Who-told-you-that?"

"I heard it at a café." I replied.

"Ha! For-sure, my-boy, the-cafés-are-co-lle-ges, aren't they?"

After another pause and with a feigned sternness in his face, he leaned close to me and asked, "Who-was-Pe-ri-cles?"

I didn't answer.

"How-a-bout-So-cra-tes, who-was-he?"

"I don't know."

"So-lon?"

"I don't know."

"Ly-cur-gus?"

"No," I replied and silence followed.

I felt guilty that I was so ignorant. A minute of silence passed, I felt compelled to volunteer something I did know.

"But I can tell you about the Old Man of Morias."

This statement startled my uncle, and he started laughing so loud that he almost fell off his chair. His cloudy eyes widened with surprised joy.

"And-who-do-you-think-was-the-Old-Man-of-Morias?"

He leaned closer to me and with giddy anticipation, listened carefully.

I was embarrassed that he was speaking so loudly, and I didn't want to answer him at first. But when I saw that he kept waiting for an answer, I leaned towards him and whispered, "Kolokotronis."

War!

"Ko-lo-ko-tro-nis!" he roared. Then he howled for his daughters, "Ma-ria! Ka-ti-na! Come-here-im-me-dia-te-ly."

The girls rushed in, frightened that something had happened to their father.

"Li-st-en-to-what-Sa-ran-ti-said. He-just-told-me-that-the-Old-Man-of-Mo-rias is Ko-lo-ko-tro-nis! Say it again Sa-ran-ti."

"*O geros tou Moria* was Kolokotronis," I quietly repeated. Relieved that the man had not fallen off the balcony, they laughed and told me how smart I was.

For the next several weeks, this is how my visits went with my uncle. I liked being around the man and his unconditional love so much that I visited him every day. In his choppy voice, he spoke to me about many subjects and then would ask me out of the blue questions like:

"What do you like the most, Saranti?" "What's important in life?" or "Who do you like best?"

After a series of "I don't knows," he would tell me repeatedly, "Sa-ran-ti, the-mind-needs-cul-ti-va-tion. Did-you-know- that? Al-ways-cul-tiv-ate-it!"

More than once, I tried to come up with something noble to tell my uncle, like how I liked to share my food with the poor, or how I wanted to alleviate the suffering of people like Bousoulas, Mougos, or Bililis. But I could never quite get the words out.

Once, when he pushed me for an answer to some question about what I liked best, I said something like, "I like to play." That prompted him to ask another question. "What-hap-pens-when-your-friends-do-not-want-to-play-with-you?"

"I would be sad if my friends refused to play with me. And then they would not be my friends because friends always play together."

When I said that, Theo Dimitri leaned back and smiled. Apparently, he liked my response.

"My-wish-for-you-is-that-you-are-al-ways-sur-roun-ded-with-good-friends-in-life. May-you-live-to-be-an-old-man-like-me-with-ma-ny-friends!"

Theo Dimitri's positive attitude always made me feel welcome and happy. But unfortunately, my visits with him came to an abrupt end. One morning, I sat with him as he told me a story about his youth.

He stopped and asked, "What-do-you-say-Sa-ra-nti, would-n't-it-be-nice-if-we-had a slice-of-bread-with-some-fig-mar-ma-lade-to-eat?"

Before I had a chance to respond, my uncle called into the house, "El-e-ni-bring-Sa-ran-ti-and-me-two-big-sli-ces-of-bread-with-some-fig-mar-ma-lade-on-top."

Theo Dimitri continued his story.

When several minutes passed and neither Eleni nor the fig marmalade appeared, Theo Dimitri called out again, "E-le-ni, bring Sa-ran-ti and me-two-sli-ces of-bread with some-fig-mar-ma-la-de."

Once again, nothing. When Eleni failed to respond to this second request, I could see Theo Dimitri become agitated. He began to lose his focus.

"What hap-p-p-e-ned to-that-girl? Has-she-fal-l-l-l-en-as-le-ep?" He mumbled. When still nothing appeared after a few more minutes, he cursed. "Damn-that-girl, what-is the mat-ter-with-h-h-her?"

He called out again. After yet another unanswered request, Theo Dimitri was visibly angry.

"Damn-it, E-le-ni-come-out-here."

That sparked Eleni into action because she appeared on the balcony and immediately took the offensive.

"And why are you screaming for all of Gargaliani to hear over a stupid piece of bread? You are a blind old fool; you've lost your mind. Stop yelling! In any event, you have no business eating bread and marmalade now. Lunch is almost ready. You will ruin both your appetites."

Eleni stood in front of her father with her hands on her hips. Not surprisingly, her response failed to calm the situation. Her words caused Theo Dimitri to become so enraged that he began to stutter.

"C-c-c-come h-h-here you ung-g-g-grateful girl. Aren't you a-sh-sh-sh-amed to talk that w-w-way to your f-f-f-father? Come here and I-I-I'm going to t-t-t-tear you a-p-p-part."

Theo Dimitri rose from his chair and with a swift motion, slammed the table with his cane so hard that it knocked me to the floor and back into the balcony's railing.

"You s-s-s-stupid ungratef-f-f-ul girl. D-d-d-damn you. Where are you? C-c-c-come-here-r-r-right-now."

Theo Dimitri's curses continued and the aged man began to

employ a vocabulary that I had rarely heard before and then, only words that had previously come from the mouth of Spyro's older brother.

"I-I-I'll t-t-t-tear you in half."

He lunged to grab Eleni, who ran from the balcony and into the house. Apparently able to follow her with his ears, Theo Dimitri ran after her, through the bedroom and into the dining room where he swung his cane in the air in his desperation to hit Eleni. And with each swing, he bumped into furniture or hit some decorative piece.

Theo Dimitri's curses continued and then, as I still lay on the floor of the balcony, he called out to me in a thunderous staccato stutter, "S-S-S-Sar-an-tis, w-w-where i-i-is she? H-h-help m-m-me f-f-ind her!"

I looked through the bedroom into the dining room and saw Eleni standing silently frozen.

"S-S-S-Sar-an-ti, w-w-where i-i-is she?" he yelled.

Scared to death, I remained silent.

He stuttered louder yet again, "S-S-S-Sar-an-ti, w-w-where i-i-is she?"

I arose and raced into the dining room where I saw my uncle's intense and useless eyes trying to find her. And there, right in front of him was Eleni, as motionless as any armless statue, standing atop the dining room table holding her breath. Her only movement was the darting of her eyes, like an animal at the moment it realized it had been cornered by a predator.

Before I could say anything, Eleni jumped off the table, landed directly in front of her father, dodged his desperate reach, and darted past him through the doorway and out of the house. When he felt her pass him, Theo Dimitri swung his cane in a vain attempt to hit her and let out another barrage of invective.

"Eleni, you d-d-dirty d-d-dog. You *p-p-p-poutana*! You- will l-l-live a l-l-life- of-curses-and- t-t-t-tur-moil, do- you- k-k-k-know that? And- at- the- end, you- find- a b-b-burn-ing- h-h-hell w-w-w-wai-t-t-ting-for you."

When I heard "b-b-burn-ing- h-h-hell," I too ran out of the dining room, out of that house and didn't stop until I ran into my home.

When I told Mother everything that happened, her face fell.

"Saranti, I told you about Eleni. This whole thing was her fault. There is nothing more important for us to do than to honor our mother and father. God will punish Eleni for the disrespect she shows her father. Do you understand me Saranti?"

"Yes," I replied.

"One of the worst things a person can do is to show the people who gave him life disrespect. Do you understand?"

"Yes."

Mother thought for a moment.

"Actually, I feel sorry for Eleni, Saranti. She has a lot of trouble ahead of her. As for your uncle, stay away from there for a while. Let things calm down a little. You can go there next week."

"Yes, Mana."

That was the last time I saw Theo Dimitri. Within a few days of that ugly incident, he fell ill and died. Whether or not Theo Dimitri's sudden death had anything to do with what I had witnessed, I don't know. But the episode left me shocked, unable to comprehend how anyone could ever speak to a parent so disrespectfully. My family, of course, didn't operate that way, and the episode led me to an acute understanding of what my Father had always told me, that my world was my immediate family and that not much else existed beyond my mother, my father, and my brother Stathi. Indeed, everyone outside of the four of us, no matter how closely related, was, to a degree, a stranger. When push came to shove, I realized, we were alone in the world.

Chapter 11
ITALIANS!

After the Germans invaded Greece, they advanced in a motorized column toward Athens, and in anticipation of their arrival in April 1941, King George II and much of the Greek government fled Athens for Crete. However, foreseeing the fall of Crete, many Greek officials bypassed it and headed directly for North Africa. On April 27, 1941, German tanks rumbled into a seemingly deserted Athens, and the Germans raised their swastika atop the Acropolis, an act that made our country's occupation official.

Within days, many began to worry about the country's food supply. Among other calamities, the invasion caused inflation and plundering in larger cities and led to hoarding by shopkeepers. Hoarding caused people to suffer and die of starvation. And these deaths were generally not in the quiet of a family's home, with family present and quietly whispering prayers. They were instead, oftentimes, undignified and public, with people collapsing on the once-cosmopolitan boulevards of Athens. For the first time in recorded history, people in Greece were dying faster than they were being born. It became common for parents to watch, one by one, their children die from hunger. At the same time, it wasn't uncommon for children to watch their parents die, one at a time. Such widespread, horrifying death began to create society-wide insanity.

People affected by hunger and on the verge of death often become deranged, talking to themselves and seeing apparitions. Wading through the harshness of dead children lying on the streets of Athens awaiting, along with the other dead, for municipal carts to take them away, was too much for most to bear. Only adding to the burdens of the living was that people could not care for their dead. They couldn't afford to bury them, to pray for them or even to honor them as mandated by the Greek Orthodox Church and its traditions. Death brought with it a horrifying realization to those whom it had yet to visit—the recognition that one's instinct for self-preservation can snuff out his sensitivity to the suffering cries of others.

When the dust settled, Germans, Bulgarians, and Italians occupied Greece. They quickly spread atrocities everywhere, with the Bulgarians guilty of the most egregious. In northern Greece, they undertook a systematic attempt at its de-Hellenization. They murdered teachers and clergy and sent the women and children out of the country to work as forced laborers. Many Bulgarians were so brutal that they surprised even the Germans.

Slowly but surely, the war advanced into the Peloponnesus and worked its way toward Gargaliani. It arrived one afternoon in May.

"There are Australians hiding in the olive groves," Father announced as he ran into our home.

The olive groves Father referred to were located in the five-kilometer strip of land that sat between our town and the Ionian Sea. Fighting alongside the English, the Australians had battled the German invasion, and with Greece's fall, they heading south toward Pylos to catch sea passage out of our fallen country. With Axis forces pushing hard, some Australians had made their way to Gargaliani.

When Mother heard Father's announcement, she was immediately concerned.

"What in the world are the Australians doing in our olive groves? What do they want with us here?"

After thinking for a few moments, she turned to Father.

"That must mean that the Germans and the Italians are upon us. We are all going to be killed!"

"I don't know about that. I hear the Australians are looking for transportation out of the country. The Germans and Italians are after them. Someone said the English soldiers are all over Peloponnesus and are looking to get out. My guess is that they are headed to Pylos. I'm sure we'll see more of them." Pylos was a port town a thirty kilometer drive to the south of Gargaliani.

In the days that followed, we began, for the first time, to hear gunfire. The Germans and Italians had learned where the fleeing Brits and Australians were hiding and began to fire at the olive groves. We could see foreign war ships off the coast that quickly moved to sink any vessels considered unfriendly or suspicious. Looking for soldiers, German pilots shot at farmers while they tended to their fields. When one overzealous such pilot dove so close to one farmer's field that he lost control of his plane and crashed into an olive tree and died, the locals rushed to cover up the wreckage, afraid that the Germans might blame them and retaliate.

Though most of the British and Australian soldiers escaped from Greece, those that remained received covert assistance from Greeks everywhere.

Late one evening in May, a firm knock on our door woke us up. When we opened it, Nikos Halazonitis stood in front of us with a group of foreign men.

"Kyrie Panagioti," he said, "we would like you to help us speak with these fine Australian soldiers."

Father nodded his head in agreement.

"Please tell these men that tomorrow, we will escort them sixty kilometers east through the mountains to Kalamata and to a place where they will be more likely to get safe passage to Crete."

Father, happy to help and be part of the action, complied. When he shook hands with the young soldiers as they departed, we were overwhelmed with patriotic feelings. Instantly, we were helping our country, in however small a way. We were proud of the fact that warriors had called my Father's language skills and fluency in English into action, and that he performed so eloquently.

Day after day, we could hear the strafing near the beaches intensify. Italian planes became a common sight, flying overhead, surveying the area, and continuing to fire into the olive groves. The sudden ubiquity of planes caused the town to create a warning system whereby residents rung the church bells at the first sight of a plane. The bells rang one morning when they spotted Italian planes moving in on a Greek merchant ship stranded several hundred meters off the coast of Marathos. People watched as the planes tried to sink it. That the old vessel was empty, abandoned with mechanical problems, didn't matter. In a screaming fury, the fascists dove in and dropped their bombs on the impotent boat. With the first pass, we heard huge explosions and saw water thrown in gargantuan cascades that flew everywhere. But as the first pass concluded and the planes began to circle back, the settling waters revealed that the ship remained unscathed. A crowd gathered on the west end of town to watch the invaders sink the ship. And we watched bomb after bomb fall around the ship, blowing water into the air. After fifteen full minutes of bombing and violent explosions, the planes flew away. But the ship remained, dignified and defiant.

The spectators began to laugh at the Italians.

"What kind of invaders are these?" one asked.

"This is going to be one interesting occupation," said another.

"I have a feeling we are going to be the ones who occupy them!" someone else yelled.

That night, people in the plateia debated whether the Italians would try to sink that boat again. They joked and made bets.

The following morning, the town's people began to congregate near the chapel of the Prophet Elia, which provided a clear view over the valley, of the town of Marathos on the coast, and of the lone boat. The day was clear and sunny, and the vessel stood anchored in a calm sea at the south end of Proti, the small alligator shaped island that sat several kilometers off the coast of Marathos. It awaited its fate. Sometime later, an Italian squadron appeared in the distance, heading straight for the craft. The planes circled it from an altitude of roughly two-thousand meters and as if on cue, started bombing. As before, bombs fell everywhere, and water flew in every direction. Some of the bombs fell on Proti, disturbing the peace that had existed there longer than anyone could remember, throwing smoke, dirt and fire into the air. In less than ten minutes, it was all over, and the Italian planes turned around and in formation, headed back north. And once again, there stood that intrepid boat, untouched.

If everyone laughed the day before, now they were hysterical. Money changed hands and everyone cheered for the boat.

"Our occupiers can't sink an anchored, abandoned boat on a clear sunny day," one man said and the crowd roared.

"This is truly embarrassing," said another.

But the fun ended quickly. Out of nowhere, two German Stukas appeared. They headed directly for the boat, and the crowd watched in amazement as the first plane spun and dove toward it, followed by the second. Each dropped several bombs. The sea exploded and completely engulfed the ship, which in an instant disappeared. The Germans had bailed out the Italians once again. And the message was clear: Italians were one thing; Germans were something else entirely.

War!

Though we were unaware of it, in June 1941 and in what turned out to be a foolish move, Germany executed its Operation Barbarossa and invaded the Soviet Union. Within weeks of that, we began to hear rumors that the Italians were closing in on Gargaliani. Around that time, roughly a dozen Italian Military Police, "Carabinieri," quietly arrived at the edge of town. To everyone's surprise, they appeared to take great pains to avoid imposing themselves on anyone. They set themselves up in a residence and during the day, stayed below most people's radar. At night, they conducted military style marches in groups of four. Dressed in their Napoleonic hats, their appearances were stern. These men seemed to be all business.

A week later and about the time we had become accustomed to the rhythms of these Italians, more began to arrive. And within a few more weeks, over six-hundred Italian soldiers arrived in Gargaliani. Suddenly, they were everywhere. Italians walked around our streets, stood with their weapons in our plateia, and took over many of our town's buildings. In need of places to sleep, they co-opted people's homes. An elite Italian Alpine artillery unit moved into our neighborhood and bivouacked temporarily in the open field adjacent to the giant oak tree near our home. Why the Italians sent this particular unit to southern Greece, I don't know, but after it arrived, Niko, Kostas, and I sat under that tree and watched in silent amazement as the invaders settled in. The men moved animals around, loaded and unloaded carts, and loudly spoke a language that none of us understood. We must have been quite a sight because as we stood mesmerized, an Italian soldier came over to us.

"*Piccolo!*" he said to me. I sprang to attention. The soldier handed me a canteen, and by his gestures, I gathered he wanted me to fill it with water. I took the canteen, ran into the house, and sank it into the barrel of water Mother kept near the side door. I returned it to the soldier who smiled.

"*Grazie, piccolo.*"

I returned to my friends and we smiled at one another. Indeed, we were right about the Italians. It seemed we had a lot in common with them.

Troops continued to move into Gargaliani. A flurry of activity hit the town and Niko, Kostas, and I watched as much of it as we could. Soldiers haphazardly pulled horses and mules full of supplies in every direction. Amid the chaos, officers shouted orders directing their men this way and that. Some soldiers tied down their animals while others untied theirs. When one tied several mules to our oak tree, we headed home.

One evening, several soldiers and an interpreter knocked on our door. Mother answered, and the interpreter announced that the soldiers had come to inspect our house. Mother showed them our rooms and led them to the basement. The men spoke amongst themselves.

"The officer declares that this house is too big for just a family of four," the interpreter said.

The men spoke some more, and the interpreter pointed to the older section of the house.

"You and your family will be permitted to live on that side of the house. You may also use that side of the basement."

Then pointing to the "new" side, the one Papa Sarantis had built, the interpreter continued, "The Italian army will reside in this side of your home."

Before we knew it, the Italian army was moving into our house. A soldier nailed shut the doors that would separate their side and ours, leaving us with the north end of the house, which included one bedroom, the dining room, the kitchen and the bathroom—so much for having our own rooms. The Italians would live in the south side, comprised of two large rooms. At some point, we learned that they would use their half of the basement as the army's brig.

"What a lousy jail our basement will make," Father commented. "The floor down there is so uneven and its ceiling so low that no one can stand up. What a mess."

Within days, non-commissioned officers moved into our house and unruly soldiers quickly filled our basement, entering from a separate entrance on the south side of the home. Though the nailed doors allowed us to maintain our privacy in our half of the dwelling, deep foreign voices echoed through our home.

The Italians weaved themselves into our town from one street to the next until they had completely taken it over. They took over the first floor of the home of Kyria Matsouka, the woman who lived directly across the street from us, turning her dwelling into the Italian

Army's infirmary. Just around the corner and across the alley from Theo Dimitri's house, they converted the ground floor of another home into the barn where they housed a dozen or more of their mules. The animals quickly demolished that home's wooden floor, kicked out the front door, ate all the window and door casings, and created a stench that filled the entire block.

Soon after they took over our home, I saw Gargaliani's electrician running a wire into the Italian side of the building. A short time later, he knocked on our door.

"The Italians instructed me, as a courtesy, to run a wire into your side of the house as well."

Mother thanked the electrician who installed a long electrical wire that ended with a single light bulb that she hung from the bedroom door. For the first time, electrical light entered our home. Unsure of exactly what to do with it, we followed Father around as he held the light bulb in his hand and walked from room to room. That bulb burned so intensely and was so blinding that it revealed details in every room that none of us had ever seen before. I noticed for the first time that walls all over the home were cracked, that paint in a number of areas was uneven, and how dust and dirt filled the corners of all our rooms.

When Father returned the bulb to the door, we took out our books and began to read in bed, something none of us had ever done before. But the light burned so brightly that we found sleeping almost impossible that night. Father didn't know how to turn the light off and for the next few days, we struggled to sleep in our bedroom with a blinding light, until Father learned that he could unscrew the bulb.

For the most part, the occupation of Gargaliani went as expected. At least in our town, the Italians turned out to be compassionate people whose similarities to us were much more pronounced than any differences. We quickly found friends amongst the rank-and-file soldiers who understood our plight and helped us whenever possible. We saw that the officers and soldiers were almost as much victims as we were and helped them when we could. I remember once how a soldier from the infirmary knocked on our door and began agonizing efforts to communicate to us in Italian that he peppered with the few Greek words he had picked up. When Mother figured out that the man was trying to cook something, she invited him into the kitchen and watched him curiously as he tried to tell her what he wanted.

"*Thelo—thelo—*" he said, and then made two circles with his hands. Then he repeated, "*Thelo—thelo—*" and made the same two circles.

Mother and I looked around the room and tried to figure out what the man wanted, to no avail. Mother tried to help him by picking up various items and showing them to the man.

Then suddenly, he remembered the word and with great excitement yelped, "*Thelo—thelo ena tigana.*"

When we heard him butcher our language, we laughed and Mother pulled her frying pan out of a cabinet and handed it over.

"*Grazie, grazie,*" he replied as he took the pan, smiled and went on his way.

Several moments later, he returned.

"*Thelo olio.*"

Mother was able to figure that one out and handed him a small bottle of olive oil.

"*Grazie, grazie,*" he said again.

Later that evening, the soldier knocked on our door and returned the pan. Inside was a piece of fried liver and some bread, an unexpected and welcomed treat that we quickly split and devoured. To show her appreciation, Mother filled the soldier's pockets with raisins. Everyone was happy.

Gargaliani quickly learned that being a soldier was not a major priority for most Italians. The ones in our town had no respect for Mussolini and used every opportunity to malign him and to curse him for sending them to a foreign land. Indeed, after they settled in, the soldiers quickly became preoccupied with non-military activities such as organizing social events, figuring ways to get ahead by beating their own system, and perhaps more importantly, having fun. They appeared to be perpetually churning some angle in their heads.

There was so much activity near our house and its surrounding open lots that it seemed from my perspective we were the epicenter of the Italian occupation of Greece. The Italian army's organized activities began before the town awoke, in the very early morning hours. From the depths of sleep, I could make out the sound of the

War!

occupiers' horse-drawn wagons, their braying mules, and the spray of Italian profanities that were everywhere.

"*Unjale! Unjale!*" the soldiers would shout at their animals to direct them. Throughout the occupation, I must have heard someone yell *Unjale!* several thousand times.

And with their animals in tow, soldiers in small groups would march around performing various military exercises, with some heading toward the plateia and others toward the farms to the east. At the infirmary in Kyria Matsuka's house across the street, sick soldiers seemed to be everywhere, spilling out its front door and into the street, in line to see a doctor. If a soldier could get a doctor to declare him sick, he would get the day off from his usual chores. When the noon hour approached, and regardless of what was happening, the fascists, sick and well alike, dropped everything and reported for lunch, usually some sort of macaroni soup. Afterward, they returned to their barracks to nap. And while they slept, all of their activities ground to such a halt that it would be hard for a visitor to believe that Gargaliani was in the midst of an occupation.

They would sleep until well after the hot sun had settled into its decent and the cicadas had ramped up the early evening's rhythmic whines. That's when the infirmary's door would re-open, and its supervisor would stick his head out, survey the sky to get a feel for the time, and if he decided it was late enough, cacophonously thrust open the windows and doors. I was always curious at how the afternoon nap miraculously healed the sick soldiers of whatever illness had paralyzed them only hours before. Like clockwork, someone from the infirmary, in an effort to settle the dust in the air and to cool the street off a little would emerge and sprinkle the area with water. That momentary coolness would attract soldiers to the infirmary to socialize and wait for the bugle that announced dinner.

After dinner, the soldiers would return to the area near the infirmary and continue their socializing. Oftentimes, they would then engage in loud discussions that I can only guess dealt with politics. When such gatherings became very intense, or when one of the soldiers became visibly angry, someone, out of nowhere, would start to sing in a loud operatic voice. And once a soldier started singing, others would join in, putting an end to whatever hostilities might have been brewing. Oftentimes, the singing would prompt someone else to break out an accordion, sit down at the steps of the infirmary, and provide the background music. Abrupt clapping and yelling would follow, and the best singers would move to the forefront and begin belting out some aria. We used to watch these shows from our window and observed how the singing caused our entire neighborhood to congregate on the street for entertainment. On occasion, the soldiers would ask our local girls to dance, but the girls refused, not wanting to be scandalized.

The Germans made their base just eleven kilometers north of us in Filiatra. Though they rarely came to Gargaliani, they did occasionally stop in for a few hours, just to sternly walk around, visit the chapel of the Prophet Elia to admire the view of the valley and the sea, and then leave. And whenever the Germans were around, the Italians were all business and on their best behavior, neatly dressed in their uniforms and busily performing military-related tasks. One day that summer, the Italians' festivities morphed into a comedy show when one of the soldiers emerged from the infirmary dressed as a woman with enormous breasts. One by one, the rowdy soldiers began to dance with her causing everyone in the crowd to become hysterical. When someone taped a sign to her back that read *"puttana,"* the crowd hooted and whistled at the town's new prostitute.

But the fun didn't last very long. Out of nowhere, an Italian ran up and reported that a German officer had arrived in Gargaliani and was headed toward the infirmary. The soldiers began to scatter. But before they could, the German officer appeared in front of the infirmary. He was impeccably dressed, walked erect and stood tall. His arrival was so instantaneous that most of the soldiers didn't have enough time to get away or even to hide. So the men lined up as best as they could, shirt tails out, some out of uniform, others out of breath, and one with large breasts. When the German saw the disarray, he glared at the men for several moments as if they were offal and walked away in disgust—apparently wondering how they could possibly be allies.

The psyche of the Italian soldiers was an amalgam of a lack of investment in their mission and an overwhelming desire to return home to their families. These were not the components of a lean and mean fighting force. But there were, of course, exceptions. One lieutenant named Rossini was a true Fascist and, as if personally instructed by Mussolini himself, took his position of authority very seriously. This executive battalion officer set a fine example for the officers. Tall, immaculate, and clean-cut, Lieutenant Rossini spewed forth a singular zeal for order and discipline that separated him from the rest. His beard was so well manicured that Mother nicknamed him, "Yenatos," the bearded one. Had Il Duce looked like him, he would have indeed rebuilt the Roman Empire.

Yenatos was the owner of the most handsome horse any of us had ever seen. Black, muscular, and trained to execute perfectly the most complex of prances, that show horse drew the starkest of contrasts to the sorry slouching workhorses of our town. Yenatos employed a full time aide whose sole job it was to take care of that horse. The aide stayed with the animal, fed and watered it, combed its tail and mane daily, and walked it several times a day. That stallion was extremely alert and sensitive. When too many people surrounded it, it would become agitated, air would rush through its nostrils, and its huge muscles would twitch, forcing the aide to chase everyone away until he could calm the beast down.

The duo moved through their ranks and Gargaliani with impunity. But as Mother and the other locals knew well, there was one thing that neither could combat, a force that, if thrust upon them, would bring a quick end to that dynamic duo—what was known as the *mati,* the evil eye. Indeed, Yenatos, his perfect uniform, and his singular horse, were a remarkable sight. When the two appeared, all would gather in amazement to watch the closest thing to Alexander and Bucephalus anyone would ever see. The sight impressed even Mother so much that when they passed in front of our house with their majestic gallop, she crossed herself and whispered a prayer to the Virgin Mary to protect them.

"All that admiration for Yenatos and his horse is not good, Saranti," she'd say. "For sure, those gawkers are giving them the *mati.*"

While one might expect the powers of the *mati* to be most commonly triggered by a sinister leer, the opposite was in fact true—receiving the *mati* was usually the result of someone's excessive admiration. So if someone, say, kept staring at someone's hair and talking about how beautiful it looked, no one would be surprised if it suddenly rained and the style was ruined. One's only hope to neutralize the deleterious effects of excessive admiration would be for some quickly to spit at or near the recipient of praise. So it is not uncommon to see someone complement someone, only to see her feign spitting, "*tu—tu—tu*," at the person just complemented. And as Mother's comment about Yenatos's horse demonstrated, the *mati* was powerful enough to affect people, objects, and animals as well. That put the neighborhood on edge with regard to Yenatos and his horse.

Shortly after the Italians settled in and around the time Yenatos and his horse were prancing through our streets, Stathi, who by that time was almost four years old, ran into the house holding a kitten he found near Theo Dimitri's courtyard.

"This kitten kept following me when I was playing," he reported. "Let's give it some food."

Mother examined the cat and for reasons unknown, seemed to like it.

"Well, Stathi, who do you think it belongs to?"

Overhearing, Father chimed in, "Who does it belong to? There are cats all over this country. Maybe it's Mussolini's."

"Stathi, you can keep it here if you want, but if someone asks for it, we'll have to give it back."

Mother picked up the cat and stared into its face.

"Now, we have to give it a name."

A silence hung in the kitchen as everyone thought about what we would name this new and unplanned member of our household.

Then Mother announced, "We'll call him Benito."

Father laughed. Stathi and I liked the name, and Benito quickly became a fixture in our home.

Benito had the run of house and neighborhood and grew to be a beautiful animal. When Mother tied a red ribbon around his neck, he became quite the local celebrity. People learned his name, and Benito, as if he knew who he had been named after, liked to sit on a window ledge that faced the street and soak up the public's constant admiration. And whenever people passed him, complements were in no shortage.

"What a beautiful cat!"

"Look at that cat!"

"That's an amazing cat!"

War!

Everyone loved Benito, with the exception of Father. He hated the poor beast. Perhaps it was because Benito whined and begged us for food whenever we sat for dinner.

"I don't ever want to see anyone feed that damned animal," Father declared almost daily. "Let him be hungry so he can go in the basement and eat the mice down there. If you feed him, he'll be lazy and won't do anything."

Or perhaps it was simply because Benito ignored Father as he pompously paraded around our home. When we ate, the cat often moved through and around our legs, whining and begging for food. Despite Father's tirades, Stathi, Mother, and I used to sneak Benito a morsel here and there. Our actions most certainly kept him around and brought Father, who was otherwise to a fault the most placid and peaceful of persons, well past his boiling point.

"*Ai gamisou* and your Mother and your Father you damn cat! Get away from here," he would begin.

If Benito didn't listen, Father's anger would ramp up.

"I said leave! I can't stand looking at you! Go into the basement and find some mice to eat!"

Though at first frightened by Father's wrath, Benito became accustomed to the outbursts and ignored them completely. His insouciance only made Father even more upset and compelled him to either grab Benito and throw him out the window, or to just kick him in the belly when he couldn't catch him.

"Go to the basement and eat the damn mice!"

When Father's abuse got out of hand, Stathi would cry and Mother would intercede.

"You tyrant! Of all the things in our life to get upset about, you're incensed about the cat? Have you gone crazy? This is absurd!"

Such comments often caused Father to feel remorse.

"Don't cry for the cat, Stathi. Nothing will happen to him. Remember, cats do not die easily. That goes double for Benito. You see how smart he is. Most cats have nine lives, Stathi. Benito here probably has twenty."

Father must have been right about Benito's multiple lives because no matter how much he abused him, how hard he kicked him, or how far he threw him, Benito always bounced right back. Within minutes of being abused, we would see Benito, as if he was the dictator of our home, trotting back through our kitchen again as if nothing had happened, back to being everyone's loyal friend.

Before long, even the Italians began to notice Benito. Sounds of "*Bon giourno Benito*," "*Bona cera, gato*" became common. In fact, the Italians paid Benito even more attention than any of the locals ever did. That worried me. My fears were confirmed one day when Stathi and I were playing in front of our home as a group of soldiers stood quietly in front of the infirmary across the street. Suddenly, an orderly swooped up Benito who had been quietly sunning himself nearby and began to stroke his head. Stathi and I froze. The orderly laughingly showed Benito to some other soldiers who began to touch and talk about him. Then, with the drama of an auditioning actor, the orderly began to dramatically feel Benito with his fingers, first his thighs and then Benito's underside. The others laughed. The orderly turned to his buddies and said, "No, no, no," and then he held up his thumb and index finger as if to say Benito wasn't ready yet, that he was still too small. The men laughed and the orderly let Benito jump from his hands and dart away.

"They want to eat him!" I told Stathi, who grabbed his cat and ran in the house crying.

"Mana, Mana, the Italians want to eat Benito."

But before she could answer, Father spoke.

"Nitsa, that cat belongs in the basement chasing mice, not in our window with a bow on his head for everyone to admire. Everyone who passes and complements him has given the stupid animal the *mati*. If the compliments don't stop, Benito's finished."

Chapter 12
IN BUSINESS

One of the effects of the occupation on Gargaliani was the suspension of most commerce, something that became a little more and more pronounced every day. People quickly emptied stores in the agora from staples like beans and lentils. Even potatoes became scarce items. Macaroni, coffee, and other foods disappeared completely. People improvised however they could, say by substituting wheat for coffee beans and grape syrup for sugar. Bililis, that poor deranged beggar I spent my youth watching collect money only to throw it in the air at the urging of the neighborhood's teens, starved to death around this time. Indeed, Bililis had the distinction of being Gargaliani's first citizen to die from what was throughout Greece: widespread wartime starvation. And though tragic, I don't believe anyone in Gargaliani shed any tears for Bililis, because in a perverse way, people deemed the evil done to him as acceptable, as if God had created this poor man for the sole purpose of serving as the town jester.

Death from starvation made Mother and Father worry more than ever about how we would get enough food to survive. And with Father's ability to feed everyone diminishing steadily, he ignored our occupiers and focused his efforts solely on working the fields, leaving the management of the Italians to Mother. Every night, he returned home, carrying his usual sack of greens, several bundles of wood for cooking, and whatever else he could get his hands on.

One afternoon, Father brought home a man he met in the agora, a peasant from a small village roughly ten kilometers to the east called Mouzaki. Father told the man, who claimed to be interested in purchasing dowry items for his teenage daughter, that we had a household of such things and were interested in bartering them for food.

"There are some beautiful things here and here and over there," Father said to the man as they entered through the front door.

Father placed several items on the dining room table for the man's inspection. He looked at them, and I watched the man survey the rest of the room. His eyes stopped on the Singer sewing machine Father had brought Mother from the states. He pointed to the machine.

"What about that?" he asked.

"I'm sorry, that is not for sale," Mother replied.

"Kyrie, my wife is right. That is not for sale. But you missed some items over here," Father said as he pointed to the table.

But Father's diversion only sharpened the man's interest, and immediately, Mother knew they would make a deal.

"This is one of the latest items in America," she began. "This is a Singer sewing machine. It was made in America. Believe me when I tell you that Singer is known around the world as the premier manufacturer of sewing machines. Singer is the best in the world and for sure, this is the only one in all of Gargaliani. To tell you the truth, this is the perfect dowry item for your daughter or for any young woman. Just look at it."

The man examined the contraption from every angle and touched it with the same care one touches a newborn.

"But as I said, Kyrie, I could never part with this item because my husband bought it for me when we were married. Besides, I rely on it to clothe my family. Look around you, what would these people wear if we didn't have this? For us, it's priceless. The sewing machine is not for sale."

As Mother spoke, she removed the machine from the corner and set it up in front of the man. Then she grabbed some pieces of cloth, sat in front of it and began to demonstrate the ease with which it worked. The peasant stood wide eyed and didn't require any more convincing.

"I will give you one sack of potatoes for the machine."

Mother ignored the offer and continued to talk about the merits of the sewing machine, how it worked, how the foot pedals operated, where the thread went, and so forth, and in the same breath, told the stranger that it was not for sale. Never before had I seen Mother and Father work together so harmoniously. It was as if they had previously orchestrated everything. When Mother uttered the phrase "not for sale," Father would tug on the man's sleeve in attempt to lead him back to the dining room table. But the man from Mouzaki was relentless, just as my parents hoped he would be. He wanted the sewing machine and everything else on the table and in the house had become inconsequential.

"I'll give you the potatoes and a bag of corn for the machine," he said.

"Watch how easily this handles even the thicker fabrics," Mother replied as she quickly stitched together two denser swatches. "I love this machine. I'm sorry but it's not for sale."

Father once again pulled at the man's sleeve and this time, in an emotional desperation, the peasant shook Father's grip loose.

"I'll give you *two* bags of potatoes and the corn!"

"Look," Mother replied, "we cannot sell this machine. I need it for my family. This is a machine that I have used for years and will continue to use for years. It's a Singer! This is not something that we can just trade for a sack of potatoes that will be gone in a week."

Mother stopped talking and silently began rubbing her chin, as if she was thinking of a way she could help the man.

"All right. Keep the second bag of potatoes and give us a goat. Then the sewing machine is yours."

"I'm sorry, Kyria. That is impossible. You know how expensive animals are now in a time of war, don't you?"

Mother stared silently at the man.

"Besides, city people like you are unable to care for such animals. You will just kill the poor thing. Please, take the second bag of potatoes and we have a deal."

"I'm sorry, the machine is not for sale," Mother replied, apparently finished bartering.

She rose from her chair and began to put it away. Correctly believing that there was no other way to make a deal, the man from Mouzaki spoke.

"All right. The goat, the potatoes, and the corn. But within a few weeks, that goat will be dead. You city folks just don't know how to take care of animals."

"We'll see about that," replied Mother. "We have a deal."

My parents gathered the machine and its accessories, and Father carried it back to the agora with the man.

dandelions for Dinner

"A sack of potatoes, a sack of corn and a goat for one sewing machine? You have taken advantage of me. This was not fair."

The man griped the entire way.

Several minutes later, Father returned with the sack of potatoes, the sack of corn and a goat, which he left outside, tied to our home's front door. We rejoiced as our food problem had been resolved, at least for a few weeks, and we gleefully rushed to examine the goat. But the poor animal was not what I expected. She was a dirty white hue with large brownish-red patches littered over her body.

"What's wrong with her?" I asked. "Her face is crooked and slanted to the right while her nose and jaws are slanted to the left. C'mon Father, that thing is deformed. And where are the horns? Without them, she'll never win a fight with another goat."

Mother examined the animal.

"Sure she's a little small and won't be able to produce too much milk, Saranti, but she's fine. The goat is fine. What do you expect? She's just a goat."

Mother smiled, pleased with the deal she pulled off, trading a dormant asset like the sewing machine for one that would produce at least some food for us on a daily basis. She crossed herself and thanked God.

"Do you see what God has done for us? He knows about our suffering and has brought us this goat. Praise God. This animal will make our lives a little more tolerable."

My triumphant Mother looked at the goat for a moment.

"Look at her brown spots. From now on, we will call her Kanella."

We agreed that the name, which means "cinnamon," was appropriate and went inside. As for poor Kanella, she was either scared or upset about the transaction and cried her lungs out for the rest of the night.

Shortly after Kanella's arrival, Mother began pushing me to visit Papa Christodoulos.

"Your grandfather was a priest, Saranti. He spent his life on the altar and it's time for you, you who have his name, to begin to serve as well. You will go to Papa Christodoulos and become one of his acolytes."

"But I am too ashamed at how I look to do that," I replied. "For the past year, I haven't worn any shoes and don't want to be the only barefoot altar boy. And what about my pants? Look at them. I outgrew them a long time ago and they are covered with patches. How can I serve in front of everyone like this?"

"Saranti, our Christ was born into poverty and lived his life with nothing. He knows about us and our challenges. And for sure, he is not concerned about what we wear when we serve him."

"I know Christ is great, Mana, and I do not have any problems with Him. What are the other kids going to say when they see me like this? It's them that I worry about."

I had seen before the children who helped Papa Christodoulos, all individuals I perceived as being from affluent families. To me, they were immaculately dressed and for sure, I didn't want to be the only barefooted one. But Mother would listen to neither my pleas nor my excuses and had her own reasons for sending me to the priest. She knew that if Papa Christodoulos was anything like her Father, putting me in his inner circle would open the door for me to receive occasional handouts.

"Don't worry about any of these things, Saranti. Keep your faith in Christ. He will take care of everything."

Mother prevailed as usual and I reported to Papa Christodoulos. At first, he welcomed me and gave me one of the garments to wear, a shiny golden robe equipped with a matching ornate belt. One of the other altar boys took it and helped me wear it, wrapping it around my waist and crisscrossing it over my back and around to my chest. To the other boys' credit, none of them said anything about my feet or my pants. In a way, my condition had become the common dress code of the day. There were many like me. After a few Sundays, I learned and performed an altar boy's duties very well. I also went to the church on Sunday afternoon for Papa Christodoulos's religious study group, and then, also with Mother's prodding, I began to go to his house to help him with various errands. I watered his garden and swept his floors. When I finished whatever job he had for me, he would give me a piece of bread and send me home.

I enjoyed all of this until one day, after I had completed my chores, I rushed into the priests' house to get my piece of bread. When I found his office empty, I ran into his parlor only to find Papa Christodoulos, along with a number of young men from the high school, giggling and laughing at me, apparently at my decrepit clothing. From the smirks that hung frozen on their faces, I knew that I was not part of their group, their cabal not one I could join. Then Papa Christodoulos quickly rushed to me, took me by the arm, handed me a piece of bread he grabbed from his kitchen and led me out of the back door of his home.

"Thank you for your help, Saranti. May Christ be with you. Now go home, my child."

Though I couldn't understand what exactly happened, I felt that my presence was no longer welcome and I never returned to Papa Christodoulos's home and never again served on the altar.

That fall, the jail in our basement became a very busy place. It seemed that at one point or another, every Italian soldier in town spent a few days in it, usually for insubordination or violating some regulation. The prisoners were always a curiosity to me, but the jail something I had been repeatedly warned never to venture near. One afternoon, as I was fetching olive oil from one of the urns we kept on our side of the basement, I heard a faint but persistent call coming from the jail door. When I moved closer, I realized that it was a prisoner, directly on the opposite side of the door, whispering to me. Though I could not understand what he was saying, I kept hearing him say "*la porta—la porta—la porta,*" words that sounded similar to the Greek word for "door." I deduced the whisperer wanted me to open the door, so I ran out of the basement and told Mother what I heard. Mother hurried to the basement and began speaking with the Italian through the door. She called him by his name, Rafael, and after only a few minutes of tortured conversation, turned to me.

"Run upstairs and get me a piece of paper and a pencil," she ordered.

When I returned, she slipped them both under the door. Several moments later, the prisoner slid them back and asked Mother to give the note to one of the local girls in town. Mother, always the entrepreneur, understood the opportunity that had presented and placed the note in her brassiere. She hurried up the stairs and through Gargaliani's streets. When she found the girl, she handed her the note.

"Thank you, thank you, Kyria Nitsa," was the joyfully surprised young lady's reply.

And as Mother slowly turned to leave, the girl grabbed her arm.

"Please Kyria Nitsa, wait one minute."

She disappeared into another room and, when she returned, handed Mother a bag full of fruit and homemade noodles.

Mother returned home very pleased with the quick profit she was able to turn for such little work. We ate well that night.

The following day the girl came to our home, handed Mother a note and asked her to deliver it to Rafael. Mother agreed. Before long, the other prisoners had their own delivery requests for Mother, who, one by one, accommodated them all. For the next several weeks, Mother became the town's undercover courier. It was an easy job for her and with the notes tucked away inside her bra, the Italian commanders remained unaware. And every successful delivery brought to us an influx of at least some food, a fact that pleased Father. But he was worried.

"If the Italians find out what's going on here, *we* will end up living in our basement," he once said.

Mother was euphoric and quickly dismissed Father with a wave of her hand. But Father's worry grew and grew, and several weeks later, had reached the point of no return.

"Enough of this. You will close down your business, Nitsa! And you will do so immediately!"

Mother relented when her work took on a life of its own with the prisoners endlessly knocking on our door and slipping her notes. Everything reached a head when a young woman burst into the house carrying a large bag full of food she handed to Mother.

"I demand to see one of the prisoners," she loudly announced.

Mother froze. Not only did Mother not know the woman, but this was the first time anyone had asked to actually see a prisoner. Worse was the woman's audacity, which struck fear in Mother's heart. Mother was well aware that carelessness could rain ruin on everyone.

"I don't know what you are talking about," Mother responded. "It is not possible for me to grant your request. Who do you think I am, the jailer?"

But the woman proved to be as relentless as she was reckless.

"Don't play dumb with me Kyria," she replied. "Everyone knows what's going on here. And everyone knows your reputation as a woman who can get things done."

Mother stood dumbfounded as the woman silently stared at her.

"Okay, I get it, I promise to bring you another bag with food tomorrow."

"No, Kyria, that's not it. What you ask for is not possible. It's impossible. It's impossible! I am sorry. I cannot help you. Take your food back."

An argument ensued and the more Mother resisted this woman, the more intrepid the woman became.

"Even if I wanted to do this for you, the door to the jail is nailed shut. There is nothing that I can do. The Italians have sealed it. There is nothing that anyone can do. Go ask the Italians if you insist!"

When the woman saw she wasn't getting anywhere, her composure changed completely. She buried her head in her hands and began to sob so uncontrollably and so loudly that people outside could hear her cries.

"If I don't see my Giovanni, I will die, Kyria Nitsa. I don't know what to do. I'm desperate. You have to help me."

She fell to the floor.

"I am dying. I am dying. God help me! God help me! Only you can help me, Kyria Nitsa! You must help me. At the very least, let me talk to my Giovanni through the door. Let me hear his sweet voice. Please. Please! I beg you. Please!"

It is always easier to maintain resistance against a person who is being pugnacious than it is against someone who throws themselves at your mercy. And wanting to put an end to this dangerous episode, Mother relented, apparently deciding the harm in letting this woman speak to her Giovanni through the door was less than sending her away sobbing and screaming. Mother was wrong. As she led the lady down the stairs, Mother directed her to keep very quiet and pointed to the door.

War!

But knowing that Giovanni was only a few feet from her was apparently too much to handle, and she bolted to the door and clawed at it as she hysterically shrieked in Greek and broken Italian, and even more loudly than she sobbed upstairs, "Giovanni! Giovanni! Are you there? Can you hear me my sweet Giovanni?"

"I am here, *agape mou*," he replied through the door.

Giovanni was in control and spoke softly and calmly. Mother let the two speak for a few minutes and then rushed the lady out of the house, relieved that she had kept things under control and avoided a disaster.

"Don't you dare mention this to your Father, Saranti," she ordered.

The next day, the woman appeared again at our home, but when Mother and Stathi were out running errands. Father opened the door and the woman stood in front of him holding a basket filled with beans and flour. Father thanked the lady for the food but was overwhelmed with horror when she demanded a direct audience with Giovanni.

"What are you talking about?" he asked in disbelief. "You want to see a prisoner? That's impossible! There are Italians everywhere. Do you want to get us killed?"

"I only want to see him for five minutes, that's all. I was here yesterday. There is no one on your side of the basement. No one will know. Please, I beg you. I have to see my Giovanni. The Italians don't care anyway. Everyone knows what's going on here. If they cared, they would have shut you down a long time ago."

The woman's words left Father, who had thought Mother was winding down her secret business, in a daze. And before he could say anything, the woman made a break for the door that led to the basement, ran down the stairs and toward the prison door.

"Giovanni, Giovanni! Are you there my sweet?"

Father and I chased after her.

"I am here, *agape mou*," Giovanni responded through the door. "*Ti amo bella.*"

In the basement, Father grabbed the woman by the arm.

"Please, *despina,* if the Italians find out about what is happening here, we will all be killed. This has to stop right now. We cannot do this anymore."

Father's words fell on deaf ears, and the lady continued to speak with her Giovanni through the door while Father pulled at her and pleaded with her to leave. That was when a nail in the door jamb caught Father's eye, causing him to suddenly realize that the door to the jail was secured only by a single tiny nail that he, in an inexplicable momentary lapse of judgment, pulled out with his hand. The door to the jail swung open, bringing us face to face with Giovanni and the silhouettes of several other prisoners directly behind him. They looked even more shocked than we did. Giovanni and his lover ran to one another, embraced and began to hug and kiss. Father froze. The other prisoners meandered into our side of the basement and Mother, who had just returned home, heard the commotion and came running down. When she saw the chaos, she sprang into action and began to frantically pry the woman away from Giovanni.

"Wake up, Panagioti! C'mon!"

Mother threw the woman to the floor and my parents began to push the Italian soldiers back into their jail cell.

"Why in the name of God would you open that door?" she said to Father. "You must be insane! You are all going to get us killed."

Mother turned to the soldiers.

"Now, everyone back in the cell! Are you all crazy? They will send you directly to Hitler, but if you are lucky, they'll only hang you in the plateia. Have you lost your minds? We are in the middle of a war here. This is not a bordello! Everyone back in the cell. *Unjale!*"

For some reason, the enemy soldiers obeyed Mother's orders. Giovanni and the other men reentered the jail as the woman, still on the floor, sobbed uncontrollably. Giovanni must have recognized the danger because he began to speak in Greek and Italian in soothing tones to the girl.

"The lady here is right, my love. We must return to jail. But I will not be here forever. I will be out in only a few days, *agape mou*. Then we will be together forever."

"Yes, Giovanni. In only a few more days, we will be together."

Mother nodded in agreement and led the disheveled girl upstairs. Father closed the door to the jail and nailed it shut with several dozen large nails. Then he reinforced the door with steel rods he stretched across the top and bottom and finished by filling the large crack under the door with mud, an action that marked the official end of Mother's profitable but brief business enterprise. For the next several weeks, we lived in fear that someone would betray us or that one of the solders in the jail would inform a superior about what had happened. But when no one approached us, we figured we had either dodged a bullet or that someone, somewhere, gave us a pass.

Shortly after the end of Mother's delivery service that fall, we once again found ourselves without food. With Father bringing home no more than a few dandelions from the fields and with no money to buy what little was available in the agora, our hope for another meal became more and more bleak. There were few job prospects for Father with the exception of the occasional emergency carpentry job, like fixing a broken flight of stairs or plugging a leaky roof. With the occupation in full swing and food scarce, no one performed any carpentry above and beyond what was absolutely necessary. Somehow, we eked by.

On December 7, 1941, Japan attacked the American naval base at Pearl Harbor, Hawaii. In a speech before congress the following day, President Franklin Roosevelt reported what had happened and prepared his nation for all-out war. Three days after that, Germany and Italy, understanding that it was only a matter of short time before the United States' entry into the European War, declared war on the United States. On December 11, 1941, the United States Congress reciprocated and declared war on Germany. The Americans were in the war.

Back in Gargaliani, everyone did what he had to do to stay alive. My friends and I quickly learned that the infirmary across the street would give us food whenever they had some extra. Getting near the front of that line required a keen eye as all the children in the area competed to get whatever morsels were available. Though the soldier's food—macaroni soup—was good, even better was the food the Italians had prepared for their own patients. That food was healthier, of a wider variety, and better yet, much tastier. So twice a day, we would wait near the door for a chance to get a share of the infirmary's leftovers. And the Italians always tried to help us, scraping the bottoms of their pots to try to give us at least something. Individual soldiers would leave food for us when they could. Indeed, whether we received any food usually depended on how much the

dandelions for Dinner

Italians ate. Sometimes I brought home a plate that was filled. Other times, there was nothing.

By the fall of 1942, the soldiers routinely checked into the infirmary as a way of avoiding work. One morning, so many soldiers filled the infirmary that they spilled out the front door and into the street. Though the staff busily handed out quinine tablets and urged men back to duty, nothing seemed to reduce the number of sick. Niko and I watched the spectacle as we played in the street in front of our home. We suddenly froze when we heard the singular clap-clop of an animal we knew meant only one thing—Yenatos on his majestic horse. We watched as he strolled past us and as he gently stopped his animal at the infirmary door. From the saddle, he surveyed the area, and I watched as a look of caustic displeasure and disgust settle on his face.

Then without any warning, Yenatos began to berate the soldiers. Though I had no idea what he said, you didn't have to speak Italian to know that the man was not happy. I can only guess he was upset about all the claimed illnesses because without missing a beat, he jumped off the animal and began to push everyone out of the infirmary. To those who moved too slowly, Yenatos helped them along by driving his boot into their backs. In the midst of his rage, he turned to the children who milled about looking for handouts and shouted orders at them as well.

"*Va via! Va via!*" he said. Everyone scattered when confronted with Yenatos's palpable rage.

I ran into our house and continued to watch from a window as enraged Yenatos re-entered the infirmary and hollered and kicked some more. The sick Italians slowly staggered onto the street, some wearing boots and pants, others barefoot, and others shirtless. Then Yenatos lined them up at attention in the street, mounted his horse, and marched them toward the outskirts of the city. The soldiers spent the rest of the day digging ditches. I watched as other Italians, who Yenatos could not see, laughed uncontrollably at the sight of Napoleon on his horse leading their pathetic counterparts out of town.

After the men were gone, the kitchen staff began to sweep the infirmary and to scrub its floors. Two cooks arrived and dropped off a large pot with the noon's macaroni soup and left. With the men gone, it was clear the soup would go uneaten. I grabbed Stathi and two plates and we ran to the infirmary door, each holding one in our hands. As the other children who Yenatos had scared away still hadn't returned, Stathi and I were the only ones asking them for their extra food. One of the men told us to wait. We watched as a few men ate several bowls of soup. When they were finished, the orderly turned to me.

"Take it all, piccolo," he said as he signaled to me to take the entire pot and to return it cleaned.

"Thank you," I said as Stathi and I took the half-full pot and dragged it across the street to our house.

Overwhelmed with joy, we pulled it around to the kitchen door and wrestled it up the three steps that led into our kitchen. After we managed to get it to the middle of the kitchen floor, we were suddenly faced with a unique opportunity. We could eat as much food as we wanted. As our parents were out, I sat Stathi in his seat at the table and then set a bowl for each of us and lined up our spoons. I filled each bowl with soup. Stathi was excited and I watched a look of the most joyous, lip licking anticipation on the boy's face that I had ever witnessed. Then, Stathi and I, seated at opposite sides of the table, began to eat. And we ate and ate and ate, one plate after another. Neither of us stopped and neither of us talked. We just ate, swallowing spoonful after spoonful of soup.

After plowing through a number of bowls, Stathi, with his chin barely over the table and with his spoon near his nose, looked up at me.

"My stomach hurts. I don't want anymore."

Stathi's statement caused me to survey my own body, and I realized that my bloated stomach hurt as well. I stopped eating and with great difficulty, arose from my chair. My head began to spin and I felt so tired I could hardly walk. Though I couldn't believe I was going to stop eating while food remained on the table, I grabbed Stathi's hand, helped him onto the family bed, and we passed out.

Noise from the kitchen woke us up several hours later. Stathi and I staggered in only to find Mother preparing an evening meal from the soup we hadn't eaten.

"Bravo, Bravo to both of you. You ate well, I see. Excellent job."

Mother put two bowls on the table, and Stathi and I happily sat and ate some more.

Chapter 13
MOUZAKI

On November 8, 1942, the Allies launched Operation Torch, landing on the west and northwest coasts of Africa. Prior to that invasion, the Allies possessed no real ground at all in Western Europe or the Mediterranean. But though closer than ever, help was still a world away from us. We remained at the mercy of the occupation and occasional handouts of food alone were never enough to sustain our family.

Starvation had already killed tens of thousands of Greeks, and survival would not only require grit but every tool in our arsenal including intelligence, craftiness, determination, perseverance, and hope. Those who quit would surely die. When Father realized that our hope for a regular supply of food had reached a completely new level of futility, he pulled my brother and me into the kitchen for a talk. Mother stood at the stove, boiling some greens. With a stern face, Father spoke.

"Boys, our food has run out. All of us must eat less, okay? We have to conserve what little we have. Do you boys understand?"

"Yes, Father," I said.

"Now, just because your stomach growls, it doesn't mean you need to eat. Mother will feed you when she's ready. You don't need to pester her. Is that clear?"

Mother quietly stirred the pot. As Father spoke, he slowly and deliberately weighed each word, as if he was sermonizing for us to refrain from gluttony.

"Now, when you do eat, you don't need to fill your bellies. If you eat each day a little milk or cheese and a slice of bread with some dandelions and olive oil, you've eaten enough. And if you add to that some raisins, you are eating a feast. Now every so often, you will get something extra like potatoes or corn. But don't ask for it.

War!

Mother will give it to you when it's time. Is that clear? Do you have any questions?"

Though I wanted to ask Father why he was telling us all this when I was already hungry all the time, I remained silent. A life of conservation was the only life I knew. But my mind drifted to Karagiosi, the Greek puppet character who was, like us, constantly hungry. One time, Karagiosi walked into a bakery and saw in front of him on a large table a huge pile of freshly baked loaves of bread.

As poor Karagiosi was starving, he turned to the proprietor and asked, "Are all these loaves of bread yours?" When the proprietor answered affirmatively, Karagiosi asked, "Then why aren't you eating them?"

I found Karagiosi's question extremely logical as my ever-increasing hunger had created in me an incessant and extreme desire to eat. Eating was my sole focus, the subject, verb, and object of my every thought. I had long before gotten to the point that all I wanted to do was to eat without stopping, to eat until I had devoured every piece of food in Gargaliani. I could not imagine *not* thinking about food. Mother owned a French cookbook, and I would stare for hours at the pictures of raw chickens for sale in piazzas, baked briskets, and the like. I fantasized about lavish banquets replete with every food imaginable spread across our dining room table. Often, such images would permeate my dreams, and I would awaken with the taste of dirty wool in my mouth, only to discover I had been gnawing on my stringy blanket. Even though the Italians often gave us food, it was never enough. They fed themselves before they fed the locals.

As the silent weight of Father's words hung in the room, Mother, apparently disgusted with what she heard, suddenly spoke.

"What are you talking about Panagioti? Children cannot live on dandelions and such fasting. We have to do something else. What you are saying is not an option for the children."

As she spoke, Mother walked around our home and picked up various items that she placed on the dining room table. She picked up bed sheets and pillowcases from the bedroom, a massive wool blanket and a number of items from the kitchen.

"Panagioti, the children cannot and will not live on raisins and dandelions. We will not sit around and wait idly for God to throw down some manna from the sky to sustain us. Christmas is only a few weeks away. Don't you remember last year? We didn't have a decent meal to celebrate Christ's birth. We will not repeat that this year. No, this year we will do whatever it takes to have a proper meal."

Mother continued moving around the house, picking certain things up, putting some back down and transferring others to the kitchen table. She was obviously upset, well past the point of motivational dissatisfaction. She began to talk to herself.

"How long can we endure this? How long are we going to remain in this damned place that God has long ago forsaken? What did we do to deserve this? I knew this would happen, and I told it to my sister and to Papa Ntres. But no one would listen to me. Why in God's name did I listen to them?"

When Father heard Mother's questions, he looked at her and, as if without giving it any thought, replied in his quiet, matter of fact manner, "Well, there's always America."

Father's words were the last words anyone spoke that night as Mother, so tired of being a victim, sprang into action. She moved quickly, silently appraising our household goods. She gathered the only food we had, some onions and raisins, and then boiled them together on the stove, creating one of the most appalling concoctions I have ever seen. When she served it to us, we found it so offensive that we couldn't eat it, even though we were starving. Everyone went to bed hungry that night.

By the following day, I saw she had placed various items on our table and she told me that I would accompany her that day on the ten kilometer trek eastward to Mouzaki.

"When we get there, we will sell as many of these things as we can, Saranti" she said.

"How long will it take us?" I asked.

"Two and a half or three hours of walking. It's not too far."

I knew that walking to Mouzaki was a trek that would lead us through fields and over rocky crags. I panicked when I heard how long it would take as such trips for me were endless journeys into a painfully boring and tiring abyss. Even before we left the house, I was overcome by the mental fatigue of even contemplating walking such an ungodly distance. The farthest I had ever walked before was to Theano's farmhouse by the sea, a little more than one hour

War!

each way. But at least with that walk, boredom was overcome by the anticipation of meeting friends and playing at the beach.

And though I knew the sacrifice Mother was making for us and also knew that she could not make the journey alone, I still couldn't stop myself from mumbling, "We'll be walking all day."

We left through our front door and headed out of town, toward the same road Father used to walk to our fields. Slung around my neck and under one arm was a bag Mother had filled with bed sheets, pillowcases and some other smaller items. She carried a much larger bag, one filled with our rug, various kitchen utensils, a pot, pillows and some jewelry, mostly dowry items she inherited from her Mother. No sooner had we passed St. Spyridon church and the Italian sentry on the eastern edge of town and exited the city when Mother began to have difficulty with one of her sandals. When we were out of town and reached a slight bend in the road, Mother sat on the fresh stump of what was only recently a huge oak tree the Italians had cut for firewood. Such stumps were everywhere. As she sat, Mother sighed and examined her feet. She showed me a huge blister that had erupted, apparently from the rubbing of the strap of her sandal on her foot. She removed both sandals and stuffed them into her bag. I watched as she quietly examined her naked feet, her now overgrown nails and her tender and protruding bunions. We sat there silently and tears began to gently roll down Mother's cheeks and into her lap.

"How did I let this happen to me?" she quietly whispered.

My heart ached for my mother as I watched her momentarily lost in her private realization of how far she had fallen. We sat there for several minutes until she quickly gathered herself, sprang up and with full determination, continued walking, now without shoes. Even though I had been without shoes for over a year, I didn't like watching my Mother walk barefooted, an unbecoming state for any woman. My mind drifted to how I had outgrown my last pair of shoes and I became embarrassed when Father told me we couldn't afford to have Gargaliani's cobbler make me new ones. I realized that from that point forward, I would have to walk around barefoot. Kostas, who had long been without shoes, showed me and Niko, who was also newly shoeless, the ropes of our new found state. He removed thorns from our feet and showed us how his soles had become hard like hoofs and speckled with holes left by the countless thorns he had stepped on as he ran around Gargaliani.

"It is not as bad as it looks," he explained. "Look how tough my skin has become. Only the longest thorns can penetrate this, and most of those just snap when they hit my foot."

When Kosta said that, I looked at my clean feet and hoped they would never look like his.

These thoughts circled my head as I watched my shoeless Mother walk. I felt ashamed and wished I was twice my age so that I could help my family survive our difficult times. Mother sensed my concern.

"Don't worry about my feet, Saranti. This is nothing. We are going to trade these things in Mouzaki and get lots of food for all of us to eat. This is only another challenge for us to overcome."

As we continued our barefooted trek, Mother kept a lookout ahead and whenever she saw someone approaching, quickly put on her sandals. It was one thing for me to see her walking barefooted and another thing altogether for someone else to see her.

We entered the small village of Floka and passed by the barely discernable dirt road that led to our fields. Passing that road marked a milestone for me as I was venturing into new territory. From time to time, a vehicle passed us and stirred the road's dormant dust into a small storm that engulfed us, covering us from head to toe with a powdery white film that made us unrecognizable. As we proceeded, the terrain remained the same—irregular and full of vineyards littered with the occasional fig tree. Our journey was not as difficult as I had originally feared. In fact, time passed quickly because Mother kept talking.

"These bad times that we are experiencing, Saranti, are only temporary. Everything in life is temporary. This war, like every other war before it, will not last forever. And when it is over, we will leave Gargaliani and move to America, to the Promised Land, to the place where the streets are paved with gold. Then, your Father will work hard, but he'll have something to show for his work. He'll earn money. Here, we work and work and we are starving to death. Your Father used to live there and as soon as we can leave, that's where we are all going to live."

Mother's comments marked the first time she discussed our future in terms of America with me. Prior to that, she had made a habit of pointing out local people in town saying how I would be like this pharmacist or that teacher. She often told me that after I finished high school, she would take me to Theo Plato's family in Athens, to people who would help me become "someone." But Mother had had enough of Greece, the meager existence it provided us, and its hopelessness. And there was no commodity more valuable in these times of struggle than hope. And our only hope—our hope to survive, our hope to live a life beyond scrounging for food, our hope to move past being barefoot—was to leave Greece, its history, its beauty, our roots, the only place we belonged, for a new place, a place I only knew by name, a place only Father had been, a place called "America." Mother's talk that day of our move to America created in me a new, though flickering, hope. The abstract thought of leaving Gargaliani for an unknown utopia comforted me; the theoretical end of our struggles was a welcome change to my thought processes. Though we had been told over and over about how life in Greece would improve after the war, Father was suspicious of such notions as news of Allied victories in North Africa and Russia hadn't changed our lives at all.

Before Mother spoke of America, time dragged on and on for me as monotonously as a skipping record that keeps whining the same verse. No matter what happened at the national and international levels, my tomorrows were only continuations of my todays, my yesterdays days to forget, and the weeks and months reruns that peeled away in a crawling, never-ending eternity of anticipation. Mother's talk of America changed that and planted the seed that our future would be lived in a place where we could achieve our potential and where our hard work would reap benefits. It gave me hope that things would get better, that the day would come when our lives would transcend our present lowliness. But still, the very thought of going to America was so abstract and remote that it proved well beyond my ability to fully grasp. Nevertheless, it gave me hope, something we all needed, the only fuel that could keep us struggling.

By the time we approached the town of Pirgaki, white dust completely covered us.

"This is where my mother, your grandmother Eleni, was born.

This is where your grandfather, the great Papa Saranti, first saw her and fell in love with her."

Lacking any strategic importance, Pirgaki remained unoccupied and stayed completely as it was prior to the war, its citizens carrying on much as they had before. Just as we were about to enter the town, we passed in front of a beautiful house surrounded by well manicured gardens and sculpted trees. In front stood a neatly dressed, dignified-looking woman, clad in a flower patterned dress and starched white apron. When she saw us approaching, the woman waived at us to stop. Mother reached down and put on her sandals. The woman crossed her garden swiftly and then opened her home's main gate.

"Can I see what you are selling?" she asked.

Our dusty appearance, combined with this unexpected encounter, embarrassed Mother and for the first time, she was speechless. Whatever it was, whether the woman's immediately identifying us as peasants looking to barter, the appearance of this matriarchal woman just outside grandmother Eleni's village, or that Mother saw the woman as the mistress of a prominent household, a position she herself had enjoyed for many years herself, I cannot be sure. In other such situations, Mother could quickly play the hyper-subservient and manipulate her counterpart's kindness and vanity, a move that quickly gave her the upper hand in any encounter. But here, I am certain that for an instant, Mother allowed herself to be overcome by a long-forgotten prideful fever as she was so abruptly reminded, once again, of how far she had fallen.

"Everything we have has already been sold," Mother said. "I'm sorry. It has all been promised elsewhere."

It took me years to figure out why Mother hadn't traded any of our things with that woman and even longer to forgive her. As hungry as I was, I would have traded everything we were carrying for a single piece of bread.

Fifty meters or so past that house and just before we entered Pirgaki, we veered onto a dirt road that continued due east. We quickly passed an arrowed sign that indicated Mouzaki was straight ahead and we continued eastward toward the mountain Ayia that stood directly above our destination. Mouzaki was a village occupied by several-hundred, people who spent their time farming and raising livestock, mostly goats. Set at the foot of the mountain

Ayia, Mouzaki's hilly terrain made mules the preferred mode of transportation. When it rained, water quickly filled streams making Mouzaki even more isolated from the chaotic world, its wars and its occupations, and certainly off the radar of the Germans and Italians. Mouzaki's contact with the outside was limited to Sundays, when its villagers loaded their mules with skins, wool, produce, and dairy products and walked them to agoras in outlying towns like Gargaliani. Whenever they hit our town, the Mouzakians created a festive atmosphere as they boisterously screamed out their deals and loudly negotiated their bartering.

"Saranti, do you remember the man who bought our sewing machine?" Mother asked.

"Yes, Mana."

"We are going to find him and sell him many of the things we have here. Hopefully, he hasn't married off his daughter yet. We have many beautiful things here for her dowry."

"Do you think we'll find him?"

"We'll find him. For sure, we will. We have to find him. This Christmas, we will eat more than onions and raisins. We have no choice but to trade these things."

As we approached Mouzaki, the church of Panagia that accented the peak of Ayia was no longer visible. We walked under some broadleaf trees that grew on the outskirts of town and increased our pace in anticipation of the adventure that lie ahead. Mother slipped on her sandals, and because she couldn't remember the name of the man to whom she sold our sewing machine, she began to speak to everyone we passed.

"Do you know where the man with the sewing machine lives?" she asked one person. "Do you know where we can find the man who recently bought a sewing machine?" she asked another.

After several attempts, she hit upon a certain young woman.

"Yes, yes, I know the people well. I've seen the machine. They've showed me how it works. Come with me. I'll take you to Kyrios Koropoulos's home."

"Thank you, thank you," Mother replied.

The young woman dropped what she was doing and led us to this man's home. And she couldn't stop talking about the sewing machine.

"Everyone in town has seen that machine. It is really amazing. I hope that one day I will have one of those as well. No one here has ever seen anything like it."

When we arrived at the house, we knocked on the door. It creaked open and in front of us stood a motionless, austere looking woman. She was slightly taller than Mother, slender, and wore a long dark blue peasant dress partially covered with a dirty yellow patterned apron. On her head was a handkerchief tied under her chin and from under which protruded stringy strands of uncombed brown hair. Without uttering a word, she stared at us, exhibiting no facial expressions. Only a slight glimmer of perspiration on her temple caused me to think she was alive. Convinced we had knocked on the wrong door, I moved closer to Mother for protection as it appeared obvious that selling anything to her would require God to work a major miracle. Slowly, she opened her stiff mouth.

"What do you want?"

"Good afternoon, Kyria. I am Kyria Nitsa Stamatis. This is my son, Saranti. We have come to you all the way from Gargaliani. You may remember us. It is from us that your husband purchased your Singer sewing machine. I want you to know how grateful we were to your husband for trading your goat Kanella for the sewing machine. Of course, I miss the sewing machine, you can imagine. My husband gave it to me as a wedding gift. But our Kanella has given us milk and has saved my family— my husband and my two children—from starvation."

When the woman heard the words "sewing machine," a half-smile appeared on her face.

"Indeed, the sewing machine has been quite a blessing for our family. I have made many items for my family with it. I learned to make my daughter a dress and have made clothes for my other children."

"It makes me very happy to hear that," Mother replied.

"And, as I am sure my husband told you, the machine has been promised to our daughter as part of her dowry. It will be hers when she gets married."

Her brief smile quickly faded.

"So what do you want?" she asked.

Slowly and with great deliberation, Mother spoke, "As I said

Kyria, my son and I have walked here all the way from Gargaliani. We have brought a number of other items to sell that I am sure will be just perfect for your daughter's dowry. Take a look at these..."

The woman abruptly cut off Mother.

"Kyria, my husband paid too much for that sewing machine. He should have never made the potatoes part of that deal. Do you know what a high demand there has been for potatoes? We have had quite a difficult time since we gave up all those items for just a machine that sews."

The pettiness surprised Mother.

"Kyria, don't be foolish. While the goat has saved us, it was not of very good stock at all. Her breasts are so small that the expenses of keeping and feeding her is barely worth the milk she produces. Everyone keeps asking us why we don't just slaughter and eat the poor thing."

"There was nothing wrong with the goat. You city folk just don't know how to care for animals. If you did, if you fed it properly, then it would produce much more milk for you. The size of her breasts doesn't matter."

The woman's tone was businesslike and stern.

"I would be happy to buy the goat back at the market price."

Mother saw that this conversation was going nowhere and that unless it took a sudden turn for the better, we would be carrying our things back to Gargaliani. So rather than argue any more with her, she stopped talking and began to gently smile as the woman continued to pontificate about potatoes, corn and the ineptitude of city dwellers with goats. Mother's smile was not a happy, joyful or even mocking smile, but the type of sweet serene smile one sees only exhibited by the humblest and most enlightened of monastics. Her calculated sincerity must have had an effect on the woman because her countenance changed completely.

"Well, Kyria, why don't you return in a couple of hours. My husband will be back from our fields and you can talk to him then."

She closed the door.

By the time we left that house, we were extremely tired and hungry, still not having eaten anything that day. We staggered to a nearby tree where Mother sat me down and told me to rest. Then

Mother began to canvas the area for some kind of deal. After what appeared an eternity, she returned with some feta cheese that we quickly devoured and washed down with water we drank from a nearby stream. I was still hungry. We walked around town and Mother traded a few of our linens for some vegetables. The farming season was ending and we watched Mouzaki's farmers prepare themselves for ground-crushing fall rains that were coming and the winter that would follow.

Several hours later, we returned to the Koropoulos house and found Kyrios Koropoulos tending to some of his animals and unloading farm implements and what looked like the season's last produce from a cart. Sacks filled with beans were everywhere as were baskets of green tomatoes that would ripen slowly, providing the Koropoulos family with tomatoes for almost the entire winter.

"Kyrie Koropoulos!" Mother called out.

Obviously briefed by his wife, Koropoulos dourly waived at us to wait until he finished up his work. We quietly stood near the entrance to his home. The wealth of the Koropoulos household was obvious. The ground floor was filled with the products of their fields: what looked like enough beans, corn, tomatoes, and olives to feed the Spartan *and* Athenian armies. I don't think I had ever seen that much food in someone's house before. We watched with interest as he placed mounds and mounds of food into his storage shed and as he led his animals into his barn. When he finished, he approached us, and without any reservation or hesitation and before Mother could get a word out, he began.

"Kyria Stamati, I am sorry you came all this way. This year's harvest was poor and I'm sorry but I will not be able to trade anything with you."

We stared at him dumfounded.

"I am afraid we do not have enough food in storage to get my family to the next harvest. I am sorry."

To get him through the next harvest!? I thought to myself. *Can't he see we are starving right now? Can't he see that while he's worried about what he's going to eat in June, we need something to eat right now?*

Kyrios Koropoulos's comment brought to light the stark contrast between our two views of the world, polar opposites even though we lived only a few kilometers from one another. Koropoulos thought of and lived in the future, whether he and his family would have enough to eat in six months. No doubt in six months, he would still be worrying about the next six months. We, on the other hand, were so consumed with the present that we never spent any time worrying about the future, acutely aware that if we didn't fill today's requirements to live, there wouldn't be a tomorrow. When Mother saw that we weren't going to make any deals with Koropoulos, she thanked him for his time.

"Hurry back home," he said as he lit an oil lamp. "Look at the sky. There is a storm coming. The rainy season is upon us. You have to hurry because the water can quickly overwhelm you. Many animals die during the first rains of the year."

But Mother absolutely refused to leave totally empty handed.

"What a blessing it is for you people who live in these villages. Your life away from town's likes Gargaliani is a life lived constantly in God's presence. In times like these, it is people like you, people with no need for towns and governments and their follies and worries, that help the rest of us survive. Take my home, for example. It has been taken over by the Italian army. They just came in and took it over. Ever since the Germans captured and imprisoned my husband, we have had just such a difficult time. And even then, our troubles didn't end. When my daughter caught malaria, I thought I would die from the stress. You met little Katina, didn't you?"

Koropoulos shook his head.

"Oh, I wish you had! She's an angel. We almost lost her, you know. But what can I do. Look at my family. I have to keep forging ahead. This is the cross our Lord has given me. I am comforted by something my Father, the great Papa Sarantis, used to say, that our God gives the biggest crosses to the strongest. But I wished he had asked me before he gave me all these crosses. They just seem too much for me to bear."

I couldn't understand what Mother was talking about. My Father captured by Germans? And I had a sister? A sister who was sick with malaria, no less? But before I could say anything, I looked at Mother and saw that as she spoke, she cried. Huge tears flowed down her cheeks and to the ground. Mother's soliloquy must have touched Kyria Koropoulos's heart because then and there, and because what I suspect was a desire to be done with us, she reached around for her husband, quickly grabbed Mother's bag and filled it with flour. In another, she placed a loaf of bread and some noodles.

"Now please, Kyria Stamati, get moving. A storm is coming and you do not want to get caught in it," she said.

"Thank you, thank you." Mother replied as, with a triumphant look on her face, we headed home.

Not only had Mother accomplished her mission of getting food for her family, she did so without having to give up any of our household items.

Once out on the street, the sky instantly flashed with lightening quickly followed by earsplitting thunder. Mother became frightened and grabbed my hand and returned to the door of the Koropoulos' home.

Mother knocked, "Please Kyria Koropoulos, let us stay the night with you. This terrible storm is coming and we don't want to get caught in it. Please."

But Kyria Koropoulos would have none of it, perhaps feeling that Mother had gotten the best of them a second time.

"I am sorry Kyria, that is not possible. Please hurry and get out of Mouzaki before the rain comes and the streams swell."

"Can we at least sleep in the barn with your animals?"

"Kyria Stamati, please, hurry and go before the rain comes. You have to get moving. There is a terrible storm coming."

We left the Koropoulos home and began to run. When we reached the edge of town, enormous rain drops began to hit our heads and the ground in front of us. Then, as if someone had flipped a switch, gale force winds instantaneously howled in every direction so intensely that the enormous trees in front of us began to bend as if they were made of soft rubber. Sheets of rain engulfed us and were so heavy that they reduced visibility to only a few meters. Water suddenly seemed to be everywhere, up to our ankles and rising. Mother held my arm firmly and led us toward higher ground, to where she thought she would find cover. But we were completely disoriented, and Mother reversed directions. We were suddenly knee deep in a stream that pushed us toward a larger, faster stream. The food we received became soaked, too heavy to carry. As Mother yanked me along, the food slipped from both our hands and the rushing stream carried it away. We desperately moved against the current toward a low line of trees and found temporary refuge. As we clutched some branches, I could hear Mother screaming.

"Most holy Panagia save us! Have mercy on us! Dear God, save us!"

More and more water flowed everywhere and quickly rose to the tree line. Mother surveyed the area for a new refuge but in the rain and the wind, we couldn't see anything. We couldn't see which way was up. We were doomed. Amidst the chaos, I discerned a voice returning Mother's prayer.

"Kyria Stamatis, Kyria Stamatis!"

"We are here," Mother replied.

When he saw us, Koropoulos made number of daring rock-to-rock leaps and landed beside us.

"Thank God I found you. Thank God I found you," he kept repeating.

He grabbed us and as he led us to higher ground, began to scold Mother.

"Didn't I tell you to get moving and to get out of this town? These rains are deadly. You should never try to travel at this hour. They come down so hard they can crush stones."

Mother, just happy we had been saved, said nothing.

"Don't you know that floods in times like this are common? We are going to lose much livestock tonight."

"Thank you for coming for us, Kyrie Koropoulos. Thank you. You and your wife had done so much for us that we didn't think it right to impose on you any further."

Koropoulos led us across the high ground and to his home. When we arrived, his wife welcomed us with open arms, as if we were lost relatives they thought were dead.

"Thank God you're alive, glory to God. I don't know what we would have done if anything happened to you."

She directed us to a large room on the second floor of the family's home where a warm fire blazed in a huge stone fireplace. We took off our clothes and hung them. The hot and penetrating fire quickly dried them.

"I'm hungry," I whispered in Mother's ear.

"Don't worry, there's food on the way," she whispered back.

Several moments later, Kyria Koropoulos appeared, carrying a large tray with our supper. Before my eyes was something I can only describe as a phenomenon: lamb in an egg-lemon stew with potatoes and an unlimited supply of bread and cheese.

"*Bon appétit!*" said Kyria Koropoulos as she left us alone to eat.

It was a meal truly fit for a king. As I silently consumed every bit of food in front of me, I thought about the people of Mouzaki. Why didn't we live here? These people are truly blessed. If I could eat like this twice a week, I would be in paradise, I thought. When Kyria Koropoulos returned to take the dishes, she found them spotless as I had eaten every bit and then wiped every drop of the egg-lemon sauce completely from each plate with my bread. And though I was totally content, my stomach full, I could have eaten still more.

Later that evening, Mother prepared a place for us to sleep near the fireplace with blankets Kyria Koropoulos had given us. I crawled under them and instantly fell asleep with the glow of the cozy fire warming my face. Mother woke me up the next morning, and Kyria Koropoulos once again fed us and equipped us with a fresh loaf of bread and homemade noodles. We were off.

And as we walked away, Kyrio Koropoulos announced, "I'll be in Gargaliani Sunday and I will bring you some corn, Kyria Stamati!"

"Thank you, Kyrie. May Panagia be with you all!" Mother replied.

Chapter 14
THE MATI

By the late fall of 1942 and after almost a year and a half in Gargaliani, it was clear that the Italians were as sick of the occupation as we were. Nevertheless, as a nine year old, I had become pals with many of the soldiers, addressed them on a first name basis and was eager to run little errands whenever asked. And they helped me with handouts when they could, usually when they were eating and I was hanging around.

Though most of the Italians and Greeks realized we shared similar struggles and recognized the importance of maintaining cordial relations with the locals, there were no doubt exceptions. For example, the immaculate Yenatos was never approachable. I stayed out of his way and if I found myself in his path, I would literally turn and run in the opposite direction. Another example was an Italian private we had nicknamed Hondros, the fat one. From his dour and unkempt appearance, Hondros was the polar opposite of Yenatos. Not only was he overweight, but his face was round and so terribly pockmarked that we assumed he had suffered from some terrible childhood disease. He rarely spoke, but when he did, formed words in such an awkward way so as to telegraph that he was, at best, as intellectually out of place in the war as he was physically. His comrades must have agreed because they teased him relentlessly, an action that only encouraged the local children to do the same. And whenever we chimed in, Hondros would lose control of his temper, verbally berate and stumble after us. When he did that, the other Italians would laugh even harder at him, an action that only further fueled his awkward outbursts.

Perhaps even more out of place than Hondros was a toilet that sat on an outside wall, several meters into an alley off the main street and only a quarter block from our home. The outdoor toilet was a relic from the Ottoman days and for at least a century, had remained dormant. In need of additional latrines or perhaps just feeling nostalgic, the Italians resurrected the old toilet, cleaned it, restored its primitive plumbing and installed a burlap curtain in front of it for privacy. But as a person sitting on that artifact could be seen by anyone moving through the alley, I have to believe that using the toilet was a last resort for anyone—anyone except, of course, Hondros.

Shortly after his arrival, Hondros and that toilet formed a special bond—so intimate that several times a day, he sat his bulbous body upon it, using it not only to relieve himself, but ostensibly as his personal retreat from war. Indeed, it got to the point where almost every time we passed the toilet, we would peek under the curtain and see Hondros's thick legs, with his pants sloppily bunched around his ankles. And whenever we saw him, we never missed a chance to laugh at and make fun of the man.

"Look at him," we would hoot. "Look at those legs. He's there again! The man is constantly crapping—doesn't he ever get tired of it?"

It was bad enough Hondros was ordered away from his home to occupy a foreign land he likely never even wanted to visit; the war forced him to endure the constant ridicule of that land's local children.

By late 1942, Hondros had had enough of everyone's abuse and one day, waited in the alley for one of the children to pass by. I was oblivious to his presence and strolled by alone. When I realized that he had been hiding and waiting to attack some child, and that the child was going to be me, it was too late. He appeared, grabbed me by the wrist, pushed me to the ground, and began to drag me down the alley. We passed the side of my house.

"Help! Help!" I yelped in vain.

Hondros continued to drag me, by the stables, and then toward an abandoned house when he stopped. Near its entrance sat a dry, shallow well. Unsure if I was dreaming, Hondros picked me up and dropped me in. I fell to the bottom with a thud. When I realized what had happened, my assailant was gone and I stood at the bottom of the well, its walls too smooth for me to climb. I was trapped—Hondros had gotten his revenge.

"Help! Help!" I screamed.

War!

After what was probably only a few minutes yet seemed like an eternity, I looked up and saw the faces of several barn workers appear. They quickly fished me out, and after I told them what had happened, reported Hondros to his superiors. His superiors immediately transferred him, and no one saw him again.

I told Father that evening about what had happened.

"Well, Saranti, the vineyard was bad to begin with, so you shouldn't be surprised that a donkey ate it. What did you expect?"

I had no idea what he meant, but figured he was probably right.

Indeed, the war, the occupation, famine, and an uncertain future were the centrifuge that distilled and revealed the substance of each of us, Italians and Greeks alike. Another case in point was Nikos Halazonitis. Ever since his return from war and despite my Mother's advice to the contrary, Nikos unknowingly served as my primary role model. Whenever he appeared and though he was oblivious to me, I stopped whatever I was doing and watched him, aware that for sure, something interesting was bound to happen. Mother must have felt the same way because whenever he approached, she would try to intercept him to learn our town's latest gossip. Though she didn't want me to be like him, she definitely liked talking with him. In a town filled with characters, Nikos's singular charisma and ability to control others and events left me in a perpetual state of wonder. But though Nikos was likable, he was obnoxious enough to ruffle the feathers of even the most apathetic of Greeks. And he wouldn't hesitate to turn on anyone, no matter who they were, whenever he thought the need arose. Indeed, there were no sacred cows in his world.

Around Christmas of 1942, Mother and I watched Nikos, out of breath and full of excitement, run past our kitchen window and into his yard. When Mother tried to catch him to learn his latest scoop, he had already ducked into the back door of his home and vanished. But rather than chase after him, she patiently remained in the kitchen, knowing that one way or another, she would hear what had happened. Sure enough, several minutes later, Kyria Garifalia walked out of her back door and into her yard. Obviously distressed, she looked up into our kitchen window and waved for Mother's attention.

"Nitsa, Nitsa, I don't know what I am going to do," she began.

"What happened?"

"He's done it again. If it's not one thing with that boy, it's something else. I don't know what to do with him. I can't believe it."

"Tell me, what is it? What happened?"

Kyria Garifalia shook her head from side to side.

"Just now, he came into the house, and do you know what he told me? He said that he just punched Leonidas Didoni in the mouth and broke his jaw."

Mother, truly shocked, also shook her head from side to side.

"And do you know why he did that? He said he punched Didoni because Didoni called Nikos a loudmouth and a *malaka* in the plateia and because Didoni said it loud enough for others to hear."

Leonidas Didoni was from one of the most prominent families in Gargaliani. His father was a well-respected, wealthy landowner. For Nikos to punch the man's son was an act of disrespect to Leonidas's father and to the entire Didoni clan. For sure, it would not reflect well on Nikos or his family.

"How could he have done this? Doesn't that kid use his brain?" Kyria Garifalia rhetorically asked.

Just as Kyria Garifalia's lamentations began to ramp up, there was a knock at the gate that led to her backyard. When she opened the doors, Kyria Garifalia stood face to face with the victim's father, Kyrio Didoni himself, a bespectacled, middle-aged man dressed in an immaculate, brown, three-piece suit and tie.

"Kyrie Didoni," she began, "Welcome to our home, please come in. I heard what happened and I wanted you to know how …"

Kyrio Didoni waived his hand, and Kyria Garifalia stopped talking.

"I want to speak with Nikos," he declared in a sober, businesslike manner.

Apparently stunned at the man's presence, Kyria Garifalia hesitated.

"Nikos is not home."

At that very instant, Niko burst out from the back door and into the yard. I watched him walk right up to his victim's Father, extend his hand with a warm greeting and lead the man into his home.

War!

Kyria Garifalia scurried after them and into her house. Mother and I retreated from the window.

The Didoni and Halazonitis families shared many things in common. Both were well to do and owned substantial swathes of land that included hundreds of olive trees and acres of vineyards. But perhaps even more important was that both families were politically conservative and supported the return of the king to the throne of Greece after the war, a fact that mattered more and more with each Allied victory. After several minutes, we saw the door swing open and watched as Nikos, his mother, and Kyrios Didoni exited the house smiling and shaking hands. Later that afternoon, Kyria Garifalia told Mother that all was well and that her Nikos felt terrible for what he had done and that he had already apologized to Kyrios Didoni and to poor Leonidas.

"Nikos has assured everyone that he feels sick about what he did, and that nothing of the sort will ever happen again," she happily declared.

Apparently, the disgrace of Nikos's own actions had tamed him.

That evening, with the drama over and as the sun set over Gargaliani, I heard the sound of a familiar guitar drift into our home through the kitchen window. It was Nikos, sitting on his patio, strumming the instrument as he leaned back in a straw chair, against the wall of his home. After a few strums, the chastened Nikos began to sing disjointed and extemporaneous verses, loud enough for the entire neighborhood to hear,

Once upon a time, a man named Niko,
Broke a jaw with a single punch;

Nikos sang verse after verse that night, bragging about clobbering poor Leonidas Didoni.

The hero they call Niko,
one time broke a jaw with just one punch.

If nothing else, Nikos proved that night that he was, among other things, incorrigible.

Though I had never given too much attention to the evil eye we called the *mati* and for sure, never kept track of whether something or someone who had received an overabundance of complements soon suffered some calamity, two events took place that fall that made a believer out of me. The first involved Yenatos's horse and the second our cat. First, the horse. Even General Patton himself would have agreed that the Italian Lieutenant Yenatos and his stallion were amongst the most regal of sights to behold. And by the fall of 1942, both had certainly received more than their fair share of praises. With the arrival of the cool fall breezes, the horse's caregiver would throw a blanket over the animal and walk him around for exercise. And every time he did, the locals marveled at the animal.

"What a beautiful horse," or "I have never seen anything like that animal," or "Look at the beauty God makes," were the typical comments that were directed toward the beast as it was paraded around our neighborhood.

But that fall, the horse's customary walks terminated abruptly and without explanation. After a full week where no one had seen the horse, its orderly or Yenatos, rumors began to circulate that for no logical reason at all, the horse had become ill, fallen victim to the *mati*. When the animal and its aide finally emerged one day for a walk, the beast had suddenly aged. Its head drooped, its eyes were foggy, its gait was shaky, and its skin sagged over an aged frame of bones. Whatever fuel line that fed the stallion its life had been snipped. The following day, we saw a flurry of activity near the barn and watched as doctors from the infirmary paraded in and out, as Italians moved buckets of water around.

Word quickly spread that the animal could not be saved. My friend Niko and I watched as the orderly and two other soldiers led the blanketed patient eastward, past the church of All Saints and to the edge of town. Yenatos was nowhere to be seen. From a distance, we watched the Italians pull the horse to the center of an empty field and as one of the men pet and talked to the animal as the other two produced shovels and began digging. Before long, the digging men were waist deep in a massive hole. When they finished, they climbed out, and then one of them removed a pistol from his holster, took a deep breath and shot the most magnificent animal any of us would ever see near its ear. It crumpled to the ground with an awkward thud. The three men lined up behind the horse, dug their feet into the ground, and pushed it into the hole. After it sloppily fell in, they

War!

shoveled dirt on top of it and walked back to town. The beautiful stallion, the one that had been so meticulously cared for, had suddenly and unceremoniously become food for maggots—another putative victim of the *mati*.

Within only days of the stallion's mercy killing, the life of Stathi's red-bowed and oft-praised cat Benito, also the recipient of excessive praises, took an unexpected turn for the worse. One afternoon, Father, whose dislike for the cat had only grown with time, had gone into the basement to retrieve some oil. Benito followed him. When a mouse suddenly appeared, Father hopefully watched to see the cat eat it. But the rodent's appearance initially failed to rouse Benito from his chronic indifference. Father became even more excited until he saw the mouse run up to Benito, then directly around him and out the door.

Incensed, Father began to chase and swear at the cat, grabbed a piece of wood, and hit the animal across the body so hard that Benito slammed into one of the basement walls. Assuming he had killed him, Father went to examine the corpse but couldn't find Benito anywhere. He had disappeared into thin air. After we came rushing down the stairs to see what had happened, we saw Father, befuddled and holding the board and searching in vain for the vanished cat.

"Did you see that damned cat? Where did it go?"

After it was clear Benito was gone, Father muttered, "*Gamise* that damned, useless beast."

Mother spent the next few hours looking for Benito.

"Benito! Come here, Benito, where are you?"

The evening ended after Mother, Stathi, and I looked inside and around the neighborhood for Benito. We never found him.

When we returned, Mother stared at Father in disbelief and every few minutes, asked him some rhetorical question like, "You have declared war on a cat? What's the matter with you?"

The following day, we confirmed that Benito had survived the ordeal when he strolled into the kitchen as we ate dinner. Father must have regretted his actions because even he threw the cat a few scraps of food to eat.

"How many more lives does Benito have left?" Stathi asked.

Father worked the following day as a hired farm hand for a man he called Kyrios Taso. Generally unaccustomed to being treated

dandelions for Dinner

generously and above all, humanely, Father couldn't stop praising Kyrio Taso and his wife when he returned home that evening.

"Kyrio Taso's wife cooked and fed everyone who worked for them today. Can you believe that? She made us a beef stew with potatoes and also gave us as much bread as we could eat. What nice people."

Father opened a container and showed it to Mother.

"Look at what he gave me to bring home. Kyrio Taso let all of his workers bring home the leftovers. Thank God that there are still people like this."

Mother took the food and split it between me and Stathi.

"And on top of all that, he butchered a goat and gave to each of his workers some meat to take home! Look! And this is in addition to what he paid us!"

Father handed Mother the meat, wrapped in newspaper. She smiled, thanked God, took it and began preparing it for dinner. Because we hadn't eaten meat in months, Stathi and I watched intently as Mother removed the flesh from its paper wrapping, placed it on the kitchen counter, seasoned it with salt, pepper, oregano, olive oil, and garlic, and then as she placed it on the counter while she cooked vegetables that sizzled in her sauté pan.

When I looked down, I noticed that Stathi and I were not the only ones watching Mother. The smell of raw meat and its blood had attracted Benito, who like us, had locked in on Mother. Slowly, the meat put Benito into a frenzy, causing his wild side to take over. The animal began to stalk back and forth as it stared at Mother. He held his tail and head high in the air and followed Mother wherever she moved in the kitchen. Father noticed Benito's arousal and immediately reimposed his zero-tolerance policy.

"Get out of here you damned cursed beast," he said as he kicked Benito into the other room.

But Benito was unfazed and immediately returned, making Father even more upset.

"You come back here, *gamimene?*"

Father grabbed Benito and threw him out of the kitchen window. Within seconds, the determined animal jumped back inside just as Mother added the meat to the sizzling pan that sat near the stove's intense flame.

No one expected what happened next. Benito suddenly defied

War!

whatever instincts kept him from fire and heat and reached his head into the crackling pan, grabbed the largest piece of meat and darted away. Mother screamed in horror. Father sprang up, closed the window and began to chase Benito, whose mouth had clamped down firmly on the meat, around the kitchen. I heard the "slap" of Father pulling his belt free through the loops of his pants and watched as he whipped it back and forth at Benito, who darted around the kitchen, under the sink, into the fireplace, and back under the kitchen table, all the while, maintaining his vice-like grip on the meat. Father eventually cornered Benito under the kitchen sink, grabbed a hold of the meat and dragged him out.

"Let the meat go, you cursed beast! Let go!"

When Benito refused, Father lifted the cat off the ground by the meat and tried to shake him loose. When that didn't work, he began to swing Benito back and forth. When Benito still didn't let go, Father swung the cat faster and faster in a circular motion. Father spun Benito until he finally tried to readjust his bite on the meat, flew loose and slammed into the kitchen door. Father opened the door and Benito darted away.

"Don't ever come back here you damned and cursed beast. *Ai gamisou!* you dirty cat."

Father handed the meat to Mother and she placed it back in the pan and continued cooking.

For weeks, we did not see any sign of Benito and assumed that Father had traumatized the red-bowed cat so severely that it realized he had overstayed his welcome and moved.

Then, one afternoon, Stathi ran into the house full of excitement, "Benito is across the street! The Italians have him! Come and see!"

When we looked out the window, we saw Benito in the arms of one of the infirmary's orderlies. Groomed and continuously fed, Benito now lived as royalty and was twice his previous size. When the orderly placed him down, we saw that Benito's alertness and agility were gone, his mass so hindering that his quickness was but a memory. Then we watched as the orderly picked him up and placed him in a box.

"They are keeping him in the box so that he doesn't move around. They want to fatten him up so they can eat him," Father said. "They will eat that cursed beast like a rabbit!"

dandelions for Dinner

Several weeks later, the Italians announced that Benito's special day arrived. They sold lottery tickets to one another, with the winner of the lottery being offered a piece of Benito. Despite his hatred for the beast, Father couldn't bear to see the Italians eat our cat.

"How many of those jackasses can possibly eat one poor cat?" Father asked. "I can't take this. Let's go to the fields for the day."

And that's what we did. When we returned, we learned that the Italians had placed our cat in an oven with potatoes and that five or six soldiers had eaten him in a festive and ceremonial feast, bringing Benito's run to an end and once again, proving the power of the *mati*.

War!

The plateia in Gargaliani in the 1940s

Proti seen through the haze from Gargaliani

Papa Sarantis

The Church of All Saints

Nitsa as a teenager

dandelions for Dinner

Theano and Niko

War!

Tasia and her husband Spyro Mothonios

Panagiotis and Nitsa on their Wedding Day

Panagiotis and Nitsa's Wedding Portrait

The Balcony in 2009

Papa Sarantis home in 2009

dandelions for Dinner

The Memorial of the Elli at Tinos, Greece

Theo George's Balcony in 2009

War!

Mouzaki at the foot of Ayia

Mother, Stathi and me

dandelions for Dinner

Nikos Halazonitis on his wedding day

War!

The Bell Tower at St. Spyridon

The Memorial at Manousos Bridge

A statue of Archbishop Damaskinos in Athens

Gargaliani's Cemetary

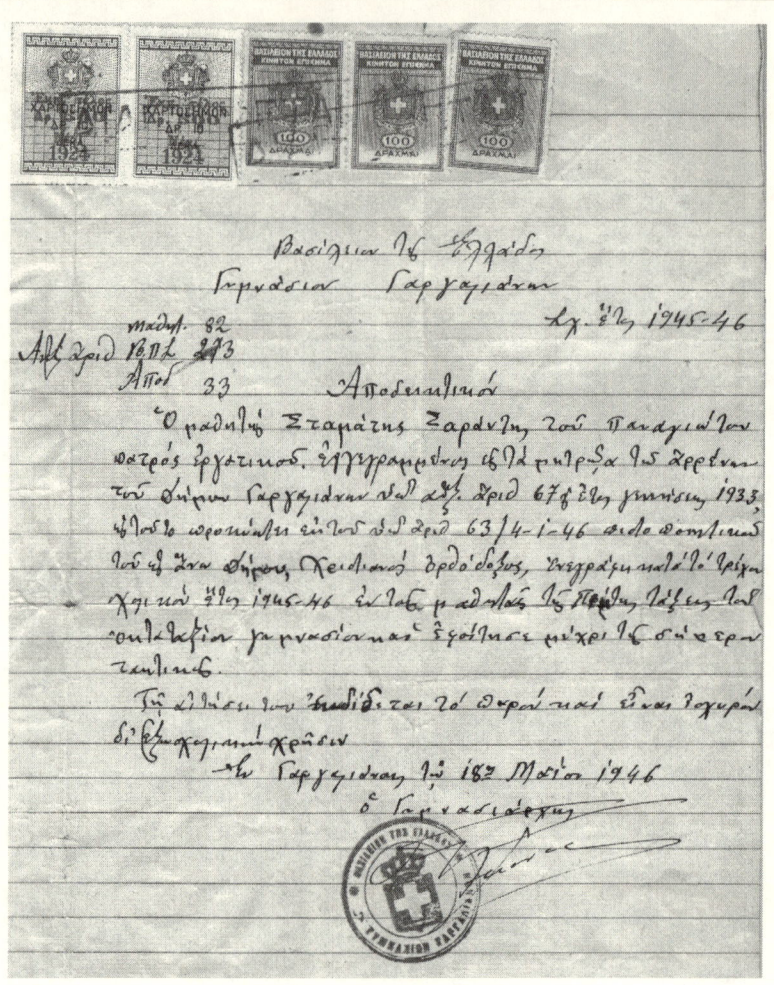

Proof of My Schooling

War!

Hard times, 1946

Nitsa and Panagiotis around 1948

The plump brothers in America around 1948

Chapter 15
LIFE GOES ON

Though wartime events on the world stage were beginning to turn, we didn't know it because nothing in our lives would change very much in 1942. In January, Franklin Roosevelt and Winston Churchill met in Casablanca, Morocco, and planned how to conduct the war. February saw the surrender of the German army at Stalingrad, and every day that peeled off the calendar seemed to make Italian success less and less likely. As for my family, we continued as we had: not knowing from where our next meal would come, only to be saved from disaster just in time, but then to immediately begin worrying again about where we might find yet our next one.

By the end of 1942, my spiritual life had begun to suffer. The more I contemplated what had happened with Papa Christodoulos, the less I wanted to be around him or his services. While my faith in Christ had not changed, my faith in Papa Christodoulos as God's able and sincere representative certainly had. I knew that for sure, he was nothing like my grandfather and so by that spring, though I had long before stopped going to the priest's house, I began skipping his church services. Sure, I would continue to kiss his hand when social circumstances required and only out of respect for his position, but I was just going through the motions. My gestures were empty and banal.

Mother became livid at my ostensible onset of faithlessness, something she told me was no more than a poisonous combination of vanity and spiritual ingratitude. When in early 1943, I began skipping Sunday school, Mother had enough.

"Tell me why you are so ungrateful to a holy man who has done so much for you—to a man who has given you work and then paid you for it? And more importantly, to a man who has done even more for you by teaching you the tenets of our faith? Papa Sarantis would be very upset with you if he knew about this. He would have never tolerated this, Saranti."

"Mana, the priest does not like me," I replied.

"What are you talking about? Of course he likes you."

Unable to tell Mother the truth, I told her an embellished version of another incident with the priest that I hoped might get her off my back.

"Well, one Sunday," I began, "Papa Christodoulos walked into our Sunday afternoon Bible class."

Our class was located in the balcony section of the church.

"For some reason, as he was coming in, he immediately picked on me to read the class a prayer. Then he pulled out a sheet of paper from his robe and pinned it waist high to the balcony railing that faces the front of the church. In front of everyone, he told me to kneel down and to extend my arms out in a position of prayer to read the prayer to my class. Kneeling there with my arms spread out and my knees hurting on the hard floor was uncomfortable. Right away, my arms felt heavy, and my knees began to ache. But I read anyway. After getting through only a few lines of the prayer, I began to stoop down, my arms fell, and I couldn't keep my eyes on the prayer anymore. I started skipping lines. Papa Christodoulos became upset with me and in front of everyone, said, 'stop butchering the prayer, Saranti.' When he said that, the other children laughed. Then I became even more nervous. I began re-reading lines I had already read. Papa Christodoulos became even more upset, and kept telling me to correct my posture and to pick up my arms. Finally, he ordered me to stop and get up. Then in front of everyone, he said 'Saranti, you butchered the prayer. May the saint forgive you.' Everyone laughed at me. Then he called on one of the girls in class and she kneeled perfectly, held her arms out, and read the prayer without making any mistakes at all. When she finished, the priest told her what a nice job she had done and how her reading, thankfully, was nothing like mine. Because of that, I don't want to go to that class anymore."

To my surprise, Mother seemed to listen very closely to what I told her, carefully weighing my words. When I finished, she thoughtfully paused for a moment.

"These types of things happen all the time. They are nothing to worry about. I don't know why Papa Christodoulos singled you out

War!

the way he did but it's up to you to read your prayers properly and to do everything as best as you can. Your missing Sunday school is out of the question. You must go. You do not have a choice in the matter."

I returned to the class and continued to attend, but from that point forward, I sat in the rear and made every effort to be as inconspicuous as possible. As for Papa Christodoulos, he left me alone, never spoke to me again and, not surprisingly, never asked me why I had stopped visiting his house on Sundays.

So with a dearth of role models for me in the church and because I was beginning to see my Father as a man who could only stand up to cats, I viewed, more and more, Nikos Halazonitis as everything a man should be. Large in size, unafraid to talk and seeming to relish exerting his will upon others, Nikos appeared to me to be everything Father was not. That spring, rumors began to circulate that Nikos would soon be married. Mother tried to get the real story but was unable to glean even an inkling from Kyria Garifalia, who adroitly avoided Mother's roundabout attempts to raise the subject. Whenever Mother directed a conversation toward Nikos's future, Kyria Garifalia became purposefully dense, refusing to pick up on Mother's conversational cues. When the subject became too obvious for her to avoid, Kyria Garifalia would offer only platitudes about her son, saying things like "my Nikos is too young for marriage" or "it will take quite a girl to tame that boy," or "in war, who can plan anything," or "in times like these, one cannot be too careful about choosing a wife."

But Mother was not so easily put off and, convinced that Nikos's marriage was imminent, executed covert operations to determine what was going on next door. Through our kitchen window, she watched more closely than ever who entered and exited the house and kept mental notes of what she saw. Amongst friends, Mother made oblique inquiries about Nikos and frequently made statements about him that she knew were at best, only partially true; this was her way of fleshing out her knowledge with what others knew when they inevitably corrected her.

Then one afternoon, Mother cracked the case and reported that Nikos would soon be engaged to the daughter of the wealthy and urbane Kyrios Katritsis, the impeccably dressed boulevardier who I spent my childhood watching pass under our balcony when the bells at the church of Panagia signaled high noon. Mother's information turned out to be correct, and within a few weeks, Nikos married Rita Katritsis. A few days later, there was a flurry of activity next door and Nikos and his Mother moved out of their home and over to the Katritsis household across town. Just like that, my hero was gone.

The Halazonitis' departure saddened me. The house next door to us, the source of so much action in the neighborhood, went quiet. Also gone was the constant flow of anecdotes and the enhanced tales of Nikos's cunning and valor. I could no longer glance next door for a firsthand look at what a man should be. I rarely saw Nikos, who was caught up in his new life and never came to visit his old neighborhood. From time to time, stories about antics he had pulled would filter their way back to us and we would sit around, talk and laugh about our town's Odysseus. These discussions inevitably ended with everyone waxing poetic about the time Nikos broke the jaw of Didoni's son, quickly made peace with the family and then rhapsodized the event with his guitar for our entire neighborhood to hear.

The Halazonitis house did not remain empty for long. Kyria Garifalia quickly rented it to a man named Manolis, who had recently moved to Gargaliani with his pregnant wife, Eleni. Because Manolis was a cobbler and accordingly a craftsman, he was referred to with the title "Master" or in Greek, *Mastro*. Mother quickly made friends with Manolis and his wife and though she tried to socialize with Eleni from our kitchen window like she had with Kyria Garifalia, it just wasn't the same. It was immediately obvious that our new neighbors would never provide us with the action of Nikos or his mother, so with the diversion of the Halazonitis family's adventures gone, we spent the rest of that spring focused solely on our day-to-day survival.

There were two events in the spring of 1943 that exemplify our continued struggle to survive and our incessant inability to turn the corner on our seemingly never-ending bad fortune. One evening, shortly after Easter, Father appeared home holding a screaming baby pig in one hand and two chickens by the legs in the other. While the piglet squealed and snorted, the chickens screamed and struggled to break Father's grip. He walked into the backyard and let the animals loose.

"What a blessed day!" Mother exclaimed. "Where did you get those?"

"Well, Kyrios Eusevios had promised to pay me with chickens for the work I did on his house and with a piglet when his pregnant hog gave birth. The hog just had a litter of eight piglets and he gave me one. We changed a lot of tiles on the man's roof, but these animals are well worth it."

We were thrilled to have the food and Stathi and I began to play with the piglet. Mother picked it up and tied a red ribbon around its neck.

"Everyone say hello to our new pet," she declared. "Now, all we have to do is to give it a name."

"We can name him Azor," Stathi said, citing a common Greek name for dogs.

"Or Kerveros," I replied, after the mythological two-headed dog that guards Hades.

"C'mon," Father retorted, "it's a pig and it should have a pig's name. How about Ali Pasha, after that Turkish tyrant?"

Everyone kept thinking.

"We should name him Mussolini," Stathi interjected.

Everyone laughingly agreed. Father turned to Stathi and me. "It's your job to feed Mussolini as much as possible. He'll grow fast and give us plenty of food to eat. Got it?"

"Yes, Father."

The following day, Stathi and I walked around with Mussolini, showing off our new pet. As it had with Benito, the red ribbon attracted much attention and caused people to laugh when they saw it. They laughed even more when Stathi and I would say his name. But even with a red ribbon and a name, a pig is still a pig and Mussolini was drawn to slop and garbage. He became so dirty, so fast, that Stathi and I gave up any notion that he would make a pet for us. Father secured him in the yard and fed him whatever scraps we had and whatever garbage he could find around town. Mussolini grew at lightning speed and within only a few weeks, had tripled in size. When Mother ran out of food only a month or so later, and much earlier than she had planned, Father took it to a butcher. Mussolini fed us for an entire week.

At the same time that Kyrio Eusevios gave Mussolini to Father, he also gave a pig to our new neighbor, Mastro Manolis, in payment for a pair of shoes the cobbler had made for him. But while we fed Mussolini what little we could find, Mastro Manolis's wife fed their pig a hearty solution of watery corn flour. And every time we saw that pig waddle into the yard, we were astonished at how much it had grown. When we slaughtered Mussolini, Mastro Manolis and his wife just kept feeding their pig and only a few months later, the animal had become enormous, so big it could barely fit through the door that led to its stall and so tall that it seemed to tower over me. It must have weighed over a hundred kilos.

Early one day, we heard Mastro Manolis barge into his backyard with two teenagers who worked at one of the butcher shops in the agora. I called for Mother and Stathi, and word quickly spread through the neighborhood that the cobbler was going to slaughter the great beast. The neighborhood became electrified. All sorts of curiosity seekers, including some Italian soldiers, meandered into Mastro Manolis's backyard to watch this once in a lifetime phenomenon. Apparently concerned that things could get ugly, Mastro Manolis chased everyone out and locked his gate, causing the gawkers to pile into our house. Our kitchen became skybox seating for the show.

My pals Niko and Kostas joined me, but because the kitchen was so crowded, we moved atop the stone wall that separated our two yards. From that vantage point, we could see everything. The pig was anxious, snorting and grunting behind the barn door directly across from us. In the center of the yard, Mastro Manolis placed a large bronze pot atop a fire and filled it with water. Before long, the water furiously boiled. Kyria Eleni fed the flames with dried wood from a nearby pile while some other women prepared the cutting table where the pig would be taken apart by setting it with knives and various other kitchen utensils. When Father approached, we peppered him with questions about what was happening and what was to come.

"What are they going to do with that thing over there?" "What's that for?"

When I asked about the boiling water, Father told us how they would use it to scourge the dead animal and to help separate its meat from its skin.

"After they kill the pig, you'll see how easy the hot water makes it to remove the animal's skin. It'll come off by just wiping it with a brush or even a rag."

In between Father's tidbits, we could hear what the two butchers discussed as they stood several feet from us and strategized about the pig's final few minutes.

"This is a big animal," one of them said. "We can either quickly slit its throat or we can plunge the knife into the back of his head. What do you think?"

From the barn, we could hear the pig ramp up his grunts and snorts, and it appeared he was aware of his imminent demise. When everything was set, the butchers, knives in hand, approached the barn. When they opened the door, the pig, now beside himself, bowled them over and battered his way into the yard. Though we sat safely atop the wall, the animal's appearance startled us, and we braced ourselves so as not to fall off and into its path. Any questions we had as to how much the pig knew about his fate were immediately answered. The animal was in acute distress and ran wildly around the yard. He was determined not to go down without a fight.

Mastro Manolis and the two butchers chased the pig from one end of the yard to the other, finally tackling it and crushing it against the yard's far wall. The beast let out such blood curdling screams that the hair on the back of my neck stood up. It's an eerie feeling to know that a life, even a pig's life, is about to end. The men herded the terrified screaming animal into a shed at the other end of the yard. Once it left our sight, we could only hear the action, the shrieks of the pig and the commanding voices of the men.

"Grab him!" "Over there!" "Don't let him move!" "This is a strong pig!" "Watch yourself!"

Then, in an instant, the pig's screams tapered off into a few grunts. And then it went silent.

The butchers moved swiftly around their makeshift abattoir. I saw the silhouette of one man bend toward the animal and cut at the motionless mass. He emerged from the shed holding a bundle of hot intestines, which he handed off to Kyria Eleni, who set them on the table in the yard and began to clean them. The next man emerged with the animal's heart followed by a parade of dark red and purple organs. One by one, the eager women received each, set them on their table, and began to wrap and prepare them for storage. With the inside of the carcass empty, the men carved and chopped it into pieces. They placed large body sections into the boiling water, and soon, the women were able to remove the skin, just like Father said, by rubbing it off with a brush.

From our kitchen window, Mother watched the enormous amount of meat that one pig produced. She saw the women work hard, preserving certain sections, making sausages from others, and wrapping still others. I saw that familiar look of dejection on her face and when she couldn't take it anymore, she chased everyone out of her home.

"Okay, everyone, the show is over. Time to go. We'll see you all later."

Mother turned to my friends and me.

"Children, time for you all to go play. Get off the wall. Saranti, take your friends and go play somewhere else."

Then she turned to Father.

"Did you see, Panagioti, the amount of food that pig produced? We should have never slaughtered Mussolini as quickly as we did. That animal is going to feed those people for an entire year."

Father listened quietly, perhaps knowing that Mother's lamentations would have to run their course and that there was nothing he could say that would short circuit them.

"I don't know why we are unable to manage our affairs better. Had we let that damned beast live a little longer, we too would be eating for the next year. What is wrong with us? Why did we have to slaughter Mussolini?"

Mother spent the rest of the evening muttering to herself, loud enough for the rest of us to hear but mostly asking more rhetorical questions.

"Is this family cursed? Why do we have to constantly starve? Is it our fate to always lack everything?"

But no matter how upbeat Father tried to be, his positive thinking fell on deaf ears.

"I have a new job changing the tiles on Kyrie Antoni's roof," he said. "I'll be working there at least five days. After that, I heard that the Agricultural Cooperative might give out new loans for the coming planting season. We will get some money then, and if we can plant it properly and have a proper harvest, we'll be just fine. Don't worry, Nitsa."

And that was that.

A second example of our shortcuts costing us dearly also occurred that spring. Almost directly across the street from our home lived the Kostopoulos family. Their house sat recessed some fifteen or so meters off the main street, just behind an empty lot. Aside from a short stone fence that encircled that lot, it was an eyesore, filled with weeds and all sorts of wild fauna.

The Kostopoulos' children had grown into well-respected professional people, and from our perspective, the war appeared to have little effect on their family. Mother once told me that Kyrio Kostopoulos was the entrepreneur responsible for bringing the first factory to Gargaliani, one that manufactured stockings. The Kostopoulos' daughter, Veta, was a kind and compassionate soul, a person who enjoyed the type of respectability and position Mother had known as a young girl. Whenever I played near her front door, she would offer me a treat, a slice of bread with marmalade, a handful of almonds mixed with raisins, or a piece of fruit. To return the favor, I would clear her yard or run an errand for her in the agora. Mother admired Veta and sang nothing but praises for her.

"Whoever marries that girl will surely be a blessed man," she would often say.

Though she couldn't have been over twenty years old, Veta knew of my family's struggles and just by looking at me—my sunken cheeks, my bony arms and legs, and the beginning of malnutrition sores on my lower extremities—she could see just how bad things were for us. One morning, Veta called me over when I was playing in the street. I ran to her in excitement, expecting a treat in exchange for some errand. Instead, Veta handed me a large bag filled with potatoes.

"Saranti, I had our sharecropper pick these potatoes for me. As you can see by looking at them, they are ready to sprout. Take them to your Father and tell him that he can plant them here on this plot in front of our house. Your family can use this area as your own garden."

When Veta shut the door, I lifted the bag with both hands and ran home. I showed Mother the potatoes and told her about Veta's offer. She became excited, walked me to the garden, and surveyed it. She pointed out how rocks covered the entire area. Indeed, rocks were everywhere.

"How can we make a garden here when there are so many rocks?" I asked.

"Don't worry, Saranti, we'll talk about it with your Father."

"I just don't see it, Mana."

I waited impatiently for Father to come home that night. When we told him about the potatoes and he took a look at the rock-filled plot, Father dripped with pessimism.

"You cannot grow potatoes here without water, Saranti. Potatoes require lots of water. They are not olive trees. They cannot grow in dry soil. Unless there is a lot of water, we should just eat these potatoes now. For sure, there are at least a couple of meals here."

But Mother was sick and tired of our chronic shortsightedness.

"Panagioti, we can use our own water, that's in the barrel on the inside of our door. We'll just carry it to the garden in buckets."

"No, there's not enough water in that barrel to handle the whole garden. Besides, who can carry all that water across the street? It's too far."

The entire venture seemed doomed, until I remembered a huge barrel of water just inside Veta's doorway, just a few meters from the garden.

"Veta has a lot of water," I screamed and without waiting for a response, ran out of the house to ask Veta if I could use her water to irrigate the garden. Though I seemed to have caught her by surprise, she quickly agreed.

"All you have to do is to turn this faucet," she said as she pointed to the bottom of the barrel. "Water will flow down this pathway, under that wall and eventually, into the street. Divert the water down there so it turns into the garden. Once you are able to control this flow of water, the rest will be simple."

My parents marveled at Veta's kindness and ingenuity. And I saw a change in Father's attitude. He seemed pleased, as if our luck had begun to change. Over the next several days, my family cleared the garden of all its rocks. It seemed a never-ending job, and yet when we finally cleared it, Father was happy to find good soil, rich in nutrients. He tilled it and let it soak in the sunlight for a few days, which he said revitalized the ground. When the ground was ready, Father removed the potatoes from the bag and inspected them. Each was covered with at least two or three sprouts and with a grin, he told me how each represented its own potato plant. "From each plant, we will be able to harvest a several kilos of potatoes," he said.

With his knife, Father surgically dissected each potato into wedges, each with buds that would sprout into new plaints.

When I moved to touch one, he sprang to life, "Saranti! Don't touch them! If the bud on the potato breaks, that is one fewer potato plant we will have."

Stathi and I watched Father carefully and expertly operate on each potato. Then, we followed him to the garden where he began to experiment with the water flow from Veta's barrel. He watered the ground, examined the soil, ran his hands over it, through it, squeezed it between his fingers, and then watered it again.

"What are you doing?" I asked.

"We cannot be too careful. The water must enter the garden from its highest point so it can flow down and water the very last plant. All the soil must be watered. We don't want any of these plants to die."

Father began planting the potatoes one by one, with each spud's sprout pointing upward. He showed us how to plant them in rows and before long, we had helped him plant some fifty potatoes in symmetric and parallel lines. Then, we saw how the rows we had created made watering the garden easy. Father allowed the water to flow down a ditch he had dug and then deflected it to each row, one at a time.

"See how easy it is? Tomorrow and for the next few weeks, watering this garden will be your job, Saranti. You will have to make sure that the soil near each potato is soaked with water every day. Even though you still can't see the plants, remember that they are there. If they get enough water, you will see them emerge in only a few days. Before you know it, they will be as big as tomato plants!"

It all seemed easy to me and I loved that he gave me responsibility. The following day, I couldn't wait for evening to arrive and kept pestering Mother about whether it was finally time to water the garden.

"Mana, it is high noon. If we don't give them water, the plants are going to die from thirst," I said.

"No, Saranti. If you water them now, you will kill them."

She took me by the arm, led me to the window, and pointed to the street in front of our home.

"Do you see the shadow line of our house on the street there?"

"Yes," I said.

"When that shadow reaches Veta's door, then you can water the garden."

I spent that afternoon watching the shadows. Nothing moves slower than a shadow when all you are doing is watching it. When it finally approached the door, I crossed the street, turned on the water, and saturated each potato in the garden, just as Father had showed me, row by row. When I finished, I rushed into Veta's yard and turned off the spigot on her barrel, pleased that it was almost empty and that the plants had gotten plenty of water.

When Father returned that evening, he inspected the garden.

"Saranti, you did a fine job. Soon, the whole area here will be full of plants. You'll see. But make sure not to water them too much and not to forget to fill Veta's barrel every morning when the town's water line is turned on."

With eagerness, I followed Father's instructions to the letter, filling the barrel every morning and watering the garden every evening. Within a few days, the plants magically emerged from the earth and within only a few weeks, dense foliage covered the garden. News of the garden spread throughout the neighborhood and everyone watched it grow, happy for us that there might be some light at the end of the dark tunnel in which we lived. When neighbors walked by, they complemented me on the job I was doing. Others offered me one pointer or another. Some reminded me to make sure I used enough water. Others warned me against the dangers of over-watering. When they saw Father or Mother, they mentioned how nicely the garden was coming along and noted that if we let it grow long enough, we would have so many potatoes that we wouldn't know what to do with them.

Before I knew it, the plants grew so big that watering the garden became more and more difficult. But with Father's encouragement, I kept at it, equally pleased to be helping the family and to be seeing results of my hard work. One evening, Father dug into the soil with a small knife and gently around a plant, exposing its roots. He let out a yell.

"Saranti! Come on over and see!" I ran to Father and saw that the roots of the plants were filled with new marble sized potatoes.

"Saranti, these potatoes will grow to be more than ten times what you see here. We are going to have enough potatoes to last us an entire year! What a blessing. Thank God."

Father continued to talk about how many potatoes we would have and how we could sell some, trade others, and eat the rest. The thought that we might have turned the corner, that perhaps our destitute days were behind us, gave us a collective feeling of euphoria.

But the euphoria was short lived. Almost overnight, Father was unable to find work causing us to eat through our few reserves. We were suddenly without any flour, lentils, or beans, and what little Father brought home from our fields was not nearly enough to sustain us. We began going to sleep hungry again. That made the potato garden our only hope, and Father began personally to handle its maintenance. He cultivated the soil almost daily, weeding away the unwanted growth and at night, checked the roots of the plants. He quickly grew impatient.

"Damn you, you cursed potatoes, can't you grow any faster than this? You damned potatoes. Grow faster, damn it!"

Father and I began to dig and inspect the potatoes so often that it seemed they were shrinking rather than growing. We were all so hungry that all we talked about were the potatoes and fantasized about meals Mother would make with them.

"Well, I can bake some of them, I can make a stew with others, or I can even fry them," she would say.

I don't know whether Mother and Father worried that we had all become too dangerously hungry or whether they just gave into a constant temptation, but without warning, they abruptly put a temporary end to our hunger, and a permanent end to our garden. One night, after Stathi and I and the rest of Gargaliani had gone to sleep, my parents quietly snuck into the garden. One by one, they pulled up each plant, dug their hands in the soil and harvested every potato they could find. They dropped each into a sack, instantly providing us with food but decimating the garden. The next morning, I awoke to a single large sack filled with small potatoes, the largest one the size of a plum. Then I ran to look at the potato garden and saw it was in shambles, as if wild animals or a hurricane had torn it apart. It made me ill. Mother told me what she and Father had done and how the potatoes would provide us with a few days' food.

"Don't tell anyone what happened. Got it Saranti?"

"But what should I say when they ask me? Everyone was watching us. They'll want to know. What should I do?"

"Don't worry about that. That is something I will handle. In fact, I'll do it right now. You just make sure you don't say anything." Mother headed for the door. "Panagioti, keep the children in here. I'll be right back."

From our window, we watched Mother walk toward the garden and could see Veta, standing on her balcony, talking about the wreckage with some neighbors who were standing in the street. Feigning ignorance, Mother rushed toward the garden as if to see what the commotion was all about. When she arrived, she let out a shriek of terror and began to cry. In a putative state of shock, Mother slowly stepped into the garden and dramatically bent to pick up one of the uprooted plants. She silently stared at it as she held it gently in her hands.

Then she looked up at the sky and with tears in her eyes, actual tears, she shouted, "The Italians destroyed our garden and have stolen our potatoes!"

The women ran to Mother's side and put their arms around her as she cried.

During those years of occupation, it was common for the Italians to raid the local's food supplies. They stole fruit and olives from trees, animals and eggs from barns, and vegetables from gardens—whatever they could get their hands on. Mother knew that something like our garden would have been a prime target for them.

"Damn those Italians! Damn them," Mother tearfully lamented. "They have brought this disaster upon us and acts like this will bring disaster upon them as well."

Mother continued on and the women persisted in their efforts to calm her. When Father thought she was on the verge of over doing it, he arrived at the scene. Stathi and I watched from the window as father looked at the garden, sadly shook his head, took Mother by the arm, and quietly led her home.

When they entered the house and closed the door behind them, Mother's face beamed with the triumph of victory.

"Did you see that? Did you? What a performance. I was brilliant! Did you see how I fooled them all?"

Stathi and I were dumbfounded.

"Only you know that you live with one of the truly great actresses of our day. No one knows it except for you. It was a performance that could only be given by Paxinou herself."

Paxinou was a Greek actress who had found fame in revived productions of the Greek tragedies.

"What a wasted talent I have. What a waste. I could have been the best actress in this country, perhaps even the world."

Mother let out a sigh.

"Ah, but God must have other plans for me. He must have some reason for wanting me to suffer like this. There must be something better in this life. Perhaps it's life in America. I don't know. But I want you to know that what you witnessed today was one of the great performances in the history of Greece. In the history of the country that created theater. Oh, what a wasted talent! Such a great talent cannot be just for a bag of potatoes. God must have greater plans for all of us."

Mother was so convincing that the sympathy of all the neighbors was with us. And as she had hoped, the neighborhood murmured about our bad luck and with the same breath, cursed the Italians. Some even brought us food. Yes, harvesting the potatoes well before their time left us with only a single bag of them, rather than with the sacks and sacks we imagined. But then again, our physical condition had deteriorated so much that one of us might not have survived if Mother and Father had waited any longer. And though the end of our garden and the hope it gave us was sad, Mother's energy and self-adoration gave all of us a boost in morale and the inspiration to continue on. Mother reinvigorated our hope that indeed, God must have prepared something better for us. It was suddenly obvious that God would not have created any of us, let alone such a great actress, just so we could die of starvation during some war.

Chapter 16
THE ORACLE

I was ten years old when news of Allied victories in North Africa petered into Gargaliani. We heard about the Allied spring offensive that put the Germans on their heels. We learned that the Allies' final assault, beginning on May 5, 1943, produced a quarter of a million Axis prisoners of war and caused the once invincible German tank commander, Erwin Rommel, to flee Africa before capture. But though the Allies seemed to be winning, one thing was for sure—such victories didn't change our lives one iota. And so news of battles won, of troop movements, and of surrenders were no more real to us than a fairy tale. The difficult lives of the Greeks continued, unchanged by any "good news" from the North African front. And it was up to each individual to take care of himself and for each family to take care of its own. For villagers with land and animals, that wasn't all too hard. But for people in cities, including small towns like Gargaliani, that was done by participating as much as possible in whatever commerce existed. Without it, city dwellers were finished.

So on Sundays, farmers from surrounding villages flooded Gargaliani's agora to hawk whatever goods they were trying to move. In fact, there were times when so many such persons entered Gargaliani in such large groups that even the Italians moved out of their way to make room for them to pass. One Sunday that spring, I stood in front of our home and watched a parade of such merchants walk past on their way to the agora when I uncharacteristically heard Mother holler at one of them.

"Where are you folks from?" she asked.

"We are from Valta," a young woman enthusiastically replied.

Roughly eighteen years old, the girl's innocent and vigorous spontaneity surprised Mother.

"Is this your first time here?"

"No, Kyria, we come here every Sunday."

The young woman stepped out of the parade to talk to Mother. Mother approached her and the two struck up a conversation. Mother learned that her name was Despo, and though I'm not exactly sure how or why, Despo opened up to Mother as if the two were old friends. In only a few minutes, she told Mother about her parents, her siblings, and that she was thinking about getting married.

"Kyria Nitsa, Vangeli is a boy from one of the small villages near Valta and has been in love with me since I was fifteen years old, and to tell you the truth, last year I began to notice him. And I have begun to develop feelings for him, especially after I heard my parents talking about him as a potential husband for me. I know my parents have a substantial *prika* to offer any groom so I don't think that it will be difficult for me to get married. But I don't think I want anyone except Vangeli."

"Bravo, bravo, my Despo. You are a young woman and these decisions are very important ones. But you must be very careful to make the right choices in your life. Who you marry will affect everything. It will determine the course that your life takes. It will determine whether your life is lived as royalty or as a pauper. Believe me. Despo, be sure to listen to your parents and to choose wisely."

"I know that, Kyria, and I am not concerned about my feelings for Vangeli. I know they are pure and sincere. But how can I know Vangeli's feelings for me? How can I possibly know if he loves me truly and not just the *prika* my parents have prepared? People know what we have. They know about our animals and our land. Sometimes I feel like I am just overwhelmed with curiosity. How can I know? How can I ever be sure? How can I be sure about anything? I don't know what my parents are up to, what they say, to whom they have spoken, or what arrangements they have made. And I dare not ask them again because all they tell me is that I will know when the time is right. Don't I have a right to know about my own life?"

Despo's comments must have hit a chord with Mother because the two spoke for some time. Mother stressed to her the importance of being prudent and of moving with caution and of listening to her parents. When Despo thanked Mother for her advice and turned to leave, Mother headed back inside the house.

"Despo, when you come next week, be sure to stop by and I will read your coffee cup. From there, we will learn all the secrets of what the future holds for you."

"Oh! Wonderful, Kyria. Thank you. That is wonderful! I will stop by. I will see you next week. Thank you! Thank you! Thank God I stopped to talk to you. It must have been God's intervention that made me stop."

"I'll see you next week, Despo."

The following Sunday, Mother readied the kitchen for Despo's arrival. She cleaned up, prepared the kitchen table by setting two demitasse cups at either end and placing next to each a glass of water and on a small plate a spoonful of fig preserves she had scrounged. When the entourage from Valta approached on its way to the agora, Mother spotted Despo holding a basket filled with various foodstuffs, dried pasta, lentils, beans, and the like.

Despo knocked on the front door, and Mother, serene and composed, opened it.

"Welcome, my girl," Mother said as she escorted Despo into the kitchen.

When Despo handed Mother the basket, Mother feigned surprise.

"Oh, thank you my child. But you know gifts are not necessary. The secrets of tomorrow are for everyone to know. You need not pay for them. But I thank you for your kind gesture."

She placed the basket on the kitchen counter.

Mother sat Despo down and moved toward the stove to prepare the coffee. She carefully measured two and one half demitasse cups of water into the pint-sized copper coffee pot. Then, she scooped in two teaspoons of the finely ground cinnamon colored coffee. Because we didn't have any sugar, she added in a teaspoon of *petimezi*, a sweet grape syrup, and stirred the small pot until the coffee began to boil up. When the coffee hit the top, she quickly removed it from the flame, turned and poured some into each cup, alternating little by little so as to ensure each had its fair share of the *kaimaki*, the bubbly foam that rests atop the coffee.

Mother and Despo slowly sipped their coffee and chatted like old friends about a plethora of topics including the war, theater, art, and Despo's family. Mother learned that Despo descended from a line of wealthy farmers and that her family owned goats, chickens, and a number of fields of corn. She had three younger sisters and confessed that she wanted to marry and that she was ready to leave her parent's home and to start her own family. For Despo, like most Greek women, marriage meant freedom, and although she loved and respected her family infinitely, she was ready to go it on her own.

When Mother finished her coffee, she looked down into her cup and saw a heavy, thick, wet coating of the fine coffee grounds had settled on the bottom. In a single circular motion, she swished the residue and turned the small cup over onto its saucer. Despo, with the dexterity that comes only with experience, emulated Mother's digital gymnastics. As the two continued to talk, the coffee grounds silently slid down the cup's inside, leaving a patterned trail of dried coffee behind. It was in that pattern that Mother would read the future of this anxious young woman.

When Despo, anxious to see what fate had designated, extended her arm in an attempt to lift the cup, Mother slapped at her hand.

"Not yet. If you lift it before the grounds dry, you will ruin it."

After some more conversation, Mother quietly turned over her cup. She gently held it in the palm of her hand and sorrowfully laughed as she carefully viewed the pattern of the grounds. She returned the cup to its saucer.

"It's funny, my Despo. I know my luck, and I know what my destiny holds. There is no point in my looking at my own grounds anymore, because for me, they always tell the same story."

Mother nodded at Despo who carefully picked up her cup and looked inside. She handed it across the table to Mother, who placed it in the palm of her hand and, without saying a word, began her pokerfaced examination. She studied the cup, slowly rotating it in her hand. She nodded, grunted, and nodded again. Finally, a smile crept on Mother's face, and she looked up at Despo.

"My girl, this is indeed an excellent cup. An excellent cup! I don't know where to begin. Nothing but happiness waits you."

"Tell me, does he love me? Will we get married? What will happen?"

Mother continued her study and remained silent as Despo sat on the edge of her seat, anxious to hear what life had in store for her.

"Come around to this side of the table, Despo, and I will show you what awaits you."

dandelions for Dinner

In an instant, Despo eagerly sat next to Mother. Mother removed a pin from her hair and pointed inside the cup.

"Do you see the line that curves and bends downwards?"

"Yes, I see it."

"Now look very closely at the beginning of the line—up and toward the right side of the cup. You see that there is nothing there but a smudge, correct?"

"Yes, I see that too."

"That smudge is in the figure of a woman. That smudge is you. Now follow the line as it curves downward and to the left. The line goes into this mark over here. That one is a man. You see it too, don't you?"

Unable to contain herself, Despo let out a gasp.

"Yes I see it! I see that also!"

"That man is clearly Vangelis." Mother looked up at Despo. "So, we have you at one end and Vangelis at the other, and you are connected by a road. My dear, your husband is in front of you. You are both on the road to one another. There is nothing anyone can do. The die has been cast."

"Oh, my Panagia, I'm going to be married soon. Thank you, Kyria Nitsa, thank you. I have to go and tell…"

Mother silently raised her hand, a signal to Despo to be quiet. The girl composed herself.

"But look at the line, my Despo. It is not a direct one, is it? Look how it twists and turns, how it runs toward the top of the cup and then darts to the bottom before reaching Vangeli. Do you see that also?"

"Yes, of course."

"It's hard to say and I'm not exactly sure what to make of this, but it appears that your road to union is not a direct one. There will be bumps in the road. My guess is that your marriage may take some time. So just be patient, my Despo. Don't rush anything. All things will fall into their proper places. The end is obvious. You have nothing to fear, my dear. Happiness and love await you. But things should not be rushed. That could spell disaster."

Mother was finished. The oracle had spoken. Silence hung in the room as Despo's mind churned what she had heard.

After a few minutes, Despo spoke.

War!

"Kyria Nitsa, now that I know for sure that Vangeli loves me—actually, it is something I have known for a long time—the decision to marry is now mine. I think I know what that curve means: that our union will take time and that there will be many curves in the road toward one another, but what's the point in waiting? Answer me that! Isn't it up to us, really, to determine our own fate? Vangeli loves me and there is nothing anyone can do about that. The cup says it. But I will not accept what it says about the timing. No, on that point, I will make my own fate. One or two years can easily turn into ten. My grandmother has told me about women in our village who missed a chance to marry someone, only to learn that relentless time had made their options disappear. Or worse, that they had forced them to marry someone they would have never married when they were young. No, no, no. That will not happen to me. Time is the enemy of every young woman. And to fight it requires brutality. I have been told and know that the years will begin to add up, that my freshness will fade and that I will never again be like I am now."

"But, my Despo, the line is not straight. Things will not be too simple. Be careful. Who knows what it means and who can avoid their fate? Who, I ask? If mighty Achilles could not, what does that say for us?"

"But if I don't act now, Kyria Nitsa, I will spend the next years vulnerable and helpless. Forget it. That will not be my fate. *I* will determine my fate. May God protect me. Kyria Nitsa, I know my head is spinning right now, but I will not let my world and my future crumble under my feet. Forgive me for leaving, but I do not need to discuss the subject with you any further. Thank you, Kyria Nitsa. Good-bye."

And with that soliloquy, the impetuous Despo abruptly arose and left. Somewhat bewildered, Mother sat back in her chair and contemplated what had happened. What she had really wanted was a little more give and take with Despo, not only conversation with a new friend, but to turn the reading into a few more counseling sessions, and at the very least a few more baskets of food. For sure, she didn't expect Despo to take what she said too seriously. And the more she thought about what had just happened, the more concerned she became that she may have overplayed her hand.

For the next several weeks, Mother hoped Despo would pass by

dandelions for Dinner

the house so that she could invite her in and mollify whatever impact the reading might have made. But the girl was nowhere to be seen. After nearly a month, Mother finally spotted her walking into town alongside her family.

When Despo saw Mother, she shouted, "Coffee, Kyria Nitsa?"

"Yes, of course," Mother replied.

Despo entered our home and sat at our kitchen table. Mother prepared and poured the coffee. Despo wasted no time.

"Vangeli and I are getting married."

"That's wonderful news," Mother replied. "Congratulations! The time is right for you. May God bless you. May you live long together."

Mother rose and gave Despo a warm hug.

"You know, I had to act fast, Kyria Nitsa. I was not just going to wait and let some coffee grounds determine my destiny. When I left here that day, I knew I had to act and force events to a quick marriage. I didn't see the point in waiting indefinitely. Thank you, Kyria Nitsa, for bringing me to my senses. I spoke with my parents and they quickly arranged everything. You see, we *can* determine what happens to us. Forget the line in the cup, Vangeli and I will be married two weeks from Sunday. And one of the reasons I came today was to invite you! You must come to the wedding. Please come, Kyria Nitsa. Please. I hope to see you there. I owe it all to you!"

When Despo sensed a lack of enthusiasm from Mother about attending her wedding, she pressed her even harder.

And in the end, Mother would only commit to not committing: "If I can make it my dear, then I promise I will try to come."

Mother didn't want to attend Despo's wedding. I overheard her talking about it with Father, about her lack of interest in walking the five kilometers to Valta, about the fact that she did not know anyone there, and about how she didn't feel like spending the day mingling with a bunch of uneducated villagers. But at the last moment, Mother surprised us by announcing that she would attend and that she was taking me with her. When she made the announcement, her voice dripped with opportunistic overtones; she would use the occasion to find some food to bring home.

So, the morning of the wedding, Mother and I walked out of the house and began heading north. Mother held a canteen of water in one hand and an empty bag in the other, one she hoped to fill. In light of our condition, even bringing home a single piece of bread would have made the two-hour walk each way worthwhile. We headed out of Gargaliani and with no path or road to guide us, we followed the cliff upon which Gargaliani sat. Our walk was especially tiring as I had to jump barefoot from rock to rock. Pebbles, rocks, and boulders were everywhere, and each step required much care because one false move could prove excruciatingly painful. Peaks and valleys surrounded us, and the terrain was so rough that one would have thought we were the only humans to have walked there since the Helots twenty-five-hundred years before.

For Mother, the lights that guided us to Valta were piles of horse manure that were littered here and there. We followed pile after pile which eventually led us to the peak of a hill from where we saw a small valley speckled with a half dozen or so homes.

"That's Valta," Mother declared.

From several blocks away, we could hear that the town was in a festive mode. We saw horses and mules loaded with the bride's dowry, the family's way of showing off the bride's personal wealth, the depth of her *prika*. Several animals were loaded for the journey to the groom's house and were adorned with beautiful harnesses. As we neared the homes, music from the bride's house became louder and louder. It was obviously the nucleus of the festivities. Like most rural homes, the first floor of the house was a barn that sat under the family's living quarters. When we arrived, we climbed the dozen or so stone steps up past the barn and to the dwelling's second floor. It was packed with people.

"Do you recognize anyone?" I asked.

Mother shook her head.

"Where's the bride?"

"I don't know my boy. Be quiet. You see that the celebration has begun. We must have missed the wedding."

Mother led me down to the end of a narrow corridor that ended at a "T" with the kitchen on the right and the home's parlor on the left. We entered the kitchen, which we found to be immaculate, without even a crumb. Mother led me back out toward the entrance to the parlor.

"Stay here," she said. "I'm going back into the kitchen."

dandelions for Dinner

I stood alone and within seconds, Mother emerged and with her palms up, shrugged her shoulders. She couldn't find any food.

"Wait here Saranti. I'm going to check over there."

I had full view of all the festivities in the living and dining rooms. Directly across from me sat a group of musicians that included a bag piper, a clarinet player, a flautist and a drummer. The quartet played some local music I had never heard before and the guests danced some steps I had never seen. Roughly thirty people milled around the room as the half a dozen dancers stood in the center in a semi-circle. In accordance with the beat of the drum and the squeaks of the clarinet, the dancers stepped, turned, and kicked. I became so lost in the music and the dancers that I forgot about Mother, not to mention our mission. The musicians picked up steam, and I became transfixed on a young man who, though diminutive, led the dancing with high jumps, kicks, and an unflinching smile carved into his face.

When a new song began, which, unlike the gaiety of the previous one, was slow and deliberate in tempo, the dancers downshifted and moved slowly, stomping along with each beat. And that's when the man with the stone smile really got going. Hanging from a handkerchief he held in his left hand and the adjacent dancer held in his right, he lowered himself into a crouched position and spontaneously sprang high into the air, nearly hitting his head on a ceiling beam. He perfectly timed his jump because his hand, forearm, and feet hit the floor together with an earsplitting "boom," just as the musicians played their sonorous downbeat. He performed this move again and again, and with each one of his "booms," I felt the floor of the entire home vibrate. Dust long hidden in the crevasses of the floor planks sprayed into the room and caused swirling clouds to dance in the rays of sunlight that streamed through the parlor's windows. As the band played, the crowd that encircled the smiling dancer became more rowdy, goading him to continue his primate-like acrobatics with even more vigor. The man obliged and ramped up his act, jumping even higher and crashing to the floor even harder. All the while, I watched from the doorway just outside the room.

Then, the unthinkable happened. The smiling man jumped so high that his head actually brushed against ceiling. The giddy crowd cheered, and when he descended, he hit the floor with a thunderous crash so hard that the "boom" turned into an earsplitting cracking sound that was followed by another "boom." In a flash that my brain was unable to process, the living and dining room floors split open down the center and instantaneously spilled the contents of the both rooms, everything, and everyone, into an abyss below. The room was suddenly gone.

The destruction that lay before me was incomprehensible, and the crack was so large that the floor sheared off right up to where I stood in the doorway. I instinctively braced myself. It was a miracle that the hole didn't suck me down with the rest. By the time I realized what had happened, the moans of the injured people and the grunts and snorts of the maimed animals in the barn below overwhelmed me. I stared into a chaos of dust, broken wood, blood, people, animals, and smashed furniture.

The startled animals begin to buck and move wildly, and a man rushed to open one of the barn's doors to let them out. As I became lost in it all with my mouth open, I felt Mother's hand grab me from behind and pull me away from the doorway.

"Let's go," she said.

Mother led me down the stone steps and we sprinted from the house like thieves, up the hill and out of town. And as we ran, I looked back and could see the dazed and injured milling about as their cries of agony cut into the noon sky.

I wondered why we were running so hard and remembered Father's aphorism, "Saranti, it's always the guilty that run and hide."

Only when we reached the acme of the hill that led out of town did Mother stop running. We sat on a large rock to rest, and I could see that the empty bag Mother had carried was now full. I was pleased to see that we were leaving Valta, a place I would forever associate with calamity.

"Did you see what happened, Mana? I was standing right there. Can you believe it?"

"Forget that, Saranti. Look what I found," said Mother as she opened her sack.

She had filled it with various foods, bread, cheeses, desserts, and the like.

"Where did you get all that, Mana?"

"Well, there was a storage area and I helped myself to a little bit of this and a little bit of that until our bag was full."

A few minutes of silence passed, and my heart beat began to return to normal.

"But isn't that stealing, Mana? And isn't stealing a sin? And why are we running? Shouldn't we be trying to help those people?"

"First of all, we did not steal anything," Mother snapped back, raising her voice. "I only took what was owed to me for services rendered. Besides, never forget that God has compassion for people like us who are in need and always looks the other way when we take just enough to help us survive. And that's doubly true when we take our subsistence from reluctant givers."

"No, we did not sin today by taking this food. To tell you the truth, at the very least, we helped those reluctant givers find their salvation. Yes, we helped them help us. There is nothing worse than a rich person with no feelings for the poor and the starving. Their callousness is one of the greatest sins of all. God will never forgive such people, and they will all burn in hell. We probably saved their souls."

Mother reached into the bag, removed a loaf of bread and some cheese, and handed me some. We sat silently for several moments, eating and watching the turmoil below.

"My boy, I warned Despo about moving too fast, about challenging her fate. And look at the horror that followed. None of us can avoid our fate, Saranti. And the more we try to fight it, the more we strive in vain. Our time is better spent praying, asking God to be merciful to us, insignificant as we are. Do you understand that, Saranti?"

"Yes, Mana."

For the next half hour and as if we were in a theater, we ate and watched as bloody victims staggered and were carried about. When we finished our meal, Mother thanked God for saving us from the calamity below and for providing us with enough food to last a few days. Then, we walked over the crest of the hill and put Valta out of our sites.

Mother whispered under her breath, "Good luck, Despo. May the Panagia protect you."

Then, with a renewed sense of urgency, Mother turned to me.

War!

"Saranti, let's hurry home. The Italians are commemorating one of their saints tonight, and for sure, they will be eating macaroni with tomato sauce. We have to try to get some."

I spent the walk home replaying what I had witnessed that day—the anticipation of the wedding, the smiling-jumping-dancing man, our dip into the wedding's food, and our abandonment of the injured. My mind contemplated each event in turn, and then all of them together. As for the dancer, I couldn't help but marvel at his agility and dexterity. I thought that if I were ever able to dance like him, I would be certain to make sure I was on a strong enough floor. When I thought about the broken floor, I was unable to get the images of the bloody injured and their cries out of my head. I wondered if anyone was dead and kept visualizing how the floor had broken right up to my feet, how close I had been to joining those who had fallen. As for the food Mother collected, I had a much harder time rationalizing our actions than she did. But I accepted her explanation and concluded that, indeed, it was only fair for the rich to be generous toward the poor and that the poor were within their rights to take from the rich what they needed to stay alive. Since our survival depended upon eating, we had no other choice but to take from reluctant givers what we needed. Would it be better for us to die instead of stealing? What was the point in that? Surely, God, our loving Father, would not want us to perish when food was so close by.

As I hopped from rock to rock and over boulders, I thought about how so many people hoard what God gives them, personally taking credit for their good fortune and concluding it must be the just reward of their own work or cunning. As for the poor and destitute in their midst and on the verge of perishing, most pay them little concern and failed to recognize that God entrusts them with a commission of largess. As we approached Gargaliani, I became convinced that Mother and I had every right to take what we did that day, that it was God himself who gave us the means to live at least a few more days. And for that, I was thankful.

Chapter 17
KANELLA

In June 1943, we found ourselves entering the third summer of Italian occupation. Food continued to be an elusive commodity, and if it hadn't been for our goat Kanella, with her constant though limited supply of milk, we probably never would have made it. Even though I hated Kanella's milk—its smell made me ill and thrust me to the verge of vomiting—Mother did everything she could to get me to drink it.

"Look at how I drink this milk, Saranti. It's so good for me. Mmmm. And look at how Stathi drinks it."

Oftentimes, she would add something to the milk in an effort to make it more appealing to me.

"Try this. I have added honey to this milk. It's delicious. Smell it now. It smells good!"

She would also add *petimezi*, her grape syrup, or even bread. But it was all for naught, because I just couldn't drink that milk no matter how she served it. Though I could handle the cheese Mother would sometimes make from Kanella's milk, the quantities produced were never enough for Mother to make it on a regular basis.

To keep her milk supply going, Kanella needed to be fed well every day. That was easy when Father worked in our vineyards, because he would take her with him and tie her to a tree with a long rope. From there, Kanella could graze all day long. But when Father worked away from the fields, the responsibility of feeding Kanella had, by the spring of 1943, fallen upon me. No matter what I was doing and no matter where I was going, I had to drop everything when it was time to feed Kanella.

One morning that spring, Father left early without taking Kanella, making her my responsibility for the day. Just before sunrise, Mother roused me from my sleep.

War!

"Get up and take Kanella to graze. She's been bellowing all morning and waking up everyone. Hurry up. Go!"

I staggered toward the kitchen door and could see Kanella struggling and kicking up her legs against the stone wall that separated our yard from Mastro Manoli's house. She was either attempting to escape or to grab the branch of a rose bush that had slowly crawled over to our side of the wall.

Poor goat, I thought. *She is starving. She's really no different than me. She's just hungry. I am hungry too. I am going to take Kanella to her food, and she will eat and be satisfied. But what about me? What will I eat? Kanella will be filled, and I will still be hungry.*

I ran down to the yard and untied Kanella. With a sudden jerk, the goat instinctively darted toward the open door, pulling me to hurry along behind her. She galloped up the few steps that led to the street and then pulled me to the left with all her might, toward where I had taken her to feed a few days before. That field was close to the northwest side of Gargaliani, near the end of a narrow dirt path that circled the hill called Anemomilos and was a place lined with rich vegetation, including wild berry bushes and tall grass. On the right of that area was a drain ditch and then a wheat field. On the left, a cliff led straight up to Anemomilos hill. Kanella liked to feed on the wheat and intensely to snap up the mulberry bushes, thorns and all, without ever pausing to take a breath. She would eat as fast as her mouth would let her.

Though Kanella pulled to the left, I had to be ultra-careful to avoid not only an encounter with the owner of that wheat field, but to also steer clear of the entity that was the bane of every young Gargalianian's existence—a beast of mythical proportions who tortured young and old alike, who devoured anyone who happened to cross his path for no other reason than he liked to reaffirm his physical supremacy. The monster was Petros Zobolas, and I had had two terrifying encounters with him only a few days before.

Zobolas was our school bully. Roughly my age and not quite as tall as me, he struck fear in the heart of anyone who strayed too close to him. More agile than a jackrabbit and as strong as a ram, he was always ready to strike the unaware and could perform physical feats no mortal thought possible. This young Hercules could outrun and out-jump people twice his age, would gladly wrestle anyone, anywhere, anytime, and seemed to relish the opportunity to establish and then reestablish his position as the region's supreme male. When one combined Zobolas's physical abilities with his desire to dominate everyone, he was unchallenged in his quest to perpetuate a reign of terror of his own creation. Teachers so feared him that they rarely, if ever, punished him. They even left him alone the day he challenged everyone in the school to a fight, and then, when not even the sixth graders met his challenge, he picked a fight and beat up some poor kid anyway. As for me, I saw Zobolas as infinitely worse than the Minotaur, the mythical Cretan half-bull, half-human who ate Athenian sacrifices in his underground maze. When it came to Petros Zobolas, my modus operandi was as simple as it was straightforward—I knew I would never be the Theseus who would conquer him and so I avoided him at all costs. My strategy had proved successful until the very last day of school.

Caught up in the spirit of the end of another school year, some students and I were standing around in our classroom, waiting for our teacher, Kyrio Eugenio to come in and wind things down. When he burst into the room, we instinctively scattered, making quick moves for our desks. I spun directly into Zobolas, catching him by surprise and causing him to lose his balance. I watched him fall backward onto my desk, then to the ground. As if in slow motion, I witnessed an open ink bottle slide down from the desk and fall onto him, covering his hands and shirt with ink. It was over in an instant.

But Zobolas quickly gathered himself, immediately sprang up, put his face right into mine, and ominously whispered, slowly, deliberately, and with his teeth clenched, "Black and blue, Stamati; black and blue."

Total and complete terror paralyzed me. And as I stood, nose-to-nose with this irrationally frightening menace, visuals of my face—deformed, black and blue—darted in and out of my mind. I could picture Zobolas pounding on me with his bear-like claws, hammering away with the monotonous rhythms of Gargaliani's blacksmith. Zobolas repeated "black and blue" several more times as we took our seats.

As I sat in class that day, fear overcame me. My entire world, my life as I knew it, my peace of mind, crashed in an instant. As Kyrio Eugenio spoke, I was unable to understand him. His words

War!

entered the air as sprays of incomprehensible gibberish and dissolved into ethereal vapor. No longer did anything in my life carry any importance and things I had considered sacred quickly faded in the background of irrelevancy. My mind raced to mundane things: my Mother, my Father, my brother, our vineyards. I thought of the Italians, my friends, and the transitory nature of this life, the peace of mind I had for so long taken for granted.

"Panagia, please help me. Please get me out of this situation."

I was sure I would not survive this ordeal.

Why did it have to be Petros Zobolas? I wondered.

In a fight with anyone else from my class, I stood a chance. Though I couldn't think straight, the irony of Kyrio Eugenio's discussion that day about the plight of Athanasios Diacos, the monk who had so become a thorn in the side of the Turks that they finally captured him and roasted him like an Easter lamb, was not lost on me.

But at least that monk got to live many years longer than I did, I thought.

Fighting Zobolas was never an option and so I quickly began to devise schemes to escape my imminent death. I could jump out the window at the end of class, or I could run out the door before anyone knew what happened. I even considered simply apologizing to the boy, but I knew that if I did that, he would only mock me and kill me anyway. Besides, to apologize in order to avoid a confrontation would have been an act of cowardice reserved only for the lowest of the low, those who lacked not only familial pride, but any bit of self-esteem. Running away was preferable.

Through the entire day, an enormous weight settled on my shoulders. Zobolas sat in the column of seats directly to my right and several seats behind me and I could feel the heat of his penetrating eyes on the back of my right shoulder. When I turned to see whether one of Kyrio Eugenio's stories had prompted Zobolas to laugh and put our encounter behind him, I only saw the menace growling at me with a mocking, evil smile, holding his right hand in a fist with its index finger between his teeth. He seemed delighted to have a fight on his schedule and giggled about it with the boy next to him. There was only one thing for me to do.

I was in a full sprint before the first ding of the dismissal bell and ran out of my classroom, bounced off the third grade teacher, moved through the courtyard and onto the street. Though out of breath, I made it all the way home, ran inside and locked the door. However temporary, I had outfoxed Zobolas. Once home, I was able to relax and decided that I was safe at least until the beginning of the next school term; provided, of course, I could avoid running into Zobolas over the summer. Thankfully, he lived on the other side of town.

But such matters are never so simple. Only a few days after that unfortunate episode, I took Kanella to graze near the Anemomilos hill. While she scarfed down weeds and mulberry branches and I daydreamed, stones the size of walnuts began mysteriously to rain down upon us. I looked up and saw that they were coming from atop a bluff to our rear. When I moved away from the base to discover their origin, I saw, to my great dismay, Petros Zobolas himself, holding a slingshot and shooting at birds. I froze when I realized he hadn't seen me. Adrenaline buzzed up my spine, and I watched Zobolas very carefully as Kanella kept eating. I slowly turned to leave and quietly reeled in the rope tied around Kanella's neck when suddenly, one of Zobolas's pebbles hit Kanella's rear. Startled, she let out a curdling screech and jerked her head from me so hard that the rope slipped through my hand.

Kanella ran directly into the wheat field and though in a state of painful surprise, couldn't resist the temptation to stop and feed on the luscious growth that surrounded her. She began to eat with an appetite I had never seen before. Every time I moved in toward her to grab the trailing rope, she was smart enough to know I had closed in and moved a few meters further into the field, only to stop and continue eating. Then, I heard a shout and saw the owner of the field standing some one hundred meters from me, holding a club.

"*Kerata!* You bastard! *Gamimene!* You son of a bitch! Get that cursed goat out of my wheat field. That animal is going to ruin everything. Are you insane?"

The farmer moved toward us, swinging his club.

"Damn you and your damn goat. Come over here. Who do you think you are, letting your goat feed in my field? Come here right now! What's your name?"

As he closed in, I dove for Kanella's rope, grabbed it, and began to drag her out of the field as fast as I could. Kanella resisted, leaving a trail of ruined wheat behind. The farmer began to run.

"Stop immediately! Stop right now *gamimene*!"

His piercing voice roused Zobolas from his preoccupation and caused him to notice my encounter with the farmer.

Suddenly, I heard Zobolas roar, "Stamati! Is that you? I am going to kill you. Get over here you bastard. You *malaka*! I am going to tear you apart!"

Before I knew it, I was running from both the irate farmer and Petros Zobolas, who was, thankfully, trapped atop the hill, unable to figure out how to descend toward Kanella and me. I ran as fast as I could and pulled Kanella who, though clueless as to the danger, began to gallop behind me. Zobolas, stuck on the bluff, began to fire projectiles at us with his slingshot. Kanella and I ran toward town as fast as we could but the farmer gained ground, screaming and waving his club over his head. As we passed the first house on our way into Gargaliani, our running excited a couple of stray dogs who joined the chase after us. One of them nipped Kanella's leg, fully awakening the goats' defense mechanisms and causing her nearly to double her speed. I don't know which was worse, being chased by Petros Zobolas, the farmer, or the dogs. I looked down to my right and saw Kanella, now in a full sprint, catch up to my side, her tongue hanging from her mouth and her inflated breasts swinging wildly behind her hind legs. She passed me and began to pull me. Kanella and I were suddenly like a couple of marathon runners—a boy and his goat, two melded into a single unit before the backdrop of Gargaliani. We must have truly been a sight to behold.

Before long, the dogs gave up their chase, but when I looked back, I was surprised to see the farmer, though falling back, still coming after us. I could only guess he wanted to see where we lived. So rather than provide him with this information, Kanella and I dodged left and right through the maze of Gargaliani's streets, turning here and ducking there. We finally surreptitiously entered our backyard where I closed the door, secured Kanella and sat down directly under our kitchen to catch my breath. I immediately fell asleep. Sometime later, I awoke and found Kanella blissfully sitting next to me, regurgitating and re-chewing her heavy meal, indifferent to whatever danger we had faced.

dandelions for Dinner

That had been my previous adventure with Kanella. And I knew there was now no way I could take Kanella back to the path to feed—dealing with Zobolas, not to mention that farmer, was not an option. When we passed through the back door and onto the street, Kanella instinctively pulled me back toward the wheat field. So I gave her a quick kick in the belly and pulled her in the opposite direction to a field I knew was on the other side of our old neighborhood, near where Mother used to take me to watch sunsets. Not wanting any of our old neighbors to see me pulling a goat, I moved quickly through the old neighborhood and past our old house. After a few more turns, we reached Gargaliani's western city limits and stood near the steep decline that led down to the valley that separated our town from the Ionian Sea. I found an ideal strip for feeding Kanella and guided her through the lush vegetation.

As I stood and looked down at the valley and at the dawning day, I was overcome by a feeling that the things I looked upon were awesome. Though I had lived in Gargaliani my whole life, I realized that the view in front of me was overwhelming, its panoramic beauty transcending our lives, the war, the world, and the mundane rhythms that dominated the day. Even Kanella had become mesmerized, frequently pausing from her meal to lift her head and seeming to admire the magnificent display of nature set before her. For the first time, I noticed what I had heard many visitors to Gargaliani comment on, the beauty of our town's sunrises and sunsets. Though I had seen countless numbers of them, I had never before paid any attention. How many times had I watched the sun peek through the mountains that lie east of us, just south of Ayia? I realized that sunrises are God's gifts to early risers. I watched as the sun almost instantaneously illuminated the darkened valley below, and then, its fingers stretched to the sea, energizing it into a sparkle of blue and white. Tranquility reigned as I contemplated how all living things, from the lowest insects up to Kanella, were involved in a sacred quest, their own version of a blissful partaking of the good things in God's paradise. I saw the perfection set forth in front of me and realized that the world was an orchestration of divine music, directed by an invisible conductor. All living things played a part in God's score.

A sudden pull of the rope refocused me onto Kanella and I followed behind her as she led me to a different grazing spot a few meters away. Despite my lofty thoughts, and without warning, a sudden and uncontrollable urge came over me to relieve myself. I tied Kanella's rope to a nearby bush, looked around to make sure I was alone, pulled my pants down and squatted. The relief was instantaneous. When I pulled my pants back up, I observed that I had left an enormous pyramid shaped pile on the ground. I admired it, wondering how it was so large when I knew I really hadn't eaten anything to speak of for a number of days. The sharp hunger pains in my abdomen only made me wonder all the more.

Just then, out of nowhere but as if on cue, a dog nonchalantly trotted toward Kanella and me, sniffing here and snorting there. It was hungry too. Still terrified of all dogs, I froze and readied myself to fight it, assuming a combative posture and watching every movement the animal made as it approached. When it passed, I was ready to give him a quick kick. But it ignored me and went straight for the pile. Then it stopped, sniffed and circled it. It apparently liked what it saw because to my astonishment, the dog began to eat it. It lapped up every last bit and liked it so much that after he swallowed it all, he began to lick the ground, apparently not wanting to let any bit of it go to waste. Then he happily trotted away. And as the dog left, I looked at it and then at Kanella and couldn't help but feel a little jealous.

Fine, both of you have eaten, I thought. *Now what am I going to eat?*

It occurred to me that Kanella and the dog, through no effort of their own, were being fed by God without having to do anything.

Why are goats and dogs eating while I am suffering? I thought. *Why aren't I a part of God's bounty? Where is His compassion for me? Why am I preordained to suffer?*

The scream of a shepherd's whistle abruptly roused me from my self-pity. I looked up and saw a man waiving at me to come toward him from the top of the hill. I gave Kanella's rope a pull and moved cautiously toward him.

"Who told you that you could let that damned goat feed on my land you little bastard?"

He quickly moved toward me, and I could see the anger on his face.

"You let a goat graze in my field, *kerata*?"

The man then raised his arm across his chest and readied himself to strike me with the back of his hand. To avoid his blow, I quickly stepped back, tripped on a stone, and fell to the ground.

"Kyrie, I didn't know that the field is yours. It doesn't look like it belongs to anyone. It's just a vacant piece of land. Anyway, I just got here. My goat hasn't eaten anything." My lie seemed to have saved me because the man backed off.

"If I ever see you here again with that animal, I will break your legs. I'll cut them off!"

I headed home that morning feeling more alienated and dejected than ever. On the one hand, I was in charge of Kanella and my family was relying on me to keep her fed so she could keep us alive. On the other hand, every time I took her for food, it seemed someone vilified and threatened me. And then, there were God's creatures who enjoyed the seemingly perpetual bliss of oneness with Him. I thought about one of Mother's favorite sayings during those days, "God has all," and I wondered why He seemed to be sharing his abundance with goats and dogs but not with me.

When I entered our home, mother had a bowl of lentils waiting for me, which I quickly swallowed, and then followed up with another. And with nothing else to do, I put behind the world of rancorous adults and ran out to find Nikos to play.

PART 3
GOOD RIDDANCE

Chapter 18
ARRIVEDERCI, ROMA

By the summer of 1943, we had become accustomed to our Italian occupiers, and yet, none of us forgot that they were foreigners, military occupiers of our country. From time to time, they instilled curfews, marched around, and even berated some locals. But the Italians were generally good natured and benign, nothing like the Germans or Bulgarians. Politically speaking, the Italians were Fascists and sat on the super-extreme right of the political spectrum. They advocated the placement of total political control in the hands of one Caesar-like tyrant, in this case Il Duce. Their antitheses, their sworn enemies, were the growing number of Communists, who favored placing property and power in the hands of "the people." The Italians were always on the hunt for Greek Communists and would occasionally mobilize and capture one in town or out in the villages and imprison him in Patras. The number of such Communists seemed to grow, even though Metaxas, prior to his departure, imprisoned every one he could find.

Communists aside, the Italians had become used to the rhythms of our town after two years of occupation. So accustomed, that many of them adopted our ritual of taking naps after the afternoon meal and remaining indoors until roughly 5:00 p.m., after the relentless midday heat had subsided. In a sense, the Greeks had changed the Italians more than the Italians had changed the Greeks. But there were still a few soldiers who decided not to nap, half a dozen or so, and they routinely congregated near the shaded, breezy side of the church of All Saints, just around the corner from our home. Those men passed their time by socializing, booming their echoing voices through the streets, and filling the quiet of those sleepy afternoons. Oftentimes, children who didn't nap mingled with them, joked around and played games. When I didn't sleep and was able to skirt Mother's ever-watchful eye, Nikos and I would drift toward them and check out the scene from a distance. If we recognized one of the soldiers, we would approach and join the fun. If we didn't or if we saw that kids from another neighborhood surrounded the men, we would just hang back and watch, which was our way of avoiding confrontations.

On those steamy days, the off-duty Italians battled the heat by wearing sleeveless t-shirts and shorts. "*Ciao, piccolo!*" they would say when a child approached and communicate by using hand signals and the few words of Greek they had picked up. Sometimes, one of the soldiers would perform magic tricks while the others would just talk and talk and talk. Though we never knew what these men discussed, we always enjoyed being around and listening to them, thoroughly entertained by their charisma, the lightning fast speech, and how their voices vacillated instantaneously from sober deliberations to jovial laughter and then back again.

We quickly noticed that there was one word those men repeated over and over, a word that, like their cigarettes, was present on every Italian soldier's lips, no matter what the mood, tone, or tempo. That word was *migia*. The men seemed to use *migia* to emphasize every point they endeavored to make. *Migias* were the bookends of every concept, the beginning and end of every thought articulated. When one Italian said something and another wanted to disagree with him, he would arise and begin his retort by saying, "*migia, migia.*" *Migia* was the seal that gave weight to one's words, the secret term that lent gravitas to any phrase. It was as if without the imprimatur of *migia*, your words were empty and what you said didn't count. No matter what the occasion, it appeared *migia* was always the right word.

When the soldiers mentioned Mussolini's name, *migias* flew everywhere. They used the two words together so often that we thought they were somehow related. Before long, we began to speculate about what *migia* might mean. Some of us wondered whether *migia* was just another name for Mussolini or perhaps his middle name. Others thought it was another word for Italy or for Italian pride. When we finally decided to find out, Niko asked one of the older boys, who whispered the translation into his ear. Niko let out a scream and began to howl with laughter.

"What is it? What is it?" I asked.

"They are talking about testicles. *Migia* are testicles!"

We roared.

"A war is going here and all these men are talking about is their testicles?" one of the other boys asked. We laughed even harder.

At first, I couldn't figure out why the word "testicles" enjoyed such a place of primacy amongst Italians. But the more I thought about it, the more I began to realize that the Italians weren't the only ones with a testicle fixation. Many Greeks were as well. Men in Gargaliani talked about their *archidia* all the time. In fact, inebriated patrons of Gargaliani's tavernas even used to sing about their endowments,

My testicles are moving
to the right and to the left.
Just look at them,
my bags of golden nuggets.

From that point forward, we began to pay even closer attention to the Italians' conversations, waiting for them to say *migia*. When we saw one of their cooks arise and emphasize a point by spitting out, with machine gun rapidity and with his palms up toward the sky, "*Migia, Migia, Migia*," we loved it. And we laughed even more when one of the boys pointed out that the cook's shorts were so short that his *migia* hung down into full view. Indeed, we soon realized that the *migia* of all the Italians were visible, hanging freely out for all to see.

"Look at their *paparia*!" One of the boys exclaimed. "You can see all of them!"

At one point or another, we had seen all the men's *migia*, and though we never knew who won the heated arguments they always seemed to engage in, to us, the big winner was always the cook, the man we identified as having the biggest *migia* of all. It is ironic that those soldiers earned our respect not because they were an occupying army, but based on the size of their *migia*.

Around the late spring of 1943, perhaps to reinstitute some discipline in their bored ranks or just to get their minds off their *migia*, the Italian officers decided to take all the men on maneuvers. For several days, Niko and I watched them prepare themselves. We saw the men clean their uniforms and weapons and then prepare and store their field meals. After several days of preparations, the army, led by their officers, who were followed by infantrymen, marched out of Gargaliani. Carts with artillery pieces and other supplies followed them. Judging by the amount of gear the Italians took with them, it didn't appear they were planning to return any time soon.

After they marched away, an eerie quiet settled in Gargaliani. With the exception of a few soldiers here and there and the sentry who stayed back to guard the headquarters, the Italians were gone. Curious, Niko and I asked a lone guard where his colleagues were headed, but when we approached him, a harsh voice boomed from the window on the floor above.

"*Va via, va via!*" Lieutenant Yenatos yelled at us in an enraged fury as he motioned for us to leave. Apparently accustomed to have his orders followed faster than we moved, he again yelled "*Va via!*" and dumped a barrage of "*fangulos*" and "*migia*" on us. Somewhat shaken by the man's tirade, Niko and I fled.

The following day, we learned that the army had bivouacked at the foot of the mountain range near Mouzaki, not too far from Ayia. It stayed there for several weeks to sharpen whatever skills of war had become dull by living with us. I visited the farm with Father one day and could hear the faint boom of canon shots and the cracks of rifle fire in the distance. When I asked him what all the shooting was about, Father was candid.

"They are probably killing goats."

I laughed.

"I'm serious," he replied. "There are a lot of goats out there, and the Italians are opportunistic. Those cat eaters won't let a chance to eat something other than macaroni soup get away."

"I miss them," I said. "Things are too quiet around here without them."

"Don't miss them, Saranti. Never forget that the Italians are our enemy. They don't belong here. They are an occupying army in a land that doesn't belong to them."

"Well, how much longer will they stay?" I asked.

"They will be leaving here for good soon. The war isn't going well for them. The Italians are part of the Axis, and the Axis is losing the war. The Italians and the Germans will leave Greece much sooner than any of us know."

Father talked about the war and tried to explain which country was on which side.

"The Americans are beating the Italians and the Germans. It's almost over. They will leave. And we will also leave this place. Greece, Saranti, is not what it used to be. And this war will end soon. And Greece will never be our home again. Our family does not have a future here. There is nothing here for us. There's nothing here for you and Stathi. Our future is in America. Remember that. Yes, we will go to America. Did you know that in America, the buildings are so high you can't see the tops of them? And that many of the streets and buildings are lined with gold? And that people there are able to work and take care of their families and are able to buy beautiful houses in which to live in and to buy food in enormous stores that have more food than anyone could want? Did you know that?"

I shook my head.

"Oh, yes, Saranti, in America, there are wonderful schools for you to go to. You will be educated. And best of all, Saranti, there is no war in America."

Several weeks later, the Italians returned. They were a welcome sight for me and I was pleased when they quickly fell back into their old routines. As far as I was concerned, their presence brought Gargaliani back to normal. But that normalcy was short lived. News soon filtered into town, mostly through Greeks with secret radios, that the Italians were losing ground every day. On July 10, 1943, we learned how British and American forces invaded Sicily, landing in the southeast corner of the triangular island, near a city called Syracuse. The American Seventh Army, led by General George Patton, fought its way northwest and by July 24, took Palermo and the island's entire western half. The following day, July 25, 1943, we learned the unthinkable, that Mussolini was no longer the leader of Italy. When we heard that, we cheered. But our glee paled in comparison to that of the Italians, whose reaction can only be described as total and complete ecstasy.

"Mussolini is gone!" they cheered. And with that announcement, the Italians suddenly changed. Spontaneous jubilation, pandemonium, let loose. News spread quickly and soldiers and officers spilled into Gargaliani's streets celebrating, shouting and dancing. That day turned into a festival, a complete celebration over the fact that Il Duce's reign had ended.

"We're going home," the men shouted.

Even if they had won the war, the Italians could not have been happier. I watched soldiers swear at, urinate on, and burn pictures of Mussolini.

In the midst of their jubilation, the Italians began to prepare to leave. Soldiers gave their possessions away, apparently whatever they didn't want to carry home and handed out things like cigarettes, shoes, and clothes. When Mother realized what was happening, she positioned me to get whatever I could. Some of the more opportunistic soldiers began selling and bartering their extra items. I saw one Italian sell a fountain pen. That evening, I heard someone say that the Italians had opened up their supply room, and Mother and I ran to see. We found a soldier handing out sheets, blankets, canned food, and other miscellaneous items.

In the craziness, I ran into my friend Niko. We were curious to see what was happening elsewhere, and we ran from our neighborhood to the plateia. There, people bantered about all kinds of rumors. Some said that Italian ships were docked at Pylos, thirty kilometers south of Gargaliani, waiting to return the soldiers to Italy. Others, perhaps the more sober ones, voiced concerns about possible German reprisals.

"Will the Germans let their ships cross the Ionian now?" I heard someone ask.

"Aren't the Germans and Italians enemies now? Watch the Germans kill these men while they march to Pylos," someone else commented.

Many Italians agreed and began to plan the unsanctioned termination of their military careers. And, as many Italians had trustworthy friends amongst the Greeks, they sought help from the locals.

A number of Greeks foolishly considered the Italian withdrawal from Greece as a sort of Greek victory, as if the Greek Army had crushed the Italians in some heroic battle. These men saw an opportunity and spontaneously gathered in the plateia. Members of various underground resistance groups that had formed during the occupation organized and marched through town, through the plateia and toward the Italian headquarters. As they marched, other like-minded boisterous men joined in and soon, a mob presented in front of the command center. They demanded a meeting with the Italian colonel, which the Italians refused, instead sending down an emissary to calm the situation.

Good Riddance

"We demand you give us arms before you leave," one of the Greeks told him.

"All of you know as well as we do that now the Germans are both of our enemies. Give us arms so we can fight them!"

The emissary took the message into the headquarters.

Several moments later, another officer exited, stared at the men and commanded, "*Va via, va via!*"

As if they were obeying an order, the Greeks complied, retreating to a taverna near where Kyrios Ladas and his clerk used to count off his sardines. They regrouped, drank some more, and strategized. Amongst those men was my first cousin, Theano's oldest son, John. He stood with the other men in that taverna and took an oath of allegiance to liberate Greece from the Germans. He also swore to take from the Italians, by force if necessary, the weapons the Greeks needed for their new and holy mission. After the oath and a few more drinks, the men enthusiastically left the taverna and headed back toward the Italian headquarters, waving Greek flags and singing songs.

When John, who was holding a huge revolver, saw Niko and me following the men with our mouths open, he snapped at us both, "Saranti, go home immediately. It's too dangerous for you to be out. Get out of here before I cut off your *archidia*."

Successfully deterred, we ran back to our neighborhood where Greeks and Italians alike continued their celebration of Mussolini's fall. I saw Mother holding two blankets under her left arm as she held out her right and solicited handouts from the jubilant Italians. I ran up to her and quickly whispered what Niko and I had witnessed. She immediately grabbed Father and Stathi, and we retreated into the safety of our home.

The mob headed toward the Italian headquarters, brandishing their long-forbidden pistols and hunting rifles. They crossed the plateia and passed directly in front of Tsironis's and Kokonis's cafés. Patrons in those establishments emptied into the mob, which more than doubled its size. When it returned to the Italian headquarters, the men spread into an aggressive semicircle around its entrance and began to shout slogans like, "Long live Greece!" "Down with the Fascists!" "We want guns" "Long live Greece!"

When the sentry realized what was happening, he left his post, slipped inside the compound, and locked the door behind him. With no guard in front, some of the men fired their weapons into the air and others, perhaps the more determined, shot directly at the building, perforating its walls. This entire episode was at best, comical, and at worst, a true display that a mob is the antithesis of logic.

Situated across the yard, a block or so from the entrance to the headquarters and outside the high school, sat a machine-gun nest. The weapon had been there since the beginning of the occupation and though everyone was aware of it, none of those Greeks must have thought about it that afternoon. Or perhaps none of them thought the Italians would use it, especially since they were preparing their retreat. So as the men chanted and shot their weapons, an Italian began to fire bursts from that machine gun, into the air, just over the men's heads. The startled mob scattered. To their credit, the Italians handled the altercation superbly, avoiding a bloodbath by showing restraint in the face of those disorganized but high-spirited, inebriated young men.

The celebration continued into the evening, when we heard a knock on our door. Father answered it and stood face to face with two Italian soldiers, one of whom he knew.

"*Signore*, will you help us? We do not want to leave here with the army tomorrow."

"What are you talking about?"

"We need your help, *Signore*. We are concerned that if we leave with everyone tomorrow, we will never make it back to Italy."

"*No capito*," Father replied.

"We think that the Germans will not allow us to return to Italy. We don't want to leave with everyone else. The war is over for us. We can go home later. Can we stay here with you tonight? Can you hide us? *Signore? Prego.*"

Without hesitation, Mother and Father agreed and hid the two enemy combatants in our basement. Others in our neighborhood did likewise, turning their homes into safe-houses for deserting Italians.

The following morning, the Italian Army loaded its belongings on horses and mules and then left our town. A garrison of roughly fifty armed Germans that had arrived in town that morning escorted the soldiers. When I asked Father why the Italians needed an escort, he told me that the Germans and the Italians were now enemies and that the Germans weren't willing to let their guard down.

And just like that, the Italian Army was gone. Afterward, the deserting soldiers donned civilian clothes and moved in the opposite direction. After everyone was gone, Father walked to the door that separated the two halves of our home and removed the nails that had kept it sealed shut for over two years. Once open, Stathi and I burst through it and I quickly remembered the rooms I had long before forgotten. The Italian's barracks reeked of the intense body odor of the ten men who had lived in those two rooms and wasting no time, my parents sprang into action. Mother opened the windows and fresh air began to move through the stale home. Father carried in several buckets of water and began to scrub the floors. After that, he white-washed the scuffed walls with a solution he had made from water and asbestos.

That very afternoon, Gargaliani's electrician arrived unannounced and disconnected the electricity the Italians had connected two years before.

"Was it necessary for you to come so soon?" Mother asked.

The man said nothing and in no time removed the wires from our house. By nightfall, we had finished cleaning the home. Mother liked what she saw.

"Panagioti, these rooms are as clean and as fresh as an egg," she said.

Mother and Father let Stathi and me sleep in one of the empty rooms that night. It was quite the adventure, and we loved it. The lack of furniture gave us the feeling that it was enormous. The following morning, the sun's sudden beams shot into the room through a large crack in the shutters. The light bounced off the white walls and in an explosion of reflected light, created a brilliance that instantly woke us up.

Several days later, we heard rumors that the Italians had never made it back to Italy, that the Germans had sunk their ships, killing all the soldiers. I don't know whether that actually happened, but the German murder of garrisons of Italian soldiers, mostly unarmed, is well documented. On the island of Cephalonia alone, it is believed that the Germans massacred some five-thousand Italian soldiers following Mussolini's ouster.

"We rented the Italian half of our house to a banker from Athens," mother announced one afternoon. "His name is Kyrio Saki. He works for the National Bank of Greece. He is an important man, someone you should try to be like. Kyrio Saki is a bookkeeper. He has a big position with the bank. You watch him. Watch what he does and how he handles himself. He is a good example for you. He earns a living by using his brains. He doesn't have to kill himself in the fields like your father. Like I have told you before, education is the only way to get ahead. There is no other way."

Kyrio Saki, who couldn't have been older than thirty, was not my kind of guy. Bookish and taciturn, he was the polar opposite of Nikos Halazonitis and frankly, I couldn't figure out what Mother saw in him.

Why would I want to be so boring?, I wondered and sighed as I listened to Mother's incessant chirping of the man's praises in the kind of soliloquies I had heard only hundreds of times before. While I liked the idea that my life's work might amount to no more than lifting a pencil and writing things down, such a future seemed so distant, so remote, that Mother's speeches never created any sense of urgency in me.

"Kyrio Saki is a person who others respect. This is what education brings. It earns a person respect. You and your brother will be educated people. So not only does education help you live and take care of your family, it automatically gains you respect. An educated man is instantly someone that others look up to. My grandfather, my mother Eleni's father, was a brilliant man. The Greek government brought him here to educate people. Everyone respected him and everyone looked up to him. Remember that though his mother gave him life, his teachers gave him his good life. Aristotle said that. You know that, don't you?"

For the next few weeks, Kyrio Saki was Mother's pride. She couldn't say enough about him and was quick to point out his good points.

Good Riddance

"Look at how clean the man is, Saranti. Did you see how orderly his things are? Notice how courteous he is. Did you hear how he always speaks to me in the plural tense?"

In the Greek language, the plural tense is used as a formal tense and indicates respect, not to mention it serves as a signal that the speaker is an educated and refined person. But Kyrio Saki's superstar status didn't keep Mother and Father from taking advantage of the man. Oftentimes, when he was at work and depending on how hungry we were, they would sneak into his immaculate room and with a knife, carefully cut slices of bread and cheese from Kyrio Saki's private stash, thin enough that he never realized what had happened.

In the end, however, poor Kyrio Saki could not live up to Mother's lionized image. A month or so after his arrival, noises began to emanate from his side of the house during siesta time. While the rest of Gargaliani slept, we could hear the main doors opening and closing, the sounds of steps in the hallway, and low whispery conversation. When I overheard Mother telling Father of her concerns, I kept quiet, even though I had noticed a woman on a number of occasions sneak into the house and move swiftly down the corridor into Kyrio Sakis's room.

Before long, Mother figured out what was happening.

"How dare that man bring *poutanes* into our house?" I heard her ask Father one afternoon. "He has soiled our home. We have to get a priest in here. What audacity is that? Does he have no shame? Does he think he can just do whatever he wants in our house? What does he think this is, a bordello?"

"I wonder who the woman is," Father quietly and thoughtfully replied.

With her discovery, Mother had uttered her final praise for Kyrio Saki. Suddenly, she couldn't stop telling me what a lout he was and reserved for him only the harshest of adjectives.

"He's a bum, Saranti, an unethical bum. He's just another stupid villager. I don't care how educated his is. A hillbilly is a hillbilly, no matter how you dress him up."

Kyrio Saki's love life effected not only his afternoon sleep but Mother's as well. She became obsessed with his affair and refused to permit it to continue in her home. Unable to rest and worse, not knowing the identity of the woman, caused Mother to lose her mind. For the next week, whenever she heard the faint click of the door, the swift walk down the corridor, and the click of the door into Saki's bedroom, she would try to sneak a peek at the mystery woman and would wring her hands and agonize over what was happening just on the other side of our wall. Her agony ceased only when she heard the door click again, the signal the mystery guest had left the building.

With each day that passed, Mother's anxiety increased.

"What are they doing in there?" she would ask Father.

"When I see them, I'll be sure to ask," Father once replied with his wry smile.

Mother finally resolved to put an end to the encounters and knew that in order to do so, she would first have to uncover the identity of the mystery woman. And to do that, Mother invited my late Theo Dimitri's daughter Maria over for coffee one afternoon. As Mother filled her in on the background, I could hear the two of them whispering and giggling over coffee in the kitchen, a sharp contrast to their usual conversations, which were boisterous, full of loud talk and overwhelming laughter.

"Don't worry, my Nitsa, I will get to the bottom of this. Don't you worry one bit."

The following day, Maria came over just before siesta time. I was in the bedroom feigning sleep and wondering what the two had planned. They sat in the kitchen until they heard the familiar click, the steps, and the second click.

"I'm going to go now, Nitsa. Wish me luck," said Maria.

Maria climbed down the stairs and into our basement. At one end of it was a crawl space that sat directly under the floorboards of Kyrio Sakis's bedroom. Somehow, Maria hoisted herself up into it and then shimmied on her back across the dirt floor until she was directly under Kyrio Sakis's room. From a large crack in the floor board, Maria got a clear look at Kyrio Saki, his guest, and their tryst. Sometime later, she climbed back up the stairs, and with spider webs in her hair and her clothes covered with dust and dirt, Maria retreated into the kitchen with Mother, whose anticipation had reached a fever pitch. Mother was unable to contain herself.

"Who was the woman?" Mother asked. "Did you see her? Do you know who she is?

Good Riddance

"I could see her. Nitsa, I could see everything," Maria replied.

"Are you ready for this?"

"Yes, my God. Of course I am."

"It's Kyria Despina. The woman is Kyria Despina!"

Just then, I walked into the kitchen on my way to the bathroom and could see Mother's face was pale with shock. When she saw me, Maria quickly gathered her things and with a smile, slipped out the back door.

When Mother heard it was Kyria Despina, everything suddenly made sense to her. Kyria Despina was a woman in her early thirties who had married a man in his sixties. She was one of Mother's newest friends. When Kyrio Saki had arrived in town, she had invited him, along with our family, to her house for dinner. It was her way of welcoming her new neighbor. And with the pervasive famine, such dinners were unheard of. But Kyrio Saki had apparently caught the woman's eye to such an extent that she slaughtered her chicken to make a special meal for us.

Mother was livid at the overwhelming immorality and could not contain herself. Apparently unable to accept that a friend of hers was having an affair under her roof with a tenant, she reported everything to Father when he arrived home that evening.

"Can you believe that woman? And do you remember that when he moved in, she had us all over to her house."

Father smiled and nodded.

"What would her poor husband do if he ever found out?" Mother asked.

"Be careful, Nitsa," Father replied. "Whatever is going on between these people is none of our business. I do not care what they do in their private lives. And neither should you."

I never learned exactly what happened, whether Father and some others had run the man out of town, but that day marked the end of that affair, at least the last time it took place in our home. And then, within a few days, I noticed that it was quiet next door. When I told Mother, we checked the apartment and saw that it was empty. Like the Italians, Kyrios Sakis was gone. But unlike the Italians, he left without ever saying good-bye.

Chapter 19
THE DAY AFTER

Although it might have appeared that with the Italians gone, Gargaliani had returned to its prewar tranquil state, such serenity was only skin deep. Underground, the seeds of strife and upheaval, which had long before been planted, germinated and darted toward the surface in a race to break through to the light. While the sun is certainly the best disinfectant, it also provides food for weeds. And after the Italians left, the weeds grew and grew.

Of course, everyone wanted the Italian army to leave Gargaliani, perhaps no one more than the Italians themselves. But it seemed that few in town really understood what would happen after they were gone. And for sure, everyone had underestimated how bad things could get. Many thought that Germans would fill the void the Italians had left and occupy Gargaliani. But that didn't happen—the Germans apparently saw fit to contain the town from their bases in Filiatra, eleven kilometers to the north, and Pylos, some thirty kilometers to the south.

The absence of an occupying force left a power vacuum in Gargaliani, a black hole that the extremes of Greece's political ideologies began to fill. Gargaliani became an open city, an unsettled safe haven for both those on the far right and those on the far left of the political spectrum. This forced many of Gargaliani's citizens, most of whom were moderates, to pick between the extremes of total Communism and total monarchy. In Gargaliani, perhaps because they were louder, the Communists seemed to have the upper hand. They were audacious and vocal about denouncing their former nemesis, General Metaxas, and relentless in their condemnation of the Greek monarchy, their hatred of which they promulgated in their slogans, songs, and graffiti. The only proper government, they claimed, was "by the people" and "for the people." To them, that meant Communism.

Kappa Kappa Epsilon, the Communist party of Greece, fed an alphabet soup of suborganizations. Three of those were EAM (Ethniko Apeleftherotiko Metopo, or the National Liberation Front), EPON (Eniaia Panelladiki Organosi Neon or United Pan-Hellenic Organization of Youth), and ELAS (Ethikos Laikos Apeleftherotikos Stratos or Greek People's Liberation Army). EAM was the home office, the political organization comprised of elder Communists. As Kappa Kappa Epsilon's brains, EAM served as the nerve center that planned and ordered the actions of its subservient organizations, including EPON and ELAS. EPON was the youth group, the "young Communist" section of EAM. My cousins, Theano's sons John and Saranti, were members of EPON. Though lacking any sophistication in political matters, I doubt that either of them were Communists, but instead, like many others, likely ran with EPON to receive an occasional handout, usually a loaf of bread, some cheese, or olives.

Then there was ELAS, EAM's real muscle, its guerilla warriors, the Andartes. The Andartes were Greece's battle-hardened mountain fighters who had spent the war working with the British to disrupt German transport lines to ships at the port at Piraeus. They plotted ambushes of German trucks, killed whenever possible, and planted roadside mines aimed at German convoys. The Andartes' philosophy was simple—hit hard and keep moving. And they were usually indifferent to what they knew was the typical German response to their attacks, reprisals, the random execution of ten Greek civilians, whether men, women, the elderly, or children, for every German killed.

The ideas the Communists espoused—democracy, an end to exploitation, and equality—appeared rooted in traditional Greek values and held a great appeal for the masses. Indeed, everyone in our part of the world understood the plight of the poor farmer and his suffering in a system he didn't understand from a fate he couldn't control, in a world that only bred more of the same. The Communists claimed that the blame for this failed system was not with the Greeks themselves, but with the other governments of Europe. They saw the Greek monarchy as Euro-Fascism, the king as no more than Europe's lackey, and the true cause of Greece's suffering in its century of independence from the Turks.

The slogans that Kappa Kappa Epsilon chanted in the plateia

still ring in my head. They were the advertising campaign for a radical, new, social order, one they shrouded in traditional and universal values everyone understood. Some of the chants equated Communism with tradition and common sense: "Kappa Kappa Epsilon!" and "Whatever the people want!" and "The people own the country!" Others equated Communism with freedom and self government: "The time of freedom has arrived!" and "The people have begun to govern!" and "The people are the rulers!"

The rest were no more than diabolical prayers for Kappa Kappa Epsilon's political enemies: "Death to the king!" and "Death to the Fascists!" and "Death to the Germans!" Kappa Kappa Epsilon members also sang songs, endless songs filled with hope, duty, and nostalgia for things like Greek pride, the homeland, and motherhood.

We are leaving our village behind and saying good-bye to our relatives.

We are going to guard the honor of our people.

We are all *leventes*

The Andartes of ELAS.

Into the fire

With a strong heart.

We will fall into the battle.

And if our fate writes that

Here we will be buried,

Good-bye life,

Lost because of the tyrant's sword

The Andartes ramped up their activity in Gargaliani after the Italians left. And all the action—songs, the slogans, the seeming fixation on things bigger than all of us—excited me. The commotion, not to mention the passionate political discussions in the plateia, mesmerized me. I used to watch such animated debates, men who were so sure of what they said that they would stand up from their chairs and pound their fists as they made their point. But, when I hoped and waited to see Father show everyone how smart he was and how much he knew, I was always disappointed. Father never took any stands, never drew lines in the sand, and never gave anyone a piece of his mind.

Why doesn't he stand up to these know-it-alls? I wondered. *Why does he always have to be so damn quiet? Why does he only swear at things like cats and weeds?*

But at our dinner table, Father was anything but quiet. Better read than most of his peers, Father absorbed books, periodicals, and just about anything else he could get his hands on. Even Mother deferred to him on political matters. He had read plenty about the Communists, the writings of both Lenin and Trotsky, and had learned about what happened in Russia during the revolution. Father equated Communism with a stifling lunacy.

"At least under the king, we could speak our minds," he would say. "If we say anything about Communists that they don't like, they'll cut our heads off. What kind of rule by the people is that? What these 'freedom fighters' are really pushing is Russian-style Communism. Stay away from them."

Father equated Communism with a bloodshed that would extend well beyond World War II.

"There is a lot of blood on the hands of those Russian Communists. And there will be blood on the hands of these fools as well. I don't care if they are fighting Germans now. They won't be satisfied after the Germans leave. They are getting ready to turn on us. They say the people will rule? That's a joke. The Communists will rule and kill anyone who stands in their way. They say the people own the country? I own the country? If I own the country, how come I was hungry yesterday, am hungry today, and will be hungry tomorrow? And if the Communists take over, that won't change—we'll still be hungry. Their promise of a democracy of the people is a lie. It is no more than the dictatorship of the few."

What a letdown I felt when Father told me these things. Those slogan-wielding nationalists in the plateia seemed so strong to me, their songs so aggressive and macho, just the kind of thing our country needed.

"But don't worry about them too much, Saranti. Those people are only after those with wealth and those who are educated. We don't qualify to be killed. But you don't have to be educated to know that Communism means bloodshed. And that for the next few years, there will be nothing but turmoil and civil unrest here. Many won't survive. Now everyone listen to me carefully. This goes for everyone in this house. No one is ever allowed to talk of any of these matters in public. Is that clear, Nitsa? Saranti? This conversation stays at this table. This family will keep its mouths shut and its ears open. We will all mind our own business. Remember, our future is not in Greece. We are going to get out of here as soon as we can. Our future is in America. In order to get to America, we have to survive. For us to survive, we have to stay out of everyone's way. We don't belong here anymore. We are not part of any of this. If any of you talk politics in public, that will be the end of us. Never forget that these Communists are much more dangerous than the Italians. Maybe even more dangerous than the Germans. Remember what we are. We are starving farmers. Don't get caught up in the songs and the poetry because no matter who comes into power, no one will be there to give us a helping hand. We have been and will continue to be on our own. All we have is each other, the family that lives in this house."

In the weeks after Italy's departure, the Andartes became a formidable force. Having eluded Metaxas, Italians, and Germans for years, they had become organized and highly experienced in guerilla war tactics. And since the beginning of the occupation, they had been quietly armed by, among others, the British, who were so caught up in arming the enemy of their enemy that they somehow ended up arming their own future enemy. But before EAM and their Andartes could take over Greece, they had to first show the Germans the door. EAM turned Gargaliani into a nest of unrest. It was from our town that its members planned and promulgated their orders to the Andartes. The Germans soon figured this out, and whenever they drove on the main road that passed just to the west of town, in between Gargaliani and the sea, they focused their binoculars on Gargaliani and the cliff-side caves that sat just below the town, the perfect positions from where the Andartes could harass the German convoys. And the German convoys, usually ten or twelve trucks carrying men and supplies between their bases in Filiatra and Pylos, would spray bullets at the caves and at anything they saw moving.

Father warned us constantly about the Germans.

"Although we really haven't seen too much of it here, brutality is second nature to them. The Nazis are barbarians. Don't forget that. They will kill anyone for any reason. Never get too close to them. I know those people well. They have no compassion for anything or anyone. They go out of their way to terrorize."

Good Riddance

The Germans were always on an aggressive offensive and were quick to pick up and interrogate anyone for any reason.

"If they pick someone up, forget it," Father used to say. "You'll never see that person again. They'll either send him away to work or they are more likely to tie him to a tree and shoot him in the head."

On occasion, it was hard, even for Father, to live perpetually braced for conflict with Germans. One afternoon that summer, a convoy of Germans on its way to Pylos entered Gargaliani and stopped at the plateia to rest. The men must have been traveling for a long time because when they jumped off their trucks. Father and I could see that white dust from the road covered them. When Father saw the men sprawled around the plateia, he suddenly forgot his own advice and got the urge to see if he could still communicate with the Teutons as well as he had during World War I. So he approached the men and said hello to the first German he encountered. The German, apparently amused, reciprocated and asked Father how he learned the language so well. The two struck up a conversation. When Father ran out of things to say, an awkward silence fell and Father felt compelled to keep talking and began peppering the German with questions.

"So your convoy is on the way to Pylos? This looks like a large convoy. How many men are in it? Where did you come from? Why are you going to Pylos? How many men are in Pylos?"

As the words came out of Father's mouth, he began to realize that he was asking the soldier detailed military questions that could most certainly get him killed. He panicked.

"*Danke, danke,*" Father told the German. "*Auf Wiedersehen, Auf Wiedersehen.*"

Father scooted from the plateia as gracefully as he could and when he was out of site, sprinted home, entered the house, closed the shudders, and told us everything that had happened. Terrified, he hid under the basement stairwell for the rest of the day, until well after the convoy left town.

As the summer of 1943 turned into the fall, hostilities between the resistance and the Germans increased. Around the Peloponnese, the Andartes plotted ambushes, planted mines, and blew up roads and bridges. The Germans retaliated by continuing to kill ten

Greeks—men, women, children, whatever—for every German killed. To avoid such a fate and any surprise, Gargaliani established a warning system, posting a man around the clock at the chapel of Prophet Elia whose job it was to watch for German vehicles on the road that ran northward toward Filiatra. When any convoys approached, the sentry would ring the church's bell, which would cause sentries in other churches, All Saints, St. Spyridon, and the Church of Panagia, to ring their bells. Whenever the bells rang, the town shut down: businesses closed, people retreated to their homes, the streets emptied, and known members of the EAM would run out of the city and head for the hills. After some period of time, perhaps a quarter hour or so, the Germans would motor into Gargaliani. And when they did, they would pass the plateia and find what appeared to be an abandoned, lifeless city—a ghost town. More often than not, the Germans would remain in their vehicles and just drive through. We preferred it that way. And within minutes after the German exit, the bell towers would ring the "all clear" and the people would pour back out into the streets, businesses would re-open and Gargaliani would resurrect.

The warning system had a weak spot, and that was the east side of Gargaliani. There, the sentry sat in the bell tower of St. Spyridon where his visibility was, at best, no more than a few kilometers. Provided the sentry paid close attention, the town had fewer than ten minutes after the first bell to shut down. And if the sentry lost focus, something that was easy to do because the time between German convoy visits from the east was random and oftentimes weeks, all could be lost.

Though the Germans were well aware that everyone retreated when they approached, retreating was nevertheless the best course of action. On one occasion, a convoy had stopped in town to find Gargaliani shut down. As we peeked from our partially open shudders, we could see a German patrol in the distance, stop and linger about a block away. All the nearby businesses had closed, with the exception of a taverna down the street. Its owner had served in Germany with Father and was a man we knew well. We called him Barba Sotiri. Like Father, Barba Sotiri spoke German. For reasons unknown, he didn't close down his taverna that afternoon when the Germans appeared but instead, invited them in and offered them drinks. The Germans were overwhelmed by his adroitness with their language and even more so at Barba Sotiri's unusual hospitality. Perhaps it was their first taste of Greek *philoxenia*. We could hear the echoes of men talking and laughing with Barba Sotiri, really enjoying themselves.

But the fun quickly ended. Barba Sotiri kept a towel atop his bar and when one of the Germans picked it up to wipe something, he found two loaded pistols underneath. What possessed Barba Sotiri to keep two pistols under a towel on top of his bar that afternoon remains one of Gargaliani's great mysteries, but suffice it to say the Germans didn't like it. We suddenly heard echoes of sharp angry voices, shouts in German, and then the racket of the occupiers beating Father's friend. Finally, we heard several shots and saw the Germans drag him out from the taverna and into the street. He didn't appear to have been shot but he laid on the ground as the Germans beat him with their fists, their boots, and the butts of their rifles. Then they picked him up, kicked him in the stomach, pushed him to the ground, and beat him some more. Barba Sotiri's body helplessly absorbed blow after blow.

The soldiers dragged Barba Sotiri back into his taverna and a short time later, pushed him back out again. This time, he was carrying what appeared to be a huge sack of raisins on the back of his shoulders. And then, in a sort of perverted passion play, the Germans punched and shoved him from German to German. They mocked him and when one of the soldiers pushed him again to the ground, we could see the weight of the sack of raisins on the back of his head drive his face into the dirt. Then they picked him up and punched and kicked him some more. When it seemed he wouldn't get up again, the men hoisted Barba Sotiri up and forced him, raisin sack and all, toward the plateia. We learned later that the Germans had loaded him into a truck and drove him toward their base in Filiatra. Somewhere between Gargaliani and Filiatra, they found Barba Sotiri tied to a tree and shot in the head.

Father was distraught at what we saw and spent the following days muttering about the foolishness of his friend.

"What in God's name possessed that man to have guns in the presence of those Germans? He knew all too well what they are like. The man committed suicide. Why would he do that? What was the point of that?"

Father's rhetorical questions went unanswered.

All in all, the Germans only occasionally stopped in Gargaliani. Their absence allowed the Communists to add to their ranks and before long, EAM revealed its true colors. While the organization's primary order of business seemed to be frustrating the Germans, it also undertook the systematic harassment of anyone EAM considered a "reactionary." And EAM's definition of reactionary was anyone who wasn't a Communist. This meant that anyone unmoved by EAM's hymns, and that certainly included the town's wealthy and its intellectuals, suddenly lived with bulls-eyes on their backs. And to eliminate the reactionaries, EAM set EPON loose.

The youth of EPON became more and more public in their harassment of reactionaries. They knocked on people's doors in the middle of the night and put the fear of God in the town. Indeed, our status as "nobodies," coupled with Father's ostensible lack of appeal to any organization (he was too old to join ELAS, his sons were too young to offer to EPON, and everyone equated our poverty with a lack of intellect on Father's part) formed the basis for the world's perception that Father couldn't help anyone's cause. It is ironic that while the Communists claimed to want to help poor farmers like us, they had not the least bit of interest in us.

EAM began to use Gargaliani as a staging ground for attacks on Germans. And the best way to do that was to frustrate the flow of German trucks between Filiatra and Pylos. None of us approved of this because we knew that the threats of reprisals were real and that our enemies would inflict them upon people like us. The Andartes didn't seem to care, and the more time passed after the Italians' departure, the more intrepid the Andartes became. One day, rumors spread through town that the Andartes had something big in store for the Germans.

"I hear those lunatics are going to try a major attack against the Germans," Father reported. "What a disaster that will be. Don't they know that for every one of them they kill, the Germans will kill ten of us? And then those Andartes will just hide in the hills. That will leave the rest of us to serve as the victims. What idiocy."

Greeks can be terrible secret keepers and before long, Father reported all the details of the attack.

"They are planning to ambush an entire German column on

Good Riddance

the road below the cliff, about a kilometer north of town. Do you remember, Nitsa, where the road winds out of the olive groves just before it begins its incline into Gargaliani? Well, near that rocky terrain, where all the tall weeds grow, and in front of the chapel at Koutsouveri, ELAS has fortified this little hill with their British-made machine guns. Right now, the Andartes are waiting for the German column of trucks to pass to attack."

"Ambush an entire column?" Mother asked. "I can't believe they would do that. They have gone insane. They are going to get all of us killed. I can't believe their audacity." Mother shook her head.

"If the Andartes pull this off, hundreds of us will face a firing squad. Then, they'll burn our city," said Father.

Those who knew what was coming left Gargaliani and headed for their farms. But we couldn't figure out where to go and just stayed in our house. The Andartes waited in position for many days but for reasons unknown, the Germans never appeared. Fearing someone might have betrayed them, the ELAS fighters finally gave up their plan and retreated to the hills with all their heavy weaponry. On their way, they proudly displayed their arms in the plateia. Everyone, especially Father, was shocked to see how well stocked the Andartes were.

"Saranti, those are English weapons. The British have been arming these men for some time. What they don't realize is that they are arming their enemy. I have been hearing about how English planes, I think from their bases in Egypt, have been flying in at night and dropping weapons to the Andartes near Ayia. Those are the plane engines we sometimes hear at night. They are making a big mistake. They are arming Communists. I wonder if they even know it. They will be very sorry one day."

The following morning, the weapons were gone, and the Andartes instincts about a betrayal turned out to be correct. Within a day or two after they had abandoned their post, the watchman at the chapel of the Prophet Elia spotted a German unit a number of kilometers away, motoring toward Gargaliani. Within seconds, the church bells rang, and everyone retreated and the locals moved indoors. When the Germans approached the base of the hill upon which Gargaliani sat, they let loose a barrage of prophylactic machine gunfire at the caves that sat just below the city. There was no doubt they had come to confront the Andartes. But the Andartes were gone, and so the German bullets were wasted. And then as if to be sure to drive their message home, the barrage ended with a grand finale, a mortar launched into town that landed right in the plateia, not far from Hilas's pastry shop where Mother had fallen years before. Though no one was injured, windows were shattered and people were shaken. The Germans had made their point to everyone except the Andartes.

Before long, Andartes were again in our midst. Across the street from our home, the Matsukas girls rented the space formerly occupied by the Italian army's dispensary to a widow and her eighteen-year-old son. Mother referred to the woman as Kyria Agni and told me her son's name was Pavlo. Kyria Agni was around forty years old and Pavlo no older than twenty. He was an attractive young man, fresh faced with a soft smile and dark black hair.

"Her husband died in Albania, Saranti." Mother told me. "She has been a widow for two years now. Thank God that she at least has her son."

Kyria Agni and Pavlo were the antithesis of the garrulous Italians. Quiet and low key, they lived inconspicuously and kept to themselves. Pavlo, who appeared to spend his time helping his Mother, was eager to please. A few weeks after their arrival, Mother made an announcement.

"Kyria Agni told me that her son has joined the Andartes. She's very happy about it. She's proud to say that he will one day free Greece from our current oppression. Pavlo seemed happy too. People were coming by all day to congratulate him, even calling him 'comrade.'"

"Oh, no," replied Father as his head hung low. "That's terrible news. Having an ELAS member across the street from us can only bring us trouble. And that kid isn't exactly smart. If he is stupid enough to be a Communist, he should just join EPON and be a young Communist. Who convinced him to join ELAS and become a guerilla fighter?"

"But she is convinced he is going to fight to liberate the Greeks and to bring us democracy once again," said Mother.

"Oh, sure," said Father. "ELAS is going to fight to liberate Greece? Let me tell all of you something. People like them don't know about democracy and know even less about liberation. That kid hasn't had a father for the past three years and has no doubt been brainwashed by those people. Pavlo is simply incapable of understanding his newly acquired power. He'll choose flexing his muscles and showing off before exercising discretion. This is a bad development for sure."

Father's head hung low.

After a few minutes of silence, he looked up.

"Remember, none of us talks about these things outside of our home. Is that understood? We have to be very careful. The last thing we want is to be on anyone's list. Especially the list of EPON. All it takes is one word to be misconstrued, and before we know it, they will be knocking on our door."

That fall, Pavlo left his mother's house to live with the Andartes.

"They are training him to be a strong soldier," his Mother proudly reported. She would occasionally offer Mother an update, something like "right now Pavlo is fighting the Germans," or "last week, Pavlo's unit killed ten Germans," or "Pavlo is the best fighter in his unit." Mother always smiled and nodded at such reports from the front, adroitly changing the subject or moving indoors to avoid any extended encounters.

As the spring of 1944 set in, Pavlo returned to Gargaliani to the delight of his mother, who was thrilled to have her heroic son home. I didn't share her feelings because when Mother pointed Pavlo out to me, I couldn't recognize him—he was completely transformed. Pavlo wore a uniform that had obviously belonged to someone else. Several sizes too big, its sleeves hung below his fingers, and its pants were so baggy that he needed a rope to tie them around his waist. But even more striking was that Pavlo was so filthy. It looked as if he hadn't bathed since he left Gargaliani. His stringy, unwashed hair stuck out in a number of different directions from underneath his cap and a thick, untamed beard covered his face. Crisscrossing Pavlo's chest were two munitions belts.

In just a few months with the Andartes, Pavlo had undergone a complete metamorphosis. Whether he was still human was debatable. Everyone in our neighborhood saw him as an animal and looked at his mother with distain. Though Mother continued to be on good terms with Kyria Agni, she couldn't help but agree with our neighbors' assessment.

"Pavlo spends his days just hanging around his mother's house," Mother told Father. "Then in the afternoons, some other Andartes appear, and they all talk."

"I'd give anything to know what they are talking about, what they have planned. Maybe some mission," replied Father.

"That's what his mother keeps telling me. She says that Pavlo is awaiting word from his superiors to lead some ambush somewhere."

"Oh, this is terrible news," said Father. "Those damned kids are going to bring ruin to us all. If they succeed, they will not have helped their cause, but will only elicit reprisals. They'll bring ruin to us all."

"Well, I just wonder how they could entrust such a mission to kids. They'll only get themselves and the rest of us killed." Mother replied.

Within a few weeks, the wait was over. Mother entered Kyria Agni's apartment one afternoon to find a number of Andartes present in a party-like, jovial atmosphere. The men drank, joked, smoked, and celebrated as if they had won a lottery. When Mother asked Kyria Agni what all the fuss was about, she motioned to Mother to follow her outside their front door.

"He is going on a mission," she furtively reported. "The men are planning to ambush a column of Germans at the bridge near Hora." Hora was a small town just six kilometers to the southeast of Gargaliani. "They are planning to attack …"

Just then, Pavlo opened the door.

"Mana, have you gone insane? Shut your mouth. Don't you ever speak to anyone about the cause's plans! You are betraying the freeing of Greece from the German yoke. You are jeopardizing the freedom of all Greeks! Who are you? Efialtes?" Pavlo asked, referring to the Greek who betrayed the three hundred Spartans at Thermopile several thousand years before.

Pavlo pulled Kyria Agni back into their house and slammed the door on Mother. Mother scurried home, terrified that we had become a target for the Andartes, now that she knew of their secret plan. And from our home, we could hear Kyria Agni's sin had thrown her house into turmoil.

"Please, please, my Pavlo, don't leave. Please! I know I shouldn't have said anything, but don't worry. These people are all Greeks, and the Greeks are with you. They won't betray you. They are your people."

Pavlo said something we couldn't hear, and Kyria Agni frantically pled with her son as he walked away from his mother and his home.

"Pavlo, stop! Come home. Where are you going? I am your mother. There is nowhere for you to be other than with me. They haven't called you yet, Pavlo. Stay here!"

Pavlo kept walking, leaving his mother crying in the street in front of her home. That was the last time I ever saw him.

Though Pavlo had every right to be upset at his mother for telling a neighborhood woman, namely my mother, about the Andartes' risky plans of an attack on Germans, his rage was wasted, if for no other reason than every Andartes in town had told *his* mother about the attack, who in turn let her friends in on the secret, one at a time and with a promise not to tell anyone. Father heard about it that afternoon at one of the cafés and hurried home to tell Mother about what she already knew. We weren't nearly as worried about the Andartes as we were about the German reprisal that was sure to follow. That prospect threw Father into a panic, scaring him like I had never seen before.

"For every German these animals kill, they will kill ten of us," he repeated for days.

And every day that followed, we waited to hear whether the dreaded Manousos bridge ambush had taken place. And with each day that passed, tensions only increased. Conflicting rumors flew around town that the ambush had taken place or that it *would* take place the following day. Father heard that there hadn't been an ambush because there had yet to be a German column to pass through the Filiatra-Pylos corridor. But after even more days had passed with no ambush, the consensus at the cafés seemed to be that the Andartes cancelled it. Many speculated that someone had again tipped off the Germans.

Then suddenly, and to everyone's disbelief, it happened. And what was worse, the attack was successful. As the Andartes waited near the town of Hora, a column of twelve German trucks appeared. The Andartes attacked with small-arms fire and machine guns around the bridge at Manousos, just as we had been told. The attack took the

Germans by surprise, and a fierce battle ensued. The Andartes killed every German in that convoy, one hundred eighty in total, losing only eighteen of their own. Then, they stripped the victims' bodies and trucks of anything remotely of value and carried the loot back to the mountains to resupply other guerillas.

Terror filled Gargaliani. Mother and Father could barely speak.

"They will come for us, Nitsa, you know that don't you? For every German that's killed, they'll kill ten of us. That's one thousand, one hundred ten people from the villages and from Gargaliani. We'll never make it. That bloodshed will make its way here."

"Panagioti, we have to leave."

"I know we do, but where will we go?" Father thought for a moment. "I know."

My parents quickly grabbed Stathi and me, gathered whatever food we had into a satchel, and we headed out of the house. We walked west, descended the hill upon which the town sat, toward Marathos. Half way through the olive grove-filled valley between Gargaliani and the sea, we came upon the farm of one of Father's second cousins, my Theo Vasili. Theo Vasili lived at his farm year round with his wife, Agathi, and their two children. He welcomed us warmly, and when Father told him what had happened, Theo Vasili invited us to stay with them as long as we wanted. Thankfully, this was one of the few of Father's relatives who Mother actually liked. And so we stayed.

From Theo Vasili's farm, I had a panoramic view of Gargaliani as well as of the road that headed toward it, as it zigzagged up the hill. From the farm's safety, I kept a constant eye on the road, well aware that the German response would come from Filiatra.

"Stop looking at the mountain," Father said. "When the Germans come, it'll be obvious. You won't miss anything, believe me."

As usual, Father was right. The following day, heavy machine-gun fire interrupted the tranquility of the valley. On the road, we saw several trucks, which we speculated were the Germans looking for their missing men, heading south from Filiatra, toward Gargaliani. As they began their assent up the hill and into Gargaliani, they fired heavy machine guns, aiming it into the rocky hillside caves that sat just below the north end of town. The machine-gun fire continued as the trucks motored up the hill. They gunned down anything that moved. They even shot and killed small animals. The trucks entered Gargaliani, continued through and out the east side of town and toward Pylos. The sounds of motors and gunfire faded as the convoy exited the city and headed for the ambush battleground.

Several hours later, the Germans passed back through town, their trucks filled with the bodies of their dead. The smell of death was everywhere. In the days that followed, we learned that the Germans had killed anyone they could find in the area near the Andartes' attack. And then they burned a couple of nearby villages. But for reasons we didn't know, they spared Gargaliani and its immediate surrounding area. We learned later that Gargaliani got a pass because of a man named Stoupas, a person whose name I had never heard before.

After their victory at the Manousos bridge, the Communists sang a song in Gargaliani's plateia and its cafés. Kids like me picked up on it:

And at the bridge of Manousos
Twelve trucks he had sent.
They were all hand-picked,
New and frightening,
But none of them returned, to give a report to him.
Oh, what a bad thing
Without giving it thought
It almost blew my mind.

In late 1943, ELAS Andartes killed seventy-eight German soldiers near a town in northern Peloponnesus called Kalavrita, the place where the Greek war of liberation from the Ottoman Turks began in 1821. The following morning, the Germans gathered all 2,500 of the townsfolk on the edge of town. After they locked the women and children in a school house, the Germans forced 511 men and boys to watch their town burned to the ground. Then the Germans sprayed *them* with machine gun fire, killing each and every one. After that, they lit the school house on fire, but a German officer moved by pity unlocked a door and allowed the women and children to escape with their lives. That the Germans did not level Gargaliani and kill us all after the Andartes attack at Manousos Bridge is truly a miracle.

Chapter 20
STOUPAS

By the time the fall chill of 1943 settled in Gargaliani, nighttime harassment and beatings became the Communists' new modus operandi. In the midst of a world war, the center of a murky ocean where the only certainty was that politics can, without question, always trump life, EAM dispatched EPON, its young Communists, to knock on the doors of suspected Royalists in the dead of the night for a quick word. They grabbed and dragged those who refused outside. There was little morality in the promoting of Communism. I was often awakened by nocturnal screams that pierced the quiet of our neighborhood. The ghostly and ephemeral crack of a firearm usually truncated such screams. The panic EAM's vampires caused could be heard everywhere and made those who were King George's supporters tremble with fear, consumed with dread that they might be on EAM's hit list.

Though I never got used to them, the night-time cries eventually became common and fell into a pattern whereby each morning we would learn who the Communists had executed the night before—the day's first order of business. Oftentimes, we knew the victim. And growing each day in confidence and stature, EAM augmented its assassinations with a campaign to replace Gargaliani's civil servants with known Communists. I remember once hearing that they summarily sent home the town's judge and replaced him with the town's charcoal salesman, a man whose only qualification for the job was that he was a Communist.

In the middle of all this, as people did what they had to do to survive and to live their lives, Mother was greeted with news that one of the daughters of my late Theo Dimitri, Mother's cousin Maria, was going to be married. Ever since Theo Dimitri's death three or so years earlier, our family's relationship with his family had been at best, bumpy. Mother was friendly enough with the girls, but there was always an uneasy tension in the air, a stiffness perhaps caused by the fact that no one ever seemed to be able to let down her guard in the presence of the other. It was as if Theo Dimitri's wife and daughters knew that Mother gossiped about them when they weren't around and that Mother knew the girls gossiped about her when she wasn't around. And, of course, they were all correct. That made for a chronic awkwardness amongst the family members that in turn led to a preference for avoidance. Mother wasn't shy about lambasting any of them at the drop of a hat.

"Those girls shouldn't be trusted with anything," she used to say. "They are so stupid. And have you seen how they talk? Va va va va va. They act like everything they have to say is so important."

Mother thought manipulating them was child's play and laughed at how easily she could extract whatever secrets my cousins happened to be carrying around. And it was in one of those manipulative conversations with Maria that Mother learned of a relationship between her and a young man named Panagi. Mother knew the boy and told Father that she approved of him and especially liked his stable trade as a cobbler.

"He is made from good material. He will make a fine husband for Maria," she said.

Maria and Panagi's engagement became official when the couple participated in a ceremony that included Papa Christodoulos. The priest blessed the couple and the engagement rings they would wear on the ring fingers of their left hands, until their marriage when they would wear them on the right. Surprisingly, Mother actually participated in the engagement ceremony, an unexpected honor. It was nice to see her, for the first time I could remember, involved in a family event that transcended my immediate family's survival. It had been a long time since we had felt part of something bigger and that made us, especially Mother, happy. The togetherness caused everyone to let their guard down, and Mother took part in Maria's wedding preparations, helping the girl make decisions about various details. At home, she often lamented about what a shame it was that my Theo Dimitri wasn't there to partake of all this joy. As for me, I was called upon to run little errands. I loved the festive atmosphere almost as much as the feeling of importance my responsibilities gave me.

As the big day approached, the neighborhood began to swell with excitement. With only the mention of the coming day, the Pavlovian mouths of the neighborhood children watered in anticipation of the unimaginable sweets that would be doled out. But as had become a pattern for us, the big day became just another let-down. The night before the ceremony, after the neighborhood had gone to sleep, murmurs that pierced the quiet of the night soon awoke me. At first, the sounds frightened me and I wondered whether ghosts had appeared.

"Mana," I called.

"Soot!" she replied. "Silence!"

In the darkness, I could see that my parents were already awake and standing on top of their bed with their ears pressed against the wall that separated our home from that of my late Theo Dimitri. With their ears so positioned, they could clearly hear the conversation next door and figured out that our relatives were having a family meeting prior to the wedding, going over various details. The dour and unapproachable Thea Fotini, my late Theo Dimitri's wife, barked out orders to her daughters and even from across the room, I too could discern some of what she said.

"Make sure there is enough food out for everyone to eat. And enough for everyone to drink. When the children from the neighborhood show up, don't give them more than one thing to eat. And above all, all of us have to keep an eye on Nitsa."

There was a pause.

"Nitsa's pushed and shoved her way into this wedding, and I am sure she is up to something. Eleni, it's up to you to be sure to keep an eye on her at all times, especially if she goes near the kitchen. We don't need any surprises tomorrow. Nitsa will rob us blind if we let her. She'll take all our food, and we can't allow that to happen."

As Thea Fotini spoke, Mother, obviously stunned, repeated what she heard as an amalgam of distress, sadness, and anger wrapped her. All the joy, all the anticipation, the innocent feelings of family togetherness had, with only a few words from my aunt's mouth, became instantly petrified. When Mother regained her composure after a few minutes, she erupted in a stew of hurt, anger, and cynicism.

"Those lousy *poutanes*. I have been doing so much for those stupid girls, and this is my thanks?"

Father remained silent.

"That's it. Fotini doesn't have to worry one bit about Eleni or any of those useless girls having to watch any of us."

Mother spoke with her eyes so wide open and so piercing that I could almost feel the heat coming off them.

"None of us will go to the wedding tomorrow!"

This soap opera, however troubling to Mother, caused Father to giggle. He pressed his ear harder against the wall, and I could see he was smiling.

"You're right, Nitsa, you're right. Yes, those stupid girls. I can't believe what I'm hearing. This is an outrage. None of us will attend the wedding tomorrow. Is that clear? Saranti, that goes for you and Stathi as well. When the wedding is going on next door, we will all stay home."

Though Father giggled some more at Mother's dysfunctional family, I wasn't laughing. I knew that my fun with my aunts, my feelings of belonging, and most importantly my anticipation of eating every kind of treat imaginable, had ended.

The following day, Mother pulled Theano aside when she saw her sister heading toward the festivities. She told her what had happened, what we had heard, and why we would not be stopping by our neighbor's house to wish the new couple well. Theano, in turn, passed the information along to Thea Fotini, apprising her of the fact that she need not worry about keeping an eye on her sister that day.

Once again, the actions of these irrational adults left me in the dust. Commanded to stay away from my relatives' home and relegated instead to watching the other neighborhood kids eating treats from the reception was the very definition of agony. While I knew I no longer belonged at the celebration and that my carefree feelings of love and belonging were illusory, my head swirled in a confusion of how everything had changed so much, so fast. So I stayed back and watched the wedding house as Gargaliani, dressed in smiles and its Sunday best, paraded in and out to congratulate the newlyweds. I nearly vomited when I watched children emerge and sloppily shove pastries in their mouths, pastries I had been planning for weeks to eat myself.

At one point, someone must have told Katina that I was outside watching her house because she came to the porch and called me in,

"Come in, Saranti, I have prepared some sweets for you, c'mon my boy."

But I ignored her, stood motionless and didn't respond. When Katina persisted, I sadly turned and entered my house. Mother, who witnessed the exchange, must have felt for me because when I came in, she hugged me and brought me into the kitchen where she consoled me with soothing words and a little fig preserve to eat.

One morning that fall, Father entered the house with an ominous announcement: "They killed Barba Mitso last night."

Barba Mitso was a farmer of means. The man had ten times the land we did and, unlike us, had such good harvests during the war that his family had not known hunger. Barba Mitso's holdings were enviable, and he never had a problem feeding himself or his family. I can only guess the man's success and wealth had carried a sense of impunity because Barba Mitso wasn't shy about telling the Communists what he thought of them when they knocked on his door for support. Brash Royalists with money like him were number-one enemies to the Communists. Barba Mitso had long before become a marked man, most likely during one of his typical rants at one of the cafés. Father had heard him pontificate many times.

"I can't stand listening to that 'rule by the people' and that 'people are the masters' garbage," Barba Mitso used to say. "It turns my stomach when I hear it. We are going to listen to the people who made the charcoal salesman the town's judge? What stupidity!"

Perhaps there was nothing more important to survive the war than to keep one's mouth shut. In order to avoid a fate like that of Barba Mitso, Father had long before begun avoiding extended stays in coffee houses, opting instead to work long hours at our fields. Each night, he returned home exhausted, only to wash up, eat whatever food we might have scraped together, and go to sleep early. He tried as best as he could to live this routine.

"Carelessness in the cafés is the quickest way to attract visitors to your home in the middle of the night," he used to say.

While the Andartes stepped up their attacks on Germans in the fall of 1943, they became even more aggressive toward Greeks who threatened them, typically people like Barba Mitso, garrulous Royalists with means. Bullying and killing without repercussion, EAM became filled with hubris and excess—what Greeks millennia before had identified as man's most fatal of flaws—and paraded as if they were on top of the world with their highhanded tactics. But EAM couldn't escape the fact that most of its henchmen were no more than young deviants, adolescents intoxicated by a political ideology they used to mask a brutal and base lust for power advanced with a corrupt intrepidness. Their thoughtlessness quashed whatever rationality might have existed within them, and so it was with great zeal that the Communists stepped up their pursuit, one by one, of "reactionaries." And in their wake, they left behind a red river, a body of tainted water filled with the blood of their fellow Greeks, human beings whose lives they indiscriminately took the liberty of truncating. And it was in the deep scarlet of that river that the Communists left the widows and orphans of their brothers to drown. As bad as the depression, the famine, the Italians, and the Germans were to the Greeks, Greek Communists were worse—much worse.

With the Communists challenging the status quo even more than the Italians, something had to give. Some Royalists, fearing they might be next on EAM's to-do list, fled Gargaliani one night and made the eleven-kilometer trek north to the German base at Filiatra. They knocked on the door of the German command and asked the Nazis for protection. They laid out for them the situation in Gargaliani: the polarization of left and right, the nighttime killings, and the opportunity the Germans had to enlist the Greeks in help quell the Communist insurgency. The Germans had no illusions that these Greeks were pro-Nazi, but they welcomed any Greek that might help them keep the disruptive Andartes off balance. They had already recruited a famous Andartes killer from Mouzousta, a small village south of Gargaliani. His name was Stoupas.

Stoupas made a name for himself when, shortly after the commencement of the war, he shunned invitations to join EAM. He had been an intrepid fighter in the Greek army and apparently disliked the Communists so much that he sided with the Nazis, identifying an alliance with them as the quickest way to return King George II to his throne. Stoupas killed many Andartes, and the Andartes made killing Stoupas a priority. But he was elusive, always on the move, and impossible to pin down. He was also heavily armed and traveled with fierce bodyguards who never left his side. Also, it has been said that Stoupas traveled with a piece of *ton tymion stavro* on a chain around his neck: a small piece of the actual cross upon which Christ was crucified, a sliver of wood that was said to protect him wherever he went.

With the Nazi's blessings, Stoupas and his men conducted raid after raid in south-central Peloponnesus. They were so successful that people literally called Stoupas the "Andarte-killer." One afternoon, I found myself in the middle of the plateia when a truck filled with fifteen or twenty Andartes pulled up to Kokonis's café. The men inside the truck were armed, and an enormous machine-gun sat atop their vehicle. Someone said they were on their way to Mouzousta and that one way or another, they were finally going to bring Stoupas to justice, dead or alive. I didn't recognize any of them and heard someone say that this posse had been made up of the toughest men from other towns for this specific mission. Amongst the Royalists in Gargaliani, Stoupas had earned an almost mythical, Achilles-like warrior status and the thought that his run was about to end made everyone in the plateia that afternoon somber and sober. I watched as the truck's engine cranked up and as the determined, hard-faced men loaded in, rumbled off, and disappeared.

I happened to be in the plateia several hours later when that same truck returned and pulled back in front of Kokonis's café. People there gathered to watch the anticipated unloading of Stoupas's body. Instead, they watched the Andartes unload, one by one, their own newly dead, clad in their ragged clothes with their ragged clerical beards. I saw the Andartes lay the bodies, side by side, at the edge of the plateia right across from the café. Most had been shot in the head with a single bullet. I later heard that Stoupas knew the Andartes were coming, outmaneuvered them, and with his men, he killed nearly all of them. It was a miracle that some survived.

A few days passed, and a detachment of Germans came through town. Without stopping, they steered south toward Mouzousta where they picked up Stoupas and some of his men and returned with them to their base in Filiatra. Stoupas became the German's main organizer of a collaborating force of Greeks that the Germans formed to counter the increasing Andartes threat.

One afternoon that fall, Stoupas and the Germans made their move on Gargaliani. We heard them coming when the sentry at the outpost of Prophet Elia chapel noticed an unusually long column of German trucks weaving in and out of the olive groves and heading south from Filiatra toward Gargaliani. There were more than fifteen vehicles including two sedans with officers seated inside. The sentry rang the bells, which prompted the other sentries in the other towers to ring their bells. Filled with the clangs of the bell towers, the town shut down within minutes and EAM's high command fled to their designated safe zones north of the city and away from the main road.

The German column worked its way into town and, rather than proceeding through to Pylos as expected, stopped in the plateia. Uniformed Germans and Greeks in regular Greek Army uniforms fully equipped with the King's insignia spilled out of the vehicles. When the officers emerged, there was Stoupas himself with various members of the German high command. They barked out orders and the soldiers secured the square and then fanned out into the streets, on the hunt for members of EAM and ELAS. German and Greek sentries assumed positions around town, and within an hour or so and without a single bullet being fired, the town was under Stoupas's and German control. Soldiers returned to the plateia with captured Communists, sent home whatever stragglers they found in the tavernas, imposed a general curfew, and searched the homes of suspected EAM members.

The following day, the German-led occupation remained in town, but things somewhat returned to normal. Stores re-opened and people resumed their regular routines. Father and I left the house for the fields with Kanella in tow. Careful to avoid our new occupiers, we left Gargaliani through a back way near the water reservoir in hopes we could remain incognito. But at the reservoir, two Greek soldiers immediately stopped us.

"Who are you?" one asked.

"I am Panagioti Stamatis, and this is my son. We are going to our fields to work."

"Where do you live?" asked the other.

"We live right over there. I was born here."

The man looked at his list, apparently full of the town's "wanted" people and when he didn't find Father's name, his demeanor changed.

"Thank you, Kyrie. You may proceed."

"How long are you going to be here?" asked Father.

"As long as it takes to make sure that those Communists never come back. They have killed many. They have even killed members of our families. They won't kill another Greek unless they first go through us."

"Long live Greece," Father replied.

"Yes, long live Greece."

Father smiled at the soldier and we continued walking toward the farm.

"You know, Saranti, it's a good thing that those men are here. Now things will settle down a little."

"I hope that the beatings and the killings will stop," I replied.

"No, Saranti, the beatings and the killings will continue. The only difference is that the Communists will now be the victims."

"But at least those Communists will be getting what's coming to them," I replied.

Father's face fell when he heard me.

"No, Saranti, killing only begets more killing. Don't forget that. In the end, all we will have is two opposing forces killing each other. It won't matter who is on which side anymore or who pulls the trigger, because the more killing there is, the more reasons each side will have to continue the killing. And both sides will point to the other's atrocities as evidence that their killing is just. None of it will make any sense. If you really think about it, Saranti, the Royalists aren't so different from the Communists. Both are the agents of governments outside of Greece. The Communists are really only the agents of Moscow—the Royalists, of the Germans. What's the difference? What Greece really needs is once and for all to be governed by Greeks. Here we invented democracy and still, we can't get ourselves out of the mindset of being occupied. The Turks were here for four-hundred years, Saranti. Now the Russians and the Germans are trying to take us. What's the difference? Any government has to be comprised of Greeks and must serve the Greeks. It can't be any other way."

The more Father spoke, the more fire filled his eyes and the stronger his voice became.

"Saranti, it saddens me to say that Greece will remain polarized for many years. Strife and turmoil will reign here for a long time. But your future is not here, Saranti. It is in America. All of our futures are in America."

Within a few days, the German soldiers returned to their base in Filiatra, while a small contingent of the Greek protective forces remained in Gargaliani. And after they secured the city and continued to jail the opposition, they looked to enlarge their ranks through a recruiting effort. For the next few weeks, men from the town lined up to join the Royalist fighters. Most of those who tried to sign up were no more than known Royalists who understood that their greatest strength lie in banding together in numbers and that they would be crushed under the iron fist of Communism if EAM came out on top in the end. The men who were accepted received a uniform that included a new pair of boots and berets emblazoned with the King's insignia. They were immediately sent to training.

But there was another group eager to enlist in the protective forces: the hungry. It was well known that Stoupas and the Germans fed each of their soldiers two meals a day plus a loaf of bread. That alone prompted a number of Father's friends to sign up and to rave to Father about how well they had been eating. That was when Father came home one night with his head filled with ideas of enlisting in the king's army.

"You're going to do what?" asked Mother.

"That's right. If I join them, I can ensure some kind of food supply for us. At the very least, I'll be able to bring home a loaf of bread every day."

Mother thought about it for a moment.

"So you'll eat the noon meal and bring the bread and the evening meal home to us to eat?" said Mother.

Father's plan, specifically the prospect of eating a loaf of bread every day, excited everyone. For reasons I don't know, none of us, including Mother, worried about Father getting hurt, or even worse, that the Communists might in the end win, leaving Father most certainly dead and the rest of us at their mercy. But bread tends to trump everything, and we were thrilled about the prospect of a regular supply of food.

So the following day, Father groomed himself as best as he could, put on his American suit, shined his decrepit shoes, set his hat on his bald head and walked to the Royalist's recruiting office, situated in Gargaliani's mayor's office. The officers there examined Father's record and quizzed him about his political affiliations, specifically his loyalty to King George. The interview went smoothly until someone in the office asked if Father was related to the Communist "Stamatis," a man who had been imprisoned in Patras. Though Father knew of this other Stamatis, a distant third cousin, he adroitly denied any involvement with him, declaring to the recruiters, "I do not know him." Then, when all systems seemed to be a go, one of the bureaucrats found Father's name in the town's birth registry.

"Panagioti Stamati? Are you the Panagioti Stamati, the son of Anthony? Were you born in 1893?"

"Yes," said Father.

With the cut-off age for the protective forces set at fifty, Father was a few months past the deadline. I don't know why such rule rigidity was applied to him at that time, but his age was immediately deemed to preclude his participation in the forces. Father was, once again, rejected. When he returned home, he told Mother what happened, about his disappointment and his dashed hopes. But I can't help but think that deep down, Father was at least somewhat relieved. What good was a loaf of bread to keep you alive if you were just going to be shot to death?

Mother greeted Father's news with unusual compassion and clear-headedness.

"Panagioti, we are going to leave here as soon as we can. What's the point in our publicly taking sides now? It can only make us vulnerable. We have made it this far in this odyssey. Let's not be seduced by the siren that sings about bread. With God's help, we will continue to survive. God will provide. God is omnipotent."

Within a few weeks, the new Royalist troops were in place, a force of over a thousand fighters. Although from their perspective, the Royalist's mission was noble, they also knew that unless they collaborated with the Nazis, they were finished, that Greece would fall to the Communists. Accordingly, the left branded them as traitors

Good Riddance

and collaborators. But the fog of war lay thick in Gargaliani, so thick that it was nearly impossible to tell whether collaborating with the Nazis was a good or a bad thing. And while the Royalists were able to quell the unrest and put an end to the night-time killings, they also gave the Nazis the breathing room they needed to organize their retreat from Greece. When citizens began to finger Communists to the Royalists, their ostensible policy of an eye for an eye and a tooth for a tooth caused them to act much like EAM had before. Father was right when he said one oppressor would replace another and that parasitic violence would be alive and well no matter who happened to be running the town.

As far as we were concerned, whether Germans, Royalists, EAM, ELAS, or whoever happened to be on top, our plight did not change. We remained as hungry and as destitute as ever and nobody cared.

Chapter 21
SURVIVING A WAR

By all accounts, 1944 would be a very bad year for Greeks across the country. While a number of questions existed on a larger level—who would win the war, who would rule Greece after the end of the war, who would run Gargaliani—our focus remained simple: to stay alive. And while I look back today and wonder how we did it, how we survived it all, the answer is absurdly simple. We remained focused only on surviving the day. Our chronic shortsightedness, a perspective that had brought us to destitution, eventually saved us. Indeed, surviving the war meant living a life of dealing only with whatever fire burned the hottest and closest to us. Our continued survival required patience, determination, and the ability to live on little or no food, not to mention a readiness to change and adapt.

We did what we had to do to survive, but even so, we were still slowly starving to death. Indeed, all over Greece, people were dying. For a number of reasons, the government still doesn't know how many people died during those years, as most deaths went unreported by families who merely dumped the bodies of their dead at cemeteries so they could hold on to the deceased's ration cards. Indeed, surviving meant taking advantage of opportunities and doing everything possible to make the most of them. Many of those who didn't starve still wouldn't survive the war, either by the hand of another or by their own.

We would learn years later about what happened in the town of Distomo, situated in northern Greece near the temple of the Oracle of Delphi. There in the spring of 1944, German soldiers cut down 218 men, women, and children in a door-to-door massacre, purported in reprisal for various Andartes attacks. We would also hear about how a town in western Greece called Komeno, where German soldiers, with nary a single bullet being fired against them, entered and, after a few hours of work with machine guns and hand grenades, killed three hundred seventeen men, women, and children. The lieutenant in charge of the massacre, a man in his twenties by the name of Roser, had ordered his men to leave "nothing standing" in a town erroneously tagged an Andartes lair. Roser even personally shot the town's priest when he approached to see what was happening.

But not all the war's atrocities were so grand. When I was in the plateia one day, my eyes were drawn to a woman in a second floor balcony directly across the street, roughly twenty feet from where I stood. I didn't pay any attention to her, but then, just as I stood and watched, she threw herself from the balcony and with a sound that was the combination of a thud and a crack, smacked into the street in front of me. Unsure whether what I had just seen was reality, I stared at the woman, and she stared back at me. And as if I were her messiah, she focused directly into my eyes and reached out her hand to me. The woman and I remained locked in that eternal moment until people surrounded and carried her away. I learned later that she died, the apparent victim of her own insanity. She was the second person whose death I witnessed after a balcony fall.

In early 1944, we learned the protective forces would be creating a soup line in our town. Though the gesture was certainly a token one, we were elated with the opportunity to get something to eat. We learned that the distribution of soup would take place every day at noon near my school under the canopy of a half-constructed but abandoned building. When the opening day arrived, I saw men preparing large pots of bubbling soup. In anticipation of this coveted noontime nourishment, crowds of people with bowls and newly issued ration cards began to congregate in the area as early as ten o'clock. The ration cards contained personal information including the name of one's family, the names of each person entitled to a serving, and various dates. No card meant no soup. Officials carried a list of locals to whom ration cards had been given and at noon began to read off the names.

I stood in the soup line that first day, fully equipped with our family's ration card and a pot. According to the card, we were entitled to four ladles full of soup, one for each one of us. I stood in the line and quickly discovered that the soup was being distributed in alphabetical order and because our last name began with sigma, the eighteenth letter of the Greek alphabet, I would be amongst the last to be served. When they finally called "Stamati," I gave the official our card. He looked at it, scribbled something, returned it to me, and signaled to the cook to pour four ladles into my pot. Because I was hungry, the soup smelled as good as anything I had ever smelled in my life. I hurried home as fast as I could, struggling with each step not to let anything spill from the pot. As I approached, I saw Mother waiting for me near the door to the house.

With a look that said I had taken too long, Mother grabbed the pot, carried it into the kitchen and began to prepare lunch. She reheated the soup and had already boiled some dandelions. The lunch was a feast. Though a bowl of soup a day was not sufficient to sustain anyone, the food did provide us some much needed nourishment, but perhaps even more importantly, gave us at least something to look forward to.

Right after the soup line opened, Mother reconnected with Kyria Papageorgiou, the pharmacist's wife. She lived in a large house on the other side of the plateia and had recently begun inviting Mother to her home. Mother and her regular stream of anecdotes about Papa Sarantis, not to mention the latest gossip, thoroughly entertained the woman. Before long, Mother helped her with her household chores and in return, received some food for us. On one occasion, Kyria Papageorgiou gave Mother her dead father-in-law's dress shoes as a gift for father. Though the shoes seemed twice as big as father's feet, Mother graciously accepted them anyways. On another occasion, Mother triumphantly entered our home.

"Look everyone what I have!" she said. "Look what I have here. We are going to feast on soup. Kyria Papageorgiou gave us her family's ration card! She says they don't need it. So she gave it to me."

Mother carefully pinned the new ration card to the back of our card and emerged from our kitchen with an even bigger pot.

"Have them fill this one up, Saranti," she said.

I took the pot to the line and when the supervisors finally called "Stamati," I handed the cards to the coordinator. He carefully examined them, looked up at me, and then shouted to the man with the ladle, "eleven helpings!"

I could not believe my eyes as I watched the server pour ladle after ladle of soup in our pot, one after another, until the number reached eleven. The pot was so full and so heavy, I could barely lift it.

I headed home, carrying it only a few meters at a time, only to set it down until I could catch my breath and then pick it up and continue a few more meters. I must have taken even longer than usual because when I was only half way home, Father came looking for me. When he saw the pot, a big smile erupted on his face, and he picked it up and we hurried home.

That afternoon, we didn't stop eating soup until our stomachs were completely bloated. And even then, there was plenty left for dinner. The next two days were a replay. It was the first time in my life I remembered all of us going to sleep with a full stomach three days in a row. But on the fourth day, the authorities figured out that people were gaming the system—we weren't the only ones—and collected everyone's cards after distributing the soup. The following day, Kyrios Patas, my fifth grade teacher called people's names off his list and then located the corresponding card that had been collected the previous day. When he got to our cards, he immediately saw the second card pinned behind it. He carefully removed Mother's pin and when he saw Kyria Papagiorgiou's name on top, turned to me.

"Why do you have Kyria Papagiorgiou's card here?"

I knew the party was over.

"Kyria Papageorgiou said she didn't need the card and so she gave it to my family to use."

He examined the cards closely, looked back at me, and then back at the cards. Then he paused, handed me only our card, returned Kyria Papagiorgiou's card to his pile and turned to the man with the ladle.

"Four helpings!" he exclaimed.

But alas, the procedures and the scrutiny in the end came to nothing, because for reasons I do not know, they ended the soup program within only a couple of days thereafter.

Later that year, stimulated by a frustrated taste of success I had previously enjoyed selling some pears for a neighbor who then cheated me out of my share of the proceeds, Mother determined it was time I helped Father put bread on our table.

"Saranti, you are going to be eleven years old soon. You have seen the difficulties your Father has had taking care of us. He has faced all these great challenges alone. Now it is time for you to help him. Your Father's income is too uncertain. You can help him now."

Though I was well aware of our challenges, Mother's declaration caught me off guard.

"What can I possibly do?"

"You will become a peddler in the plateia. There are a number of things you can sell. Don't worry about that. I will help you get everything together."

"But what about school?"

"Of course, you will continue your schooling. School always comes first and will never be compromised, Saranti. You can work in the afternoons, the evenings, and on Sundays. That will be enough for you to make a difference here. Remember Saranti, our very survival depends how well you do."

The vocation Mother had chosen for me was anathema to my very existence. I hated the very idea of being a peddler, of being conspicuous, out in the open, of coming out of the protective shell of anonymity. Being so exposed was well beyond my nature and far outside my zone of safety. I had neither the desire nor inclination to approach strangers and ask them to buy something, let alone to compete with other hostile and more experienced peddlers. Mother's proclamation sparked a number of scenarios to play out in my mind, each one worse than the previous. I flashed back to when I was a child forced to swim naked in full public view, and then to when I was forced to recite that stupid toothache poem. The thought of leaving my shell, of putting myself in front of everyone to judge and condemn, intimidated me to such an extent that I frankly preferred starving to death.

But of course, I relented—it was impossible for me to refuse Mother, and I knew well that there would be no point in resisting. When the woman got something in her head, she would pound away at me repeatedly until I acquiesced. In this case, seeming to understand my trepidation, Mother was predictably persistent, constantly bringing up one aspect of the plan or another.

"You will be able to keep one-half of whatever you sell, Saranti. You will bring that money home, and we will use it to supplement what your Father earns."

None of my attempts to avoid or change this subject were

successful, and Mother arranged everything within days. She worked out deals with a cigarette merchant named Kyria Niovie and a baker named Barba Vasili, a man known for his tasty *koulouria*, something akin to the combination of a sesame bagel and soft pretzel. Mother directed Father to make me a display container that I could strap around my neck and hang in front of me. She was so excited about my becoming an entrepreneur that she floated around the house with an excitement I had rarely seen before.

But whatever joy Mother felt, I experienced the exact opposite. As her plans moved from discussions to reality, my anxieties grew exponentially. She took me to visit my suppliers, and I learned I would be selling their products on consignment. I would get the goods, sell them, and only then pay for them.

What will my friends say? I wondered. *How will I get in front of everyone and shout slogans to sell what I have? How can I so upset my status quo, go beyond the impression others have of me? Can I really venture from the safety zone where I have been compartmentalized and where I am comfortable? And besides, what do I know about selling?*

Father must have sensed my anxiety because he repeatedly tried to put me at ease.

"Don't worry about selling, Saranti. You won't have a problem selling the cigarettes. Smokers will always buy them. Cigarettes sell themselves."

Father spoke from experience. An avid smoker, he loved his cigarettes, which were an important part of his life. He bought them only one or two at a time; I never saw him purchase a pack of ten. Though he was typically peaceful to a fault, we knew to avoid him when he was without a cigarette. Father even grew a few tobacco plants, and though they occasionally saved him, they were never enough to support his habit. And when he became particularly desperate, he would experiment by smoking whatever he could. In a moment of particular desperation, I saw Father smoke dried fig leaves he rolled in rectangular pieces of newspaper. But he put away such experiments for good after inadvertently lighting his mustache on fire. Smoking was a calming ritual for Father. When he had a cigarette and wanted to smoke, he would stop whatever he was doing, sit down, gently fish through his vest pocket with his index finger, carefully retrieve a cigarette, roll it between his fingers to ensure its circularity, smell it, and then push it into a small cigarette holder he carried, a contraption that allowed him to smoke the filterless cigarette all the way through, leaving nothing. After he smoked every last bit of tobacco, Father would clean his holder by tapping it and blowing out any remaining residue. Only then would he return the holder to his vest pocket, ready to return to whatever he was doing.

In the end, my crisis of introspection was ignored, and before I knew it, I was walking through the plateia on a Sunday evening with Father's display rack filled with Kyria Niovie's cigarettes and Barba Vasili's koulouria. In shock and awe, I meandered through the crowds, numb at the thought of becoming known to my peers, of being recognized, and of receiving the scathing judgments that I knew were sure to follow. By the time I had finished my first lap around the plateia, I thought I had already endured a number of stares, points, and giggles. So, I just kept walking, and before long and to my surprise, nobody seemed to care that I was there. Some people even bought my cigarettes. Apparently, the people of Gargaliani had things to focus on other than me. When Niko and some other kids from the neighborhood saw me, they were surprised to find me working.

"Saranti, how can you stand there with all those *koulouria* in front of you and not eat them? Why don't you give us one, c'mon, Saranti. You have so many there, no one will notice if you give us one," he said.

The other kids nodded in agreement with Niko, their eyes wide open with anticipation.

"*Va via!*" I yelled, chasing them away. "And don't come back unless you have some money!"

As more and more people approached me to buy smokes, my mind drifted away from my torment, and I slowly began to focus on selling. Most of my sales were cigarettes, one or two at a time, that my customers lit up immediately. I accepted the money, made change and buried what was left deep in my pocket. Here and there I sold a few *koulouria*, mostly to parents trying to quiet a crying child.

In the end, my first day as a salesman went much better than I had expected. My manufactured fears of exposure, embarrassment, and torture were no more than the creations of an overactive imagination. When I arrived home, Father was impressed.

"Saranti, you didn't sell too many *koulouria*. Those are best sold near the cafés early in the morning. Make sure that you canvass the coffee houses before you go to school tomorrow. But see how easy it is to sell cigarettes? They sell themselves."

The following morning, I headed for the plateia's cafés as Father had instructed. Despite the war, protective forces, and the like, the cafés were still busy places. But in contrast to the evenings, its morning congestion was all business. People hurried toward cafés for their morning coffee (or a course substitute made with roasted wheat kernels when coffee beans were unavailable), vineyard growers moved through the plateia negotiating with day laborers for services, and others just rushed through on their way somewhere. I was happy to see that just about all the men were smoking, our era's surest mark of manhood. Competition was everywhere and with a little gusto, I sprang into action.

"Cigarettes! *Koulouria*! Cigarettes! *Koulouria*! Cigarettes! *Koulouria*!"

Despite the other peddlers, my first morning was a busy one. I sold many cigarettes, and like before, mostly one or two at the time. No one seemed to have enough drachmas to buy more than four. Indeed, while people appeared able to go without food, no smoker was able to go without his cigarettes. And a man in need of a smoke had the sympathy of all and could usually find some kind brother to rescue him from his misery. I sold the cigarettes for one thousand war-inflated drachmas each, or five for four thousand. Each buyer took his cigarettes and placed them in a safe place, usually in a shirt pocket for later ignition. By the following morning, I had sold everything. My pockets were stuffed with money and when Mother and I counted it, we organized it into two piles, one to pay our suppliers and the rest for us.

"Now run and pay Kyria Niovie and Barba Vasili and refill the case," she ordered.

Soon enough, I enjoyed being a peddler and being involved in the plateia as part of the center of the town's action. But in this line of work, for better and for worse, I was exposed to many glimpses into the darker sides of life that adults often participate in but wisely know to keep from children. In the plateia, I met and made friends with another peddler named Laki, a boy roughly my age. Both thrust into the same occupation, Laki and I sold our wares in the plateia and played around his house during off-peak hours.

As I got to know him, I learned that Laki's Father had been killed in Albania with the initial Italian invasion and that he and his mother lived alone. Oftentimes, we played near Papa Christodoulos's house and became so unruly that the priest would holler at us and chase us away. Laki and I quickly became pals and began to knock on one another's door with ease.

That all changed one afternoon. I knocked on Laki's door and when his mother answered, her appearance was unlike anything I had seen before. Her lips were painted red and her face padded white with powder. I looked past her into the house and saw a man inside I did not recognize.

"Oh, Laki," she said. "Saranti is here. Why don't you go out and play?"

When I looked at Laki, his face fell, and I could see that he wanted no part of playing with me that day.

"No, Mana," he said. "I don't feel well. I want to stay home."

"Oh, my Laki, Saranti wants to play with you. Go out and have fun. Don't turn him away. He'll be sad if you don't play with him."

"Mana, no. I don't feel good. Please, don't make me go."

Then the mystery man stood up, reached into his pocket and pulled out a few thousand drachma.

"Here my boy, take your friend to the store and buy yourselves something to eat."

When Laki appeared to resist, the man arose, forced the money into his hand and sternly said, "Now go and buy yourselves some candy!"

A frown appeared on Laki's face as he froze and looked down, straight at the floor. His lips began to quiver. Then I saw his mother visibly become angry.

"You ungrateful bad boy, don't you have any respect at all for your elders?"

She grabbed Laki by his left ear and pushed him out the front door, shutting it behind him. Out on the street, Laki's head hung low. It was obvious something was wrong. He didn't want to speak.

"Leave me alone today, Saranti. I don't want to play, I don't want to go the plateia, and I don't want any candy. You go home, okay? I have to stay here with my mother. She needs me. That man hurts her, and I have to stay here to protect her."

As I walked away, I turned to wave at Laki and saw him sitting with his back against the wall next to his front door. His knees were bent, his head hung between them, and his hands were clenched. My friend was crying. My arrival at Laki's house that day let me in on a family secret that Laki and his mother carried alone, a secret that neither I nor anyone else was meant to know. I saw Laki again here and there in the plateia, but whatever shame he felt at my unintentional participation in that unfortunate episode must have been too much for him. And I can't blame him. Sadly, our friendship ended almost as quickly as it began.

I made friends with another boy named George, a peddler who was two years older than me. Even though he was a competitor, George and I got to know one another as we crisscrossed the plateia hawking our goods and checking each other's trays to see who had sold more. One afternoon, I complained to George about the lack of business during afternoon siesta time.

"Come with me, Saranti. I'll show you where to sell your cigarettes."

George led me out of the plateia, down a small street in the direction of Thea Theano's house. We stopped after several hundred meters, in front of a door I had noticed many times before, but never dared to venture inside. On the door hung a foreboding sign that read, "Private Club, Entrance Forbidden." We opened it and waded into a room filled with layers of smoke that danced in seductive swirls through tubes of sunlight that shot through the building's few windows. Fifteen or twenty rough masculine men sat around several tables dealing and looking at cards and then throwing money in the middle of each table. Money, liquor, and ethereal smoke were everywhere in that dimly lit den.

One of the men spotted us and hollered, "get those damn kids out of here."

"Let them sell their cigarettes," replied another. "We need some more cigarettes."

George and I moved through the room. One man called me over and asked me for five cigarettes. When I laid them out before him, he reached for his money, which he kept in front of him on the table in a number of rolls, each containing what he told me were four thousand drachmas, his bundles of ante. He handed me a bundle. As I walked away, I examined the roll and could see that it contained only three thousand drachma. He had cheated me one-thousand drachmas and he was apparently doing the same to the card players. I hesitated for a split second, but then just took the money, shoved it in my pocket and moved on. Something told me that challenging him in front of everyone else could not possibly end well. I continued on and sold a number of cigarettes and even a few koulouria that afternoon. Being conned out of a thousand drachmas was a small price to pay for entrance to the club.

When I arrived home, I excitedly told Mother about the club. But as the words emerged from my mouth and before I could brag to her about how much I had sold, her face went blank.

"Saranti, you are never to enter that place again! What possessed you to go in there? Do you know what kind of place that is? Do you know who is in there? I'll tell you—the bottom of the barrel. The scum of the earth. The lowest of the low. The people in that club are bums. They have no ethos and are setting a bad example for you. Stay away from that cursed place!" she ordered.

But for some reason, I didn't listen. Perhaps it was the sense of adventure I felt when I entered the club, or more likely, it was the sales I was sure I would make with little effort. If those men were anything, they were cigarette smokers. So for the next couple weeks, I went into the club almost daily, sold my cigarettes, and heard them talk about things that I mostly didn't understand. Business was brisk and by my family's standards, lucrative. If I learned nothing else in that club, I learned that there are quick profits to be had when dealing in vice.

One afternoon, when I entered the club, I heard someone call my name. When I looked up, I saw Nikos Halazonitis. What a joy I felt as I ran over to his side.

"Saranti! How are you my boy, good to see you," he said as he tousled my hair.

We exchanged pleasantries, and he asked me about my parents, the neighborhood, and some of our neighbors. Then he bought a handful of cigarettes, more than ten, and overpaid me for them. In front of the other players, Nikos was all smiles and put on his usual grandiose show. But when he put his money in my hand, he clamped down on it firmly.

Then, in the most menacing of voices, he whispered in my ear, "Saranti, are you listening to me?"

I nodded my head yes.

"I don't ever want to see you in here again. If I ever catch you here, I will break your legs. I mean it. Do you understand me?" Nikos stared directly into my eyes.

At that moment, I had no doubt I was finished if I didn't obey him. I gathered myself and my things and ran out as quickly as I could. I never went in the club again.

I limited my work to the plateia and before long, became another one of its fixtures. Many came to me to buy their cigarettes. Though whatever I made wasn't much, it did augment my Father's income and enabled us to eat somewhat regularly. Mother had the bright idea to expand my line to include sewing accessories, needles, threads and the like, only to learn that people in the plateia were not interested in buying such things. I couldn't move any of those products but Mother insisted I continue to pitch them despite Father's efforts to save me.

"No matter how hard he tries, Nitsa, no man will ever buy needles and pins in a coffee house."

Chapter 22
DIVESTING ASSETS

June 6, 1944, marked the commencement of the long-awaited Allied ground invasion into Europe, "D-day." It was around this time that the German army began its drawn-out departure from our region of the Peloponnese. My job as peddler in the plateia put me on the front line of the area's rumor mill, and I heard a play by play of what was happening. In staccato bursts that spanned the subsequent weeks, I heard that the Germans were pulling out of the port at Pylos—that their trucks were heading north to Filiatra—that they had linked up with the remaining German troops there—that they there were continuing north, presumably toward Patras and then on to Athens.

And just like that, the Germans were gone. Though we were relieved at their exit, the German departure from our region of Greece had the unintended effect of intensifying the conflict between EAM and the Royalist forces. With the main deterrent to open an obvious activity gone, the Communists recognized the arrival of their big opportunity. And while Royalist forces set up shop in both Filiatra and Pylos, their real numbers were in Gargaliani, making our town a main target for the Communists.

Father was thankful when the Royalist forces established a secure foothold in Gargaliani.

"Now at least they won't just walk in here and take us over," he'd say. But not everyone agreed. To many, there was no act that trumped the Royalist's sin of collaborating with the Germans, no matter what their reason. And by this time, the country had become irrevocably polarized with Communists on the left and Royalists on the right. There was suddenly no middle ground, no room for compromise. Indeed, the existence of battle-hardened extremists in a country with no legitimate central authority made fertile soil for the insanity that would lead Greek to kill Greek and take pride in the notion that he was doing the right thing.

ELAS sprung into action. Under the direction of one of its leaders, Ares Veluchiotis, ELAS quickly sought to become the dominant force all over the Peloponnesian countryside, mostly by consolidating its position and eliminating any "traitors." As they successfully moved through the land, news of each success trickled into the plateia. We heard about the methods the Andartes employed elsewhere to achieve their goals—the same tactics they had used in Gargaliani, including intimidation, beatings, and assassinations. Like a gathering storm, the Andartes moved through the countryside and amassed an army. For those who stood in their path, the choices were simple—one could offer them succor and be considered a comrade, a friend of the cause, or one could refuse and be labeled a German collaborator, a reactionary, and a person who needed to be promptly killed as there would be no room for Royalists or their sympathizers in post-war Greece.

Before they left, the Germans strengthened the armament of the Royalist fighters in Gargaliani by leaving behind caches of heavy weapons and munitions. They knew that without sufficient weaponry, Gargaliani would quickly fall to the Communists and so they left, among other things, two mortars, shells, several machine guns, and an enormous fixed automatic large-caliber weapon. In the weeks that followed, Royalist forces gathered and enlisted more men, building their ranks to more than a thousand to defend Gargaliani. The increased numbers consisted primarily of fathers, sons, and brothers of the Royalists, the people who stood to lose everything in the event that the Andartes came out on top in the battle to come. Families throughout Gargaliani began to house Royalist fighters.

Even worse, the German departure from the Peloponnese led to a financial crisis unlike anything anyone had ever seen. During the occupation and ostensibly under the direction of the Germans, the Greek government printed more and more paper money, a way of keeping the economy going. But the bills had no real backing, causing hyperinflation. As the drachma lost value, the government responded by printing more and more bills in larger and larger denominations. Hence, my thousand drachma cigarettes. But when the Germans began to leave, the paper currency lost whatever remaining value it might have had, and people stopped accepting it as payment for goods and services, resorting instead to a barter system. Customers would show up at, say, the butcher with a container of oil. The butcher would take it, look at it, trade some quantity of meat for it and then pour it into a large nearby barrel. The paper currency became so worthless that the National Bank of Greece in Gargaliani dumped huge bundles of freshly printed drachmas into the streets. At first, the dumping was a novelty and children played with it.

"Look, I'm a millionaire," we said.

But before long, the worthless paper money was so omnipresent that playing with it wasn't fun anymore, and it just blew all over the town. Even worse, the lack of any currency had a devastating effect on my business, making it impossible for me to peddle my cigarettes and koulouria in the plateia. There wasn't any way I could sell a cigarette for oil, vegetables, or a piece of meat. I was out of business.

The only thing my family had to barter was the little oil from our thirty or so remaining olive trees, all from the grove Mother had inherited from Papa Sarantis. Because the harvest of 1943 had been inordinately strong, Father hoarded as much of that oil as possible, leaving us with some to barter here and there. But because Gargaliani's primitive harvesting methods caused our trees to produce usable olives only every *other* year, Father knew we wouldn't have any oil production during the fall of 1944. Without any new oil, our ability to survive was further called into question.

So, shortly after the Germans left and the economy went to pot, Father announced we were going to sell our olive grove, the remaining jewel of our family. Divesting ourselves of it was no easy decision, and at first, Mother was dead against it. The topic came to a head one afternoon when my parents discussed the pros and cons of selling out.

"Over the years, the grove has given us oil to eat and to barter, Panagioti. I know we won't have any production this year but we may need olives down the road. Those trees have saved us many times. It would be a sin to let them go."

"But the next few months will be crucial to our survival," Father replied. "I don't think we have a choice. If we don't get rid of them, we may die. The Germans have left the Peloponnese. The Allies are winning the war, and at some point, relief will be on its way here. We have to survive until the relief arrives. And the Andartes are coming. What good will trees do us when that happens? We need food, and we need it now. We have to do whatever it takes to survive and to the extent that we can, stay healthy. The trees won't give us any new oil this year."

"But Panagioti, the olive grove has been in my family since my grandfather Spyro came to Gargaliani. He bought the trees. And then he gave them to my father. We can't sell the grove."

"We have to sell it. What's the point of keeping the trees if we are going to die? The olive trees are here to serve us, not the other way around. We have to live long enough to get out of this country, and we have to do what we have to do to take care of these children."

And that's pretty much how it went. Father spread the word that we were interested in selling the trees and almost immediately, several buyers surfaced. Not surprisingly, they were bottom feeders, people looking for deals in a time of war. Each offered Father less than 10 percent of the value of the property.

When Mother heard the low-ball offers, she took offense and ranted for several days, "How dare they try to take advantage of us like this? How dare they be so unfair? God will most certainly pay them back in kind for their actions."

One afternoon, we heard a knock on our door and when Mother opened it, I saw an enormously tall man holding two bags of food. And once he started talking he didn't stop. And the more that garrulous man spoke, the more I focused on his inordinate height, not common at all at the time, and even more so on his enormous nose, by far the largest I had ever seen.

"Good afternoon, Kyria. I have heard that you are looking to sell some olive trees. Kyria, I am willing to buy those trees and to show you that I am serious, I offer you these two bags of food as down payment."

His bags were filled with wheat, potatoes and the like.

"Now don't worry about the price of the land, Kyria. You want to sell it, and I am willing to pay handsomely for it. Just look at these vegetables. As you can see, this food is of the highest quality."

Mother took the bags of food from the stranger, hurried to the kitchen and hid them from view. She returned to the front door, invited the man inside the house and led him the dining room table.

"Have a seat, and I will prepare you some coffee."

Mother moved into the kitchen and emerged with a tray that carried two cups of coffee, set it on the table, and sat opposite the man with the large nose.

"Thank you for the down payment," she began. "But for us to have a deal, more, substantially more, is required. You see, these are not just any olive trees. These trees belonged to the great Papa Saranti."

"Of course, Kyria, everyone knows that."

"Well, then you see that selling them will not be easy for us and will only be for a generous price. We are not desperate to sell but are considering moving abroad and have already begun to divest our holdings. I'm sure it comes as no surprise that you are not the only person to recognize this singular opportunity. Accordingly, it does us no good to talk to you if you are just another one of these wolves who have been crawling around trying to take people's land for a bag of onions during a time of struggle. God will deal appropriately with such people in his time."

"Not at all, Kyria mou, not at all. I have only the best intentions and am willing to pay you appropriately for the land. I too inherited land from my father and understand the ties we all feel to our land and especially to our olive trees. These trees, the trees of Messenia, are the trees that provided the oil that Socrates himself put on his salads."

Both laughed.

"Well, if you are serious, Kyrie," Mother began, "we will sell this *farma* to you, of course we will. I don't need to tell you that these olives are the best in the world. These trees will be a great blessing to you if you buy them, but only if you pay the appropriate price. Otherwise, they would be a curse, and no one wants that. The trees have produced great quantities of oil, more than enough for my family of four. And I am glad to hear that your two bags of vegetables are only a taste of an appropriate down payment, that you are not one of those cursed opportunists. I would say such an offer is insulting if I didn't see that you are a man of integrity, of course planning to offer much more."

The man, apparently as shrewd as Mother, played right along with her, all along avoiding any discussions of any definite price for the grove.

"Of course, Kyria, of course. I would like to discuss these matters with your husband. It is my sincere hope you will advise him of the sale and that I will be back soon with an additional down payment."

Mother nodded in agreement and after some more banter, the tall man with the prominent nose arose and left. Mother waited patiently for Father to return home that evening, chomping at the bit to tell him what had happened. But when he arrived, he cut Mother off before she could get out a single word.

"Nitsa, Nitsa, I have good news. Dr. Papathomopoulos is interested in purchasing the olive grove. I don't know too many details, but he told me he is interested and that he's willing to pay a fair price."

Dr. Papathomopoulos was one of Gargaliani's doctors. Father knew him to be not only a man of integrity, but also a rabid Royalist. That he wanted to purchase the trees was a good sign because more likely than not, his price would be a fair one.

"But Panagioti, today a tall man with an enormous nose came by and said *he* wants to buy the property."

Although the man's name was Kyrios Giorgos, Mother had already nicknamed him.

"Kyrios Big Nose knocked on the door and brought us those two bags of vegetables. But you should have seen his nose. It was enormous, unlike anything I have ever seen. Anyway, we didn't agree to any specific price, but he thinks we are going to sell *him* the trees and will come back with more food. I think we can get a lot more food from him."

Father listened quietly as he rubbed his chin.

"Two serious prospects. What a blessing," he said as he thought for a moment.

"But what will we do about the food from Kyrios Big Nose if we sell the grove to Papathomopoulos?" Father slowly and quietly asked.

Mother didn't answer.

Within days, Father and Dr. Papathomopoulos met at Tsironi's coffee house where the doctor laid out the terms of his offer. He described how he was willing to pay various sacks of corn, wheat, and potatoes for the trees, enough food, Father silently calculated, to carry us for at least a few months. Father told him he wanted to think about it and reported everything to Mother.

"I know, Nitsa, it's not easy to sell those trees for a couple month's worth of food, but what choice do we have?"

"My father and grandfather were able to hold on to those trees for half a century. What's wrong with us? We are giving them away because our backs are up against a wall right now."

"Yes, Nitsa, and the way I see things, the offer is still not even for twenty percent the value of the land."

Around the time my parents were mulling over the doctor's offer, Kyrios Big Nose returned to our home holding yet another couple sacks of food. Once again, Mother invited him in, prepared him coffee, and gladly accepted everything.

"I'm sure my husband would like to talk with you now," she said. "He works constantly and, of course, has the final say in all such matters. Only he, you understand, can consummate such a deal."

"Of course, Kyria. Thank you. And I want you to know that it has been a pleasure meeting you and working out this deal with you. I look forward to wrapping things up soon. In times like these, there are many uncertainties. I want to conclude these matters as quickly as possible," said the man.

"Yes, Kyrie, I know my husband is equally ready to wrap things up as well. You will be able to find him in Tsironis's café. He works constantly, from sunrise to sunset, so your best bet is to find him on Sunday afternoon."

"Thank you, Kyria, thank you."

The following day, Father came home with good news.

"Nitsa, I spoke again with the doctor and he increased his offer a little bit. I accepted it, and he'll bring us the food we discussed. There are, of course, some papers that have to be completed but the deal is done."

"Eh," Mother replied. "Sell it. What can we do? We are doing what we have to do to survive. Now, what do we do about Kyrios Big Nose?"

"I'll deal with that when the time comes," replied Father.

The following week, as Father sat in the Tsironi's café, a tall man with a large nose approached him.

"Kyrie Panagioti, I am Kyrios Giorgos. As I am sure you are aware, your wife and I have discussed the purchase of your olive grove."

"Yes, Kyrie, yes. Please have a seat. Nice to meet you in person. Yes, I am sorry that deal didn't work out for you."

Kyrios Big Nose was taken aback.

"What do you mean that deal didn't work out? Of course it's worked out. I have given your wife a down payment for the grove, and she has accepted it. We have a deal, Kyrie."

"No, Kyrie, I'm sorry. We have already sold the grove to Dr. Papathomopoulos. How could we not? He offered us triple what you offered. And in times like these, every little bit means a lot."

"But I had a deal with your wife! I came to you house with down payments for the grove, and that woman accepted both of them. If she wasn't going to sell me the land, then why did she accept the down payments? You people are thieves."

"Calm down, Kyrie, there's no need to get upset. Besides, you never spoke to me about it. My wife has no authority to sell our land. You know that."

"But I trusted her. She told me that the deal was done. She is the daughter of Papa Saranti. I never imagined that I would be cheated by the daughter of that great man. Your wife tricked me, Kyrie. She accepted my down payment and even asked me for more. And I complied. I brought her more food. Now you say there's no sale? Tell me how you are going to make that right?"

"Kyrie, I don't know what to tell you. I don't know what you and my wife agreed to, but I make the decisions in my family. The land has been sold. I don't have it to sell to you anymore. What else can I do?"

"You can return my down payment to me, that's what you can do."

"Okay, fine, I'll see to that."

"You'd better see to it," said Kyrios Big Nose as he arose and left.

In the subsequent weeks, Mother made it a point to avoid Kyrios

Big Nose, who she knew was looking for her. But her luck ran dry one afternoon when she was entering the house.

"Kyria Nitsa," he said with a strange smile. "I thought we had a deal. What happened? You stole from me, and your husband has promised that you would return to me the down payment I left for you. When can I expect it?"

"Kyrie, what can I do? My family has already eaten most of what you left. There is nothing right now. You understand that we are all in the middle of very difficult times. There's a war going on here. You shouldn't be so inflexible."

"Inflexible? Kyria, you led me on to believe that we had a deal when you knew that we did not. Now your husband has promised me the return of my down payment, where is it?"

Mother thought for a moment.

"Kyrie, you know we don't have that now. You performed a Christian deed by helping a family in a very difficult time, a time of need. Indeed, you have done truly Christian work. And when we Christians give, we are to do so in such a way that our left hand does not know what our right hand has done. Neither advertise nor regret your charity, Kyrie, and the Almighty will reward you handsomely."

"Charity? Are you insane? This was a business deal. Kyria, you cheated me, and I expect my payment back."

"Come, come now, Kyrie. Don't be so melodramatic. You are making all this fuss over a sack of corn and a few potatoes? For that, you are ready to declare war on us? As my father used to say, God sees everything. Your good deed will never be forgotten. Don't spoil it. He will reward you, and we will pay you back. It's quite a good deal for you—great favor from God for only a few sacks of food. And on top of that, we plan to pay you back."

The man became slightly befuddled and stood quietly for a moment.

"How do you plan on doing that?"

"The war is almost over, Kyrie. Soon, the doors to America will be opened. We have many wealthy relatives there, and they will soon send us riches from their country: dollars, packages, and the like. When that happens, we will be able to pay you back several times over."

While it all sounded good, Kyrios Big Nose was unconvinced and frustrated. He gave Mother a wave of his hand, a gesture that showed he didn't believe anything she said. He turned and walked away.

And as he headed off exasperated, Mother could hear him curse himself, "How did I let another woman get the best of me?"

Chapter 23
RETURN TO MANI

After the Italians and Germans brought war to Greece in April 1941, most thought that when they left, war would leave with them. But the wounds they created, including the normalization of violence, political turmoil, and starvation, would not be healed without much pain. Indeed, cancerous, wartime mindsets had been permitted to metastasize for half a decade and amputating them would be a barbaric surgical procedure, one performed with butcher knives and without anesthetic. Perversity can carry its own desire to perpetuate itself and often fights relentlessly for its continued existence.

In the spring of 1944, I was eleven years old and could see that things were happening fast. The Andartes worked their way from village to village and town to town on their way to Gargaliani. A Communist attack upon us was imminent. While we spent our days trying to win our daily battle against starvation, the Royalist forces in Gargaliani girded for war. They placed weapons around the town, dug trenches, moved men here and there, and recruited whoever hadn't already been recruited. I remember finding one of the Royalists' large-caliber weapons positioned at the top of the hill where I often took Kanella to graze. Kanella ate near it as the weapon pointed over the wheat fields below, positioned for a direct shot at the mountain range that sat just beyond the water reservoir. It was through there that the main thrust of the Andartes' attack was expected.

We watched the Royalist forces move their prisoners, mostly Communists, from site to site to perform whatever manual work was needed. One afternoon, as Mother sprinkled the ground near our home's entrance with water, she saw the Royalist guards leading a group of prisoner-laborers past her. When she looked at them, she recognized none other than Dr. Zorbakos, the doctor who had stood by us so many times before, the man who was present at Stathi's birth. The soldiers pushed Dr. Zorbakos along as he held a shovel in his hands. Not wanting to embarrass the doctor by his being seen disgraced, Mother darted into the house. And we watched through the slats of our dining room window as he and the prisoners passed our home. They had been beaten, and their clothes had become rags.

"How do they have the strength to dig ditches all day?" Mother lamented that evening. "And look at how they are treating the good doctor. That man is a gentleman. What a shame."

"He may be a gentleman, but he's also a registered Communist," Father matter-of-factly replied.

So, with political affiliations trumping everything and the social fabric of our town beginning to tear, my parents looked ahead toward the autumn and realized that the near future held little hope for us to obtain locally the food we needed to survive. And so, after much discussion, they determined that there was really only one option—for the two of them to walk the hundred or so kilometers to Boliana, the region of Mani where Mother's grandfather Spyro Petropouleas was born. How they determined that walking to Mani was their only option, I have no idea.

"When we arrive in Boliana, Saranti, your Father and I will find my cousins. They are our family, you know. They will greet us with open arms. The Maniates have a great sense of family and honor. They have immeasurable *filotimo*—they always do what's right. I hear that the Maniate villages have been left alone by the invaders, and that means they will have food to share with us. Those people won't let us die. And in a sense, by giving them the opportunity to be charitable with us, we will be doing them a great service. We will be offering them the chance to earn favor in the eyes of God, to help them secure their own salvation."

"How long will you be gone?"

"Well, your Father and I have planned this trip carefully, but we have to wait to see what we find. Walking will be the hardest part of the journey, and that will take at least five or six days each way. So we will be gone at least two weeks. I know it's a long time Saranti, but this is a sacrifice that you and your brother will have to endure. The two of you will stay with Thea Fotini. They are down at their farm, near the ocean, and they will have plenty of room for you there. You'll be out of the city and that will be good for both of you. Your Father and I are making an enormous sacrifice for our family by taking this trip."

"Thea Fotini? But we haven't spoken to her since the wedding. I thought we didn't talk to them anymore, Mana."

I would have much rather stayed with Thea Theano and her family, but they were apparently living through their own hard times and Mother determined that Fotini, who was at least somewhat emotionally stable, was the only choice.

"Why do you have to be gone for so long?" I asked almost crying. "What are we going to do? What am I going to do with Stathi? There's nothing for us at Thea Fotini's farm."

"Saranti, that farm belonged to your great grandfather Spyro. It was the farm he gave to Papa Saranti's brother, your late Theo Dimitri. Two weeks is not that long, Saranti. You'll like staying at your great grandfather's farm."

"Well, what about the Andartes? Aren't you worried about them?"

"What are the Andartes going to do to us? Father has planned his trip to avoid them, but why should we worry about them? We are nobodies. In fact, we are the very proletariat they say they are fighting for. Saranti, it's settled. We are leaving."

When the day of their trip arrived, I saw my parents carrying sacks of various personal items they thought they could barter for food. It reminded me of the trip we took to Mouzaki the year before. For Stathi and me, Mother had packed a bag of various foodstuffs they were able to scrounge together that included a large loaf of bread and a few vegetables. When they were almost ready to start their trip, Father signaled to Stathi and me that it was time for him to take us to Thea Fotini's farm while Mother stayed back to continue preparations. The several kilometer walk took us through town, down the bluff upon which Gargaliani sat, and southwest, toward the sea. We traversed olive grove after grove until we hit the dirt road that ran though Marathos and continued south to Pylos. We stopped at a café that sat in the middle of nowhere for a drink of water and continued through vineyard after vineyard to Thea Fotini's farm, which sat roughly a full kilometer from the sea.

When we arrived, a quick survey of the area revealed a whitewashed, two-room abode comprised of a kitchen and a roomy bedroom. Outside sat a patio, next to which stood an enormous fig tree. Above the patio was a wooden structure covered with a canopy of crawling grape vines, vegetation that provided shade. As we approached the house, Fotini and her daughters ran out to greet Stathi and me while Father handed them the sack of food. After they exchanged a few words, we said our good-byes. Father waved, and we watched him walk away, through the vineyard, behind some trees, and then out of sight. What an empty feeling. It was with only the greatest effort that I kept from crying, having been left in what I thought was a hostile environment. Stathi, apprehensive and quiet, hung on me, in anticipation of what might happen next.

I thought of my late Theo Dimitri and couldn't help but wonder, *If they killed their blind old Father, what will they do to Stathi and me?*

As soon as Father left, Fotini's family, like hyenas stumbling across a fresh carcass, descended on the bag of food. One pulled out the loaf of bread and examined it while another removed the other items.

"Saranti and Stathi, we are so happy you are here," Eleni quickly said.

And as she spoke, all I could think about was how "wickedly smart" and "dangerous" Mother always said she was, not to mention the invectives I saw Eleni hurl at her poor Father when he asked for a piece of bread. For sure, I didn't plan on asking her for anything.

"Saranti, you know about Thea Fotini's stomach problem, don't you?"

I had no idea what she was talking about. I shook my head.

"Oh, Saranti, she suffers so much with it. You know the doctor has put her on a strict diet. All she can eat are boiled vegetables and whole-wheat bread. Doctor's orders."

Though I was surprised that Eleni was letting me in on a family secret, it didn't take me long to see where she was heading.

"The loaf of bread your father brought is such a blessing Saranti. It is just what the doctor ordered for your aunt's stomach. We will save it just for her, all right? You and Stathi will eat the same bread that we eat. Besides, the ingredients in our bread are more nutritious than the bread your father brought."

"Oh yes, Saranti, Eleni is correct," Katina added. "Our bread is made from various seeds that we have ground into flour. It's delicious and very good for your health."

I didn't believe them but agreed anyway. Far be it from me to object to taking care of my aunt's tender stomach. When we sat down to dinner that evening, my cousins served Stathi and me the ground seed bread with a plate of potato stew. The bread, dark green in color, wasn't even remotely edible. It tasted like a dirty rag. But when I looked up from my plate, I saw everyone staring at me, their eyes wide open, wondering what would happen.

"Go ahead boys, it's good for you."

Stathi and I forced a little down, just enough to make them happy. After dinner, we were sick to our stomachs, and I couldn't help but think I had figured out the source of my aunt's gastric problems.

At bedtime, Fotini put us at opposite ends of a small cot and covered us with a single blanket. We instantly fell asleep. When we awoke the following morning, I saw that everyone was gone and the other beds in the room made. Stathi and I wandered out of the bedroom only to find Thea Fotini cooking the noontime meal.

"Did you sleep well children? You must have since it is past eight o'clock."

She fed us the green bread and sent us out to the patio.

"Now stay on the patio. You are not allowed to leave it for any reason, all right, children?"

"Yes, Thea," we replied.

Boredom quickly became enemy number one. With the exception of Thea Fotini, who generally stayed back to tend to household matters, the whole family was off during the day, laboring in their vineyards. Stathi and I were left to entertain ourselves and quickly explored just about everything near the patio that there was to explore in five minutes. There was a chicken coop, a bathroom in back of the house, and a fig tree. And that was about it. The tree was full of figs, but they were green and were inedible.

"These won't be ripe for another month," I told Stathi.

When I tried to climb the tree, Thea Fotini scolded me from the kitchen window, "You'll fall and break your neck."

When I moved close to the well, "Stay away from there, you'll fall in and drown," she yelled.

When we walked around the back of the house near the chickens, she nearly had a heart attack, "Don't go near the chickens, you'll scare them and they'll stop laying eggs."

So with nothing else to explore, everything off-limits, and no kids around, Stathi and I nearly died from the boredom. I had feared the days might move slowly during my parent's absence, but I had no idea just how slowly they would creep along. With the only break in the day Thea Fotini's call for lunch, there was nothing to look forward to. No one was around, Thea Fotini didn't talk to us, and Stathi and I were forced to bury our personalities under cloaks of silence.

When I once told Thea Fotini that I was hungry, she replied, "You'll spoil your appetite if I give you a snack. Wait until that shadow over there reaches that step over here."

Stathi and I spent day after day doing nothing but watching shadows slowly creep across the patio. In fact, we saw so many shadows that I became an expert in their properties. Early in the morning, when the sun first rose above the mountains to the east, the shadows were long. But as the sun moved across the sky, they shrunk until noon or so, when it was directly overhead and the shadows had disappeared. But then they quickly reappeared, when the sun made its descent in the west. I saw that Father was right when he told me how the lengths of the shadows alter more rapidly during the early morning hours but how their movements during the middle of the day are hardly noticeable. Even so, there is nothing more boring than watching, hour after hour, day after day, shadows move. It is the very definition of suffering.

Every so often, Stathi would ask, "Where is Mother now?"

I would try to answer the boy as best as I could with a guess.

"I bet she is somewhere in Mani taking refuge under the shade of an apple tree," was one of my typical responses.

Twice a day, we ate. The first meal was lunch, after everyone returned from the vineyard and washed up. That meal was usually tomato salad with green bread. I would eat the tomatoes but never the bread and was always shocked to see how Stathi put it down, bread and all, no problem, and how he would mix it with the vegetables and the salad and then wipe his plate clean with it. I was amazed at how the kid would often take a chunk of the bread and stuff it in his pocket for later.

After roughly ten full days of shadow watching had passed, Stathi and I had reached our limit. Early one morning, when everyone departed for the vineyards and Thea Fotini was preoccupied in her kitchen, I took Stathi by the hand and did the unthinkable. We not only left the patio, we left the property. We walked away from the house and its damned shadows and headed toward the main road. Once there, we turned south. There was not a soul in sight and we walked and walked, on the lookout for a certain dirt path I had become familiar with over the years, a path Mother had shown me and that I knew would take us to the sea.

We quickly reached it and followed it down toward the water. When we hit the top of an incline, we could finally see what we had been looking for— Theano's house by the sea. Stathi and I began to run. When Thea Theano saw us, she screamed with happiness and ran to greet us. It was all hugs and kisses. We told her about Thea Fotini, the bread, the boredom, and our daring escape.

"Stathi and I walked here and we are not going back to Thea Fotini's house. We're staying here. That's it! My parents can come here to get us," I declared.

"That's okay, my boy. You'll stay with us," Theano said.

Theano directed us to sit on some steps that led to the sea and gave us some bread—real bread—that we ate while we watched the waves crash on the beach. Later that afternoon, the three male members of the family returned home from their day of work. Theo Nikolaki and John had been working in the vineyards, and Sarantis had been cultivating the garden. A little later, Eleni showed up.

If there was one thing this family was *not,* it was boring. After only a few minutes with all of them, we knew that our careers as shadow watchers were definitely over. Eleni spent the next day with Stathi and me at the beach where we gathered shells, swam, and ate. The water was Greece's singular azure, the sun gentle, and the sky innocent. I soon made contact with my friend Niko, who had been at his family's farm nearby. We began to meet every day at the chapel of

Agios Sotiros, a church that sat only fifty or so meters from Theano's house. Niko and I would hang around there and delight in ringing its large bell. After that, we ran and swam and played until our hunger pains became intolerable.

After nearly a week or so of this idyllic life, I heard Theano tell her husband that they were running low on food. So Theo Nikolaki mounted Kitsos, the family donkey, and headed to Gargaliani to bring back some provisions. Anything more than lentils or even beans were luxuries no one expected.

"Don't come back here until you have plenty of food for everyone," I heard Theano yell at her husband as he left.

Theano knew Nikolaki didn't have any money, but also knew he was cunning enough to make something happen when he had to. In a sense, Nikolaki was the antithesis of Father, who would rather quietly starve than impose himself on someone. Theo Nikolaki had the gift of oratory, and when that was combined with his gifts of persuasion, he was able to extract credit from merchants well beyond the dictates of prudence. But talk can only get a person so far and with the economy in shambles, even Nikolaki was finding it difficult to feed everyone. The poor man was so riddled with debt that his promises to pay held little weight with merchants. Even so, we were curious to see what he could do.

Several hours later, we saw Nikolaki, pulling Kitsos, returning to the beach house. He was jovial, laughing, joking, and singing in full voice.

"Everyone come over here! Come and see what I have done."

We ran to see Kitsos absolutely loaded with food, enough to carry everyone through the rest of the summer. We were giddy and helped him unload several bags of wheat flour, corn flour, potatoes, several loaves of bread, several kilos of beans, and a large sack full of vegetables. There was also a large leg of lamb, wrapped in newspaper. I couldn't believe what I saw. It was one of the most cheerful atmospheres I ever experienced, one of the happiest days of my life. While we took inventory, Nikolaki turned to me.

"By the way, Saranti, your parents are back from Mani."

When I heard that, my heart jumped out of my chest. Stathi screamed.

"But where are they? Why didn't they come here to get us?" I anxiously inquired.

"They were too tired to come, Saranti. They are going to rest a little first and will be here in an hour or two," he said.

"We will celebrate today with a feast!" Theano said as she laughingly busied herself storing the food in the kitchen. "I'll make the lamb with noodles."

After an hour or so, Theano placed our lunch on the table outside in one of the most beautiful spreads I had ever seen. There was lamb, salad, bread and cheese, vegetables, and fruit.

We sat and enthusiastically began to eat. After a few moments of silence, Eleni spoke up.

"Father, how did you get all this food? How did you do it?"

Because Eleni was the first to vocalize what everyone else was wondering, we turned and looked at Theo Nikolaki. He didn't answer.

"Yes, Niko, tell us how you got all this food," said Theano.

Nikolaki remained silent, and I could see the expression on Theano's face begin to migrate away from its happy state.

"Niko, we want to know, how did you get this food?"

Nikolaki still didn't answer.

"Damn it, Nikolaki, what did you trade for all this food?"

Theano became visibly upset.

"All right, all right! I'll tell you! I traded the food for the Persian rug we bought in Chicago."

"You did what?"

"Well, I tried to eat it on a number of occasions but couldn't get it down," replied Nikolaki.

The children laughed. Theano didn't think it was funny, and I saw her face turn. When that old familiar look emerged in her eyes, she grabbed a saucy piece of lamb from her plate and threw it at Nikolaki. It hit him square in the chest. Then she threw anything she could get her hands on at the poor man. First it was cups and utensils. Then, whatever food she could grab.

"You should get lost, you lousy son of a bitch! *Bastarde*!" she shrieked.

I had never seen anything like this. Frankly, Theano scared me more than the Italians, the Germans, and the Andartes combined. Poor Stathi just sat there with his mouth open.

"Please Mana, stop! It's okay! It doesn't matter! Forget the rug!" said one of her children.

But the pleas were to no avail. Theano had become so consumed in her anger that she had lost her mind. She threw anything she could get her hands on, the bread, the cheese, the lamb, the salad. I began to shove food in my mouth as quickly as I could and Stathi did the same. In an instant, the boredom of Thea Fotini's house didn't seem so bad.

When Theano's anger only escalated, I shoved a few more bites of food into my mouth and grabbed Stathi. We huddled and crept away from the table and scampered toward the end of the patio, just past the well. We took cover behind it and watched as Theano, the only person on offense, continued to throw everything not nailed down while the rest took refuge behind the table or in the house. Food and plates were everywhere. I began to think about what our next move would be when a figure suddenly appeared behind us. I looked up and to my relief, saw Father. He looked down at us as if to say "what are you two doing here," and then looked up and saw Theano going berserk. He shook his head and motioned for us to follow him. We rushed away from the battle zone.

Several hundred meters from Thea Theano's house, Father stopped and hugged us. He looked back toward the ongoing melee and shrugged his shoulders.

"Eh, what did you expect from Theano?" he said. "Let's just hope she doesn't kill anyone."

At first, we quietly walked home. As we hit the main road and worked our way toward Gargaliani's hill, Father began to tell us about his trip. When my parents walked out of Gargaliani, they headed toward Kalamata, the largest city in southern Greece and the capital of Messenia. Along the way, they stopped to eat what little they had and traded for food whenever the opportunity arose. At night, they slept outside on blankets they had brought. My parents passed Kalamata and continued east. After several more days, they finally made it to Mani, asked for directions to Boliana, and somehow made their way to my great grandfather's village. Asking again and again for the Petropouleas family, Mother was able to locate people in the

dandelions for Dinner

town who went by that name. By our standards, they were affluent, flush with land, productive fields and plenty of food. Father said that the war hadn't affected those Maniates all that much.

But contrary to my parents hopes, they were not greeted with the open arms that they had imagined. Worried that they had come to Mani to steal from them, the Petropouleases placed my parents out in their family barn to sleep. So much for the famous Maniate *filotimo*, the loads of hospitality they were purported to have. With the passage of time so great, my parents couldn't find anyone who had ever heard of her grandparents Spyro and Maria, the vendetta against Spyro, nor of their late-night escape from there. So after a day or two with nothing left to do and no one left to find, my parents accepted the little food they were given and began the walk home. In the end, they walked twelve hot days for a sack of onions. A big effort doesn't necessarily mean a big payoff.

As for the Andartes, Father told us that they were all over the countryside and had interrogated my parents a number of times. But each time, the guerillas saw my parents as no more than members of the Greek underclass and allowed them safe passage. Father told us how the German absence caused towns in the countryside, one by one, to fall to Communist control. And each had its own story of Communist brutality to tell. But the Andartes they met were giddy at the proposition of taking Kalamata and then Meligala, a town only forty kilometers to the west of Gargaliani.

"Don't worry, Kyrie," one of the Andartes told Father, "after Meligala, it will be no time before we are in Gargaliani. Hang in there. You will be liberated before you know it from the yolk of the Fascists!"

"They say they are coming to liberate us," said Father as we arrived home. "Boys, there is a big battle coming to our town. And it's all a complete joke. Who are they going to liberate us from? These animals act like they are fighting for us. They don't even know why they are fighting!"

Chapter 24
THE BATTLE OF GARGALIANI

When we returned home, we saw that much had changed in Gargaliani during our absence. Royalist forces had become further entrenched, readying the town for an attack that was sure to come. Leftists and their followers were branded, interrogated, tortured, and even killed. The heads of female Communist sympathizers were shaved, and such women paraded around the plateia, an act designed to embarrass and disgrace them, their bald heads just rewards for sleeping with the enemy.

While organized Andartes units worked their way toward Gargaliani, smaller Communist bands lived in the rugged terrain outside of town, near Mouzaki and other nearby villages. These guerilla fighters would assemble, perform some raid for supplies or food, and then retreat to their hideouts. Royalists roamed the countryside on the hunt for them, usually on tips they received from locals. And from time to time, they would return from such missions with a prisoner or two, people they had already beaten and interrogated, only to beat and interrogate them some more. This questioning oftentimes took place on the second floor of a building across from the plateia, adjacent to Piliotis's café. The prisoners' cries pierced the plateia and eventually became so loud that the torturers were forced to enlist the help of a trumpet player to mask their screams. But the trumpet player betrayed the intensity of violence because the louder the victim cried, the louder he blew.

The music became so absurdly comical that the kids in town joked about the songs and the beatings saying things like "Woo, listen to that trumpet play the national anthem. The guy they are beating must be a real patriot," or "Did you hear that? I'll bet that poor fellow is a real music lover."

One afternoon, I was walking through the plateia when the trumpet player began to blow a famous Greek marching song. As

I approached the torture building, the music abruptly stopped. I looked up and saw a man in the torture room run toward the balcony and jump off it. He landed right in front of me, his body hit the ground just a few feet away. As he lay there experiencing the final seconds of his life, he looked at me. Though I had never seen him before, our eyes met without any pretense, just like the others, as if he knew that I was the last human being he would ever see. We stared at each other, and I wondered what he was thinking. Did he want to leave a message for someone? Perhaps a good-bye to his mother? A word to his wife? But our momentary bond ended abruptly when a crowd surrounded the man and quickly carted him away. This was the third person that I saw die right in front of me, proving mother's maxim that "everything happens in threes."

Life was never as cheap as it was at this time, and it became clear, at least to us, that the safest thing to be was exactly what we were—insignificant. In Mouzaki, Andartes visited Kyrio Koropoulos, the man who had traded us Kanella for our sewing machine and the man Mother and I visited two years before. When Koropoulos, who the Andartes had labeled a "Fascist plutocrat," didn't want to share his food with the Andartes any more than he had at first with us two years before, they shot him in the head and took what they wanted anyway. They similarly visited Papa Yianni, the priest who purchased and then dug a well on a "useless" piece of our vineyard in the summer of 1936. They killed him too. People on both sides were being killed everywhere.

Around this time, British policy in Greece began to shift. Up to this point, the British had supported EAM, strange bedfellows drawn together because of their common German enemy. English airdrops to the Andartes, coordinated oftentimes by British field agents on the ground, were common, and we had heard and even seen some of them.

"Those idiots are arming their own enemies," Father used to say.

But whether or not the British were brainless for arming EAM, their strategy was certainly slowing the German withdrawal from Greece, the positive effects of which were felt elsewhere on the European continent. A number of factors played a role in the English policy shift, including the impending defeat of Germany, the

Russians on the verge of conquering Eastern Europe, and a division of postwar Europe in the offing.

Nothing pushed the Brits over the edge faster than their recognition of EAM's true colors, which came into full focus just sixty or so kilometers from Gargaliani. On September 10, 1944, Communist forces hit Kalamata. The carnage was merciless and beyond words. And the leftist victors and their obsequious followers were so frenzied that when they paraded the former governor of Messinia and some other prisoners through Kalamata's main square, crowds killed the captives to death with their bare hands, clubs, knives, shoes, and rocks. The three-day battle of Kalamata and its carnage scared the British so much that they finally determined that ELAS and EAM, who they knew were savage Marxists, were now their enemies. Within a week, the Andartes hit a town near Kalamata called Meligala. There, they massacred some fifteen hundred in a fierce, three-day battle that culminated with the dumping of body after body in a well near the town.

In the days that followed the massacre at Meligala, more and more Andartes appeared in the towns surrounding Gargaliani, now personally led by their brutal and fanatic leader Ares Veluchiotis, often called only "Ares." Rumors that the victorious army of Meligala was on its way to capture Gargaliani intensified. The showdown between Veluchiotis and Stoupas, the "Andarte-eater" himself, was at our doorstep. This prompted the British to send an agent by the name of Grimson to meet with Stoupas, an attempt to avoid a Royalist defeat by persuading Stoupas that his forces should immediately surrender to ELAS.

"Give up your weapons," he told them, "and wait for the arrival of Greek government from exile."

But for Stoupas, long before baptized in fire and the blood of his fellow Greeks, there was no such choice. Not only did he believe his forces could beat the Andartes in Gargaliani, he knew that his surrender meant the firing squad. Dying in battle was preferable and certainly more honorable.

The stage was set. Around noon on September 21, 1944, two heavily bearded men on horseback approached Gargaliani from the east, near the church of St. Spyridon. Fully dressed for battle with rifles slung on their backs and strings of ammunition crisscrossing their chests, they carried white flags over their shoulders and informed the sentries guarding the city that they held a message to be delivered directly to Stoupas. They were permitted to continue into the town and rode, ever so slowly, toward the plateia. When they reached the gymnasium, the men cut diagonally across an empty lot and stopped in front of the Protective Forces' headquarters, what had previously been the Italian army's headquarters. Then, remaining mounted on their horses, they silently waited for someone to come out of the building to meet them.

Within minutes, an orderly emerged.

"What do you want?" he asked.

"We have a note for your commander Stoupas," replied one as he handed a folded piece of paper to the orderly.

He took it into the building and in a few minutes, returned carrying another folded piece of paper, which he handed to the rider. Without looking at the paper, the men turned their horses around and walked, ever so slowly, out of town, their white flags continuing to wave over their shoulders.

Word suddenly spread around town as to the content of the correspondences. The ELAS riders' note purportedly demanded the Royalist's prompt surrender of their weapons and the town. Stoupas's reply, it was said, was the same terse reply that Leonidas, leader of the three hundred Spartans at Thermopile, gave to Persian King Xerxes after he and his hundreds of thousands of troops demanded the Spartans' weapons: *"Molon lave"*—come and get them."

The Communist attack was imminent. Seeing as Gargaliani sat atop a three-hundred meter bluff on its west, the only logical location of the assault would be from the east, with the St. Spyridon neighborhood to catch its brunt. That afternoon, activity was at a high pitch. Forces imposed a curfew, civilians retreated to their homes, and Stoupas, flanked by his body guards, walked through town inspecting positions, shouting orders, and encouraging his men. I watched him pass our house several times to examine his defenses. On one occasion, Mother waived and wished him good luck.

"Thank you, Kyria. We are going to eat those criminal Communists alive," Stoupas responded as he smiled and waved.

When Father heard Mother talk to Stoupas, he burst in from the other room.

"Soot, Nitsa. Don't talk to him. Have you gone mad? Nitsa, even the walls have ears. We cannot be too careful. The last thing we need right now is to expose ourselves as Royalist sympathizers. Our life is difficult enough as it is."

Morale within the ranks of the protective forces was high. And most in town were confident that they and their Andarte-eating leader would be able to do what the Royalists had been unable to do in Meligala—repel them. Night came, and we retired to bed waiting for the storm. Well before dawn, sporadic gunfire began. And by the time the sun rose, the gunfire was constant—the battle was underway. Machine-gun bursts were everywhere and seemed to originate, as predicted, from the east.

At the outset of the battle, the protective Royalist forces put their firepower to use, and their mortars played havoc with the Andartes, who were pinned down and unable to add a meter to their positions. Bits of information made their way to us from the occasional passerby.

"Our lines are holding; we are winning," we heard a number of times.

But as the battle wore on, we heard the Royalist's defenses began to crack. News quickly spread that the Andartes had set up a cannon near Pirgaki and were attempting to lob shells from there all the way into town. But the shells, many of which had been retrieved from a sunken ship, were damp and despite intense impacts, didn't explode. One of the Andartes' units broke off from the rest and attacked the town from the south. Simultaneously, another detachment moved covertly along a dry creek and launched a surprise attack on the water reservoir's defenders. After a fierce firefight, it fell to the Andartes.

Even though news from the front was spotty and for the most part unreliable, increasingly bad bits made their way to our neighborhood, giving us a sense of doom. A dead shell landed in the empty lot right next door to us and shook our entire house. Then another dud landed directly inside my friend Niko's house, entering through the kitchen window and smashing a cement sink. More and more shells landed in our vicinity, causing Father to worry that the next shell might not be a dud and worse, might land directly on us.

"Nitsa, we are leaving. The Andartes will be here soon. Gather a couple of things. Let's go."

We ran out the door and headed west. With nowhere else to turn, we went to our old house, still home to my late uncle's family. For at least the time being, we put our differences aside and our relatives welcomed us with open arms. Though slightly more distant, we could still hear artillery fire and the haphazard booms. When someone mentioned that it would be safer for us on the first floor of the home, the cellar that we had long ago used for storage, we moved downstairs. Father from time to time, peeked outside the side door to get a sense of what was happening. And whenever he saw someone pass, he interrogated him about the front, often gleaning contradictory information. One person said that the Andartes had been beaten back. Another said they had broken the lines and entered the city. Such reports continued. When we heard a lull in the fighting, we assumed the Andartes had been defeated and stepped outside to thank God we were still alive. Then we saw a man casually walking toward us. He didn't move with any sense of urgency and as he passed, we could see that though he was unshaven and rough looking, he carried no weapon and wore a clean Royalist uniform. He appeared to have been a fighter who left the front and then changed his clothes.

"How are things?" Father asked.

"Kyrie, it's all over. The battle is done."

"That's it then? The Andartes are gone?"

"Gone? The Communists have won! Or should I say, we handed victory to them."

"They won? Just like that? What happened?"

"Yes, they won. Though we had all the heavy weapons and the real fire power, we had no valor at all. What an embarrassment. The Andartes were brave and fought to win. We just went through the motions. You and your families should brace yourselves. The Andartes will be upon you in the next twenty minutes. Get ready to live under Communism."

As he turned to walk away, he confidently declared," *Zito i Ellas*"—Long live Greece.

"Where are you going?" Father asked.

"Me? I'm going home to Filiatra. I've had enough of this."

He proceeded westward and quickly disappeared.

Believing that there must be safety in numbers, several other families congregated in our building and waited with us to see what fate would bring. By now, the steady shots had turned sporadic, one here and one there. Random pops became louder and louder, telling us that the Andartes were nearing. Worried that the noises were summary executions, one of the ladies screamed that the men should immediately hide. Without thinking, the half dozen or so, including Father, retreated to a room in the rear. This dirty, dark and dank room sat directly underneath the nightmarish smelly bathroom of my childhood and was home to the building's septic tank. They closed the door.

Within minutes, people flooded our neighborhood's streets and before we had a chance to assess what was happening, a band of ten Andartes, weapons out and hot, were suddenly in the middle of us.

"Who here is with the protective forces?" one of them yelled.

"Nobody," someone replied.

"Welcome, welcome," another said. "We are all poor people waiting to be liberated from the Fascists. Thank God you're here. Thank you."

Mother froze and waited to see what the Andartes would do next. Their leader, a lightly bearded thin man in his late twenties, pointed toward the stairs with his pistol.

"Is anyone hiding upstairs?"

We shook our heads "no."

The Andartes turned to me, "You! Lead me upstairs through the apartment."

I looked at Mother.

"Go ahead. We have nothing to hide," she said.

I climbed the stairs. Several others followed behind me. With his gun pointed in front of him, the soldier searched through the entire home, under beds and behind doors. When he was satisfied that we weren't hiding anyone, he descended the stairs and turned to his men.

"Round up all these people and take them to the detention center at the high school. We can sort things out there"

As we were about to be led away, one of the women spoke up, "What about the men in the back room?"

Several Andartes ran to the back of the cellar and with guns pointed toward the septic room, screamed at Father and the others.

"Everyone out! Why are you hiding? Who are you? You are obviously all Royalists."

"No, Kyrie, we are not," one replied.

"If you are not Royalists, then why are you hiding? You're lying. You are all traitors who will be appropriately dealt with."

The women ran to the men's defense.

"No Kyrie," one replied. "We are your co-strugglers. We hid the men because we were afraid *you* were Royalists. From here, we didn't know who was winning the battle. If they were Royalists, we wouldn't have told you about these men. Thank God you've arrived."

Obviously confused, the Andartes turned to his men.

"You and you, take these men to the camp for interrogation."

One group of Andartes led the men into the street and another led the women and children. By this time, the streets were filled with scores of people being directed to various detention centers around town. We fused into the crowds and proceeded toward the high school as directed. There were so many people walking that we lost our captors, or they lost us, and before I knew it, Father was walking with us.

It seemed everyone was being led toward the high school, now within sight. Posted at the entrance of the school were several Andartes, bearded giants who directed the crowds to various places inside the compound. When we approached the building, we were ordered to walk to the right, down an outdoor corridor to a courtyard. From there, we could see the front entrance and had a clear view of at least some of the action near the plateia off in the distance. We braced ourselves for what was to come.

The Andartes continued to lead people into the school, directing them to sit in various areas. Near the entrance, the apparent paradigm of everything an ELAS warrior should be, was a ferocious looking Andarte. He was tall, rugged, and off his face hung a thick long black beard that ended near the middle of his chest. Belts of munitions formed an "x" across his torso and he held a long, black, leather whip in his right hand. No doubt, this man was formidable. Mother took one look at him and pulled Stathi and me close to her.

"Sit quietly," she said to Father. "And don't even look at Rasputin over there."

The man Mother called Rasputin, still holding the whip in his right hand, picked up a bullhorn with his left hand.

"Long live the people!" he began. "Long live the movement!" "Death to the protective forces." "We have won. We have beaten the traitor Royalists!"

As he got going, a tall, slender prisoner pushed his way through the crowd toward him.

"I'm a loyal member of EPON," he said, "and I don't belong in detention with the traitors."

Rasputin ignored him and continued to talk into his bullhorn, "Long live Greece! Long live the revolution."

The young man, apparently not taking the hint, persisted in his attempt to persuade the giant Andartes of his true colors at which time Rasputin, without missing a beat, grabbed the man's face with his giant hand and shoved him backwards to the ground.

The man sprang back to his feet and got right up to Rasputin's face.

"Why are you pushing me? I am one of you. I am with you! I don't belong here," he pleaded.

But Rasputin wouldn't have any of it and in the most fluid of motions, swung his whip at the man's head, slicing open his temple and causing a river of blood to gush forth and down his face. The victim collapsed, and several Andartes came and carried him away. And then without missing a beat, Rasputin once again put his bullhorn to his mouth.

"Attention, attention! I want everyone to know that we are all Greeks here. We are all brothers and sisters. What is done is done! No matter what side anyone is on, let us all embrace one another right here and move on! The destiny of Greece is in our hands. Now is the time to come forward and make amends. If prior to now you have been with the Royalists, come forward! Don't delay. You will be forgiven."

Emotions ran high and we sat as quietly and as poker-faced as we could. A young man on the other side of the courtyard moved toward Rasputin. As he neared the Andarte, he looked like he was going to hug him and make peace with his enemy. But before he reached him, a number of Andartes ran up and threw the man to the ground. One punched his head and his torso and the others kicked him. When the victim was barely still conscious, one of the men pulled out a revolver and shot a bullet into his head.

"Another traitor dead! We are liberated from the scum of the earth," said Rasputin. "Now who else would like to make amends?"

With a better understanding of the rules, everyone remained silent and Mother gripped Stathi and me as we stared at Rasputin and the other cold men. Off in the distance, we could hear the singing of popular Andartes' songs wafting through the air. Coming from the east, the victorious ELAS army, led by Ares Veluchiotis himself in the flesh, was making its triumphant entry into Gargaliani. Songs and cheers filled the air.

"Look at them," said Mother. "I can't believe it."

"Everyone here will do exactly as he is told," Rasputin reported with his conical bullhorn. "The screening process has begun. All those people whose sons are fighting for the glory of ELAS, come forward now."

Many rose and walked toward the Andartes, who directed them to a line near the high school's side entrance where we were standing. The line was queued up to a table, behind which sat a screening committee. Those who the committee was able to confirm were truly members of the ELAS "family" were released and immediately directed to return home. Rasputin moved down his list, calling forward those with EPON affiliations and then those with EAM affiliations. In light of the many Communists in Gargaliani, the process seemed to take an eternity. Not affiliated with any group, we didn't move. Mother quietly pointed out that men from ELAS' Andartes were burning the home of Stoupas. I watched a small fire suddenly engulf, and in what seemed like an instant, destroy the home.

As the afternoon wore on, the town quieted, and Rasputin continued directing people with his bullhorn. In the end, those left were either Royalists or people with no political affiliations. We hoped to be recognized as members of the latter group. Finally, Rasputin turned to us and ordered us to get in line. We didn't seem to interest him very much, and even before he finished motioning to us, he turned his attention elsewhere. We tensely gathered ourselves and did as we were told. As we approached the committee's table, I could see that there were a number of familiar faces sitting behind it, people I recognized from around town. And then, we saw standing up behind the committee Father's second cousin, Yiannis Mastorakis. Though I had heard Father mention that he had a cousin who had become one of EAM, the Communist nerve center's honchos, I had never before met the man. We slowly moved toward the committee's table. Just before we arrived, Father caught his cousin's attention by pulling at his sleeve. Yiannis looked at Father and Father silently pointed at himself as if to say, "Yianni, You know who I am. You know we are not in anyone's group. Please get us out of here." Yianni understood, looked around and motioned us through.

"They can go," he said to the others.

We walked past the interview table and suddenly found ourselves on the street, directly in front of Stoupas's house, which was now smoldering. Armed Andartes moved quickly through the plateia as blood, smoke, and death were splattered everywhere. It was clear that the societal rules we had been born into and spent a lifetime living by no longer applied. It was every man for himself. Gargaliani was hell. Our mission was clear—get home as quickly as possible and avoid contact with anyone. A block in front of us, near the plateia, we could see the bearded Andartes moving everywhere. Behind them, black smoke pumped into the innocent sky.

"Let's go this way," Father said as he grabbed Stathi and directed us down a back street, away from the men, and on a circuitous route home.

We moved through the streets, block by block, as quickly as we could. The random cracks of firearms were everywhere, the streets littered with the discarded dead—our neighbors, people whose lives had been ended by those next to whom they had peacefully lived for ages. When we were only twenty or so meters from our home, we were startled by the sudden appearance, directly in front of us, of Takis Pavleas, a teenager we knew well. He was flanked by two barely pubescent Andartes, their youth betrayed by their lack of facial hair. Takis grew up only a block or so from our old house. Mother never liked him, considered him an idiotic low-life and worse, resented him for being part of the family that kept an untidy barn that stunk up the old neighborhood. When Takis saw Father, his eyes darted back and forth and, as if he had located a prey, irrationally pointed at him.

"There's one. There's one right there. He is one of them."

Father froze and didn't speak, as if the wiring between his brain and mouth had been severed.

"Shoot him; shoot him now," Takis ordered.

The Andartes pointed their barrels at Father.

But before they could shoot, Mother jumped in front of her husband at lightning speed.

"Taki, what's the matter with you? Have you lost your mind? You know this man and you want to kill him in today's insanity? You know that we are the very people you are fighting for. We are the underprivileged, the deprived. Don't you recognize us?"

The men hesitated.

"Do we look like plutocrats, Taki? You grew up next to us. Have you forgotten who you are? Have you allowed all this insanity to drive you mad? You should be ashamed of yourself, Taki. I am embarrassed for you."

Takis and the men froze.

"Out of my way, Kyria, we know…"

"Taki, stop it! I'll tell you what you know—you have known my husband your entire life. You know as well as anyone that we are poor nobodies. As hungry as you and your family are, we are in the same predicament. We are the people this movement is fighting for. Now you want us killed? What kind of movement is this? What kind of justice is this? This is rule by the people? This is murder! You men have lost your minds. You have become drunk with insanity."

"But, Kyria …"

"Taki, these are not the ideals you are fighting for. If you allow this to happen, Taki, you will be killing an innocent man, and in front of his family no less, his wife and his two young boys. The action will haunt you your entire life, well after this insanity passes. Will you take care of these innocent boys? Or perhaps, *you* will," Mother said as she pointed to the man with the rifle. "What will happen to these orphans?"

"I know different," Takis said. "I know your husband was involved with the Royalists. He tried to enlist with them."

"Are you mad? Taki, stop this lunacy and get out of here. If you do this, you will be committing the greatest of sins. You will spend the rest of your life seeking God's forgiveness, and it will elude you.

None of you will ever find it. My father, the great Papa Sarantis, used to tell me about such people. They are the walking dead, bodies that carry souls in chains. Oh, you will be tortured in this life; you will become wanderers, never knowing where you are going and never arriving at your destination. And wherever you go, you will find yourselves only further from the peace you chase, so far that you will no longer believe that anyone has ever been at peace. Then, when you die, you will burn in hell. Now get out of here, all of you. Go to your homes."

Whether they were shocked by Mother's intrepidness, whether her sermon hit some nerve within them, or whether she reminded these young men of their own mothers I do not know, but Mother's statement was a hard and fast injection of clarity into the fog. Both Andartes lowered their rifles and looked at Takis. Suddenly, he wasn't so sure anymore. Mother sensed his confusion.

"Taki, we are going home. You all move on."

She grabbed Father by the arm, and we continued toward our home. The men obeyed Mother and walked away.

"We will check you out, and we will be back. You hear me, we'll be back," Takis exclaimed.

We hurried down the street and quickly entered our house. When we walked in, we understood why the Andartes had ordered everyone out of their homes and held at the high school. They had ransacked our house, and I am sure everyone else's as well, taking anything of value as the spoils of their victory. Our dining-room floor was littered with everything from our kitchen utensils to our blankets and clothes. It occurred to me that this was why relatives of the Andartes were sent home so quickly— to protect their belongings from the looting. Father's suit and his only pair of shoes were gone, but in their haste, the looters left a number of our more valuable items, many of which we found spread around our dining room floor. They were apparently shopping for specific items and even left behind a number of things clearly stolen from other homes including a bag of clothes and bread.

Overall, we fared well in the battle of Gargaliani. We were alive, our house hadn't been torched, and Kanella was still in our basement. To give thanks, Mother lit an oil lamp that hung before a cluster of icons in the bedroom. Together we prayed, giving thanks to God and

dandelions for Dinner

Panagia for protecting us, as always, and asking to help us survive what was to come.

The following morning, we were awakened by distant shouts in the streets that we learned were members of EAM trying to locate and account for members of the opposition. As we slowly ventured outside, we could see that despite the carnage that was everywhere, the sky was a deep blue and the atmosphere as clear and as crisp as ever, as if it had been striped clean the day before by a terrible storm. In fact, it was the most beautiful day I had ever seen. I surveyed our neighborhood and saw dead Greeks everywhere. People spoke softly to one another and compared stories of survival, endless tales of tragedy and narrow escapes. We saw our neighbor, the cobbler Maestro Vasili, who knew and reported the fate of many in our neighborhood. It was clear that in one way or another, the battle had touched everyone. Too many to remember were shot to death. Some suffered fates even worse. The brother of the wonderful young Veta, the woman across the street from us who had given me the potatoes to plant in her front yard, had been burned alive by the Andartes.

As Mother and I surveyed our neighborhood, Niko appeared and said, "Come take a walk with me, Saranti."

"Okay," I replied.

We walked around the neighborhood, telling one another exaggerated stories of what we had experienced the day before. We explored the area, in hopes of finding a shell or two to keep as souvenirs. Ignoring Mother's admonishment to the contrary, we approached one of the wet duds that sat in the lot near our home but were promptly chased away by Niko's uncle when he saw Niko readying himself to try to pick it up.

"Have you lost your minds? That shell will explode and blow you both to bits."

We moved through the streets and toward our school. We passed several corpses who, by their uniforms, we could see were Royalist soldiers. And by their head wounds, we could see that they were not killed in battle, but had been executed. Such men were everywhere. Across from my school, two such victims lay side by side, their uniforms so dirty and oily and their faces so crusted with dried blood that it was impossible to determine on whose side they fought. Niko and I stared at the bodies and I marveled at how only hours before they were alive, their lives filled with hopes, aspirations, worries and joys, and how now they were nothing but already decomposing corpses, as if their very lives were a mistake that had finally been corrected.

As Niko and I stared at those dead men, two young women dressed in flowery spring dresses and holding baskets of flowers approached us. They spoke loudly with one another and their entire appearance was odd, like Shakespearian fools sent onto the stage to relieve a scene's dark perversity. And as if Niko and I were not there, they began to stare and talk about the corpses.

"Are they with us?" one asked the other.

"Yes, they are with us," replied the other as she began throwing flowers on the bodies of the dead men.

"No, no, no," said the first. "They are *not* with us, they are with the dirty bum protective forces."

The girls bent down and began picking up the flowers they had just thrown on the men.

Then thinking again of her actions, the second asked, "Are you sure they are not with us? Maybe we should leave some, just to be sure."

They replaced a few flowers and left on their merry way, on to the next bodies. Niko and I headed toward the plateia. On the way, we saw that the agora was busy, filled with people buying and selling, likely replenishing depleted food supplies. In the plateia, the coffee houses were filled with noisy patrons, all of whom were Communists and their sympathizers—Royalists were nowhere to be found. They talked about a new day in Greece, discussed how under Communist rule, life would finally be just, how the people would finally rule, and how the Fascists were finished. The plateia bustled with hopeful uncertainly.

When I finally returned home that afternoon, Mother told me what she heard happened to Nikos Halazonitis. Nikos, a known Royalist, was believed to have fought valiantly that morning. But when the lines broke, around the time we spoke with the man who was walking back to Filiatra, Nikos was wounded in the leg while firing at the advancing Communists. Injured, he immediately returned to his house, nursed his wound, and changed into his civilian clothes to wait out the battle. Nikos was surprised when Andartes burst into his home but did what he was told when they ordered him to walk them through his house, to open his bureaus, and show them under his beds. As Nikos, bleeding, led the men around his home, he talked and talked. And when they asked him to show them into the home's basement, he led the adrenaline-filled Andartes down the stairs. As he descended the steps, one of the Andartes fired his weapon at Nikos's head. The shot was a direct hit and thrust Nikos forward, tumbling him down the stairs. He landed face down on his basement floor in a pool of his blood. Then, the Andartes left.

But Nikos wasn't dead and on this occasion, it was once again his mouth, the instrument that had saved him so many times before, that saved him again. Indeed, as Nikos had led the Andartes into his basement, his continuous talking caused him to turn his head to the side at the very moment the pistol fired. So rather than enter his cranium, the bullet entered Nikos's head through the rear of his right cheek and proceeded through his jaw and out his mouth. Though the shot was bloody, it wasn't fatal. But when he hit the ground, Nikos played dead, which along with the flow of blood, left the shooter believing his aim was true. Because bands of Andartes would continue to roam in and out of his house that night, Nikos knew not to move. So he lay there for hours. Eventually, Nikos's Mother, Kyria Garifalia, discovered him and helped him crawl out of the house and into a nearby sewer where he spent the night bleeding from his mouth. By morning, Nikos was on the verge of death, unconscious and down several pints of blood. Then his mother, desperate to save her son, sought an audience with Father's cousin, the Communist Mastorakis. When she appeared before him, Kyria Garifalia fell to her knees and begged him to spare her only son. For reasons unknown, Mastorakis was moved by Kyria Garifalia's gesture and granted her wish. His men fished Nikos out of the sewer and administered to him the medical attention he needed to survive.

Following the Battle of Gargaliani, the surviving but humiliated Royalists fled. Many walked south while others boarded boats and rowed away to save themselves. Stoupas and three hundred of his men fled to Pylos where he planned to regroup for another attack. But Stoupas's men weren't up to it—their morale too low. Many simply surrendered to ELAS. Rumors spread that Stoupas and his closest followers took refuge behind the walls of Pylos's Venetian fortress. So the Communists surrounded it and with his capture imminent, Stoupas took his own life. Legend has it that Stoupas placed a gun to his head and pulled the trigger a number of times to no avail, until someone reminded him that he was still wearing the piece of the Holy Cross around his neck. He promptly removed it and only then did his pistol fire. And just like that, the Royalist forces faded away with most of its leaders dead and its infantrymen returning to their homes to face the formidable task of surviving the days ahead.

When it was all said and done, six hundred or so locals lost their lives in the Battle of Gargaliani and its aftermath. Though few had died at the hands of the Italians and Germans during the occupation, the town lost roughly ten percent of its population the day the Communists won, keeping churches filled with the widows and orphans of the dead. How we survived the battle is as obvious as it is ironic—we survived because Mother's fears of marrying a poor nobody like Father came true. We survived because we were nothing more than the world's mediocrity, the very people who played no role in anything over and above their own relative insignificance, people who were not even a footnote to footnotes in the story of this struggle. Indeed, it seems that in times like these, the best thing someone could be was a nobody.

Chapter 25
NOTHING BUT HOPE

After the Battle of Gargaliani, ELAS moved to consolidate its position and to become masters of the entire Peloponnese. Fighters travelled from town to town and from city to city killing any Royalists they could find, often in mass executions. In one of the more infamous massacres, the Andartes gathered eighteen local professionals who would not switch to the Communist worldview and told them they would be taken to Pylos for further processing. Among these eighteen was Dr. Papathomopoulos, the doctor who had only months before purchased our olive grove. But just outside of Gargaliani, all of them were shot dead. Many Greek soldiers, including those who were protecting the rear guard of the fleeing Germans, quickly capitulated to the Andartes. Others escaped to Athens with their lives, finding refuge there as they waited for the arrival of the former government from exile in Egypt.

On October 9, 1944, Churchill and Stalin discussed the division of the Balkans.

In a quick conversation that ended months of negotiations, Churchill made it simple: "Let us settle about our affairs in the Balkans. So far as Britain and Russia are concerned, how would it do for you to have 90 percent predominance in Rumania, for us to have 90 percent of the say in Greece, and go 50-50 about Yugoslavia."

Churchill memorialized the percentages on a piece of paper and handed it to Stalin. Stalin looked at it, checked it off with a blue pencil, and the deal was done. That check mark was the first nail in the coffin for Communist rule in Greece.

When it became evident to EAM's leaders that the Soviet Union was not going to support its efforts to take over Greece, EAM performed a shocking political about-face, ignoring the strategy of its most violent proponent, Ares Veluchiotis himself, and seeking instead to seize power through political means. EAM joined the still exiled National Unity Government, which was at that time led by George Papandreou, and then accepted what they had refused to accept before, only six out of fifteen cabinet seats and to harness their guerilla fighters.

On the morning of October 12, 1944, the German occupation of Greece officially ended when German officers lowered their swastika from atop the Acropolis, offered a last salute to the tomb of the Unknown Soldier, and handed the city of Athens over to its mayor. And as the Germans left town, seas of long-suffering Greeks spilled into Athens's streets behind them, oozing with an ebullience that neither anyone had ever seen before nor would likely to ever see again. By noon, Syndagma Square was packed with celebrants who sang with ecstasy, hugged and kissed one another. Three days later, British troops entered Athens *en masse* and three days after that, the National Unity Government, under British protection, finally returned to Greece.

Order needed to be established, and once in Athens, Papandreou's government moved to consolidate its power. It formed a police force and began reassembling the Greek Army. The Communists initially cooperated and worked within the new government and even tried to rein in the recalcitrant Veluchiotis, who by this time, was riding around the Peloponnese on a white horse assassinating "traitors." But the harmony didn't last long. The Communists soon saw the new government as catering to the Royalists and in doing so, paving the way for the return of King George, and thus Fascism. This perception was exacerbated when, on November 10, the pro-monarchy Third Mountain Brigade, a unit of the Greek Army-in-Exile, marched through Athens in battle formation with the new government's blessing. Fears reached their acme when the government ordered all Andartes to demobilize and surrender their weapons between December 10 and 20.

Reconciling our country after a world war, an endless occupation, a brewing civil war, and a brutal famine was no easy task. Despite the new government in Athens, Gargaliani remained firmly under EAM's control, led by people who weren't shy about offering their view that the National Unity Government was neither national nor unifying. Bullhorns roared:

This government is no more than the same Fascist plutocrats from before.

This government wants to keep us down!

This government wants to bring back that cursed king!

This government plans to keep the farmers destitute—in slavery to that evil foreign king!

Father used to say that the continued polarization made Greece's unification impossible, that a far right and a far left with no political middle would cause much blood to be shed before people could be softened up enough to compromise.

"Water and oil can never be mixed," he said, "and there is little hope the criminal Communists and the collaborators will ever work together for the good of Greece."

On December 2, 1944, in protest of the demobilization order, the Communists resigned from the Papandreou government and planned a demonstration for the following day in Athens. British officers learned of it and were instructed to consider any such leftist gathering an offensive military move. They girded for battle. On December 3, several hundred EAM members assembled in Syndagma Square and shouted antigovernment slogans. At some point, shots were exchanged. Who fired first is a matter for debate, but at the end of the day, anywhere from eight to twenty-eight civilians were killed and numerous others injured.

The deaths touched off a storm and some sixty thousand people poured into Syndagma Square in protest. The dead were hailed as martyrs as handkerchiefs dipped in their blood were paraded through the city, further inflaming the people. That night, the Battle of Athens began when Communists stormed and took over a number of the city's police stations. At first, many British were hesitant to fight the Andartes, the same people they had supported and with whom they had fought with for so long against the Germans. But when Churchill sent the British general in Greece a cable ordering him to "act as if [he] were in a conquered city where a local rebellion [was] in progress," British troops went to work.

Urban fighting erupted, and in these battles, the lines were blurry. Women fought on the ELAS side, some ELAS men moved about in civilian clothes, while others wore British uniforms, making it nearly impossible for the British to identify the enemy. Before long, the British were behind. Incredibly, on Christmas Day 1944, at the height of the Battle of the Bulge, Winston Churchill left his war office in Britain and travelled to Greece. He surveyed the situation and determined that the British could not overcome the Communists with firepower alone. He searched for a political solution and settled on orchestrating the appointment of the universally popular Archbishop Damaskinos of Athens as the country's regent, until a vote could be held on whether King George would be allowed to return.

Churchill's instincts were right-on, and the New Year's Day appointment of Damaskinos caused the country's moderates to shift their support away from the Communists. And despite an orgy of massacres at the Communists' hands that January, EAM realized it had been outmaneuvered and soon agreed to come to the negotiating table in the Athenian suburb of Varkiza. Though extremists like Veluchiotis were dead against negotiations and any agreements whatsoever, in early February 1945, the right and left reached an accord that included the surrender of the Andartes's arms. In the end, despite the fact that the Communists appeared to have the majority of the country's support, it was clear that Churchill's political moves, beginning with the agreement he struck with Stalin the previous summer, had beaten them. Varkiza marked the end for Veluchiotis, who, branded an outlaw, was hunted down and killed, some say following an epic battle, others say by his own hand. Either way, the man who triumphantly rode into Gargaliani wearing the laurels of victory in September 1944 was dead within only a matter of months.

Though Father was elated when he heard that the British had prevailed over the Communists in Athens, we remained consumed by simply avoiding starvation. Our struggle became more and more acute after the Battle of Gargaliani and the Battle of Athens, causing Father to work tirelessly to get us something to swallow: boiled weeds, a handful of raisins, a couple of nuts. By January, malnutrition had caused open sores to develop on various parts of our bodies, manifold wounds that we knew would never heal without a proper diet. Stathi and I had them on our legs while Father had them on his back and Mother on her upper arms and legs. Though Mother constantly admonished us not to scratch them, I couldn't resist the urge, and scratched when I couldn't stand it anymore, only to open fresh bleeding wounds. When the sores became especially acute, Father instructed me to spread olive oil on them, a dubious home remedy that caused the scabs to fall off prematurely, leaving open wounds underneath that began to bleed again. The sores caused my parents to become frantic with worry because they knew that they were the harbingers of death. We had seen many people with malnutrition sores develop swollen joints, usually around their ankles, and then quickly die. Father, desperate to get us something to eat, began to forage even harder and harder for dandelions or whatever he could get his hands on. But without bread, which was usually missing from our diet, greens could never sustain us. In an effort to provide some extra nutrition, Mother ordered us to swallow a tablespoon of olive oil three times a day. Everyone in the family complied except me. Just the thought of drinking plain olive oil caused me to dry-heave uncontrollably, a reflex that incensed Mother.

"We are all starving to death, and he won't drink Kanella's milk and he won't drink the olive oil! What are we going to do with this child?"

As I walked the streets alone during the first few months of 1945, I couldn't help but think of the good old days when I worked as a peddler, and we had at least one meal a day to eat. On such walks, I was always struck by how many jovial people there seemed to be eating and drinking in Gargaliani's tavernas. Oftentimes, I stared at them while they ate, lost in a fantasy that I was sitting and dining with them. Oh, what it would be like if I could share in their meal just once, if I could eat as much food as I wanted and fill my belly, if I could eat until I didn't want to eat any more!

These strolls caused countless questions to swirl around my head. How was it, I wondered, that those who ate regular meals had figured out how to survive when we were starving? What was their secret? What were they doing that we weren't doing? Had they somehow won God's favor? And why did God let certain people die and others live? By what criteria did he make such decisions? I asked Mother these kinds of questions.

Her answer was always the same: "God has all, my boy. God has all."

And my response to that had become as hackneyed as it was predictable.

"If God has everything, then why are we so hungry? Why does he let us suffer? Why is God's abundance always reserved for others? Why aren't *we* on his list?"

One afternoon that winter, as I walked barefoot toward the plateia, I passed several tavernas where patrons were jovial, drinking, eating, and laughing. In a daze, I stopped at one and must have been lost in thought for some time because I jumped when the owner threw something at me, hitting me square in the chest. When I picked the object up, I could see it was the hard outside shell of a block of cheese. I looked at the man and he motioned at me with his arms, as if to say, "take that and get out of here, kid." It was obvious I wasn't welcome, so I took the cheese rind and ran to a secluded area not too far from Kokonis's café.

The rind was no larger than my hand, and when I smelled it, I was overcome by the strong aroma of *kefalotiri* cheese, a delicacy I had not eaten for years. One side of the rind was soft and tacky, clearly the side that faced the core. The other was waxy and hard. I tasted the inside portion and methodically began to scrape it with my teeth. And though the outside was difficult to bite, I gnawed and gnawed at it as well until before long I had eaten the entire thing—inside, outside, shell, and all. The chunk of cheese shell satisfied my hunger, and I realized that throwing the cheese at me was an act of philanthropy. And just then, a flush of guilt filled me as I realized I had greedily hoarded a piece of food I should have brought home and shared with my family. I never told them about it.

In those days, my hunger reached such epic proportions that I began following funerals and attending memorial services for the dead. And with people dying left and right, there was no shortage of either. Funerals had to take place within a day or two of a person's death, prior to the onset of decomposition. Memorial services occurred at various intervals after burial, usually at the forty-day mark, the one-year mark, and so on. I attended such services, not to pray for the dead, but to angle some of the *koliva*, typically distributed. At funerals and memorial services, *koliva*, or boiled wheat, was piled in the shape of a grave onto a rectangular plate placed directly on the altar. It was made mainly of boiled wheat, sesame seeds, almonds, ground walnuts, cinnamon, sugar, pomegranate seeds, raisins, and parsley. Each ingredient symbolized some aspect of life, and together were a reminder that we come from and will return to the earth and a metaphor for Christ's teaching that "unless a wheat grain falls into the earth and dies, it remains alone; but if it dies, it bears much fruit."

Oftentimes, my friend Niko would attend the memorial and funeral services with me, and we would spend our time eyeing the *koliva* plates, well aware that any *koliva* we could score would be a bonus. Waiting through a liturgy for a memorial service to begin was always agonizing, requiring more patience than either of us was given at birth. So when it was over, we were chomping at the bit to battle our way up front for our share of the spoils. Invariably, the family of the deceased would try to block-out scavengers like us.

Other times, they just berated us: "Get out of here you lousy bastards. You can't have any of this food. If we give it to you, we will only be memorializing more of our own dead."

One cold, rainy, gray afternoon at the cemetery, Niko and I stood at the head of a grave, near a *koliva* plate. It was nearly freezing, but we stood there, clad only in our short pants, with bare legs and bare feet, and covered in only small spring jackets. As the priest said the prayers for the deceased, we held our arms tucked in close to our shivering bodies. The family of the dead, perhaps from a level or two up the social ladder from us and obviously not destitute, looked at us with supercilious disdain. I could clearly hear them talk.

"Look, the lousy little bastards have shown up. Why did they have to come here?"

Then one of them turned to us.

"Get out of here! Go somewhere else! Go to another grave. We can memorialize our own dead here. These people don't need your prayers. Go pray for someone else."

But all I could think of was how fortunate I was to be positioned in front, right next to the *koliva*, and Niko and I were unfazed by the slights. Hunger turns insults into trivialities. After the service began, the scene must have been darkly comical, with people weeping for a person who was already dead while simultaneously maintaining total disregard for the suffering of the living, those who were dying right in front of them and could still be saved. When we heard the priest wind down the prayer by chanting three times the final prayer, "eternal be his memory," our Pavlovian mouths began to water. Just then, another boy, maybe sixteen years-old or so, flew in from the ether and made an end run for the *koliva* plate. Before anyone could react, he dug his enormous filthy hands straight into the pile and began shoving as much of it as he could into his mouth. The shocked relatives began to curse him, but the hungry boy was determined and kept on struggling to grab and eat as much as he could. *Koliva* flew everywhere. When they finally contained the boy, the deceased's family began to crawl on the ground and pick up, one by one, the fallen wheat kernels returning each to the plate. Niko and I were out of luck.

Our situation deteriorated even more, and most nights, my family somberly and quietly went to bed with nothing but acid in our hollow stomachs. On the occasion that Father was able to get us some food, he put us into jovial moods that caused Stathi and me to spend such evenings peppering my parents with questions about our futures. Hope-filled talks about America fueled such sessions, which typically took place in our dining room as Stathi and I sat near our portable stove, the *magali*, for warmth.

It was Mother who got these happy talks going, usually by saying something like, "If you liked today's meal, wait until you see what we are going to eat in America."

A comment like that was all it took for Stathi and me to be off to the races.

"Are we going to eat weeds there, too?" Stathi would ask.

"Weeds? No, not weeds, Stathi. Forget those. In America, we will eat much better things. In America, we will eat vegetables, pastas, and meats like steaks, lamb chops, and pork chops.

"How about bread?" I would ask. "Will we have bread?"

Somehow, a meal was only proper when there was bread to go along with it.

"Bread? Of course there will be bread. Our home will be like a bakery, Saranti. There will be bread everywhere."

Sometimes, talk of America raised more questions than it answered.

"We'll have hot dogs to eat in America," Father once said.

"They eat dogs in America?" I replied. "The Americans are like the Italians?"

"No, Saranti, they don't eat dogs in America. Hot dog is just the name of something that is like a sausage that you eat with bread."

"They make sausages out of dogs?" I asked.

After endless discussions about the food we would find in America, Father used to try to explain the economics that awaited us.

"Everyone in America works and earns money, boys. And they use the money to buy food, clothes, and a place to live. And they make so much money there that after they buy their food and their other things, they have money left over, money that they are able to save."

During these months, one of the things that worried Father more and more was a rumor that he had heard that U.S. citizens who had returned to their countries of origin for over two years had forfeited their American citizenship. Whether or not it was true, I don't know. But Father would have never forfeited his citizenship; it was the ace up his sleeve. Whenever his mind would run with such thoughts, that some law might preclude us from leaving Greece for America as we had planned, he would pause.

"Don't worry about any of that, kids. America will never forget her children. And we are her children. No, boys, America will not forsake us. America will take care of us. America cares about its people. If such a law exists, then America will change it!"

With the war seeming to wind down, Stathi and I asked repeatedly for a timetable as to when we would leave the country.

"When?" Father would say. "We will leave for America once the American consulate opens. When it does, I will run to them and tell them I am one of them, one of America's citizens. I will show them my papers, and they will immediately recognize that I have rights. Then they will help us get to America."

Hopeful talk of America made us glow with euphoria and bestowed upon us a feeling of detachment from our suffering, a real hope that despite how bad things were, there were bigger and better things in store for us. Discussions like these caused us to go to bed with fantastic hopeful dreams of our American lives, of food, of bank accounts, of homes, and of a limitless future. When Stathi or I asked about how we would survive long enough to get out of Greece, it was once again America that would save us.

"Your Theo Stathi in Detroit," Mother would say, "will be sending us everything we need to survive. No doubt he's been worried about us, and his packages will begin to arrive soon, as soon as our post offices get going. Remember children, your Father's brother has lived in America for a long time. He has been working there for a long time. He has lots of money. Even better, he is a bachelor and with no family, he is going to help us. We are his family!"

These sorts of talks kept us going, made us positive thinkers without portfolios, who at a minimum scraped together enough hope to muster the energy to keep struggling at least one more day.

Chapter 26
LYING LOW

Despite our hunger, war news during the spring of 1945 brought us great encouragement. The Allies had won the Battle of the Bulge, their troops were marching toward Berlin, and we could see that the war in Europe was wrapping up. On April 28, Benito Mussolini and his paramour, Clara Petacci, were executed and then hung upside down at a gas station in Milan, Italy. When Adolph Hitler learned of the news the following day, he dictated his last will and testament to his secretary and then married his mistress, Eva Braun. On April 30, with Soviet troops just blocks from the Reich Chancellery, the newlyweds committed suicide, Hitler by shooting himself in the head as he simultaneously bit into a cyanide capsule. After that, Karl Donitz the German Navy commander became president of Germany barely long enough to sign its unconditional surrender on May 7. Winston Churchill announced the end of the war on May 8, which thereafter was known as VE Day or Victory in Europe Day

Though our lives had become a struggle to avoid drowning before the tide turned, all things considered, we were faring much better than Hitler and Mussolini. And though things didn't change for us after VE Day, we were hopeful that our lives would improve and turned our attention toward the British, who we heard were coming with aid. And we waited and waited, day after day, week after week. Father checked the newspapers religiously and kept a sharp eye on incoming traffic, always on the lookout for British trucks, asking whatever vehicles he came across whether they had seen the English. And though food filtered into the town's stores ever so slowly, we still lacked a way to buy anything and lived our lives as we had, preoccupied by the uncertainly of each meal but always hopeful that the Allies were right around the corner, on their way to feed us.

While the Communists were still on the outside of the government in Athens, they remained in charge of things in Gargaliani and worked to regroup, claiming to prepare for what they called their "Third Round" of power. But even so, their actions were for the time being peaceful. When it came to eloquence, the left always prevailed. It seemed all the good Greek songwriters were leftists.

Arch-Fascist king
back again in your old nest,
You ask to return
and to govern us.
You ask for the first fascism
and the people's suffering,
But ELAS is rock.
Don't even think about a return to Greece.
You'll only find Metaxas supporters and soil tillers.
Don't fanaticize!
For the first time the rulers in Greece are the people,
Who for the first time have begun to rule.

One day that spring, Father and I walked to our field and saw a jeep and a tank appear in the distance.

"Those are English," Father said in excitement.

"Maybe they will give us something to eat," I replied.

As we approached them, we saw three men looking at a map spread across the jeep's hood. They told us that they were lost and trying to find their way to Kyparissia. Father pointed them in the right direction. They thanked him and moved on.

"Did you see that, Saranti? The English are moving around here freely. The Communists have lost the game. That means that the English are in charge and that can only mean the king is coming back. It seems the English will never forsake our king, Saranti."

Within a few days of our encounter with the jeep, the English made their first official visit to Gargaliani. We learned of their plans to speak to us and many curiosity seekers, including my family, filled the plateia to hear what they would say. EAM members were present, seemingly in full force, as were members of EPON and other leftist sympathizers. When a two-car motorcade pulled into the plateia, it parked in front of Hilas's café. Several dignitaries and their security detail exited the vehicles and made their way to a balcony that overlooked the square. When they stepped out, a British officer began to speak in English to an interpreter who in turn shouted in Greek what he heard to the people below.

"What is done is done!" the interpreter said. "We are all brothers and sisters here! The left should hold out its hand to the right and we must all embrace one another!"

But before the man could get any more words out, the plateia exploded in chants designed to drown him out. Members of EAM and EPON began to shout:

"Down with the king!"

"Democracy for all!"

"Liberty without the king!"

"Death to the traitors!"

Though the officer and the interpreter tried to keep speaking, the chants picked up more steam. Quickly realizing they were talking to people with no intention of listening to them, the men returned to their cars and drove away. Other government officials who came to town in the subsequent weeks were similarly treated.

Officials assigned a few police officers to Gargaliani, a move apparently designed to show that the new government was in charge. But these men only made the left more and more vocal about advertising its "Third Round" and seemed to bring about a renewed return to its trusty old tactics of intimidation. Classic slogans like "heads will roll," "capitalists remnants will be eliminated," "the people will prevail," and "long live the people," were slowly brought back. And so were the knocks on doors in the middle of the night by EPON thugs, as were the beatings. The police officers tried to help but they were too few and too ineffective to do any good.

Father kept reminding us to stick to our game-plan, "Keep your mouths shut and don't offend anyone. There is nothing more important, especially now, than keeping a low profile."

One night, a commotion on the street adjacent to our home awakened us. A group of youths had gathered at the gate that led to the courtyard of my late Theo Dimitri's home.

"Christo, Christo! Come out, we want to talk to you," called one of them.

Christo was the name of my cousin, my late Theo Dimitri's son. Because he had been long before partially paralyzed by polio, I had barely ever seen him. We quietly moved toward the windows to get a look.

"What could they possibly want with him? The boy can barely walk," said Father.

"They are EPON, I think," whispered Mother.

The voice continued to shout, "C'mon, Christo, come out, we want to talk to you!"

Surprisingly, Christo actually appeared on his balcony and when he took one look at the young men, he began to call "Police!" in as sonorous a voice I have ever heard, in a voice that thunderously and operatically boomed through the quietude of the night, *"AS-TI-NO-MIA! AS-TI-NO-MIA! AS-TI-NO-MIA!"*

"He's calling for the police," said one of the boys. "Stop it; we are not going to hurt you, Christo. We just want to talk to you. Come down here."

But intrepid Christo was unfazed and only yelled louder, *"AS-TI-NO-MIA! AS-TI-NO-MIA! AS-TI-NO-MIA!"*

"Poor Christo," Mother whispered as she crossed herself. "I wonder what he said to upset them."

Suddenly, an EPON member jumped over the gate and walked directly into Thea Fotini's rose garden.

"C'mon down right now, Christo. We want to talk to you."

But Christo remained unmoved and stood his ground. And like a great tenor, he continued blasting away, *"AS-TI-NO-MIA! AS-TI-NO-MIA! AS-TI-NO-MIA!"*

Before long, the entire neighborhood had awakened, oil lamps appeared in homes and shutters opened. And just as Christo's solo really got going, another adolescent ran into the garden and whispered something to the boys, a message that prompted them to flee. No police ever came that night, and the episode left us scared, wondering what might come next. If they went after an invalid like Christo, they were sure to come after us sooner or later. But Father kept his cool.

"Don't worry," he said. "We have nothing to fear. Now everyone go to sleep and forget what happened."

The following day, we were relieved to learn that my cousin Christo was not EPON's real target, but that the thugs had been looking for someone else, apparently a man who was renting a room from Thea Fotini.

Our relief was short-lived. That night, we could hear that the men had returned, and to our horror, were standing directly in front of our front door. Mother quietly moved toward the shutters to see what was happening.

"Panagioti, they've come for us," she whispered as she moved toward a window and peered out. "There are a number of them. They are right in front of our door. I think they are from EPON. Panagioti, they must be after you."

Father froze. "Keep the house dark," he whispered. "Why have they come for me? How did I get on their list?" The man could barely speak and stuttered when he tried to force a word out of his mouth, "Oh, G-G-God help me."

"Stop it!" Mother snapped back. "Now get out of here. Go into the basement and hide. I will take care of this."

Father hurried down the stairs, and Mother returned to the window. When she attempted to open the shutters to get a better look at the men, it sent forth a piercing squeak, one that penetrated the desolate street. The noise caused the loiterers, who she could now see were only teens, to flee. After several minutes, when it seemed they were gone for good, Mother walked to the stairs. "Panagioti, it was nothing. Come up here."

My parents walked out the front door and immediately discovered that the boys had painted graffiti directly on the front wall of our home. We moved for a better look and saw a wet and enormous rendition of the king's insignia. When Father saw it, he was horrified.

"Don't touch it, Nitsa! Stay back. It's still wet, and we don't want to get mixed up with any of this. It's bad enough it's on our house. We don't want anyone to think we put it there!"

The following day, the king's insignia became the talk of the town, prompting a steady stream of people to parade past our home. They were of course curiosity seekers, people who had come to see this uppercut in the country's war of politics, a true act of defiance of the left's authority. Many were pleased to see the bold statement and passed our home with a grin, hopeful that the dirty Communists were on their way to being decapitated.

"Finally, our turn has come," I heard one say. Others were not happy and mumbled profanities and warnings when they saw the insignia: "You bastards will get what's coming to you," or "just wait for the 'Third Round' to come."

That afternoon, Communist youth from EPON came to our home carrying a bucket of red paint. I expected that they would merely cover the insignia but watched them neatly and professionally paint their response on the side of our home, adjacent to the insignia. The enormous block letters read:

ΚΑΝΕΝΑ ΦΡΟΥΡΙΟ ΑΠΟΡΘΙΤΟΣ ΓΙΑ ΤΟ ΕΛΑΣ
(THERE IS NO FORTRESS IMPREGNABLE TO ELAS)

The reply prompted a new parade of curiosity seekers past our home, horrifying Father and further foiling our plans of maintaining a "low profile." And then, for reasons I will never know, perhaps because our home had become the canvass for a written war of ideologies, perhaps because we were now the center of attention, Mother felt compelled to get in on the action. And so that afternoon, she walked into the fields, gathered a sack full of wild flowers, and spent the evening weaving them into a large wreath. When she finished, she ordered Father, in the middle of the night, to hang the wreath just above the king's insignia. Though no one knew who had placed it there, the wreath brought yet another line of opinionated spectators past our home.

As the days passed, British military personnel were everywhere. They moved about freely and always seemed to be on their way to, or returning from some mission more important than feeding us. Then out of the blue one morning, an English medical team appeared in the plateia. Supported by a number of combat soldiers, it set up a camp to assess the health of Gargalianians, particularly the children. Doctors examined one person after another and later set up a film projector that ran evening movies in the plateia on the outside wall of the church. The following day, they set up shop at my school and examined the students. When it was my turn, the doctor looked me over, poked his fingers in the side of my neck, glanced at the sores on my legs, examined my scalp, and told me to return to class.

I knew the doctor was holding back the children he diagnosed with lice, and I was surprised when he told me to go back to class. I had been a host to lice for years. As long as I could remember, lice had been my constant companions, my omnipresent enemy. They lived in my hair, in the seams of my clothes, and in my bedding. Oftentimes, Mother would search me for them and crush whatever she could find between the fingernails of her two thumbs, the local execution method of choice. There were so many lice on so many children in Gargaliani that my peers used to kill them between their thumbnails while they shrieked "Between two mountains this maiden is dying," causing everyone to laugh. Any children the English doctors diagnosed with lice were taken to the back of a truck and sprayed all over with some chemical.

We began hearing about how food aid from the United States had arrived in Greece. We also learned that none of it was getting to us because it was being immediately eaten in Athens. However, clothing from various western philanthropic organizations known by acronyms like EMEL and UNTRA did begin to reach Gargaliani. My sixth grade teacher was put in charge of distributing these items and he did so by listing people alphabetically and calling off their names one by one. When our name was finally read, we were led into a room filled with piles and piles of clothes and given various things like shirts, pants and sport jackets, items we were thrilled would replace our rags. Members of EAM and EPON didn't like that locals were receiving aid from Fascist countries like the Unites States, clearly preferring items from the Soviet Union. And though many EAM families accepted the handouts anyway, the leftist spin doctors went to work, with a speed and dexterity that would impress even today's most aggressive politicos, quickly composing songs that mocked whatever emerged from their political adversaries:

Clothes, Clothes from EMEL.
EMEL gave them to UNTRA
And UNTRA gave them back to EMEL.
They loaded them on a caique
And they sent them by ship.
For every ten people a sleeve
And one shoe for the entire family.

Though the clothes were definitely a plus, we still needed food to stay alive and while the shipping lanes hadn't opened yet, Mother harped on Father to write letters to America anyway. I guess she thought that writing letters, even if they would sit in a local post office, was somehow better than doing nothing.

Father pushed back as much as he could, "The shipping lanes to America are still closed, Nitsa. You have to be patient. I follow these things closely, and as soon as there's a change, I will be there."

But as usual, Mother's nagging wore him down, and well before he wanted to and before there was open shipping, Father, by the light of the flame from a twig soaked in olive oil, wrote letters to his siblings in the states, to his brother Stathi in Detroit, to his brother Aristos in Woburn, Massachusetts, and to his sister Tasia who, as far as we knew, still lived in Chicago. He told them that we were still alive, of our plight, our starvation, our sores, and that we desperately needed money to purchase food.

Father and Mother talked endlessly about our long term game-plan, conversations that went something like this:

FATHER: I will continue to stay on top of what's happening and as soon as an American consulate opens, I will go. From there, I will do whatever it takes to be recognized as an American citizen. Once I get my papers, I will leave Greece alone for America. And as soon as I get there, I will find work and send for you.

MOTHER: That's fine, but I don't like the idea of splitting up the family.

FATHER: But, Nitsa, getting four people out may take months. The bureaucracy here will eat us alive, and I am afraid that we may get so delayed in Athens getting everyone's exit documents that we'll never make it out. And besides, if we get stuck in Athens, we won't be able to afford it. We won't have money to live on.

MOTHER: But, Panagioti, we are not solely at the mercy of God. I have relatives in Athens, my cousins, the children of my Mother's siblings. For sure, they will help us.

FATHER: Nitsa, we've tried that before. Remember our walk to Mani? No, it is much easier for one person to leave, travelling alone, than it will be for the whole family. We have to do whatever it takes to get out of here. When I get to the states, I'll stay with Aristos in Massachusetts. From there, I'll send for you.

One afternoon, Father burst into the house overcome with excitement. In his hands he held a copy of a newspaper from Kalamata:

"Nitsa, Nitsa! Look at what the paper says. Finally, Nitsa, finally! This is what we have been waiting for."

Father told us how an office for expatriates opened in Kalamata and how he would go there at once to turn in our papers and commence our exodus.

The news of the Kalamata office was the breakthrough we had been praying for. It meant that we could begin to gather the information we needed to at least figure out how to get out of the country. We hurried to Theano's house and knew that at the very least, her two oldest children, John and Eleni, would be leaving Greece as well. Both had been born in America.

"Don't even mention to me the word America!" Theano growled when she heard the news. "That place ruined me. It ruined my life, my family, everything. I hate that damned place, and I don't ever plan on going back to it. Never!"

"But your children are American citizens," said Father. "What are you going to do with them, keep them here? There is nothing here for them. Why would you do that?"

"Well, if they want to go, that's fine. I don't care. Let them go. In fact, they *should* go. From there, they can send us money to help us survive. When you go to Kalamata, Panagioti, take John here with you."

The next morning, with no further discussion and no fanfare, Father and my cousin John walked out of Gargaliani and began the sixty or so kilometer trip east to Kalamata, filled with hope of bringing about the solution to our misery. A full week later, they returned. Father seemed happy.

"The United States has opened a consulate in Athens," he reported. "People are going there and getting the documentation they need to get out of Greece. Before long, American ships will begin to take citizens back to the states."

"But what about your citizenship?" asked Mother. "Is it still valid?"

"Of course it's valid. I told them who I was, and I showed them my papers. They said everything was in order. But they also said that going to Athens now is pointless because half the country is trying to get out of here. If we go to Athens now, we'll be stuck there for months before they will even talk to us. We don't have the money for that. But they also told us that the Americans will soon be opening a consulate branch in Patras. That's perfect for us. Once that happens, I will be able to go there for our papers. And in Patras, I can stay with Dimitri as long as I have to," Father said referring to his cobbler brother. "All in all, this is terrific news."

"Thank God," Mother sighed. "What is John going to do?"

"He's already gone home to pack for Athens. He is leaving right away. He thinks he can stay there with some uncles as long as he needs to. And he thinks his uncles know people at the consulate and that they will get him to the front of the line and out of the country."

Within days, my cousin John was gone, on a bus to Kyparissia where he would board a train to Patras that, under normal circumstances would continue on to Athens. But because the rail bridge over the isthmus at Corinth had been blown up, he would have to board a bus for the final leg to Athens. Father made his own plans. He quickly wrote his brother Dimitri in Patras, told him that we were planning on leaving for America, and asked to be notified once the American consulate there opened.

Soon, we learned that the mines had been cleared from the shipping lanes between Europe and the states. Father picked up the pace of his letter writing to the states, and Mother began sending me to the post office to see if Theo Stathi had sent us anything. She was sure he would be amongst the first to send us aid. When the first packages from America began to arrive, literally manna from heaven, word spread through town like a wildfire. People sprinted to the post office, and I remember seeing person after person walk out clutching letters and packages. When I entered, I weaved my way through the throngs, my mind flush with images of biscuits, canned goods, and other food stuffs in a package from Theo Stathi.

When I reached the man who was calling out people's names, I called "Stamatis! Stamatis! Do you have anything for Stamatis?"

But as loud as I was able to yell, there were others who were much louder and taller than me. One by one, they momentarily captured the man's attention, and he handed them packages. I watched him hand out many parcels that day, gifts from God to people who had spent what seemed like an eternity stuck in the valley of the shadow of death. Then he finally turned his attention to me.

"There is nothing here for Stamatis. But come back tomorrow, my boy. From this point forward, we will be receiving packages every day."

Though I was disappointed and on the verge of crying when I told Mother what happened, she was unfazed.

"We have been patient, Sarantis. We have waited so long. Certainly, we can wait a little longer. At this point, it does not really matter anymore. We'll be leaving here soon."

Father wrote Stathi almost daily, articulating again and again what we had been through, how we were living, and that we had to survive just a little bit longer before we could get out. But day after day passed with nothing at the post office. It seemed that Father's letters were falling on deaf ears.

"Maybe he's still upset about the land we sold," Father often speculated.

"After all these years and a world war, he's still upset about that? Do you think he has gone mad?" Mother asked.

"He's a bachelor, Nitsa. How can a bachelor truly understand what pulls at a man with a family? I'm trying to keep us from getting shot or starving to death and he's upset about some trees. I don't know, Nitsa. For all I know, he died."

"I think it's more likely that he died. Just keep writing the states. Tell your sister what's happening and ask her about Stathi."

Father wrote everyone, his brother in Massachusetts, his sister in Chicago, and anyone else he knew. Then finally, after several weeks of radio-silence from our relatives abroad, and after day after day of fruitless trips to the post office, the post master handed me a letter from Detroit, Michigan, a letter from Theo Stathi.

"Give this to your Father," he said with a smile.

I ran home and from a great distance, began calling out, "Mana! Mana! Mana! We have a letter from America. We received a letter from Theo Stathi."

Before I could even hand her the letter, she snatched it from me and perused the envelope.

"Run to the plateia and fetch your Father."

I sprinted the few blocks, and when I found him, I told him that his brother had finally responded. But Father, to my shock, soberly and calmly nodded at me and continued his conversation. It was only after a quarter hour or so that he rose from his chair and in a slow and matter-of-fact manner, took my hand and calmly walked home.

"C'mon, Father, hurry!" I said. "Hurry."

"My Saranti, what's the point of hurrying? The message from your uncle is what it is. It will be the same whether or not we hurry. Hurrying won't change anything."

When we arrived home, Father took the letter from Mother, sat at the dining room table and calmly surveyed it. He checked the postage, pointed out the envelope's various notations, the handwriting, its stamps and stripes.

"Damn it, open the letter, Panagioti!" Mother scolded. "Who cares about what's on the envelope? Open it!"

Father smiled, looked around the room, and complied. We stared at the envelope and as Father slowly opened it, our eyes bulged out of their sockets in anticipation of what we might see. Two pieces of paper fell out, and Father's fingers gathered them both. The first was a letter.

"Beloved brother," it began.

Father read the letter aloud. We learned that Theo Stathi was alive, that he was pleased enough that we were still alive, but that he was still irked about our sale of portions of the family's land. He scolded Father for being a bad manager of money and pointed out how life in America had not been easy for him either.

When Mother heard that, she rolled her eyes.

The second piece of paper was what we had all been waiting for—a cashier's check for one hundred dollars, no less. When Father saw it, he turned to us and smiled.

"This family will eat well tonight," he said.

Father put the check in his pocket, arose and walked to the bank to exchange it for Greece's new currency. When he returned, his arms were full of groceries.

"Yes, we will all eat well tonight," he said.

Then I saw Father do what I had rarely, if ever, seen him do before. He removed a leg of lamb from the butcher's newspaper wrapping and placed it in a pan. Then he cut and added several enormous wedges of potatoes, followed by olive oil, salt, oregano, garlic, the juice of several lemons, other seasonings, and a cup of water. It was rare that Father ever performed a domestic chore like cooking, but today was a special day, and this was a special meal. And with a little bit of money in his pocket for the first time in a long time, Father was ecstatic.

He turned to me.

"Saranti, take this pan to Barba Vasili's community oven and ask him to cook it."

As I reached for the pan, Father thought twice about what he said.

"Maybe I'd better take it there myself."

I followed Father out of the house, and when we arrived at Barba Vasili's, he handed over our meal.

"Take good care of this," he said. "We haven't eaten properly in months."

"Of course, Kyrie," replied Barba Vasili.

Father and I proceeded to a nearby *taverna*, and Father handed the owner an empty bottle. The storekeeper took it and filled it with wine. Father handed the man a few coins and turned to me.

"Take this wine home, Saranti, and tell your Mother that I'll meet everyone there when the meat is ready. And don't spill it."

I watched Father retreat to the back of the taverna where he sat with a smile and drank a much-needed glass of wine with his friends. When he returned home later with the meat, we enjoyed a meal unlike anything any of us had experienced before. In addition to the lamb and potatoes, there was feta cheese, crusty bread from the bakery, tomatoes, and cucumbers. Everything we had dreamed about for so long.

We ate quietly. After we finished our meal, Father removed a piece of paper from his pocket and with his pencil, made some calculations.

"The way I see it," he said, "this money will last us about a month. Now, we have to be frugal. Everyone has to keep praying and perhaps even more important, we have to keep writing letters to our relatives in America."

We went to sleep that night with our bellies full and our home filled with the aromas of our feast.

Chapter 27
GETTING READY

On July 16, 1945, Harry Truman, Winston Churchill, and Joseph Stalin met at Potsdam, Germany to discuss the end of the war and to plan what would come next. Less than a month later, on August 6, 1945, Truman ordered that the Japanese city of Hiroshima be hit with a new weapon known as the Atomic Bomb. Three days later, Nagasaki suffered a similar fate.

Like other major events, none of this seemed to affect us very much, and we remained focused on the opening of the American consulate in Patras. Things were looking up. Theo Stathi continued to send us occasional aid including money and other miscellaneous items. One day, Father opened a package to find a business suit, which he was delighted to receive, having been without one since the looting during the Battle of Gargaliani. With the revival of a stable national currency, Mother plotted my return to the business world.

"You will sell your goods at the annual celebration at the chapel of the Agios Sotiros," she declared one day.

Agios Sotiros was the little chapel located just fifty meters from Theano's beach house. Each August 6, a packed celebration took place on the feast day that commemorated the little church.

"I have talked to all your suppliers," Mother told me. "They're glad you're ready to get back to work, and they promised to increase their inventories to make sure they have enough for you."

The day before the festival, the baker Barba Vasili handed over a pillowcase full of koulouria, Kyria Niovie tendered us a bag full of cigarette cartons, and Kyrios Elias gave us some other items including the never-popular sewing supplies. The following morning, Father organized our merchandise so we could carry it the two-hour walk to the chapel. He strapped my share around my shoulders, and he carried the rest. Before long, the strap cut into my shoulder and hurt my back, causing us to stop often. After several hours of walking,

dandelions for Dinner

we arrived at Theano's beach home and Father advised Theano of our plans. Afterward, we walked the hundred meters to the chapel where Father and I, the first merchants to arrive, picked out what we thought would be the best spot, adjacent to the church's entrance and on its north side. Father pulled out a hammer and began to construct the stand upon which we would sell our items. He sawed, pounded and nailed together a table-like structure. When all we needed was a top, Father returned to Theano's house and began scavenging for a piece of wood he could use.

"There it is," he said, pointing to Theano's outdoor toilet. "Saranti, come over here and help me with this."

We pried off a number of boards. When she saw what we were doing, she almost lost her mind.

"Are you insane?" she yelled at Father. "You are taking apart our bathroom."

"Don't worry. I'll fix it tomorrow. And believe me, it will be in much better shape when I'm finished with it."

We slept that night in the shed that sat outside Theano's home and the following morning, a rooster's call awoke us.

"Let's go," said Father and we headed toward the chapel.

On the way, we stopped at Theano's well, drew up some water, and splashed our faces. Father removed some pieces of dry bread from his sack, soaked them for a few seconds, and handed me one. We sat on the stone steps that led to the beach and ate our breakfast. And as we sat, we quietly stared at the sea and the clear morning sky, taking in the smell of the salty iodine saturated mist that gently blew over our faces. Behind us, the first rays of the sun began to flicker on the Ionian, God's signal to the world that his new day had begun. After a few minutes, Father broke the silence.

"Saranti, today will be a great day, I can feel it. Let's go set up our stand."

We arose from our ethereal perch and walked the short distance to the chapel. Father looked over his project and made a few last minute changes, pounding a nail here and there and moving a few things around. He retrieved some newspapers from his bag and carefully spread them to cover the toilet planks. Then he picked up the sack of *koulouria* and displayed the circular sesame covered breads around the top right quadrant of the stand. To the left of those, he laid out the cigarettes, opening a few cartons to allow his customers easy access. Below, he put the sewing accessories.

When he finished, he turned toward the church, "Now, Panagia, it's in your hands. Please help us sell all of this."

One by one, people appeared and before we knew it, the area was flooded with pilgrims. Other merchants appeared. By nine o'clock or so, the clergy had begun their services in the chapel, which had filled with people. The hymns from the chapel mingled with the murmur of those outside and the calls of the merchants.

Father and I remained focused on our mission. Business was brisk, and out of the box, the demand for *koulouria* was high. Mothers bought one after another, makeshift pacifiers for their agitated and unruly children. Father put the money he collected in his front pocket which, through the morning, steadily became more and more rotund. After the service ended, the hungry laity ambushed us, trading whatever currency they had for our products. Father's pockets continued to grow. When it was all over, we had sold just about everything we brought, including many of the sewing supplies. Father was happy, his bulging pockets proof of our success. We took apart the stand and Father rebuilt Theano's toilet, honoring his word to place it in a better condition than it had been before. We said good-bye and walked home.

The following day, Father and I began the rounds to our suppliers. Kyrios Elias slowly and methodically took an inventory of what we had sold, returning, to my surprise, the remaining items to his display case. On a piece of paper, he calculated what we owed him and handed it to Father. But then a look came over Father's face and rather than pay him, Father slipped the paper into his vest pocket, turned and left.

"We'll be back later," he said.

As we walked away, I remained focused on Father, trying to get a read on his face.

"Why didn't you pay him," I asked Father as we walked on the street, as if there was some business etiquette of which I was unaware.

"We are not going to pay him, Saranti."

"What do you mean, Father? What are you talking about?"

"We can't pay him, Saranti. We can't pay any of them. We need

dandelions for Dinner

this money for our upcoming trips to Patras. If we pay them, we won't have the money we need to get out of here."

"But they'll never sell us anything again. We'll be finished."

"That's all right. You don't have time for that anyway."

From Father's tone, I knew not to raise the matter again. And that was that—we were extended goods on credit, had a banner day of sales, and were now screwing our suppliers. What a nightmare. Father's decision not to pay anyone not only put me out of business, but also embarrassed me to no end. From that point forward, I couldn't again face my suppliers and went out of my way to avoid them. If I was, say, heading toward the plateia and about to pass one of them, I took a detour around the block, down an alley. I would go anywhere, however inconvenient, rather than face those people. When I complained about it to Mother, she was quick to rationalize.

"Don't worry about it, Sarantis. This money will help us leave here. Those people won't even miss it. They'll be just fine. Besides, you don't have time to be a peddler anyway. You will be starting high school in a few weeks and need to study for the entrance examination. Remember, there is nothing more important than your education."

"Starting high school? I don't want to go to high school. The Americans have just declared that the war against the Japanese is over. The whole war is over. We are leaving. Why would I go to school if we are leaving this place?"

"Saranti, you *will* go to high school, and that's that. I don't care what you want to do or what you think. You are going."

Suddenly, my problems were much bigger than the end of my business. High school at that time encompassed six years of schooling, roughly the seventh through twelfth grades. Despite my protests, my attending high school was of paramount importance to Mother, an event that she was sure would lead to much better things for me in life. Going to high school would put me on a real career path and marked the commencement of a holy mission that would pry me and my family out of its perpetual curse of poverty. It would immediately distinguish me from my peers, most of whom had already begun their life's work as farmers, a vocation that required little, if any schooling. In fact, out of my grammar-school graduating class of no more than twenty-five, only two or three planned to continue on to high school. And those were the children of educated parents. Mother, the daughter of Papa Sarantis, the granddaughter of Petropouleas, knew that while an education didn't guarantee riches, it did ensure a person a good livelihood, not to mention an elevation in status. Mother decided I would be a pharmacist and talked about how I would follow in the footsteps of Kyrio Papageorgiou, Gargaliani's pharmacist. Even then, Mother understood the pharmaceutical industry quite well.

"To be a pharmacist Saranti, you have to know how to buy and sell medicine. That is just like buying and selling cigarettes and koulouria with a big difference—you will be among the elite and your profits will be enormous."

Not everyone was as convinced as Mother of the benefits of continued schooling, a mindset that a story from that time captures: An old farmer and his wife struggled and saved their entire life to make sure that their only son could attend high school in Athens. When the boy returned home after completing his first year, the Father followed him around, treating him with uncommon respect as he quietly watched his son to see how the boy had changed, what secrets he had learned, what wisdom he had acquired. As the two walked around the farm together, the boy thoughtfully surveyed his father's holdings, as if he was seeing them all with fresh eyes and processing the information with his newly educated mind. He walked into the family's barn, gazed up, and holding his chin between his thumb and forefinger, began to ponder.

As the boy stood there, frozen, the father was in awe of the boy's intellect and wondered, *which philosopher he was thinking about? Was it Aristotle? Or Plato? Or Socrates?*

Then, the Father's mind momentarily drifted to several days earlier, when he had nailed up a plank to support the roof and was too lazy to first remove a large pile of dung one of the cows had left on it. The dung remained on the wood. Nevertheless, he watched his son curiously, sure he was contemplating some profound and lofty idea.

After several minutes, he respectfully turned to the boy. "My son, what are you thinking about? What is troubling you so much?"

The son replied, "Do you see the cow manure on the plank up there."

"Yes," replied the Father anxiously, "yes!"

"I am just trying to figure out how the cow that soiled the plank climbed all the way up there."

The Father's head fell and he walked away, shaking it in disgust, convinced he was wasting his money on his son's education.

Even though I was going to high school and had finished the sixth grade with a score of eight out of ten—the equivalent of a "B"—I always felt intellectually inadequate. Indeed, I was sure I lacked the brains of my classmates and was convinced I could never master grammar and mathematics. I knew high school would only be even more confusing and frightening and preparing for it was dreadful and for me, a torture. We heard we would have to take an entrance exam that would include written testing in language skills, mathematics, composition as well as an oral examination that would quiz my general knowledge of the world. A number of tutors emerged and Mother somehow managed to enroll me with one. I don't know how Mother pulled it off, but there I was, beside ten or so other bright hopefuls, reviewing mounds and mounds of material. The course was a definite plus and before long, there was no math problem I could not solve. My feeling of competence in mathematics generally increased my confidence and helped me approach the other subjects with at least some degree of optimism.

As the big day approached, rumors flew as to specific problems that would be on the exam. Upper classman circulated handwritten solutions to putative exam problems, and terror stories abounded that the test would be the "hardest ever," specifically designed to "flunk everybody." Test takers from the surrounding villages trickled into town on donkeys and horses. Many tried inconspicuously to pass on gifts to the professors in blatant attempts at bribery. When the mathematics professor passed our home one morning, Mother was ready for him and urged me to run after him with a bag of *koulouria* and a message she had made me endlessly rehearse: "Professor, my name is Sarantis Stamatis, the *koulouria* are for your coffee."

I did as ordered and without acknowledging me, the towering man took the koulouria and continued his walk. When Father saw what Mother had made me do, he shook his head in disbelief and walked away.

My studies took so much time that I couldn't tend to my chores and even had difficulty finding time to take care of Kanella. Father became saddled with the burden of taking her for her walks. One afternoon, I noticed that the goat was gone from her usual spot in the yard and when I asked Mother, she said Father had taken Kanella with him. I assumed she meant to the fields. Later that day, I saw Father approach the house holding a large paper package under his arm. Kanella was nowhere in sight. And just like that, only moments later, our companion for all those years, the little friend who Mother traded for a sewing machine—the goat that provided us with our only nourishment during our harshest struggles, our pet, the witness to so many of our trials—sat in quarters in a pan surrounded by sliced potatoes. And as we devoured Kanella that night, Stathi and I couldn't help but feel a little awkward.

"Do you think Kanella is in paradise now?" Stathi asked.

"No, Stathi. One thing is for sure and that is that goats don't have a soul. God has placed them on earth for us to use their milk and to eat them. That's why they are here."

Though I had difficulty eating Kanella, I must admit that in doing so, a great sense of relief had come over me. That goat was no longer my responsibility. I didn't have to walk her, I didn't have to clean up after her, and I didn't have to venture into hostile territory to feed her. I was liberated.

When the entrance exam finally arrived, a large crowd gathered at the high school. Parents wished their children well, offered prayers and force-fed them last minute test-taking advice. Some covertly handed out sheets with solved problems, ones they swore would be on the exam. Because I was a nobody, no one talked to me and no one handed me anything. The school doors opened, and when I entered the classroom, the proctor sat me at a desk in the back of the room and near a window. I could see that bed sheets shielded the writing on two blackboards in the front of the room, covers under which were written the math problems that would determine our futures. After the room settled down, the instructor offered general instructions regarding the test and pulled off the sheets. The children gasped and the test began. I copied the first problem and quickly solved it; then, the second—no problem. The studying had clearly paid off. As I worked the third problem, I felt something hit my leg. I looked down and saw a paper airplane. It must have entered through a vent, I thought. I innocently picked it up, opened it, and to my horror, saw the solutions to the first two problems written out. I began to sweat and became so nervous that I couldn't move.

"Psst, psst," said the boy next to me. "Give me the paper."

I realized that he and some others had been expecting the airplane's landing and wanted me to hand it to them. I looked up toward the window and saw several heads of upperclassmen coming in and out of view. They were one on top of the other's shoulders. They had apparently copied and solved the problems on the board and were flying in the solutions. When I didn't move right away, the boy grabbed the paper out of my hand. I returned to solving the problems on the board. The noise must have attracted the proctor's attention because he slowly and furtively worked his way toward our part of the room. After a quarter hour or so, and to the boys' surprise, he snatched the airplane. Then he picked up their exams, looked at them, compared them to the answers on the airplane and told them all to leave. Then he picked up my paper and compared it to the airplane.

"Keep working," he said and handed me back my test.

By afternoon, I had finished the test in math and grammar and found myself surrounded by teachers who peppered me with questions. After several minutes, one of the instructors nodded to me favorably and told me to leave.

That evening I quietly prayed to Panagia to enlighten the professors enough to see the wisdom of my test responses and to pass me. People talked about the test, discussed the questions and the answers they gave, and were quick to point out the mistakes others must have made. Days later, a crowd gathered around the high school office in hopes of learning the results. When I arrived, the list of the next high school class had been posted. People crowded around it and looked for their names. I waited for everyone to go before me and when I made it to the handwritten sheet, I looked for the "Σ" section and saw what I had been looking for—my name. I had been accepted into high school. What an odyssey and what a pleasant surprise.

Around this time, Father received a letter from his brother Dimitri with the happy news that the American consulate in Patras had finally opened. He packed a suitcase and prepared immediately to leave for America.

"Do you really think you are going to go straight to America?" I asked.

"Yes, of course. Your cousin John went to the consulate in Athens, and he's on the *Grimpholt* right now steaming across the Atlantic."

The *Grimpholt* was a Swedish ship that had already begun ferrying Americans back to the states.

"Why can't I go with you?" I asked.

"No, you have to stay behind and help Mother take care of things here."

"So you think you'll be on the *Grimpholt* soon?"

"I don't know about that. All I know is that John went to the front of the line and right onto the ship. I hope I can do the same," said Father.

Father's departure was, frankly, anticlimactic. We had dreamed for so long about leaving for America and had imagined things would change the instant he left. But as is so often the case, reality fell short of our years of hope and anticipation, not to mention our planned sense of adventure in beginning our exodus. Father just quietly boarded a bus and it drove away. There was no fanfare at all. And when he was gone, Mother, Stathi and I were left alone, wondering what hurdles we would have to pass before we could leave, too. And while we were saddened that we would be without Father, we couldn't help but feel a great relief in knowing that at the very least, our exodus had begun.

Several days later, I was playing in front of our home with Niko when I looked up and saw Father walking toward me, carrying his suitcase.

"Mana, Mana," I called. "Father is here; Father is here."

Mother ran out to meet her husband and bombarded him with questions "What happened?" "Why are you here?" "We thought you would be heading to the *Grimpholt* by now."

Father said nothing, and as we followed him into the house, we could see that half-smile on his face, the one he wore when he was holding back some piece of good news. He settled into a chair in the dining room and lit a cigarette.

"I went to the American consulate and met a man who looked at my papers," he began. "I told him I wanted to get on a boat right away, and that I wanted him to get all of your papers as well so that you could leave too. He told me that the American government would help us get back to the states, but not if we split up the family.

"So you are still an American citizen?" asked Mother.

"Of course I am. I told you that before. The consulate treated me like an American."

"Now, if we want to leave, we have to leave together. I protested but he insisted and told me to be patient. Then he sent me to another man who gave me this list of things to do before we would be able to leave. He also gave me a number of documents to complete, most of which asked for the usual data like names, addresses, who we knew in America, where we would go when we got there, and so forth. One even asked about our political affiliations, whether we were Marxists. Anyway, he even told me that Saranti and Stathi are already considered American citizens as they are my children. They can travel on my American passport. They are set. The remaining issue is you, Nitsa. For you to leave, you will have to get a Greek passport as well as a visa to enter the United States. But that shouldn't be a problem. All it will take is time and patience." Father smiled and leaned back in his chair. "Family, we are leaving soon."

Father was confident, in control, and seemed to know exactly what to do. In the following days, in order to get our documentation together, he began taking regular trips to Patras. Each time, he met with the vice consul, who looked over what papers Father already had, told him what else he needed to gather, and what else he had to do. During that time, Father took us to the local photographer, applied to have us added to his passport and gathered a number of documents. When the vice consul asked him for confirmation that he wasn't a fugitive, Father wrote Mother who had the appropriate document prepared. She sewed it into my jacket and sent me to Patras to deliver it.

When Father and I took the document to the vice consul, we learned that we needed yet another paper, and Father sent me back to Gargaliani to get it. Though I had already begun high school, I became the family courier and ended up making four such trips to Patras. I loved those journeys as they not only gave me a taste of independence, but allowed me the opportunity to be at the center of the family's action. And though on each such trip, I yearned to stop and visit my godmother in Kyparissia, Mother's sister Tasia, I was never able to muster the nerve to walk into her jewelry store and introduce myself. A couple of times, I lingered just outside and waited for her or her husband to recognize me, to welcome me and to invite me in, but it never happened.

The anticipation of leaving and the trips to Patras had a negative effect on my schooling. It didn't take long for me to get behind, so far that I was so desperate for help that I even turned to my cousin Sarantis for help.

"Fractions? Torricelli's experiments with the thermometer?" asked Sarantis. "You want me to help you with this? Oh no, Saranti. I long ago forgot what I learned in first grade. And believe me when I tell you that whatever I learned in high school is well beyond my comprehension. Find someone else to help you."

If there was an academic bright spot that fall, it was that my class and I would take part in the country's very first celebration of what would become known as *Oxi* Day," the national holiday that marked Metaxas's reported emphatic "No" to Mussolini's 1941 demand that Greece surrender. Our school made big plans for the day, patriotic displays that included marching around the plateia in formation and sitting with dignitaries. It was all so exciting that I could think of little else. In the week leading up to *Oxi* Day, the school marched in orderly formations, led by the sixth-year class, followed by the fifth year, then the fourth year, and so on. Everyone participated. We learned to move as one to the beat of a drum and to the instructor's commands.

Just before the festivities, a letter arrived from Father in Patras indicating that he immediately needed some document. The following day, Mother put me on a bus and I was off. Somewhere along the way, I contracted mumps and, when I returned to Gargaliani, was bedridden. Determined to march with my class on *Oxi* Day, though my face and neck were swollen from the disease, I got up and reported for duty. My class proudly marched last, behind the five grades in front of us. But we must have so paled in comparison to the upperclassmen that when we passed the coffee houses in the plateia, we could hear the patrons laughing and making fun of us.

"The big fish are gone. Now here come the smelts!"

As the end of 1945 approached, we were anxious to leave Greece and were becoming frustrated by the incessant hold-ups, despite Father's repeated warnings to expect more delays.

"There's so much bureaucracy here that, unless every civil servant signs off on our exit, Saranti, they won't be able to justify their salaries."

Father was finally back in his element, finished with his miscast stint as a farmer. Sure, the man could barely get a grape to grow, but that didn't matter anymore. He was quite the effective operator in dealing with matters of business, bureaucracy and government formalities. He was just what we needed now, a man proficient in working our family's way through Greece's and America's arcane emigration and immigration procedures. Mother realized that Papa Ntres had been right so many years before; father had gifts, important gifts, and they had come to light at precisely the right time.

Despite the delays, we remained so completely committed to leaving that Father abandoned our fields, making no effort to reseed them for 1946. And at the end of 1945, Father refused to leave Patras until he received word from the consulate that we were good to go. In early 1946, the vice-consul finally gave Father the green light and told him that a new ship, a troop carrier called *Marine Shark*, had replaced the *Grimpholt* and was now transporting repatriating Americans to the United States.

"The coast is clear," the man told Father as he smiled and shook his hand. "Now return to Gargaliani and settle your affairs because you will be leaving soon. Go home to your family, and on your way to Athens, stop here and pick up your passport. The way things look now, you will be leaving Greece on the *Marine Shark* sometime in June. And whatever you do, be sure to arrive in Athens at least two months before you leave for America. You'll have a lot more bureaucracy to wade through to get out of the country. It won't be easy."

In February 1946, we began to prepare in earnest for our departure. Father told us that the new Greek government had passed a law nullifying all property transfers made under duress during the war. We weren't the only ones who sold family land for pennies to buy food. We rejoiced when we heard the news and made plans to reclaim the olive grove we had sold to Dr. Papathomopoulos two years earlier. A few days later, we learned of an exception to that rule—that it didn't apply to the purchasers whose family members had been murdered during the war. And because the Andartes had killed Dr. Papathomopoulos just after the Battle of Gargaliani, his family was under no obligation to return the grove. Mother did a little more research and realized that there was no point in pressing the issue—we weren't going to get our olive grove back. But not one to miss an opportunity to show magnanimity, even if contrived, she nevertheless reached out to the doctor's widow, telling her that even though the law would allow us to reclaim the grove, in light of the hardship the late doctor's family had endured, Mother would not press the issue.

"You can keep the grove," she told her.

The widow thanked Mother and sent us two large bottles of olive oil as a token of her gratitude.

By this time, we had heard much from Theano about the hardships cousin John had encountered before he left Greece, most of which were caused by the endless Greek bureaucracy. This made Father worry even more about our running out of time in Athens. Even though we wouldn't be leaving Greece until late June, he thought we should allow ourselves a full three to four months to wade through the government's red tape. Father was discouraged when he calculated how much money we would need to live for at least three months in Athens, an inordinately expensive proposition considering the cost of meals and lodging.

Mother was impervious to such worries.

"Panagioti, we don't have time to sit around and wring our hands," she said. "Just keep writing letters to Stathi and the rest of them in the States. God will inspire them to help us."

"That's fine, I'll do that," he said. "But I don't think it will do any more good. These people have already done everything they can for us."

Mother ignored Father and forced him to press on. When she somehow learned that her cousin, the grandchild of her grandfather Spyro was living in Chicago, she ordered Father to write him as well, despite the fact that she had never met the man.

On the occasions that Mother perceived Father might be losing hope and saw negativity had invaded his psyche, she remained upbeat: "Damn it, Panagioti, we have come this far. One way or another, we are leaving this place. Staying here is not an option. We will leave with whatever little we have. We will live in the streets of Athens if we have to. Nothing will stop us now. We have overcome too many adversities to give up now. This is nothing compared to what we have been through."

Despite Mother's desire to continue to push Theo Stathi, she didn't hold out too much hope that he would do much more than he already had. So she worked parallel plans. She sold whatever she could—the dining room table, our sofa, and a few other miscellaneous pieces of furniture. But these items brought in little money, substantially less than what we needed to survive. When we had done everything we could, after we had sold everything anyone might want to buy, Father announced we were leaving in a week. With the official countdown under way, Mother stepped up my trips to the post office in hopes that someone on the other side of the world had answered our call.

When word spread that we were leaving for America, people began to snicker in disbelief.

"Those people can't grow two potatoes and they think they are going to America? Who do they think they are? Wasn't Nitsa supposed to leave a decade and a half ago? She's still talking about leaving?"

In the midst of our preparations, there was still time for me to see my friends. The lot between our house and the agora, the one that had long served as the holding facility for the blacksmith's animals, had become a popular place for children to gather and play, especially after noon, by which time the animals were usually gone. Though the animal droppings were everywhere and made the lot smell, none of us seemed to mind. Not only had the animals soiled the area, but from time to time children would relieve themselves there as well, oftentimes near a fountain located at one end of the lot. The droppings had made navigating the area often treacherous, especially when one walked up to a wall near the fountain to urinate, which the children did all the time. There was nothing worse than stepping, barefoot, in some animal's biological refuse. And whenever that happened, the victim would immediately run to wash his feet in the fountain.

One afternoon, I was playing with Niko and some other friends when the urge to urinate overcame me. I ran to the wall near the fountain, but because there were so many piles everywhere, I had to step up closer to the fountain than I would have liked. After I finished, two harridans who had seen me began to yell, claiming I had peed in the fountain and polluted the water. Rather than run to my defense, the other children joined in the curses and with a sudden surge of hypocritical civic concern over the cleanliness of the area, several older kids came toward me to teach me a lesson for my indignant act. I made a run for it, and they came running after me, cursing me and my audacity and throwing rocks at me. One of the attackers was my friend Niko.

In the subsequent days, Niko avoided me and on the occasions that I saw him, treated me with an uncharacteristic coolness, as if we were strangers. Without a doubt, his actions were devastating. A friendship that had been cultivated for so many years and through so many hardships, as well as good times, appeared to be coming to its sad end. Alienated and betrayed, I couldn't figure out how so many years of friendship and camaraderie could end by a silly impersonal act of urinating on the back of a cement fountain, an act he and I had performed on so many occasions. Though I was not the first Greek to be ostracized, that fact didn't make my situation any easier. So I was left with no choice but to focus on my studies, painfully accepting my predicament.

One evening, as I returned home from the post office, I walked past a streetlight and a number of boys jumped me in order to administer my awaited punishment. I reacted instinctively to the attack and punched and kicked each as he came near me. I scored a hit on one attacker's crotch, and he ran away crying. Eventually, the others fled in a number of directions and I saw that once again, Niko was one of them. I was heartbroken and wrote him off for good. The few remaining times our paths crossed, I ignored him and turned my face away.

By the time the eve of our departure was upon us, my family still had not heard from our American relatives. Mother had sold a few more of the remaining items, even our kitchen utensils, blankets, and linens—actions that only further cut our ties to Gargaliani and burned any remaining bridges. We would leave nothing behind, and we had no alternate plans and no strategies for contingencies.

However apprehensive, we were leaving Greece, and there was no turning back.

Chapter 28
GOOD-BYE

No one seemed to care when the day of our departure arrived that fateful morning in March of 1946. As Mother closed our door for the last time, she crossed herself. Having already given our keys to a neighbor the night before, we had completed the closing of our affairs. Father carried our single piece of luggage, that now decrepit and abused black leather suitcase from Chicago, secured with twine. We turned our backs on our house for the last time, and Father led us south for the two-block trek to the plateia, where our bus was waiting.

Dark clouds had covered the Gargaliani sky for several days and produced an intermittent drizzle that had especially unnerved Father. When the drizzle increased to a misty rain, Father, a few feet ahead, set the suitcase down, reestablished his grip, and motioned for us to hurry.

"You bastard sky, open your bowels and rain your guts out to relieve yourself from this prolonged constipation that has plagued you," he mumbled.

We hurried to the bus, a dusty, World War I vintage contraption that was to take us to Kyparissia.

Next to the bus was Bakas, the town crier. He was surprised to see us boarding, and looked wide-eyed at Father as he secured our suitcase to the top of the bus.

"We are going to America, Bakas. May God bless you. Be well," Father said.

Bakas crossed himself several times.

"Oh, my. God bless *you*. Good luck to you. Remember me, Panagioti. Remember me!"

Father smiled. Mother looked the other way and elbowed Father onto the bus. As she stepped up into the vehicle, I caught a glace of her sour face.

Good Riddance

"Did you really have to divulge our business to the bottom of Gargaliani's barrel?" she snapped, loud enough for Bakas to hear.

We settled into our seats, in quiet and stoic disbelief that we were really leaving. I sat next to Father, directly behind Stathi and Mother. After a few silent minutes, I spotted Papa Christodoulos approaching the vehicle, apparently to say good-bye to someone else leaving for Kyparissia. Father tapped Mother. Though she was still upset the priest had not accepted me as one of his acolytes, Mother rose, motioned to us to remain seated, and exited the vehicle. Through the driver's window, we watched her kiss the priest's hand, exchange a few awkward pleasantries, and return to her seat.

"What did you say?" Father asked.

"I told him we were leaving for America and not coming back. He gave us a blessing, but from the smirk on his face, I don't think he believes we are actually going to make it."

"Eh, forget it Nitsa. It doesn't matter anymore."

After several more minutes of silent waiting, my thoughts drifted to the many souls in Gargaliani we were leaving behind: my friends and my enemies as well, some old, some young. And for an inexplicable reason, I focused on poor Nikita, the late itinerant peddler who had innocently roamed the cafés and tavernas selling his roasted peanuts and squash seeds.

I thought of his nasal voice, and about how he used to sing "Roasted peanuts! Squash seeds! Roasted peanuts! Squash seeds!"

I remembered how Nikita used to entice his customers to gamble in a game he called *mona ziga*, in which he would instruct them to grab a closed fistful of peanuts and to guess whether the number of them was odd or even. A correct guess meant one could keep the peanuts free of charge. An incorrect one meant paying double.

I had come to appreciate Nikita's self-taught intelligence; the man was a voracious reader. In fact, Nikita taught himself to speak English from some books that Father had given him. In a different place and era, his character, augmented by a formal education, might have made him an excellent governor, an ambassador or a prime minister. But whatever Nikita had in character, he lacked in discretion. Indeed, Nikita was never shy about telling everyone he was a Royalist.

"Monarchy represents respectability and class, something we Greeks had lost as subjects to the dirty Turks," he used to say.

And so, the Andartes killed Nikita, even though he really was just a harmless street peddler with a big mouth—a nobody.

Suddenly, the bus driver muttered, "We are leaving," and bounced into his seat.

He closed the door, put the vehicle in gear, and pulled away.

Just like that, with no fanfare, no cheering and no civic interest whatsoever, we commenced our journey.

As the bus moved, I stared out the window, at the plateia and its empty tables. We drove through the old neighborhood, and I caught a glimpse of the quiet balcony from where I first watched the world's people, and the alley from where the Andartes rounded us up during the Battle of Gargaliani.

The bus headed out of town and descended the road that wound down the western cliff, toward the Ionian. As the driver turned the wheel left and right to dodge massive pot holes, the passengers bounced and swayed in choreographed unison. Heads nodded, as if everyone was in agreement to some lofty idea.

By the time we exited Gargaliani's city limits, the light rain temporarily subsided, but the low-level clouds and the drenched valley below only enhanced the moment's melancholia. Each meter the bus descended on its way to the base of the cliff upon which Gargaliani sat, I watched intimately. So many memories darted in an out of my mind, and I suddenly realized the great love I had for that bluff. Thoughts of Niko and the endless hours we spent feeding our goats came to mind. I realized I felt many of the same things I did when we left the old neighborhood for Papa Sarantis's house. Severing ties isn't easy.

The bus snaked though the sea of olive groves swerving from left to right to avoid the acne of potholes that were everywhere. Halfway to Filiatra, the road descended along the bank of a river. When we reached a small valley called Lagouvardos, my mind drifted to a year or so before, when Niko and I had brought our goats here to feed. While the riverbed is usually dry and overrun with vegetation, we had arrived just after a burst of rain that created a swollen river that raged with vengeance. Its fury surprised and scared us and caused us to move our animals to higher ground just when the sky burst forth with water again. We barely survived that adventure; the river nearly swept us away.

The driver rapidly swept over the bridge and immediately downshifted in anticipation of the incline ahead. Just then, the old bus sputtered, let forth a loud grunt, shook, and came to a complete stop. The engine was dead.

"Damn it," said the driver. "You stupid beast. You bastard, you quit on me now? Damn it. *Tha se gamiso* so bad you'll never forget it. Oh, I'm gonna fix you."

The subsequent litany of profanities impressed even Father. The driver tried again and again to crank up the engine, but to no avail. Then he picked up his satchel of tools and exited the bus screaming and swearing. Though it seemed he knew how to fix the problem, first he kneeled on the ground outside the bus, folded his hands and looked up.

"Would you mind telling me what I have done to you? Why are you giving me all these problems? Please tell me so I won't do it again."

Mother turned to me, shook her head, pointed to her temple, and said, "The man's lost it," she said.

"Please, stop pursuing me," he continued. "Please, I beg you. Just let me be and I promise I won't cause you any more trouble. But every time I think we have struck a deal, something happens that makes me realize you weren't a part of it. Please. I've had enough of all this."

The bus driver arose, picked up his bag and walked around the bus and swore some more. I was amazed at how the man could pray out one side of his mouth and cuss out of the other. He crawled under the vehicle with his tool bag and remained there for around a half an hour. From time to time, we could hear a bang or a ping, and some more swearing.

Mother shook her head.

"What kind of language is that?"

After some more time passed, she turned to Father.

"What mother gave birth to that beast?"

Then, she turned to the other passengers on the bus and said, "Please don't antagonize the man. He'll drive us all in the river."

Eventually, the driver crawled out from under the bus and with a look of satisfaction, stored his tools under his seat. He ran to the river, washed up and filled a container with water. He emptied the container into the radiator and with the help of some other men, cranked up the engine to an explosion of applause. We were off. The bus stopped in Filiatra, picked up a few more passengers, and continued on uneventfully to Kyparissia. The passengers were quiet, engrossed in their own thoughts. As we pulled into that town, I wondered whether we would visit my godmother, whether Mother would say good-bye to her sister. We exited the bus and headed to the train station.

"Mana, can we go visit my godmother for a minute while we wait for the train. Her store is right over there." I pointed down the street.

Mother didn't reply with words, but her expression conveyed a total distain at the mention of her sister, a clear indication that despite the fact that she was leaving Greece, perhaps forever, this old wound would be left open. Father returned with our tickets and announced that our train would depart in forty-five minutes. After a short ride, we arrived in Patras. Theo Dimitri met us at the train station and we rejoiced when we saw our relatives.

The following day, Father presented himself at the American consulate, and he received his passport and some other papers, including Mother's visa and our tickets for the voyage on the *Marine Shark*. I was relieved to see that Father was officially an American and couldn't believe my eyes when I saw that Stathi and I were as well.

"How did you pay for the tickets?" Mother asked.

"I didn't pay for anything," replied Father. "The American government loaned us the money to come to America, $594.32 all together. We have ten years to pay it back. I told you that America would not forsake her children!"

The papers made even more real the fact that we were leaving Greece and that the door to the promised land had been propped open for us to pass through. Father quelled our elation with a dose of reality.

"Everyone relax. We do not have everything yet. Of course, we need these documents but it has taken us more than half a year and multiple trips to get them. We are going to face big challenges ahead with the bureaucracy in Athens. And we won't be going anywhere unless we can each get exit visas and Mother gets her passport. I am especially worried about Mother's passport. I don't know how we are going to do that. In order to get anything these days, let alone a passport, you need to have not just *meson*, but big *meson*." *Meson*, that is "clout," was something that for sure we lacked.

Later that day, we boarded a bus to Athens. A bus was still the only way to exit the Peloponnese since the rail bridge over the isthmus at Corinth had been blown up. And as we pulled out of Patras, I thought about how I was travelling beyond anywhere I had ever been before. We drove through towns of the northern Peloponnese, towns that were previously only names I had heard in geography lessons. At Corinth, we picked up several more passengers. One of them carried a guitar and the other an accordion. As we approached the great isthmus, I saw soldiers wearing the king's insignia guarding the bridge and directing the traffic in and out of Peloponnesus. One of them directed our driver to stop. He looked around and under our bus and wrote the license number on a piece of paper. As he checked us out, I could see the destroyed rail bridge, how pieces of it helplessly hung into the belly of the isthmus.

"Why did the Andartes destroy the bridges?" I asked Father.

It looked so foolish to me. When Father didn't immediately answer, a man who sat across the aisle from me spoke up.

"The Andartes blew it up to try to disrupt the German's ability to move men and weapons into the Peloponnese during the war. They worked with the British and blew up bridges everywhere. They wanted to blow up the bridges at the isthmus for a long time but couldn't pull it off, especially after the Germans began loading their trains with Greek prisoners. Finally, the Andartes blew it up as a big train of boxcars crossed." Now, it is generally regarded that the Germans blew it up.

The bus moved toward the lip of the isthmus, and I looked across, surprised at how narrow it was. I had expected it to be much wider. We stopped at the edge and a sentry waived us through. As we drove over the rickety bridge, I looked into the void and saw a number of train cars littered around the bottom.

Once over the bridge, the driver hit the gas, and took me for the first time off the Peloponnese.

The kilometers quickly peeled off, and when we traveled the road that sat atop a cliff that overlooked the Aegean, Father spoke up.

"We are in Attica," he said, referring to the area to the south of Athens.

I had learned about Attica in school, how during ancient times it had been under the rule of the Athenians.

Several minutes later, Father spoke again.

"Now we are passing Kaki Skala. What a dangerous land it is. Look, Saranti, at how the road twists and turns. Many lost their lives building this road. Did you know that?"

I shook my head.

"It was also here, boys, that Theseus killed Procrustes."

Theseus, known for his many exploits, was the legendary king of Athens. Among them was his slaying of Procrustes, a man who forced travelers onto his iron bed. Those who proved too tall for it would have their legs chopped; those too short were stretched to fit. Of course, Procrustes career as a terrorist ended when Theseus tied Procrustes to his own iron bed and cut off his head and feet.

As we settled into our seats for the last leg of the journey, someone in the back of the bus began to sing. Soon, he asked the men with the instruments to play along. Suddenly, the entire bus exploded in song. Everyone sang, even Mother. Whatever worries those passengers carried and whatever hardship lie ahead were momentarily forgotten. As the bus entered Megara and weaved through its streets, the passengers sang the song of "Panagi," an oldie about a young man from Megara.

Where is Panagi?
Where is Panagi?
Has anyone seen Panagi?
Inside of Megara, he's residing.
He's getting engaged to all the girls,
and he's promising to marry them all on Sunday.

The passengers sang the chorus together and laughed, clapped, and shouted. It is ironic that even in the midst of misery, of famine, of starvation sores, and of poverty, there was joy and laughter amongst the downtrodden. But unlikely joy is part of the Greek character, perhaps as much a part of it as the pleasure each person felt at the antics of Panagi, the young man who outsmarted the girls in Megara and seemed to be getting away with it.

When our bus approached Athens, it was loud and raucous. People along the street stared, smiled, and waved as we passed.

Chapter 29
ATHENS

"We have just entered Athens," said the bus driver. A few minutes later, the bus pulled into the terminal that sat near Athens's Omonia Square, the end of the line. We exited the bus, gathered our few belongings, and began to walk. I was amazed at the multitudes of people, the shops, the bustle. We dragged our belongings a few blocks to the square, a gargantuan hexagonal plateia, nothing like ours, into which seven streets converged. The plateia sat in the middle of a round traffic circle where the streets fed into a single lane that circled it. In the center of its hexagon was a streetcar terminal that served as both the beginning and the end of several lines. We couldn't have looked more out of place, four rural people who had just landed in the middle of a cosmopolitan city. Mother was terrified of the traffic and concerned for our safety.

"Stay close! Don't walk here! Don't walk there! Get back here!"

I stared at the electric streetcars that darted around in organized chaos, dragging antennas from their roofs that touched overhead tangles of wires. Mother yanked me by the arm and we drifted in what we hoped was the direction of our hotel, careful not to be killed by a passing streetcar. And as we walked, people stared at us, some even nodded in nostalgic recognition that we had come from the village, perhaps much like they once had.

So this is the Athens that I had heard so much about, I thought as I gazed at the streetcars coming into and leaving the square, the surrounding buildings, the shops, and the people that seemed to be in a perpetual motion. *This town is like a river*, I thought. *It's always moving and leaving but it's always there. Who are these people? My God, where are they going?*

Mother continued to yell while Father asked someone for directions to a hotel he had heard about. Mother yanked us down a sidewalk as Father appeared to have a handle on where to go. We moved around the square and dodged a streetcar with a placard that indicated it was heading for "AHARNON," a place I had never heard of. After we walked a hundred meters or so, Mother saw the hotel and told us to sit at a sidewalk *taverna*. Father ran across the street to book our room. Mother ordered some food, and when Father returned, we sat and ate quietly. And as we ate, I thought about how pleased I was at how far we had come. We had made it out of Gargaliani, past Kyparissia, Patras, and were in Athens. And we were eating, no less—not bad.

Afterward, we retreated to our hotel room for some much needed rest. Our third-floor room was large and equipped with two large windows and a double door that led out to a balcony. As Mother prepared our beds, I stood on the balcony, looked around and noticed the taverna across the street. Mother arranged the covers so that Stathi and I slept at opposite ends of one of the beds. I lay there quietly for a moment and within a minute, Mother began to snore. By her third sonorous breath, I was asleep as well.

Before long, a great disturbance pierced the depths of my sleeping psyche, as if someone persisted in beating my brain with a bass drum mallet while a chorus of venomous sirens screamed and wailed. I turned over, tossed, and covered my head with a pillow, but to no avail. The noise dragged me from my sleep. When I came to my senses, I realized that the cacophony was driving through the open balcony doors from outside, from the taverna below, whose action, in middle of the night, was finally in full swing. I opened my eyes and saw that my parents were awake and whispering to one another in an effort to figure out what to do. Stathi slept.

Reluctantly, they closed the windows and the balcony door, an act that provided immediate relief from the noise but within a few minutes, caused the room's temperature to rise so much that we were soon sleeping in pools of sweat. It was one of those warm Athenian February days. I missed the quiet comfort and tranquility of our bed in Gargaliani. Father got up again reopened the doors and the noise returned, along with the cool night air.

"Now go back to sleep," he said. "Eventually, you'll get used to this."

Father walked onto the balcony in his long johns, leaned on the rail and watched the party below while we tried to sleep.

"Panagioti, come in right now," ordered Mother. "We don't want those people seeing you there like that. They're going to think we're a bunch of peasants from the village, displaying ourselves in our underwear on our balcony."

"Oh, for sure, the people down there who are eating, drinking, and dancing are thinking about me and my pajamas, Nitsa," he replied. Father stood and quietly watched for a few minutes. "Anyway, I think the taverna is closing. They are gathering the tables from the sidewalk."

Just then, a group of female singers began to sing what appeared to be the evening's grand finale. It was a song that I learned when I was selling cigarettes in the plateia, and though I never even thought about the meaning of the song—the lyrics were just empty words to me—I now realize today what they were talking about: smoking marijuana.

When Loulas is smoking, you must not talk.
Look around, all the guys are keeping their mouths shut.
No eye must see us and come looking for us
And if they find a reason they would put us all in jail.

When the ode finished, the party ended, and the noise drifted off. But the Athenian stillness was much different from that in Gargaliani; a residual hum remained. The sounds resembled the sigh of a tired city longing for a few hours of rest. We instantly fell asleep. It seemed like only a few minutes later that I felt Mother prodding me.

"Saranti, get up. Wake up! Let's go—we have a busy day today."

The room was full of blinding light, and when my eyes adjusted, I could see that Father was gone. Stathi, who had slept through all the action the night before was awake and nagging Mother for something to eat. Father entered and handed us each a large *koulouri*, not unlike the ones I used to sell in Gargaliani.

"Let's go," he said. As we walked out of the hotel, Father turned to the innkeeper.

"I don't understand how you people sleep with all the noise from across the street."

The man laughed.

"Kyrie, like the rest of us who abandoned the quiet of the village for fortune, tranquility and serenity are things you have left behind. Your life will probably never be that quiet again. But don't worry though, we have gotten used to it. You will too."

We walked out of the hotel and onto the street. Father carried a to-do list and talked over the game plan with Mother. We walked past Omonia Square. Father led the way and motioned for us to follow him. As we walked, the shops and endless array of treats captivated us. Father ignored our pleas to stop and buy us a toy and after an agonizingly long walk that seemed longer than the trek to Mouzaki, we reached our destination and stood before a large building, the Greek Ministry of the Interior. We walked inside and stopped in the building's lobby.

"Saranti, you stand here with your brother and don't move," ordered Mother. "Keep him right next to you, and don't let him walk even a meter from you, ok?"

"Yes, Mana."

My parents disappeared into the building on a quest to find out who could help them get whatever documents they needed. People raced past us with an urgency that indicated they could only be on their way to or from something very important. Stathi and I looked conspicuously out of place, and though we caught the attention of many, no one approached us. Finally, a man stopped.

"My boys, what are you doing here?"

"My parents are getting some papers inside, and we are waiting for them here."

"Where are you from?" he asked.

"We just arrived in Athens yesterday. We are from Gargaliani."

The man thought for a moment and shrugged his shoulders. He had never heard of Gargaliani.

"Gargaliani!" I repeated. "It's in Messinia."

"Oh, you're from Messinia," said the man as his face lit up. "Welcome, my boy, welcome."

He tousled my hair and walked away.

Stathi and I must have been waiting at least three hours for my parents when they finally reappeared. We followed them outside and drifted through some neighborhood streets until we found a grocery store near a small park. Mother sat us in the park while Father bought us some food. We ate bread and cheese until our bellies were full. We were tired and Stathi laid his head on Mother's lap and fell asleep.

Father stared at Stathi for a minute and shook his head.

"Nitsa, as you saw this morning, we have a lot of work to do here. It's too much for the boys to handle. We have to figure out what to do with them. We can't keep dragging them here."

"I know," replied Mother. "We have to make contact with my relatives if we can. It's worth the effort. If they can watch the boys, then we can get our work done."

"Well, let's do it right away. We don't have much time."

That afternoon we weaved through Athens's streets until we stumbled on one called "*Odos Ermoy.*"

"This way," said Mother. "Over there."

We approached a building with an enormous balcony that stretched its entire length. On the front hung a large sign that read, "*Oikos Kanakari,*" the House of Kanakari. Below that, the sign read "Bridal Wear and Gowns."

We climbed a flight of stairs and found ourselves in a bridal showroom lined with glass cases filled with wedding dresses. We wandered through the shop until a conspicuously well-dressed woman appeared. She looked affluent, not like the type of person who worried about her next meal.

"Can I help you?" she asked Mother.

"Yes, Kyria. Are you Kyria Eugenia Kanakari?"

"Yes," she replied.

"Kyria, I am Eugenia Stamati. But everybody calls me Nitsa. Before my marriage, I was Eugenia Petropouleas, the daughter of Papa Saranti Petropouleas, the priest in Gargaliani, Messinia. My mother was Eleni. She was from Pirgaki. My mother was your aunt, the sister of your mother, Theano. You are my first cousin! We share the same grandfather: Michael, the professor."

Thea Eugenia's mother Theano was the first daughter of my great grandfather Michael, the one he had sent to Athens to study. When she left Pirgaki, she never returned. How Mother found this cousin of hers is a mystery and a testament to her resourcefulness. Indeed, more than half a century had passed since my family had any contact with these people and for that period of time, the relationship lay completely dormant.

The revelation left Thea Eugenia visibly shaken. Mother paused to give her a moment to recompose herself and watched as the history of her family, something she had apparently not thought of for decades, emerged. When my aunt appeared to have processed what she had heard, she came to herself, happily embraced Mother, and led us to the rear of her store and prepared us coffee. Mother filled her in on our life, our hardships and our plans.

"We are going to America. There is nothing here to keep us from leaving. We have sold everything, have written everyone and everything off, and we want to go. Though we are here, we feel as if we have already left. We are in a sense like ghosts."

"Well, my Nitsa, I will do everything I can to help you and your family get ready to go. This is a blessing that we have connected here, that you found us. This must be God's will. We are here for you."

The Kanakari family was good to us. They offered whatever succor they could, mostly by keeping an eye on Stathi and me. They fed us from time to time and perhaps even more important, offered us moral support. Stathi and I became regulars at the Kanakari's house for the next few weeks, a stretch when Mother dropped us there in the morning and picked us up early in the afternoon. Mother would report her progress to us while we ate lunch, filling in on how much closer we were to getting our exit documents in order.

However, after a few weeks of this, life with the Kanakari family became difficult. Not only had our presence importuned these people, but Stathi and I became intolerably bored. It was as if we were back at Thea Fotini's farm all over again. And it seemed we were always in the way and had become a restriction on their freedom of movement. As two kids from the village, Stathi and I were out of place in their home and in their social circles. Because we were usually in the wrong place at the wrong time, Thea Eugenia began mildly to reprimand us for our bucolic blunders. It got to the point where we didn't want to be in her house anymore. We started to linger just outside her front door but since her store was in a commercial area, there were no kids around for us to play with.

Meanwhile, my parents had actually made some headway into the Greek bureaucracy, obtaining a number of papers and stamps. The final major hurdle was for Mother to obtain her Greek passport, a hurdle that had proved high and formidable. Long lines perpetually adorned the Ministry of Interior and each day that passed with no results left Mother a little more fatigued and pessimistic. Things reached a climax around the fourth consecutive week of one unsuccessful attempt after another, when Mother decided it was time for a new approach, time for her to put her talents to use. After she dropped us off at Thea Eugenia's store on morning, Mother stood once again at the end of the passport line. By the time it was her turn to speak with the clerk, the manager told the anxious line of people that the office was closing for afternoon naps and that the people should return after five that evening. The crowd dispersed.

Mother refused to leave and remained outside the building behind in line with some others who wanted to be the first served when the offices reopened. Father left to find a grocery store to buy lunch, and Mother planted herself on the side of the building to wait for him, in front of some street-level windows that separated the passport office from the outside. She sat herself directly at the window's edge, in full view of the passport office clerks. She started to weep—a silent and solitary weeping. Her tears prompted one of the workers to crack open the window adjacent to her.

"My lady, why are you crying?"

Mother acted startled and made a futile attempt to recompose herself.

"Why am I crying?" she asked.

Tears continued to flow from her face as she incredulously looked at the bureaucrat. Mother paused and the line between acting and reality quietly vanished.

"I'll tell you why I'm crying. But where do I begin? Well, I suppose the only place to begin is at the beginning. Kyrie, I was born the daughter of the great Papa Sarantis of Gargaliani, Messinia. Papa Sarantis was a great dignitary, a singular man that the most famous Greeks came to for advice. He suddenly died and my mother soon followed him, leaving me alone in Gargaliani to take care of everything."

Mother took a deep breath and sighed.

"I never wanted to get married but my family and friends insisted that I marry a poor farmer because they said he was the type of man I should be with. And in many ways they were right. But despite my better judgment, I married the man in 1929 and everything I feared

dandelions for Dinner

would happen came to pass. Though we were supposed to leave this country for the United States right away, the Depression hit, and I was unable to leave. And so we started our family in Gargaliani. We have two sons and for the last decade, have been forced to live under terrible conditions. We have nearly starved to death several times, were almost killed by Italians, then by Germans, and then by Greeks. My husband is an American citizen, and finally, after all these years, we can leave this place for a new home and a new start in America. My life in Greece is finished. Greece has not been good to me. No, it has only given me dose after dose of suffering, humiliation, and fatigue. I have sold everything anyone would buy and allowed a family to move into the home my grandfather built. I am finished here.

"And now, for the last month, I have been forced to come here every day to get some damned papers so I can leave this country, only to be turned away. It's as if Greece, the country that has been punishing me for so long, won't let me go. As if it has enjoyed torturing me so much it doesn't want to stop. And so, day after day I have been forced to leave my boys with distant relatives I never met until a few weeks ago so I can come here and do what I have to do to get out of Greece. And each day, I return with nothing. It's been a month now, and I have nothing to show for it. And today, I got to the front of the line only to have the door, once again, slammed in my face. So that, Kyrie, is why I am crying."

The stunned bureaucrat stared silently at Mother for a few moments and then raised his arm and pointed toward the door.

"Go to the entrance Kyria and I will meet you there," he gently ordered.

Mother did as she was told, and the God-sent angel escorted her in the building and to his office. He asked her for her papers and she handed over to him her entire folder of documents. He helped her fill out some new ones and to sign some others. The man stayed with Mother the entire afternoon, until all her documents were signed and stamped. It seemed nothing happened in Greece without a stamp and that day, in between Mother's intermittent sobs, the man's stamp got a workout. He took her fingerprints and to make sure she still had his sympathies, Mother produced some tears, which she wiped with her inked hands, mixing ink in the tears and smearing it all over her face. The man escorted Mother to other agencies within the building where his colleagues signed and stamped even more documents. When they were finished, he made up a list of things for Mother to do that included trips to other ministries, and instructions to take our passport picture.

We celebrated that evening with a meal.

"Panagioti, I wish you could have all seen it. I couldn't take it anymore. I couldn't possibly go there for another day and be turned away. I said to myself forget it, today is the day. And once again, it was my acting skills that saved the day. Oh, I am better than Paxinou. I'm the best actress that has ever been born. And to think I have never been on stage. No, my shows have been reserved for the select few, in times of great need and for those who never even knew I was acting, leaving me alone to serve as thespian and audience member. But that's all right. It's clear to me now that I was given these skills for a reason. And I have used them appropriately."

Mother went over again and again the highlights of what happened that day, each time adding a new nugget here and there. Her cheerful retelling of her sagacity gave us a new hope, the feeling that no matter what came our way, we would get through it. Yes, for that day, optimism reigned, and it was Mother's self-confidence that served as its fuel. It seemed our mission might actually come to pass in the coming weeks and that we would soon be on our way to America. Things were suddenly simple.

When I told Mother about the intense boredom Stathi and I were experiencing at Thea Eugenia's home, she gave me a quick wave of her hand.

"Don't worry about that, Saranti, all this will be over soon. In any event, Eugenia has connected me with another one of my cousins, the children of my mother's brother Xenophon. My grandfather Michael also sent him to Athens to study. I think I know where to find his daughter Eugenia. *She'll* have to be kind to me. We were named after the same person, my mother's mother."

Within only a few days, Mother announced that we were going to see this aunt who none of us, including Mother, had ever met. We boarded the "AHARNON" streetcar we saw on our first day in Omonia and took it all the way to Aharnon's plateia. Then, with a piece of paper in one hand, Father asked for some directions and led us a block to our destination, a single-family dwelling, elegant and indicative of the homes in the area. Mother saw that the building's balcony was filled with flowers that dripped water from a recent watering.

"They're home," she said.

We dodged the water drops under the balcony and moved toward the door. One knock, two knocks, and a maid opened and led us to a parlor on the second floor. Mother had let her cousin know we were coming and she was expecting us. When Thea Eugenia entered the room, she greeted Mother in a proper and refined manner and directed us to sit in a finely decorated parlor that held a large piano. Thea Eugenia made some small talk about her lineage, tracing it to Professor Michael from Pirgaki and beyond. She seemed genuinely pleased that we were going to America and expressed sorrow at our litany of difficulties as Mother rattled them off.

"I'm happy to help you in any way I can on your journey to America," she said. Just then, the maid brought in a tray with several glasses of water and a bowl of cherries. Mother flashed us a stern look, all that Stathi and I needed to keep us from attacking the fruit.

"Oh, thank you my cousin, I thank you. We'll, now that you mention it, there are a few other papers we need. If Saranti and Stathi could stay here just a couple of afternoons, it would allow us to finish our business. They won't bother you. They are very nice boys. We are almost finished and everything will be in order very soon."

"No problem, my Nitsa. I would be happy to have these fine boys here. It would be our pleasure!"

The following morning, Father gave me a few drachma. I grabbed Stathi by the hand, and we boarded the streetcar for plateia Aharnon. And as we rode it, I worried that the end of the line would never come, that we had boarded the wrong streetcar, or that somehow, things had changed from the day before. The streetcar took us through many strange neighborhoods, but soon enough, we reached the end of the line. When we arrived at Thea Eugenia's home, she greeted us with open arms and a slice of bread with fig marmalade. We followed her to her backyard and watched her as she worked.

In days that followed, Thea Eugenia was always nearby, a shouting distance from us while she performed her kitchen chores or worked in her garden. She was constantly talking to us and asking us questions, curious to know about our life in Gargaliani and our struggles. We eagerly told her as many such stories that we could think of, volunteering them one after another. Oftentimes, we exaggerated them to keep her interested and wanting more. When we ran out of anecdotes, she told us about the occupation in Athens.

"We had many hardships here, boys," she began once. "As a matter of fact, we had many Germans here in Athens, too. They weren't just in Gargaliani. Germans were everywhere. In fact, if you look down the street—look at that building down there, you see it?"

I nodded, and she continued. "The Germans occupied the main floor of that building. It was some kind of German station; exactly what, I don't know. Well, the Germans were there all the time, and eventually, we stopped paying too much attention to them. We had gotten used to them. As you can see, the sidewalk in front of that station is much wider in order to accommodate the newspaper stand and the pedestrian traffic. Children would often pass in front of the newspaper stand on their way home from school, congregate around it, and buy candy. Sometimes they would linger to play in front of the German station, there by the wide sidewalk. One day, the children became a little too noisy and a German officer angrily came out of the building and ordered them to leave. Most did, but a couple stayed behind, so preoccupied with what they were doing that they forgot the German's warning. Several minutes later, the same officer emerged from the building and shot the first child he met in the head with his pistol. The boy died immediately, right there. The other boy ran away. No one ever played again in front of the German station."

The story stunned us.

Thea had two children, Lela and Jimmy. They were older than us, and both had finished high school and were enrolled in special music schools. Because of our appearance, they avoided Stathi and me. Each day before lunch, Jimmy would practice his piano while Lela would sing, or more accurately scream her lungs out. I thought they were terrible and Stathi and I used to snicker behind their backs at the cacophony they produced—until Thea Eugenia reprimanded us. The following day, I overheard a conversation in their home.

"Mama, those two boys are terrible," Lela whined. "They are

crass and totally uncultured villagers. How much longer do they have to stay here? How much longer do we have to endure their presence?"

"Don't worry children, not much longer. They'll be gone soon. They'll be out of the country before you know it."

"Good. America can have them both. I only wish they'd leave now."

This conversation devastated me. It's a terrible feeling to realize you are unwelcome when you were under the impression you *had* been welcome. I turned to Stathi.

"Come with me."

Right then, I took my brother by the hand and we walked out of the house and down the street to the park.

"Stathi, we aren't going back to that house ever again. Do you understand?"

Stathi quietly nodded his head.

"We have been there too long. They don't like us anymore. Now we are going to take the streetcar back to our hotel near Omonia and meet Mother and Father there."

I reached in my pocket for my money and realized that I had left my drachmas on a window ledge in Thea Eugenia's kitchen. Going back to retrieve the money was out of the question.

"Stathi, we are going to walk."

We began to walk what appeared to be the ungodly distance to Omonia, following the streetcar's tracks and whatever landmarks we recognized. When we finally arrived, we told my parents what had happened.

"Eh, don't worry about it, Saranti," said Mother. "We invaded these people's lives, and they helped us as much as they could. And Saranti, it doesn't matter anyway. Our work here is complete. You don't have to go back to Thea Eugenia's house or anyone else's. We have all of our papers now. In two days, we will pick up my passport and the only thing that remains is for us to wait for *Marine Shark* to take us to America."

A couple of days later, Father picked up the passport. We had everything we needed for America. But it was still only the middle of May, and we had to figure out how to make it to July, when our ship was scheduled to leave. Staying in the hotel was out of the question as we didn't have that kind of money. What is more, living with our relatives wasn't really an option either. They were already sick of us after only a few days with them, and so it goes without saying that having us around the clock for two months wasn't going to work. That afternoon we had lunch with the Kanakari family who was genuinely happy to hear our good news.

"Finally, after so many years and so many obstacles the road to America is open to you," Thea Eugenia shouted. "What a blessing! God is shining on your family, my Nitsa!"

"Yes, He is!" Mother joyfully replied.

"But you still have two months here before the boat is to leave. What are you going to do here for the next two months?"

"That's a problem, my cousin. We have finished our tasks much earlier than expected. We can't go back to Gargaliani, that's out of the question. And we can't live in that hotel for the next two months. That is out of the question as well. And we couldn't do that even if we wanted, we don't have nearly enough money for that. In fact, we are checking out of our hotel tomorrow. But for some reason, my cousin, I am not worried. Nothing can stop us now."

"You are correct, my Nitsa. Nothing can stop you. These things of which you speak have been written. I can see how things are unfolding for you and your family. I hope you will allow me to offer you something. My family has a beach home in Palio Faliron. It is nothing big, but it is on the beach. You are welcome to live in it until you leave."

Mother was speechless.

"Really?" was all she could say.

"Yes, my Nitsa. It's beautiful, really it is. You will enjoy it. And after all you have been through, I think you all need it. Please take the keys and go."

Mother rose from her chair and hugged her cousin.

Chapter 30
AMERICA

Our days in Palio Faliron were idyllic, an unexpected stay in paradise after living in Hades for so long. We spent our time there as vacationers, eating warm bread from the local bakery, playing, taking naps, sitting for dinner, and then strolling in the nearby plateia. On occasion, Mother would take Stathi and me to the beach, which was a far cry from the isolated one near Thea Theano's beach house; this one was filled with people. Father did his best to stretch our drachma, and each day rolled slowly into the next. That was just fine with us; indeed, Palio Faliron was a singular time for me, one when I just enjoyed being in Greece, where I simply appreciated its natural beauty and its people.

We stayed at Thea Eugenia's summer home to the anxious end, until the very day the *Marine Shark* was to disembark the port at Piraeus. When that morning arrived, we left the house keys on the kitchen counter and hired a cab. The driver pulled up to the port, and Father handed him our very last drachma. We were out of money again.

"Good luck to you!" the cab driver said as we said our good-byes. "Good luck; God bless."

"Thank you," Father mumbled. We moved toward the port's gated assembly area.

"That's it, over there," Father said and pointed to a ship moored a half a block or so from the dock in the harbor. Printed on the front of the ship were the words *MARINE SHARK*.

"Why is it way out there?" I asked.

"Because the harbor isn't deep enough for it, Saranti. If a ship enters waters that are too shallow, it will get stuck. That's as far as that vessel can go without running aground."

We navigated through a chaotic crowd to a line where we nervously waited to be processed. After several agitated minutes, one of the port workers motioned us over and Father showed him our papers. The man quickly examined them, nodded, and waived us through to an area where scores of others waited, staring at the gray anchored American vessel. I examined the majestic ship carefully and noticed that a ladder extended from the ship's first deck to the water. Between that ladder and us was the *maouna*, an open flat top boat normally used to transport goods. Now it was ferrying people to Marine Shark.

When the *maouna* pulled up in front of us at the concrete dock, a sailor helped the passengers board, one by one. Father dragged the suitcase toward the sailor and Mother kept a strong grip on Stathi and me. When a jovial youth in front of us jumped onto the *maouna*, he raised both his arms in the air.

"Now, I am in America!" he shouted.

Everyone laughed and applauded as we jumped on the *maouna* right behind him.

A few moments later, I saw a young lady, one who must have been in her early twenties, struggle to keep a grip on her purse and her travel documents as she stepped aboard. Suddenly, her papers flew from her hands, propelled by a gust of wind and into the water. She panicked.

"Ahhh! Those are my papers!" she screamed. I need those! Without them, they won't let me leave this country. God help me! Someone help me! I need those papers. It has taken me months to get them. Please, someone help me."

We looked at her with empathy and held our belongings even tighter. Out of nowhere, a sailor rushed to the woman and in an act of theatric chivalry, looked her in the eyes.

"Don't worry, my lady. I'll take care of you."

He maneuvered the *maouna*, fished the papers out of the water, and handed them over to the still hysterical woman. The woman sobbed and thanked him repeatedly.

Mother wasn't impressed.

"Move on. All that trouble for nothing," she said, apparently not caring for the young lady's performance.

When the *maouna* pulled aside the *Marine Shark*, sailors directed us to the iron stairs and we began our assent. After we climbed, for several moments, I looked down and was terrified at how high I was.

I grabbed Mother's skirt, and she held Stathi tightly by the bicep. It was not only my first time on a boat, but the highest I had ever been—prior to that, I had never been higher than a fig tree.

"If I fall from here," I thought, "I'm finished."

At the top of the steps, we stepped onto the boat's first deck. Then I turned around and looked at the port. Piraeus was an awesome sight—tremendous, unlike anything I had ever seen before—huge and busy and active and international. Father handed our tickets to a man at the top of the stairs, and he checked us off his list. When we stepped past him, Father turned around.

"Boys, now we are in America! We are finally on American soil. No one can touch us here."

With that final step onto the boat, we had finally made it. We were out of Greece and in America; we were liberated. And all of our fears—of dying from starvation, of being killed by Italians or Germans or Greeks, of never making it out—were gone.

We proceeded on to the ship. Mother and Stathi were directed to the area for women and Father and I to the area for men, a large dormitory-style room filled with bunks, stacked two, three and four high. Father pointed to a second level bunk.

"You take that one, and I'll take this one," he said, pointing to the one above it.

We left our belongings in the dormitory, found Mother and Stathi, and returned to one of the decks to see the last-minute loading of the ship. We were excited, talking with one another about the accommodations, about how we had made it, and about America. We moved to the upper deck and from that lofty position, were able to see the port and the city, our last look at our homeland. Suddenly, events accelerated and ship personnel who would not be making the trip rushed toward the ladder and onto the *maouna*.

The ship's engines roared, and an earsplitting clamor exploded as the *Marine Shark* raised its anchors. A feeling of euphoria swept over me as the vessel backed up and rotated away from Piraeus and toward the mouth at the west end of the port. We were really leaving. The ship righted itself, the engines shifted and roared, and we moved forward through the water.

As the ship pulled away from the dock and its busy workers, it also took us away from so many of our problems: hunger; fear; the dearth of opportunities; the hard and unforgiving land; Communists; Royalists; Andartes; police; passions; blood; endless bureaucracy; and so on. Hopelessness was behind us and hope, opportunity, and a fresh beginning lay ahead.

"Good riddance," was all I could think.

We had made it through crisis after crisis to get to this point, and I felt no nostalgia whatsoever for Greece and no remorse. I was happy to be leaving and could not fathom ever wanting to return.

Several small boats trailed the *Marine Shark* while their captains blew their celebratory horns and waved. One by one, the boats broke off, with the exception of one.

"Why is that one still there? Will he be following us to America?" I asked Father.

"No. That boat will take the pilot back to land after he guides us out of the port."

I stared at Father. My look must have been a blank one because he continued.

"Look, only a captain who knows every inch of this port can guide a ship like this out. A foreigner will likely crash it or run it aground. So a pilot steers the ship out of the port, and then he leaves."

"Is he a Greek?" I asked.

"Yes, he's a Greek. There he is," Father said as he pointed toward the first deck ladder. The pilot descended the stairs and then jumped, in what looked to me like quite a daring maneuver, onto the trailing boat that quickly turned and whisked him back toward the port.

The ship revved its engines and accelerated, and I heard people saying lots of things, but specifically remember the shout of one lady: "*Sothikame!* We have been saved! Saved from this cursed land. This damned and cursed land!"

Within minutes, we heard a signal that indicated the kitchen was serving food. We ran from the viewing area, down several flights of stairs, through several corridors and toward the dining room. I imagined we would be served roasted lamb, pasta, cheeses, and whatever other foods I had lacked and craved the previous decade. But when we entered the cafeteria, we were overwhelmed by an awful stench. Many held their noses and gagged uncontrollably and left while others fought the urge, took a tray and stood in line.

dandelions for Dinner

"They are serving dog sausages," someone said with a smirk.

Stathi and I led our parents into the line. I looked up at Father and saw that ironic smirk on his face, then, turned to see what it foreshadowed and saw an enormous black man, clad in white, slap two sausages on my tray and two on Stathi's. He followed the sausages up with two scoops of sauerkraut. I had never seen anything like him before and gagged when I caught a whiff of the sauerkraut, which Father quickly covered with a slice of bread.

"It's only cabbage," he said. "Keep moving."

When we sat, two hot dogs, sauerkraut, mashed potatoes, and two slices of Butternut bread filled my plate.

"This is bread?" I asked as I examined the soft square slices.

I ate the hot dogs, which I actually liked, but didn't venture near the sauerkraut or the bread. Like me, the other Greeks tried to figure out how to get the food down. Some experimented by soaking it all in tomato sauce.

Within a day or so, the ship made its only stop at Messina Sicily, where it quickly picked up a few passengers and was off. We settled into the trip and became quickly acclimated to the ship's routines. The three highlights to each day were breakfast, lunch, and dinner. Three meals a day, every day, was unheard of for the Greeks. But still, many could not adjust to the foreign food and skipped the meals or only ate those they knew they could get down.

Within a few days of Sicily, we reached the western end of the Mediterranean Sea.

"The next time we see land, it will be New York," Mother sighed as we moved through the Strait of Gibraltar and past its famous rock.

Without hesitation, the intrepid *Marine Shark*, with a thousand or so passengers, plunged ahead into the vast and seemingly endless Atlantic Ocean.

Before long, I met some boys, and we passed our time exploring every inch of the ship. We quickly discovered that its highlight was the PX, a small shop that sold dime-store like items to the ship's crew and passengers. That cantina, as we called it, opened every day at noon, and the boys and I spent hours watching people buy treats for themselves and their children. The first couple of days, Stathi and I pestered Father for a few coins so we could buy a Hershey bar, by far the most popular treat. Eventually, Father relented and bought one with a couple of American coins he had held onto from when he lived in Chicago. But when Father did, he took it to the ship's upper deck where, much like he did with the letter from Theo Stathi months before, he slowly examined its wrapper, read every word of what it said, and only after a painfully slow inspection did he deliberately began to tear back the wrapper.

"Open the damned candy bar," Mother snapped. Father complied, tore back the remaining paper and broke the bar into four equal pieces.

"Eat it slowly, boys. You won't get another one of these for a while," he admonished.

Ironically, communists abounded on the *Marine Shark*. Most of them were American born Greeks returning to their birthplace. In a way, the boat was like a giant plateia filled with coffee and political discussions.

"You are a Communist," I'd say when I heard something I didn't like. "I'm going to give you away to the authorities."

"Oh, get out of here kid or I'll throw you in the ocean and the sharks will eat you," was typical reply.

"How did they let you Communists into the ship?" Others asked, referring to the loyalty oaths travelers were required to take before embarking. "Who did you pay off?"

Statements like these only elicited more threats.

With the exception of some seasickness, the weeklong trip on that very fast boat was uneventful. On the morning we were to arrive in New York Harbor, I awoke before Father. I left the men's dormitory and walked to the top of the ship, when the morning was at its darkest, just before dawn. The ship cut through the smooth water and a warm breeze blew through my hair. When I looked to the right, I saw mysterious lights trailing, flickering on and off, and moving in the midst of the darkness. Other glowing orbs hovered just above the sea.

"*Fantasmata!*" I thought. "Just like Gargaliani!"

I sprinted back to the men's sleeping area where I woke Father and dragged him up to the deck. But by that time, the sun had already begun to crack the horizon and the source of the *fantasmata* was evident: we were traveling alongside Long Island and the ethereal lights were cars driving up and down the New York coastline. And the water phantoms were only illumined buoys, set adjacent to the island to keep ships like ours from running aground.

"We're almost there," said Father. "Let's get our things ready."

We gathered our belongings and returned with Mother and Stathi to the upper deck to watch our entrance into New York Harbor.

"There she is," someone said, "Look!"

Mother and I stared off into the foggy morning distance. I suddenly saw the sight everyone on that ship had been anxiously awaiting, the green feminine sculpture, majestically holding her torch.

"Mana, I see it, the statue of freedom! There it is!"

What an awesome sight.

"Yes, my boy, that's it," replied Mother. "We have come a long way for that, Saranti. A long way."

Those on that deck that misty morning stared silently at the statue off in the distance.

Several minutes later, Father broke the silence.

"Let's go toward the exit," he said.

Though we would be waiting in line there a long time, at least a couple of hours, we didn't mind. With more than a thousand passengers who would want to leave the ship at the same time, Father had envisioned long delays and was taking extra precautions for our orderly disembarkation. Of course, lines didn't bother us—we were used to them. We secured our position at the front, and it quickly filled in behind us. We planned to be the first to step on actual American soil. When the *Marine Shark* approached and pulled into its dock, our spirits soared with a giddy anticipation.

But suddenly and without warning, more and more people appeared and crowded the ship's exit. They pushed and piled in, and we lost our place and drifted away from the exit. When it was time to disembark, we were pushed and shoved from every direction—entering the United States would not be orderly—and the crew jumped in and hollered at the people to get in line, to move here or there. By the time some sanity was restored, we found ourselves near the end of the queue, with the more aggressive individuals near the front. Those who were patient and orderly, like us, were pushed back and forced to congregate on an upper deck and would exit last.

Father took the injustice of it all in stride, viewing the occurrence philosophically: "We have waited so long, have come so far, have suffered so much. Waiting a few more minutes to get off the boat is irrelevant. Don't worry. Tonight, we will be sleeping in an American hotel and eating American food."

After what seemed like hours, we were on dry land and stood before a number of customs officials who sat on the opposite side of a long table. When we passed in front of them with our documents, Mother handed them her Greek passport and Father handed them his, the American one that included Stathi and me. The Americans, who appeared organized, dignified, and aloof, impressed me. They carried an unusual flair and unlike the Greeks, seemed sober and thoughtful, not emotional and chaotic, and were able to speak with hardly opening their mouths. As they looked at our documents, they mumbled incomprehensible phrases to one another. They asked Father some questions in English, and Father answered them in English. The interrogation obviously went well, putting aside my fears that America might return us to Greece. Finally, one of the mumblers looked at Stathi and me, said something incomprehensible and handed us each a piece of candy.

We were shuttled to another table identified with a large red cross. I was proud to see Father once again handle these Americans in English, something only a couple of the Greeks on our boat could do. Indeed, few of Greece's educated could speak English, having only been taught French and German in school.

Unlike the customs officials, the Red Cross people smiled. They spoke slowly with facial expressions that at least offered one the opportunity to glean some sense of what they were saying.

When Father told them we were going to Woburn, Massachusetts, one of the workers handed him $150 for fares and living expenses. Father signed some papers, and the officials said we were free to go. We breathed a sigh of relief. We were free to go. Finally.

We walked past the table and suddenly found ourselves on the streets of New York City. New York made Athens look like Gargaliani. We walked on a bustling sidewalk, with Mother gripping Stathi and me and Father dragging our suitcase. Cars and people and noises were everywhere. Though we finally had "arrived" at our destination—we had made it to America—we were at a loss, not completely sure where to go or what to do next. We were on our own in a new land, one oblivious and indifferent to our arrival, one where everyone but us seemed to know what to do and where to go. I suddenly realized that our life here would also be filled with great challenges.

With that sly grin of his, Father broke the anxious tension. Then, he did what I hadn't seen him do in a long time—he smiled. Not an ironic smirk, but a real smile. A happy, appreciative, satisfied smile. When Mother saw it, she smiled too, an act that caused Stathi and me to smile as well. Father's smile, a sign of confidence, was a much needed harbinger that we were going to be all right, that whatever lay in front of us would be minimal compared to what lay behind. I looked around me at the action, the buildings, the people, the cars, the wonder, and realized the noose had been completely removed from our necks. I thought about the stories Father had told us about America around the *magali* in our home, about the opportunities and the hope, about how, with hard work, we would never be hungry again; about how America was the place where we could accomplish anything we set our minds upon. I felt fearless and powerful and liberated. The one thing we were ready to do was work, and now that we were in a place where hard work could actually produce rewards, our possibilities were endless.

Indeed, with every cross in life, there is a resurrection.

Bibliography

Bailey, Ronald H. *Partisans & Guerrillas,* Alexandria, Virginia: Time-Life Books, 1978.

Deuteros, Tomos. *I. Metaxas - Words and Thoughts,* Athens: Exdoseis Gkobosti.

Gerolymatos, Andre. *Red Acropolis Black Terror, The Greek Civil War and the Origins of Soviet-American Rivalry, 1943–1949.* New York: Basic Books, 2004.

Kershaw, Ian. *Fateful Choices, Ten Decisions that Changed the World 1940-1941,* New York: The Penguin Press, 2007.

Mazower, Mark. *Inside Hitler's Greece, The Experience of Occupation, 1941–1944.* New Haven: Yale University Press, 1995.

Woodhouse, C. M.. *Modern Greece, A short History,* London: Faber and Faber Limited, 1991.

Glossary

Ai gamisou   Screw you.

Aloni   The outdoor threshing floor, used during harvest.

Alites   Hoodlums.

Andarte(s)   Greek communist guerilla fighter.

Apori   Poor.

Astinomia   Police.

EAM   Ethniko Apeleftherotiko Metopo, or the National Liberation Front. A political organization composed of elder communists.

Ellas   Greece.

EPON   Eniaia Panelladiki Organosi Neon or United Pan-Hellenic Organization of Youth. was the youth group, the "young Communist" section of EAM.

E tan e epi tas   "Come home with your shield or on it."

Fantasmata   Ghosts.

Feta   Greek goat cheese.

Filotimo   Honor, especially when shown through humility and love.

Hellene   Greek.

Hilopites	Small, square Greek pasta, used in soups and other dishes.
Kefalotiri	Type of cheese.
Kerata	An epithet that literally translates to "horned one."
Kinesaki	Little Chinese boy.
KKE	Kappa Kappa Epsilon. The Communist Party of Greece.
Koliva	Boiled wheat served at memorial and funeral services.
Koulouri	Large, round bread-like pretzel.
Kyria	Mrs.
Kyrie	Mr.
Kyrio	Mr.
Leventes	Strong young men.
Litourvio	Olive oil processing plant.
Livas	Libyan wind.
Magali	Wood burning stove.
Magissa	Witch.
Malaka	Jerk.
Mamee	Midwife.
Maouna	Barge.
Mati	Evil eye.
Meson	Clout.

Molon lave	"Come and get them." Said by Leonidas to the Persians at the Battle of Thermopylae after the Persians asked the Spartans to surrender their weapons.
Mona ziga	Game of chance played in plateia.
Oxi	No.
Panagia	The Virgin Mary.
Papou	Grandfather.
Petimezi	Sweet grape syrup used to sweeten our foods and deserts.
Philoxenia	Hospitality.
Plateia	The town square.
Poutana	Prostitute.
Prebytera	A priest's wife.
Prika	Dowry.
Psihi	Soul.
Sothikame	"We are saved."
Taverna	A sidewalk tavern that serves wine and some food.
Theema	Victim.
Theo	Uncle.
Thea	Aunt.
Tsibles	Eye sand.
Voltes	Strolls.
Yiayia	Grandmother.
Zito I Ellas	"Long live Greece."